Never Tell Me, '

Copyright © 2017 by Al Efron
All rights reserved.

To:
Ellen & Ellis

Great Friends Forever

Contents

Dedication	5
Note	8
My Very Early Life	9
My Early Life	20
Great Ideas That Did Not Work	22
My Early Professional Life ... and Harriet	24
My Young Adult Life	30
My Army Life	32
My New Civilian Life	58
My First Job, Building My Career	62
The Mafia Changed My Career Direction	64
My Architectural Education	68
My First Job as an Architectural Junior Draftsman	69
Long Range Planning	70
A Real Car	74
Sad Events in Life	76
Al Efron, The Hero	78
Becoming a Military Civilian	79
Discovering Jackson Heights, Meryl	82
A Bad Change In Career Path With A Fabulous End	86
Back to My Life & Staten Island	90
Always Listen To Your Children	98
Welcome to the Democratic Party	99
Joining Organizations & Networking	116
Our House On Todt Hill	120
Guns As A Sport	123
Don't Let Your Ego Gain Control	134
Learning The Art Of Presentation	137
Raise The Flag! I Have My 12 Years of Experience	140
Richmond County Country Club	149
The Firm of Shuman, Lichtenstein, Claman, Efron Architects	152
The Donald	160
More Donald Trump Stories	164
My Freeport Adventure On The Island Of Grand Bahama	167
Sailors Snug Harbor	172
My AIA Fellowship	175
My Testimony Before A Congressional Committee	177
Yonkers And The Law	179
Gay Rights	183
A Prominent Elected Official & Suicide	186
Staten Island Blind Society	187
"I Will Not Play Golf With Them", Harriet Told Me.	189
Another Dangerous Golf Adventure	190

Imelda Marcos and My Neighbor	191
New Philippine Government	193
Other Famous People	195
Paul's Famous Golf Ball	197
The Handicapped Law	198
Efron For President	200
The Law &/or Codes Are Not Always in the Public Interest	207
Times Change	213
Gentrification Of Manhattan	218
AIA Symposium To Expo 70, Osaka Japan	220
Name In The Newspaper Competition	224
The Adventures Of Boy Scouting	227
Heimlich Maneuver	233
My Invitation To The White House	234
Your Girlfriend, Not Your Wife!!!	236
Stupid Elected Officials	238
In keeping With Bad Political Stories, Here Is Another One	239
Unfair Legal Decisions	241
Bloomingdale's	247
The Story Of An Horrible Architectural Blunder	249
My Life's Adventure Into Sports.	251
Sport Number One: Football	252
Sport Number Two: Baseball	253
Sport Number Three: Boxing	255
Sport Number Four: Basketball	257
Sport Number Five: Judo	258
Sport Number Six: Golf	261
Back To My Daily Adventures	265
We All Get A Chance At Not Being Well	266
Christmas For A Jewish Couple	271
Great Wedding?	272
Thinking Outside The Box	276
South Bronx NY, Redevelopment	279
Another Sad Commentary Of Human Nature	281
Another urban renewal project	283
Armenian Earthquake	286
US/Europe Consortium	328
Un-Ethical Lawyers	329
I Am On The Hook	331
Again The Mafia?	332
BAGEL?	333
Back To Photography	335
Wild Eyes	336
National Parks Photo Shoots	339

Staten Island Zoo & The South American Amazon Adventure	341
Third-Party Lawsuits	354
Unethical Lawsuits	357
Arrogant Lawyer	358
Non Thinking Construction Workers	361
School Conversion To Apartment House	362
Non-Thinking Bureaucrat	364
The Desert Gold Diggers	365
Another Stupid Construction Worker	368
Pre-Jupiter Developers	369
Jupiter Developers	371
My Genius Brother Who Was Not Very Smart	374
Lesson One: How To Blow You Self Apart	378
Conditions Non-Locals Are Not Aware Of	380
AIA National Design Award	382
A Change In Life Style To Enjoy Life	384
Retirement	386
Harriet's Stroke, Angel Alice & Tommy	389
I Am In My Father's Footsteps	397
The Horrors Of Medicine	399
Mental Stimulation Over The Years	402
More Mental Stimulation Activity - Special Olympics	411
Democratic Politics	412
Phony Salespeople	414
After Operation Bureaucracy	417
In Conclusion	419
My Photo Gallery	421
Wonderful Memories	429
About The Author	454

Dedication

      I dedicate this book to my late wife Harriet for 63 wonderful years of marriage. We were bonded with love forever. I attribute any successes that I had in life to my wife Harriet for her support and encouragement which allowed me the opportunity to follow my dreams. We shared and enjoyed every moment of that 63 year adventure in life.

      In addition I also dedicate this book to my loving fantastic daughter Meryl who passed away much too early in life. She had a huge list of accomplishments. On a professional level, she earned the title of Doctor of Dental Surgery and had a successful Dentistry practice. She had a huge list of accomplishments throughout the community which earned her the distinction of having a street named "Dr. Meryl Efron Way" on Staten Island. She has been honored and allowed her to be remembered forever. Her passing left a huge void to our entire family.

      To the living: My son Paul has been a buddy and pal to me throughout the years. His large list of accomplishments has been amazing. We have been there for each other, which made life's adventure exciting and a joy. Our wonderful adventure in life still goes on as of the completion of this book, Paul and I will continue as long as my muscles and brains keep coordinating.

Very Special Acknowledgment

      Alice Ann Gilligan. She came into our lives as a healthcare worker to help care for my wife Harriet, who survived two debilitating strokes. From the first 5 minutes that I and my wife met Alice, we both saw the ray of sunshine that she brings into our lives. And so it was. This sunshine was accompanied with love and joy, making my wife's medical condition not a handicap, but part of life that can be tolerated. We both felt that we cannot lose this angel of mercy. I promised her a job for life not only as a healthcare worker but as our unofficial adopted daughter. Upon Harriet's passing, Alice became my health care worker who looks after me daily. With her guidance and help I can continue my busy community involvements as well as pursuit of my various hobbies and interests. That ray of sunshine is with us and will hopefully always keep shining. A special thanks to Brian Gilligan, her husband, for sharing part of his sunshine with me.

Acknowledgments

I would like to acknowledge and thank the following list of people whose encouragement, knowledge and help, allowed me to create this book.

Mary Kay Kirgis. Another one of my unofficial adopted daughters who I have known for years. Not only has she given me advice and encouragement in various endeavors that I was involved with, such as the writing of this book, she was also extremely instrumental with her advice and guidance in a life threatening condition that I was facing. Because of Mary Kay's advice and knowledge, I was able to change the course of action form a horrible negative handicapped outcome of possibly losing both my legs to a positive outcome that eliminated the handicapped condition. I am now a normal walking senior citizen. That is the first time I ever admitted that I actually am a senior citizen. I cherish Mary Kay's friendship and Council that I know will last for the rest of my days. At this point I would like to acknowledge and welcome to the family Mary Kay's new love of her life Frank Trembulak.

Tommy Bobnick. My life would be a complete disaster in the use of computers, cell phones, iPads and all other computer devices that are an essential part of everyday life, if not for the technical genius of Tommy Bobnick. I met Tommy about five years ago and realized instantaneously that I cannot survive in this world of technology without Tommy. After that first meeting, Tommy became part of my family. As a professional technical advisor, he is on call to help me with all the computer disasters that I encounter daily. He either gets into my computer from his computer using Team Viewer, or is in my studio an average of 3 to 4 days a week. This book would never happen without Tommy. Not only did he install the computer program 'Dragon' to allow me to talk into a microphone, he is always there making sure my entire computer system is working in top-notch shape. Tommy and the love-of-his-life Stephanie became very close friends and traveling companions. I cherish the various vacation trips we took including Alice and sometimes my son Paul.

Talking about lifetime friends, I have them too. I have known my two close buddies, Philip Korn and Isidore (Izzy) Shapiro, for many years. The three of us were members of the Retired Philosophers Guild. This group would meet every Friday for lunch at McMahon's Steakhouse here in Tucson. We would discuss and debate the issues of the day. We would come up with responsible solutions for the great society that we now live in. If you don't believe that statement, would you believe that we just talked together while we enjoyed our lunch? As time went on, things changed and now once a month, Phil, Izzy and I meet for an intelligent lunch and enjoy every minute of it.

    At one of our lunches, Phil announced that he wrote a book about his life. That statement blew me away! I asked Phil if I could read a copy of his book. He delightfully agreed and presented me with a copy at our next lunch. To me writing a book is a magnificent undertaking, well beyond my wildest dreams. I too can write a book. I read his book from cover to cover and was fascinated by his life story. In keeping with my philosophy that I want to experience everything in life that is available for me, I considered writing a book. I spoke to my IT genius, Tommy, who graciously installed the latest version of Dragon. All I have to do with this software it just speak into the microphone and the computer automatically types everything out. This is a godsend for me, since typing, spelling, and grammar are not my strong points. My strong point is making speeches. And so because of Phil, I actually wrote this book. With the kind words and encouragement from Izzy, I was able to complete this. What I thought was impossible; I wrote the story of my life.

                       A Special Acknowledgment
    I cannot forget my two editors Paul Efron & Deborah Patrick. My original manuscript was created with the use of the computer program 'Dragon'. All I did was to dictate into a microphone. It produced this book in one very very long run-on sentence. Spelling, grammar, paragraphs and all the other niceties of the English language were completely nonexistent. They edited the block of words into a readable book. It was the genius of those two people, who are very dear to my heart, which made this autobiography a real book.

Note

Just for the record, before I begin this literary adventure, a word about my personality. We are all born with an inbred arrangement of genes, etc. that creates our personalities and dictates how we will act and think as we go through life. The personality we each are given, whether we like it or not, is beyond our control.

Therefore, it should be noted that I am on the hyperactive side. I think fast, I move fast, and do not have time for keeping records or worrying about all those little details. I would never be able to survive in the corporate world where bureaucracy is the mainstay of daily life. All the stories I'm about to tell are accurate occurrences as I went through life. However, the dates, times, and chronological order of each adventure may be a little off, due to my lack of keeping records.

Because of my personality of not worrying about minor details and assembling a treasure trove of documentation, I could never be President of the United States. At the end of their terms in office, every President of the United States creates a Presidential Library. Since in my case they would not be able to find any written material or documentation to place in this library, this fact will prevent me from occupying that high office.

One more note before I start, I have to thank Tommy Bobnick, my IT guru who I could not live without. He is constantly helping me out with all the computer crises that I have daily. Tommy set me up with this program so that all I have to do to write this book is talk into the microphone. Therefore the original transcript of this book is all one run on sentence. I hope to get an editor to turn this manuscript into book form. (That's me, Paul Efron, his son and now first draft editor.)

My Very Early Life

The calendar on the wall indicated that the day was October 29, 1929. In the early morning, everything was quiet and normal, but by the afternoon, it seemed that the world was coming to an end. It was Black Tuesday. The Great Depression had just begun.

About three weeks had passed since the beginning of the bad times. The date was November 16, 1929 with the arrival of a new birth. Mother, Rose Efron, decided to name the new member of the family Albert. Little did Albert know that his entire preteen plus years were to be spent in poverty. Albert, or should I now referred to him as I, started to grow and enjoy being in the bliss of childhood.

I do not remember how old I was when the reality of the depression reared its ugly head. However, I do remember standing on the sidewalk with some of our furniture as the bank took our house. My father scouted around the neighborhood to find an apartment to move us into as soon as possible. Luck was with us, as he found a small apartment on the top floor of a six-story walk-up. Our new apartment was two blocks from our old house. The only other fact that I remember from the old house was our neighbor, whose daughter, a few years above my age, was named Dorothy MacDonald. In those days, men trying to make some money would go around various neighborhoods with a pony. They would then charge people to have their child sitting on the pony for a photograph. I was photographed on the pony at the age of 7, believe it or not. Dorothy McDonald was standing next to me with a big smile. That picture brought back a deep memory of being overweight my entire youthful life. I am sure that my weight was caused by my mother's simple way of staying on a diet. Her secret was to say only ice cream or cake, once in a while, as a treat. The great fact was that almost every day was a once-in-a-while treat day. Hence, no way could I lose weight.

Al with Dorothy McDonald 1937

My memory of those days through the depression was that our family, friends and neighbors were of the very poor class of society. Any fun to be had was what we were able to make for ourselves. There were games that we dreamed up using whatever material was available. The big game was marbles. I remember going to the grocery and asking the owner if I could have a wooden box that Philadelphia cream cheese was packed in. He was a very pleasant man and gave me a box so we could create the marble tournament of the neighborhood. We turned the box upside down and cut 4 or 5 inch openings in the face large enough for a marble to enter. We then labeled each opening with a different value. My friends and I took a puree (a clear marble) and the Tournament of the Century began, as we rolled the marble, aiming for the hole with the largest value. Those were very fun and exciting days, all done without spending any money that we did not have.

When I was approximately 9 years old and living in that walk up apartment, my mother became pregnant and was ready to award me with a baby brother named Edward. The best part of having a baby brother nine years younger than me, especially on a Saturday, was that my mother wanted to get me out of the way. Then she could take care of my brother and whatever else had to be done. I was awarded 25 cents and off I went. It was lunchtime, so I went to the neighborhood delicatessen store and ordered two hotdogs, or as we called them frankfurters, which cost 5 cents each. Another nickel was spent on a Coke to wash down the delicious hot dogs. I had spent a total of 15 cents. I held the remaining dime tight in my hand, to be spent on the local movie, which was about three blocks away.

The movies in those days were a fabulous bargain. Upon surrendering my dime and entering the theater, we received a ticket that contained a number, which we guarded with our lives, and in we went. We were herded to our seats by a matron, who we were sure was trained at a prison. The double feature began as all the kids started to cheer, while the matron billowed out, calling for order.

At the end of the double feature, the moment of truth was at hand. The screen showed 10 - 15 runners competing in a race. The entire movie theater was nothing but a container of screaming and jumping young people cheering on the runner with the number on his or her back that matched the ticket in your hot little hand. As they ran, the runners tried all kinds of dirty tricks to trip or push the opponent runners out of the way. Finally, when the race was over, we all calmed down. The winning number was announced for the lucky kid in the audience with the proper number.

Only once, in the total number of years of Saturday's that I went through this ordeal, did I have the winning ticket. My friends cheered me on as I went on the stage, a fat shy kid, to get my prize. To my horror, the prize that day was a beautiful 4-foot tall doll with rolling eyes, completely dressed in a gorgeous gown. As I held this doll and started to depart the stage, I heard my friends hysterical laughing and shouting out to me, "hold tight on the doll Mary".

I could not wait for the day to end. However, we still had to leave the theater and go through the lobby, where a large display table contained all sorts of small inexpensive toys, such as yo-yos or bags containing a few marbles. We were allowed to take one toy each. I now found myself in a long line, anxious to get to that table, retrieve a toy, and beat it out of there. The line moved slowly. As everyone came close to me, I did not only hear Mary, but Jane, Alice, and other female name that came my way. Young life can be cruel!!

When I finally got home, I walked in the door. The first thing my mother saw was that damn doll. She instantly fell in love with that imitation creature and put it on display in our house for as long as I can remember. Every day, I saw that doll sitting in the corner of the living room, looking at me, with a smile, reminding me of that horrible time.

My entire time in elementary school was a complete horror, harassment and torturous existence. Not only was I very heavy at that time, weighing over 200 pounds, I was also declared by my teachers as being stupid. I was not able to read, get a correct answer on any math problems, or spell at grade level. I was 'left back' two times during my elementary years. To make matters worse, I was unfortunate enough to have parents who should have never been married. They fought constantly. They both came to this country from Eastern Europe. They were of no help for me, to see if anything could be done about my lack of intelligence. The situation was just accepted; Al is stupid. Being in the depression, and not having any money, created much conflict. To worsen the situation, my father was a high-powered gambler. Any money that he was able to earn was lost at card games, horseracing, or other form of gambling. My mother was very heavy, or should I say fat and angry. She would yell or pick a fight at everyone and everything that came her way. My parents were in a constant war.

The only joy in my life during those younger years was in July and August. My grandparents on my father's side, owned and operated a small farm in upstate New York, in the town called Woodridge. Once school was out for the summer, my father moved my mother and me up to the farm, to get out of the horrible heat and depressing conditions of New York City life. That was standard operating procedure for families that were fortunate enough to have relatives running a farm out of the city. Once my mother and I settled in on the farm, my father went back to New York City. For the next two months, every Friday night, my father would get on the railroad and make the trip to spend the weekend with us. I would run down to the railroad station to meet my father when his train arrived.

The farm that my grandparents ran was a small operation. They had a number of cows, a lot of chickens running around the place, and the usual dog or two minding their own businesses. Their basic income was from milking the cows, collecting the chicken eggs, butchering chickens to sell, and making cheese and butter, etc. for sale. I remember learning how to candle eggs. It is a simple procedure of holding an egg in front of the flame of a candle so that you can see the inside of the egg. We then observed the condition of the egg to see if it was suitable for sale. I also kept busy helping my grandfather when he milked the cows. I would get him whatever he needed, while he sat on a small stool and retrieved the milk. When the milk leaves the cow, and splashes into the bucket, it creates a large layer of foam on the top of the milk. Under those rural conditions, there were a great many flies buzzing around all the area. A number of these flies would always get caught in the foam of the milk. My grandfather would swipe his hand over the bucket to remove all the fly-infested foam from the milk beneath it. He took a large ladle-like utensil, dipped it into the fresh warm milk, poured it into a glass, and handed it to me as payment for my assistance. Thinking about it now, that milk I drank, was not homogenized, pasteurized or any other 'ized'. It was pure, fresh, warm milk, and believe it or not, I never got sick.

    Our living accommodations left a lot to be desired. We lived in a large one-room, so-called apartment. It contained a double bed for my parents and a small single cot-like bed for me. As I remember, there were two closets, some furniture for storage, and a freestanding bathtub surrounded by a curtain. During the week, my mother slept in the large bed and I slept on the small cot. On the weekends my mother shared the large bed with my father. There was no running water or electricity. To get the required water for drinking and washing, we had to go outside to the well. We just dropped the bucket down the shaft of the well to the water below. When the bucket was full, we turned the crank handle to wind the rope that pulled up the bucket. Then carefully, we filled the jars and pots with water to bring back to our sleeping quarters. For light, we had kerosene lanterns and a new invention known as flashlights. The batteries for those flashlights were made by Eveready and did not last very long, but were high-tech in our world then. The high tech toilet facility was the famous outhouse with a half-moon cut into the wooden door. It was smelly, dirty, and disgusting but high-tech for the times.

    The cooking, preparing, and eating of meals was done in a separate building. The kitchen had a wood burning stove, buckets for water, and a pot belly stove for heating, plus a huge gathering of flies stuck to the ever present hanging flypaper coils. For those of you who did not enjoy life in those days and never heard of flypaper let me inform you. You bought the small cardboard canister, remove the top and pulled out a long strand of paper coated with sticky material that was about 3 or 4 foot long. You then pushed the thumb tack at the end of the coil into the ceiling and stepped back to watch the action. The flies buzzing around the place were attracted to the odor of the flypaper sticky coating. There, they got stuck to the flypaper, hundreds of them, and just hung there, swinging their legs in a fruitless effort to free themselves until they died.

    As I search my memory, I recall one day when I was about four years old. I tossed a small green apple that grew on the trees in the area up in the air and tried to catch it. I did this about three or four times and slowly backed up as I caught the apple. I did not realize that there was a large flower pot behind me. I backed up into the flower pot, fell over and ended up with a broken arm. A so-called 'doctor' was called to take care of my misfortune. The 'doctor' then set my arm in a position with my arm protruding out from the shoulder parallel to the ground and my elbow bent so my fingers were over my head. The cast dried and I was left to start the healing process. A couple days after that medical treatment, a good friend of my grandfather, who was a real doctor, saw me walking around in this awkward position. My grandfather told him what happened, and I remember him saying, "If you leave that cast the way it is, it will cripple him for life." He removed the cast, re-broke my arm, and set it in a normal position, like they would today. Thanks to that doctor, I healed normally and never had trouble after that. That's why I called the first 'doctor' a so-called doctor, because in those days, the licensing of doctors was not as it is today.

    Just a word about doctors in the communities of people who emigrated from Eastern Europe to the United States in the 1930s: It seems that when living in Eastern Europe, Jewish families lived in small communities known as 'Shtetls'. The Jewish doctors from those communities did not have the opportunity for a medical education. They just declared themselves to be doctors, and practiced as it was described, old wives' hand-me-down remedies. My great-grandfather was one of these doctors in Europe. My grandmother learned his practice of medicine and did the curing in our family. After I observed some of those remedies, I made sure that I stayed far away from my grandmother when I was injured. I remember once when my brother had a bad cut on his hand. My grandmother went out into the garden looking for a special leaf. When she had the leaf, she then, believe it or not, urinated on the leaf and wrapped it around my brothers cut hand. That was not my kind of medicine.

I am searching my memory to get the proper timeline as life developed during those years. I don't remember exactly when, but we finally did get running water to the building that contained the kitchen and eating facilities. A short time after that, the water was extended to the sleeping quarters. Real sinks, bathtubs, and bathrooms started to appear. All the farms like my grandparents had in that area were going through the same hard times.

In order to make ends meet, they started converting the farms to 'Kochalain', the Yiddish term that translates to 'cooking alone'. They would build a main building that contained sleeping accommodations to be rented out. They would build a cooking and dining facility to accommodate the people renting the sleeping accommodations. The cooking facilities contained stoves, ice boxes, tables and chairs for dining, and tables for preparing food to accommodate each of the sleeping quarters. Each sleeping quarter had its own cooking area. They rented the place for the summer to families who wanted to get out of the city's heat. This arrangement created better income than trying to run the farm. Most of the smaller operations, like my grandparents, eventually failed and the bank took them over. But the farms that were a little bit larger succeeded, and after the Second World War, ended up being major resort hotels in the area. This area was known as the 'Borscht Belt' because they were owned and run by the Jewish families that were struggling as farmers in those early days. Borsht is a beet soup that was very popular in the Jewish community.

One day at the end of a summer's visit at the farm, I remember my father telling me that we would no longer be staying at the farm in the future summers. My father said to remember the good days on the farm because it was a very important time in my life to experience life out of the city. The reason that we would not be able to visit the farm again was because the bank took the farm in a foreclosure. Needless to say, I was devastated. The only part of my life where I really enjoyed my everyday experience was to be no longer. We then went back to the city for the rest of the year.

Sometime around February or March, my mother told me that they met some friends who spent the summers at a place called Lake Hopatcong in New Jersey. They said there might be an opportunity to spend the summers at that location. I had never heard of Lake Hopatcong or where it was located. Since at that time there was no such thing as computers, Google, iPhones, etc., I started to ask people if they had ever heard of Lake Hopatcong. The answer was always the same, never heard of the place.

Then one evening, my parents invited the friends who told them about Lake Hopatcong for dinner at our apartment. During dinner, the guests told us all about that great place to spend some time. The lake was located in New Jersey, as I remember, about a 3-hour drive from Brooklyn. It was a very large lake, about four or five square miles, with homes scattered around the lake that were one-family summer-type vacation homes. These homes had a yard that extended down to the water where there was a small pier. Most of the homes had some kind of boat, like a rowboat, canoe, sailboat, or powerboat. It was a great place for fishing. There weren't too many homes around the lake and the scenery of all that wooded area was beautiful. They knew of a small bungalow colony located on the lake front that rented out those bungalows for the summer. They only had about five bungalows for rent. The rent was very modest since very few people visited that area in those hard times.

The closest town, which was a 5-minute walk from the bungalows, was called River Styx. The town consisted of four buildings. There was a grocery store, Dolly Madison ice cream store, hardware store, and a place called The Madhouse. The Madhouse only opened in the evenings on the weekends during the summer when homeowners came there to enjoy the outdoor life. The Madhouse was basically a place where young people could meet, have a hotdog or hamburger and listen to the music from some local band. If anyone had any kind of talent, like singing or telling jokes, there was always an open mic for them. This was the only entertainment in that area.

My parents checked out the place for themselves. The bungalow only had running water. There was no electricity, so you had to use kerosene lanterns. For cooking, there was a stove fed by a large gas canister on the side of the bungalow. The entire bungalow contained one fairly large room that was used as a bedroom, dining room, kitchen, and small closet. The toilet was located outside on the porch. There was an ice box, which was a real icebox. Every day, the iceman would come with his truck loaded with blocks of ice. He would take out an ice pick and cut off a hunk of ice suitable to fit the icebox. As the ice melted, it dripped through a tube to a pan on the floor under the unit. That meant every day we had to get more ice and clean out the water. That was high-tech at the time and it did help keep the food fresh for a while.

The entire situation was very basic, but also very inexpensive. I don't remember how much it cost for rent or how my parents was able to get that money since I was about ten years old at the time. My mother and brother slept in the bed. My brother was about 2 years old at the time. I had a cot to sleep in. We all lived in that one room. My father would come up on the weekends and share the bed. Living in that bungalow was tight, but the outside area was fantastic. Between the lake for swimming, and all that wooded area for experimenting and discovering, it was a delight. We kept coming up to the lake for about three or four years. The last time I spent there, I was 12 years old. A 12-year-old at that time could take great advantage of going to The Madhouse. There, I was able to meet other 12-year-old boys and girls, eat great hamburgers, and start to learn about life. When I turned 13, I decided it was time to be on my own. I never spent the summers at Lake Hopatcong anymore.

I remember one mind blowing incident that happened one summer during my family's stay at Lake Hopatcong. I remember this happening after I stopped spending the entire summer there and just came to visit one weekend. My mother, on a number of occasions, would wake up in the morning and tell my brother and I that she had an intuition. An intuition meant that she had a dream in which she saw an event that was going to happen in the near future. We never took my mother seriously because the thought of foreseeing the future in your dream seemed a little impossible. Usually, she would point to something that happened in the future that has some resemblance to her dreams. Whether it was an accurate forecast or not, we did not know and just pooh-poohed the whole idea. At that time, my uncle, Murray, my mother's brother, was serving in the Army and was in combat in Italy during the Second World War. My uncle was part of the big push by General Patton, fighting his way up the Italian country, to take complete control. My mother woke up one morning at Lake Hopatcong in a sweat and yelled that Murray had been shot. She saw Murray in combat being shot. My mother insisted that we write down the date and time of her intuition. We followed her instructions and placed the paper with the information on it on the table and put the saltshaker on top to prevent it from blowing away. To the best of my knowledge, about two weeks later, a representative of the U.S. Army informed my mother that Murray Sugarman was wounded in action, underwent surgery, and was doing fine in an Army hospital. We were all blown away. Her dream, or intuition as she called it, was right on the money as to the event, time, and date. Why and how it worked, I do not know. All I know, this was a true happening. From then on, we listened to my mother's intuition with greater interest.

Years later, after Harriet and I were married for about five years, we drove down to Lake Hopatcong so I could show her where I spent some of my youth. When we arrived at River Styx, I was in a state of shock. There was a huge town. In fact, it looked more like a city, with a great many stores like a supermarket, fast food places, parking lots, and everything else that goes with the modern city. The lakefront was crowded with all sorts of buildings that replaced all that beautiful woodland that I explored to my heart's content. It was so disappointing, that we just drove through the town, made a U-turn and went back home to reality.

One incident I remember is from when I was 7 or 8 years old. My mother was an extrovert and always the center of attention. She was just loud. She thought she was the entertainer for the evening, but she was awful. She tried to push me into also being an extrovert. In our neighborhood there was a primitive recording studio. This studio gave you the opportunity to make your own recording. My mother talked me into making a recording. She paid the fee, they put me into one of those booths, and told me to sing the hot song that was going around in those days, Chattanooga Choo Choo. I sat in that booth, all by myself, staring at that microphone and wanting to cry. However, with the Warden --- oops, I mean my mother staring through the glass window, I started to sing. I completed the song and my mother received the final disc, which she quickly played. To her horror, which also meant to my horror, for some reason due to the pressure I was under, I did not include the phrase 'ham and eggs in Carolina'. If guns were available in those days as they are today, I'm sure I would have used one to end my misery.

The only way I was able to get back to a normal state of mind was when I got home and my little dog would lick me with a joyful smile on its face. Speaking of my dog, whose name and sex I don't remember, it was very easy for me to take care of this companion. At that time, we were living in a three-story six-family apartment building. Our apartment was on the second floor. The door to the lobby at the street level was always open. Every morning, I opened the front door of our apartment and my little four-legged companion ran down the steps and out into the street. In those days, there were a huge number of vacant lots all around the neighborhood. My dog would relieve itself, meet up with some of his friends, and have a great morning. When I was ready to go to school, I would just whistle, and up the stairs that dog would come right into our apartment.

My Early Life

At the time I reached the age of 13, I sat myself down and had a long hard searching conference. I declared that I do not want to live a life of yelling, fighting, and aggravation without love or enjoyment. The only times in my life when there was some joy, was on the farm or at Lake Hopatcong. Those were the days when my father spent Monday to Friday in New York working and my mother and I, with my brother, later on, were alone for the summer. But that was only two months out of the year. I felt that we go through life just once and it should be with joy, love, and understanding every day of the year. I then came up with a number of laws to live by. I use the word 'law' so that what I am about to create cannot be broken.

My Bar Mitzvah

My Laws To Live By:
1. Learn how to do everything there is in this world that I need for my self-preservation. These items include, but are not limited to, learn how to cook, sew, clean, shop, travel, etc. In addition, learn how to use a bank and other institutions. I must also learn how to carve wood and stone, make jewelry, work with leather, and any other hobby that's available that might come in handy someday to earn money. Through the years I learned how to use row boats, canoes, sailboats and powerboats and as time passed I learned how to fly a plane, handle guns and live & survive in the woods etc. I must acquire just one hobby, and that hobby is, to

find as many hobbies as I can that might be useful in the future. I must be completely self-sufficient.
2. Never ask anyone for help unless the task is beyond my mental or physical capability. If I have to move a television set from one apartment to another, I will either lift it, or make a dolly, or find some way to move it without asking help. However, if I have to move a piano from the 12th floor of one building to the 15th floor of another building a few blocks away, then I can ask for help and get a moving company.
3. Finances: Live within your means. If you cannot afford the item, then live without it. Never borrow money or go into debt. Any money that you are able to invest that produces dividends or income becomes principal. Money that became principal can never be spent. The only forms of money that can be spent are dividends or income produced by the principal.

As of the writing of this book, I did and continue to live by these laws. When I was 13 and came up with these laws, I made up my mind to put these laws into action. I separated my daily life from my dysfunctional family and felt that I was on my own. I used my parents' house just as a place to sleep. I put all my energy into finding ways to make money and to be self-sufficient while still going to school. I was able to start by getting part-time work after school and Saturdays. I worked at a delicatessen store, a toy store where I put together package toys for display, delivered dry cleaning, helper on a moving truck, etc.

There were some other moneymaking ideas that I came up with that could be a little shady. There was a catering hall in our neighborhood. After the weekend of weddings and parties, they would put all the empty soda bottles in wooden cases and pile them up in the alley on the side of the building. Monday morning, the soda company would pick up the empty bottles to refill them for the next week. However I saw an opportunity. Since my brother was nine years younger than I and he had a baby carriage, I borrowed that carriage Sunday night and stopped by that catering hall. I helped myself to some of those soda bottles, hauling them away in my brother's carriage. The next day, I cashed in two or three at a time at different stores throughout the neighborhood. I know that it was a little off color, however stealing some bottles for recycling is a minor offense. It wasn't like mugging anybody or breaking into a house.

Great Ideas That Did Not Work

One cold windy day, I was with a friend on our way to the local deli for lunch. As we were walking, my friend was having a very hard time trying to light a cigarette in that wind. As I watched him, I noticed that there was a great opportunity. Why not design a self-lighting cigarette? Not having any engineering background or work shop to make this thought a reality, I proceeded anyway. After much brainstorming, I had the answer. Attach a cigarette filter-like cylinder to the lighting end of the cigarette. Coat the interior surface of the attachment with the chemicals on the tip of a match (Sulfur). Install a flywheel with an abrasive surface touching the Sulfur coating on the cylinder. Enjoy the moment of triumph, when you want to light a cigarette. Just inhale, and get the flywheel spinning, to create the striking effect of a match, and you have a 'self-lighting cigarette'.

Now that I have this great invention that will make me rich, I built a prototype to the best of my ability. Being very proud of myself, I put the cigarette in my mouth and took the first inhale. Nothing happened. The flywheel did not spin. I took a deeper inhale, nothing. I used all the strength of my body with a great inhale, until my face was deep dark red and I held on to the table to prevent me from falling. Nothing. After about four more of those humongous inhales, it lit and filled my lungs with the Sulphur, which started me choking. After I recovered from that disaster, I realized that much more technology was needed. A Sulphur filter and a spring-loaded flywheel should do the trick. At least I tried. Maybe in the future, with more knowledge, I will try again.

As time went by, I got another great get-rich idea. This time, I was riding in the New York City subway. The train was traveling through the long underground tunnel to the next station. Looking out the window, I noticed the steel columns that support the roof of the tunnel. As those equally spaced steel columns passed by, a great idea popped into my head. For those senior citizen readers who remember the first movies called Nickelodeon, you will know just what my brain concocted. Take a group of photographs with each one depicting a slightly changed image and stack them. When you flip them with your finger, you will see a movie. Taking this concept, instead of stacking the photos, blow them up to a large size and mount each photo in proper order between the steel columns in the subway tunnel. As the train passes by, it will create the same effect. Now you can have a movie commercial to entertain the passengers while traveling from station to station.

I took this concept and created a model to demonstrate how it would work. I contacted the New York City subway authority to find out how I could test this theory. I was notified that MacArthur Advertising had the contract for all advertising devices that were installed within the subway system. They gave me the name of the person to speak to with my idea. MacArthur Advertising had mostly cardboard ads mounted in the subway cars above the windows. They also had large three-dimensional light boxes mounted in positions for viewing while standing at the station. When I spoke to the Vice President at MacArthur Advertising he told me that it was a good idea and might work. However, it was not very practical, due to the fact that all those photographs would have to be kept clean, as well as maintaining the lights that would be needed to illuminate each photograph. That would mean working in the tunnel with the trains constantly zooming by. Any maintenance crew would have to notify the transit department to shut down the operation of the trains where the crews of MacArthur Advertising would be working. That would never happen. In addition, it would be too expensive. I hung up the phone. I sat and looked out the window. I thought to myself there must be some way to get rich quick.

My Early Professional Life ... and Harriet

One day when I was eleven years old, I met a friend named Alan Friedman. He was in the same family situation as I was, so we became partners. After we had a moneymaking brainstorming session, we decided to become photographers. I don't remember when or how we got the money to buy our first camera, a 4x5 Speed Graphic. That was the state-of-the-art in photography at that time and was very primitive.

The first challenge we had was to create a dark room. It was at this time that I realized that every day, opportunity passes in front of you. The problem is that 80% of people do not see these possibilities, 15% see the opportune and do nothing, but only the last 5% see the possibility and take action. They are the leaders in this world. I decided to be in that 5% and proceed through the day always looking for opportunities. That way I will find them. Without thinking, I said, "Let's see how we can get a dark room without paying rent".

After a day or two of putting my new theory into action, I noticed an opportunity right in front of me. In those days, all homes were heated with coal fired boilers. The homeowner would fill the boiler with coal and let it burn all night long to keep the house warm. In the morning, they would stoke the boiler, take out all the ashes, and put them in these big garbage cans. They would have to move the garbage cans from the cellar to the sidewalk for the Department of Sanitation to collect.

I noticed that our neighbor was pretty much getting to be a senior citizen. It looked like he had trouble getting all those ash cans which were quite heavy out to the street. I approached the gentleman with a proposition. I said that every day before school we would take all the ashes out and put them on the street for him. In return, he would let us use a part of his cellar as a dark room. The elderly gentleman's face lit up with joy as he said, "Kid, you have a deal". We quickly ran out and obtained secondhand equipment and set up a darkroom. We were now in business.

Alan and I, baby photographers.

The next problem awaited us. We needed customers. How could we take pictures of people who'd be willing to pay us for our photographs? A couple of days later, Alan and I were walking down one of our main streets in the neighborhood when we passed a Laundromat. As I looked through the window, I saw our opportunity. I said, "Alan, there are our customers". A little confused, he said "I don't see customers." "Look who is in there. Young mothers with their babies. We are now baby photographers. Follow me." We went into the Laundromat and asked to see the manager. I told him I had a deal for him, to get many customers without spending any money. I told him I wanted to put up a sign in his Laundromat that would say anybody who uses this business is entitled to one free 8 x 10 color photograph, taken of their child, in their own home. Yes, I know there was no such thing as color photography in those days. However, we did have Marshall oil colors. They were just tubs of a paste-like tint. All I had to do is put a little tint on cotton, rub it on the photograph, and lo and behold, it looks like a color photograph. The laundromat manager said, "You got it, kid", and we were really in business. The sign went up and the phone started to ring.

After school, we took our camera and lights on a trolley to the people's homes and photographed their babies. When photographing babies, we learned very quickly that you cannot put the baby on the floor and photograph them while standing. The results of that technique created a horrible photograph. We learned that we must put the baby on a bed or chair at the same height and level as the camera to create a great photograph. One time, I noticed when photographing a baby using this technique, that the baby was not very happy and had a frightened look on his face. I was using every trick I knew, which were not many at that time, to get the baby to smile. I turned to the mother to ask her for a toy that I could use to get the baby to smile. Then it hit me. Looking at the mother's face, I saw the same expression of fear. I realized that the baby was not afraid, but the mother was afraid that her baby might fall off the chair that we had the baby on. I realized that the baby and mother were communicating with one another without using any language.

Did I just discover something about human communication that nobody else knew? If this phenomenon is for real, and I can master it, what an advantage I can have over people. I had no idea that there was a science called body language. So, to test my theory, I observed people and tried to put their actions together with their thoughts. After about a year of observation, I was starting to get a positive feeling for understanding body language. I observed people throughout the years and was able to use what I learned to my advantage. By the time I was in my 20s, I had a good understanding of body language. Upon meeting somebody for the first time, in a couple of minutes, I am able to learn so much about that person's personality. I am not always right, but 90 to 95% of the time, I'm right on the button. Nothing in this life is 100%. I do not consider myself an expert in this field however I am an A student.

What I did learn from the experts is that the human body, as far as body language is concerned, contains two actions. The first action is voluntary. When you want to lift a glass of water, your voluntary system uses your brain and your muscles and your hand moves to pick up the glass and move it to your mouth so you can drink. That's voluntary. Involuntary actions are the systems of your body that work by themselves. You have absolutely no control. The beating of your heart, the digestion of food, and all the other hundreds, if not thousands, of actions that your body does that you have no control over. Body language is controlled by the action of your body that's uncontrollable by you. For example, if you were telling a lie, that is your voluntary system working. However you're involuntary system now knows that you are telling a lie. It will move your hands, face and other parts of your body which telegraph to the world that you are lying. Situations like that I spot very easily. Any further discussion of body language is for another book or come to one of my lectures on the subject.

Back to photography: We developed the film and made proofs to show the mother. She would select the photo for us to make the free 8 x 10 in color. We also made up what we call a mother-in-law album. This album contained six 4" x 6" photographs of the baby with a nice cover and simple spiral binding that held this little book together. When we gave the mother the free 8x10 photo, we also showed her the little mother-in-law album. Quite often, the moms would get excited and buy one for her parents and another for her husband's parents and others for the rest of the family. This was a great financial help to our business.

One of the other opportunities came to me while looking to meet girls. The state-of-the-art way young boys and girls could get together and meet in a safe environment was not like it is today. No way, in those days, would any young person go to a bar or any other unsavory institution to meet. Instead, groups like the Catholic Youth Organization, Jewish Community Center, and similar organizations had dances free of charge on weekends. That was the way young people could meet in a safe environment.

One Saturday night, Alan and I went to one of those dances to meet girls. It was winter time, so we all had hats and coats. Again, opportunity is right before you every day. You just have to see it and act. As we entered the dance hall, we took our hats and coats and dropped them on a large table and some chairs in the corner, with all the other hats and coats. Seeing this cash of hats and coats, I said to Alan, "Let's see the manager of this building". We found the manager and I said to the gentleman, "I will give you $10 at the end of the evening of the next dance, if you give us the use of one of your rooms near the entrance, so we could set up a hatcheck concession. Ten dollars was a lot of money in those days. The manager jumped at the deal and he said, "Yes. You got it."

For the next dance, we bought a roll of coat check tickets and the New York Times. The manager gave us the room at the entrance and a table to use. We put up a sign that said, "Check your hat and coat". Not having coat racks or hangers, we put the New York Times on the floor. As the people arrived and saw the sign, they checked their coats with us. We took the coats, folded them up and put them on the NY Times, with the ticket tucked in the collar. We were in business.

After all the kids were in the room and the dance had started, we had nothing to do until the dance was over. So we took our camera out and took photographs of the kids sitting at tables or dancing. Upon making a sale, the kids gave us money and we took their address to mail them the photos. We made enough money to pay the $10 for the manager. Alan & I took home about $20 each. That was a lot of money in those days. Remember, bread was 10 cents a loaf. All of this was done while we were on our way out of junior high school and going into high school.

We were now in high school with the Second World War in full blast. The depression seemed to be a thing of the past. Everyone was involved in the war effort. Alan and I had learned how to photograph weddings, which we did for local studios on the weekends. We also learned to shoot portraits and work with business people.

At this time in my life, I took a job as a bus boy at a guesthouse in a summer boys' camp in upstate New York. The camp consisted of two sections. On one side of the lake were the boys, Camp Rosemont and the other side of the lake were the girls, Camp Rose Lake. My quarters were near the guesthouse, where the parents of all the campers went when visiting on the weekends. My job was to get up early in the morning, make the coffee in large coffee urns, and go to the on-site bakery to get fresh buns, bread and cakes to be served during the day. This was the best time of the day for me. Once the coffee was made, and all the bread and buns were in the dining room, the staff sat down to breakfast. It was a great, relaxing time, before the onslaught of parents came tearing into the dining room. Then my job began. I had to take the used plates off the tables at the end of each course, and do it with a smile. I had this big tray that I piled the used dishes on, then gingerly walk them back to the dishwashers in the kitchen.

One day, after the breakfast meal was finished, the guests were gone and I finished cleaning up the dining room, I left with a smile on my face since the morning chores were done. I proceeded down the stairs on the exterior of the building to go to my quarters. When I reached the bottom of the stairs, this lovely young lady was sitting there enjoying the quiet morning. She turned to me, and like the sound of music, I heard her say, "Do you have a cigarette?" Wow!! With this beginning, a wonderful life was on its way. After giving her a cigarette, which I hated to smoke and don't know why I was smoking, she told me her name was Harriet Levine, and asked, "What's yours?" "Al Efron", I proclaimed and I sat down next to her. It didn't take long for us to become an item at the camp. It was supposed to be, as they say, 'just a summer romance'; however, it lasted for 63 wonderful years of marriage, until her passing.

Just to clarify my previous statement that I hated to smoke but did smoke. In those days, you ate food, drank liquids, and took care of all of the functions of the human body, of which smoking was just another function of living. It just did not enter my mind to stop smoking. To ease the dry throat I had from smoking, I used to suck on Pine Brothers cough drops. One evening, I was out with some friends, as everybody, including me, started to light up cigarettes. There was a young man standing next to me and I graciously offered him a cigarette. He looked at me and said in a proud voice, "I do not smoke". My goodness, is this a human being? How does he live? Then I realized, you do not have to smoke to exist. I threw away the pack of cigarettes and never smoked again for the rest of my life. And I found to my amazement that life went on much better than it did while smoking. I wondered, "Why does everyone smoke?"

Alan and I were about to graduate from high school at this time and become full-time professional photographers. Photography was to be our lives' profession. Weddings and commercial photography for small businesses were most of our clients. We managed to become the house photographers for two catering halls. One was Toffinedies on 43rd Street, off-Broadway in Manhattan. They had an upscale restaurant on the street floor and wedding facilities on the second floor. As the restaurant booked a wedding, they gave us the phone numbers of the couples to be married. We would call them and get booked to photograph their wedding. The restaurant, as they say, got a piece of the action. We also hooked up with small factories and photographed some of their products to be put in their brochures. In addition, we shot weddings for other photo studios, as a fill in. Everything was looking up to a bright future.

My Young Adult Life

When the summer was over, Harriet and I were both living in Brooklyn and started to see each other seriously. As time went on, and we all graduated from high school, Harriet went on to Brooklyn College. Not being academically smart enough to go to college, I became a photographer. One day, Harriet and I were sitting around the house and talking about our future. She looked at me and said, "I do not think that you are the stupid person that you make out to be because of your terrible experience in elementary school. I see all the things you have been doing that most people never see or think possible. I think your problem is that you are dyslexic."

I looked at her and asked, "What is dyslexic?" She described to me what Dyslexia is; a mixed dominance of your eyes. Most people are either right-handed or left-handed; the same goes with the eyes. People are either right eye or left eye dominant. In my case, I do not have a dominant eye. When I read, "the boys threw the ball", what I actually see is "the boy balled the threw", as my eyes change dominance in the middle of the sentence. That is why I have difficulty reading and doing math or spelling. None of my teachers or doctors ever picked up on this problem. Once I realized the problem, a whole new world opened to me. Knowing the problem, I can easily work around it. It took a high school kid to outsmart the medical and teaching profession.

Now that I knew I was dyslexic, and not stupid, I realized I could always find ways to compensate for my handicap, as to not interfere with my living experience. I understood that as I go through life, there will be times when I would have to speak in public. However, being dyslexic would be a terrible handicap.

To try to cope with this situation, I signed up to take a course in public speaking. During the first lesson, the instructor handed out books to each student. He told us he wanted each one of us, in turn, to get up at the front of the class and read one paragraph. This, to me, seems like a stupid way to teach somebody the art of public speaking. I was concerned that I wouldn't make sense when I read out loud. I quickly counted the people in front of me, which were 12, as I remember. I counted down to the 12th paragraph. I quickly memorized the 11th, 12th, and 13th paragraphs, just in case somebody left the room or another person entered the room. The speeches began. When it came to my turn, I was to read the 12th paragraph. I got up at the front of the class, looked at the book, and just spoke out loud from my memory, while giving the impression that I was actually reading. When I had finished, the teacher said that it was good, but the next time I should speak a little more slowly. At the end of that first session in this class, I decided that this was not for me and I would have to learn the art of public speaking on my own, and that I did. Later on in life, I would analyze every public speaking event that I attended, until I understood exactly how to perform the art.

My Army Life

After high school, Alan and I continued our business as professional photographers. We were slowly building up our business to the point where we started to discuss opening our own studio. After about three years in our chosen profession, the world scene took control of our lives. It was June 1950. The world event was Korea. Here we go again with another war. The draft was starting to build up the army by the fall of 1950. It didn't take long for us to realize our photography business might have to be put on hold. Alan, I, and some other friends about the same age, were prime targets for the draft. We were discussing what we should do for our future. Since we were all of the age that just missed being called up for the Second World War, we were on the top of the list to save the world from Communism.

The first thought that my friend came up with was that we should enlist so we could choose the branch of the service that we wanted. Nobody wanted to go into the Army. The Air Force or Navy was a better choice. I had a different attitude. I told them that I was going to wait until they called me. My hope was they would either lose my name or forget me in the bureaucratic mess. However, by the time I got home that afternoon, I found a letter from the draft board that said, "Greetings. Report to Whitehall Street for your induction physical" on a date in December noted in the letter. All men of my age found ourselves with a future that we could not control. My mother felt that if our doctor gave me a letter, describing how sick I was, they might turn me down. The problem; I was not sick. However I got a letter I brought down for my physical and hoped for the best.

The date for my induction physical arrived and I, like a good citizen, reported to Whitehall Street. Taking that physical was my first experience in learning that you could not be shy in these conditions. For the first time in my life, I was standing completely nude, with about 25 other souls like myself, facing a uniformed medical person. He instructed us to jump up and down, swing our arms above our heads, spread our legs and bring them together, as all our private body parts were flapping in the wind. At that time, we were all looking for a hole to crawl in. "Congratulations", the uniform man said, "Your bodies look pretty good to me". We were taken one-by-one for individual inspections. I handed him the hot little letter that my doctor wrote stating I was not fit for service. One of the items that he mentioned was that I was hard of hearing. When I read that, it was news to me! The doctor who was examined my hearing, read the note. He instructed me to walk to the end of the room. I followed his orders beautifully. The doctor then said to me, "Turn Around", and so I did. He said, "You're in the Army". I did not realize, but when he said, "Turn Around", that was the hearing test. For the rest of the examination, you can use your imagination to visualize the demoralizing of a young spirit. When we were all dressed and the exam was completed, I was told to report to Fort Devens, Massachusetts, to the best of my memory, on March 5, 1951. I reported as told, like a good soldier, and this new chapter in my life began.

Private Albert Efron, Top Row, Sixth from Right.

The first shock of the reality of living an army life hit me square in the face when I walked into the barracks for the first time. What I saw, I could not believe. These were going to be my living conditions for the next two years!! As I entered this two-story wooden structure, I turned my head to the right. There, before my eyes, I saw the horrors of all horrors. This room they called the latrine. On one side, up against the wall that was about 20 feet long, was a line of water closets. No partitions. No doors. They were fully exposed water closets, with rolls of toilet paper on the floor in front of some of them. As I stared at the situation, I tried to imagine myself sitting there, with everyone else doing what I was doing, making bodily noises and odors. It dawned upon me. If

33

I were sitting where there was no toilet paper, I would have to ask my neighbor to please send the toilet paper down. One-by-one, each exposed body would pass the toilet paper down, for my use. This must be some nightmare. It just couldn't be true!!

I turned my head to the left. Another fantastic shock! There was a long pipe, about 6 feet off the floor, attached to one wall, running the full length of the wall. I could see that there were a series of large holes, every few feet, where water came out. This became reality when I realized that this was our shower facility. Again, there were no walls, no doors, just naked bodies, side-by-side, passing the soap.

I took a deep breath, and hoped that when I had to use these facilities, no one had diarrhea or other stinky bathroom emergency. I just had to take advantage of the facilities, and like it or not, I had to accept it. It turns out that the 'water closets' mentioned before, were really only a platform with toilet seats on them. It was an open pit underneath. It was a totally disgusting lake of human waste floating just a few feet under our butts. A nasty trick that my fellow soldiers would play was to light some paper and float it on the lake. As the fire floated under someone's butt, you'd hear them scream and jump up, all to the crowd's delightful laughter.

After spending the first three weeks in the Army, the realities of life settled in. Up until then, I spent my entire life as a self-sufficient individual and completely in control of my actions. I really never had a boss or some other controlling person making all decisions for me. And here I was a buck private. Anyone with any rank at all could be giving me orders. I was not a happy camper. In fact, I was miserable, and tried to figure out how to survive the next two years. Evidently, my feelings were firmly expressed in my body language.

I was approached by two gentlemen. One said, "Young man, I see you don't like army life. If you would like to be discharged right away with a medical discharge, it could be arranged. It will just cost you $400 and you will become a citizen once more." This proposal sounded tempting. I thought about it for two days and realized that this offer could ruin my entire future. No, I was going to stay in the Army for my two years and hope for the best. In order to cheer me up, I called Harriet and asked her to have her father drive her up to the camp, so that I could propose marriage. She agreed, and my whole attitude changed!

On the day that Harriet and her father were to meet me at the camp, I got dressed in my Class A uniform and waited for word that they had arrived. The day slowly dragged on and no one showed up. I was getting worried. Then about 4 o'clock, I was told to report to the day room. It was Harriet with her father. "What took you so long", I uttered. She said that they were there 4 hours ago and asked to see Private Albert Efron. The response from the clerk looking through all the names on the base was that here was no Albert Efron in this Army. To make a long story short, the Army, in its infinite wisdom, had on all their forms I had filled out, a room for my first name, middle initial, and last name. Since I do not have a middle initial, I left the space blank. I did not know that on a bureaucratic form in the Army you cannot leave blank spaces. The clerk solved the problem by taking the E from Efron and moving it over to become a middle initial. That made me Albert E. FRON. That little clerical error could have ruined our complete lives.

We were finally together, including Harriet's father. We went to the PX. Harriet's father was looking at something across the room. I proposed to Harriet. There were lots of hugs and kisses. Harriet left for home with her father after our short 90-minute visit. I felt great and ready to put in my two years without a problem.

During my two years in the Army, someone must have been watching over me. I made many mistakes, some bad and some stupid decisions. They eventually resulted to work out in my favor. As I recall, this entire phase of my life, I still wonder how and why everything turned out in my favor. The first problem I had was being assigned for basic training at Camp Edwards in Massachusetts. I was assigned to an Alabama National Guard outfit. The guys in this outfit served in the Second World War and stayed with the National Guard upon being discharged in 1945. When the Korean conflict started in 1951, they were activated back in the service. These guys were pissed off for being called up a 2nd time. Just my luck, an innocent Jewish boy from New York City, was assigned to that outfit. I was the only one not part of the original Alabama National Guard unit from WWII. Being from New York City was bad enough, but also a Jew? It is hard to believe that I survived my time in that redneck outfit. The first problem was trying to understand what they were saying since to my ear they did not speak the English language. Simple terms like 'Scutidee', meaning 'it is a good idea', drove me up the wall.

In those days, I had a heavy beard. I shaved every morning. By lunchtime, my facial hairs started to show. Our Sargent was constantly getting on my back saying, "I want you to shave every day, soldier". I told him I did shave that morning. With that, he told me to empty out the coal bin, clean it so it shines. There I was, shoveling all the coal out of the bin and piling it on the side, cleaning the concrete floors and sides until they shined. I reported my work to the Sargent. He said, "Okay soldier, put the coal back in the coal bin".

Another time, the Jewish holidays arrived, and I was given a leave to go home to celebrate. The morning that I was to catch the train back to New York, I had just enough time to get to the train station after we lined up for roll call. I was dressed my class A uniform. My beloved Sergeant ordered me to clean out all the latrines before I leave for the holiday. "But Sergeant", I said, "I'm going to miss my train." He looked at me with a smile and said, "Start cleaning the latrine." Life was not very pleasant under those situations.

Finally, one day, a nice Italian kid from New York was assigned to the outfit. Now there were two of us and we felt we had some strength. To show off our strength, we came up with a brilliant idea. When we were marching, we sang a marching cadence, "Head and eyes off the ground. We're the boys from Alabam. Sound off 1, 2" etc. At the first opportunity, the two of us proudly shouted, "Make it smart and make it pretty. We're the boys from New York City. Sound off 1, 2" and at just about at the time we got to "1, 2", I never saw so many fists flying in my face and stomach before. After that, I guess we were the boys from Alabam.

All was never well in this outfit. The barracks were basically a two-story wood frame building. There was a small 2-foot overhang canopy over the windows on the first floor. The second floor had the extension of the roof going two feet beyond the face of the building, covering the second floor windows. It was standard operating procedure that when you washed small garments like underwear, you laid them out on the overhang canopy over the first-floor to dry.

One day, I had my item drying in the sun on that overhang when a gust of wind blew it past the window, but it stayed on the overhang. It was too far for me to reach by hand, so I climbed out the window and walked along the overhang to retrieve the garment. On the way back to the window, one of those redneck back-woodsman thought he would be funny by pushing my feet toward the end of the overhang. To keep myself from falling off, I grabbed the overhang above my head. It was a great joke on his part as he kept on laughing. As I came closer to the window, again he pushed my legs, and tried to knock me off the canopy. I told him in no uncertain terms, "the joke is over, get out of my way so I can get back into the building". Since I was wearing combat boots, I told him I would smash my combat boots right through the window, aimed at his head. I was very angry and all fired up. My life meant nothing to him and he kept pushing. I grabbed the top overhang above my head, swung my foot around, and smashed it through the middle of the window. I looked through the broken window and saw him on the floor, squirming as his friends ran over to see if they could help him. They saw shards of glass imbedded in his face. One of his friends quickly put him into a Jeep and they were off to the first aid station. I climbed through the broken window and got back into the building. The rest of those rednecks looked at me and stepped back as I walked toward them. They all got out of my way. After that incident, I never heard any news of what happened to that fellow with glass in his face. No one ever came to investigate what happened. All those Alabama boys left me alone after that. The only thing that happened was that a maintenance staff member came to the barracks and replaced the window.

One day, we were notified to pack our gear for a trip to Fort Bragg, North Carolina to participate in war games. These games were designed to get us ready for combat in Korea. Those two weeks playing war in the deep South opened my eyes to what discrimination really was all about. On my first day we were setting up camp in a cotton field, where we were to stay and play war. The cotton fields were worked by tenant farmers. I learned that a tenant farmer was a black family that worked and lived in the field. They were paid a very small percentage of the profit from sale of cotton. The living conditions were beyond belief. Their house, if you could call it a house, had windows with all the glass missing or shattered. There were no toilets, only outhouses. The roof looked as if it were ready to fall off the building.

I saw the women standing over a wood fire in front of the house with a large steel pot hanging from a tripod over the fire. The pot was full of water that was being heated by the fire. After the water was hot, the laundry was put in the pot. The women, with large paddles, would beat the laundry in an attempt to clean them. The children looked almost bare. Their clothes were very old and worn out. The entire situation in my eyes was deplorable. In discussing the situation with my fellow Alabama soldiers, they looked at me and wondered why I thought this scene was terrible. "They're just niggers. For niggers, that is a great set up. They're working and making money. What's wrong with that?" Since I had spent my entire life up North, I had no idea how horrible poverty in the US really was. I had no further discussion on this subject with my fellow Southern boys.

This was also the first time that I ever saw a cotton plant. I thought it would be very nice to send one of these plants back home to Harriet so she too could see cotton in plant form. I took a Planter's Peanut can and inserted the top of a cotton plant that was nice and white and fluffy. I packaged it up and sent it off to Harriet. Sometime later, I received a letter from Harriet saying she received the package, opened it, and found a little bug crawling over some stems. "What was that supposed to be?" she wanted to know. Evidently, I packed a Boll Weevil in with the cotton. The bug ate the cotton ball during the journey in the can. That just goes to prove that I am really a New York City boy.

When we started to set up the camp, out came little pup tents that we lined up in perfect rows, creating a checkerboard pattern. We were notified to make sure that we cut a small trench around the perimeter of the tent. The reason for this trench was to prevent rainwater from flooding the tent while we were sleeping. For those of you who have never slept in a tent, you must remember never to touch the inside of the tent when it's raining. The minute you touch the canvas, you break the surface tension and water starts dripping in. Since a pup tent is just big enough for one person to sleep in, you have to be very careful not to turn in your sleep and mistakenly swipe the canvas.

I set up my tent, as the rest of the men did, and stood there staring at it. I said to myself, "No way am I going to sleep in that little excuse for protection from the environment." Taps played and all my fellow soldiers crawled into their tents, as did I. I waited about 15 minutes for everything to calm down. Then, I quietly crawled out of the tent, left the field, and found the road. After a minute or two, I noted a car coming along and I flagged them down. I asked the driver if he could take me to the nearest motel in Fayetteville, a few miles away. He said, "Hop in, soldier" and away we went. Upon arriving at the motel, I thanked my newfound friend and quietly checked in for the night. I told the clerk to give me a wake-up call at 4:30 in the morning.

The next morning, after I got the wake-up call, I showered, dressed and walked or hitchhike back to the camp, crawled into my tent just before reveille. Once reveille was sounded, I came out of my tent as everyone else did, clean showered, refreshed and ready to start the war games all over again. I did this for my entire stay, without anyone realizing what I was doing. I must admit I was not a very good soldier.

It was time for the war games to begin. That first morning was very cold. My captain assigned me the job, with two fellow soldiers, to set up his command tent. We diligently went to work to set up the tent and install the portable potbelly stove to provide the necessary heat in the tent. We put firewood in the stove and informed the captain his tent was ready for use. "Efron", he said, "I am taking the men out for our first maneuvers. I want you to keep the fire in that tent burning while I am out with the men. It is your job to make sure that enough wood is always in the stove." I sat down in the tent to carry out my orders. It did not take me long to get bored sitting and watching a fire. I got this bright idea, to fill the stove with as much wood that would fit in. That would give me some free time to get a cup of coffee, maybe a snack, and enjoy these war games. I was killing time in the mess tent area when I heard my captain screaming out at the top of his lungs, "Efron, where the hell are you?" I gently put down the cup of coffee and snacks and ran out to see what the problem was. There, to my shocking surprise, was the captain's tent on fire in a full blaze. Evidently, by over-stuffing the stove, it got too hot and the exhaust pipe must have touched the tent and set it on fire. My first thought was, "How long will I be sentenced to the brig?" However, my good captain was so angry that he assigned two other GIs to clean up the mess and rebuild the tent. He stormed out, completely forgetting about me. I quietly waited the rest of the day for something to happen. Time slowly ticked away as the sun went down and the evening approached and nothing happened. I said to myself, "He probably forgot about me", so I went back to my outfit. I never heard another word from that officer again. For some reason, I was off the hook.

Cleaning my M1 rifle.

One of my army friends had relatives living in the area. He was able to get permission for a short visit with the family. Upon returning to the war games, he brought a bottle of fresh homemade moonshine. I looked at the bottle and it seemed like clear water. "No", he said, "This is the real stuff." He poured a little in a paper cup and handed it to me. "You'll love it", he said. "Well, let's be dangerous", I thought to myself as

I drank it. It was smooth. There was no burning sensation. In fact, for the first few seconds, I thought it was water. But then the kick hit me and my head started to spin. I am not really an alcohol drinker. However, I tried using alcohol to rub on my body to kill the chiggers. These are little bugs that drill into the pores of your skin and call it home. I had them all over me. Those little guys were torture all day long. My southern friends showed me the way to get rid of them. If you lit up a cigarette and held the burning end close to the skin, the little creature would crawl out to get away from the heat. Then you killed it. What an adventure.

War games were started by the army to make it feel like we were really in combat. At one point, an officer came up to me, slapped a notice on my chest, said that I was wounded, and told me to lie down. Two medics came rushing up to save my life. I hope those medics had more training and learned to do it correctly.

We then played make-believe shooting at one another, crawling under barbed wire, while the instructors were firing what sounded like live 50-caliber machine gun rounds overhead to make it feel like the real thing. I heard an officer yelling, "Keep your head down or you won't have a head". Believe me, my head stayed down. There were many other such delightful tasks. We finally completed the entire experience. Then it was time to clean up the area and make it look like we were never there.

The army wanted to make sure that we got the full taste of completely living in the field without the conveniences of home. We created field toilet facilities by digging a deep trench, placing a Y shaped branch of a tree on each side along the entire trench, and putting a log or heavy tree branch spanning the Ys. When you had to move your bowels, you rested on the branch, relieved yourself, and sprinkled some dirt into the trench, just enough to cover the deposit you left. The day before we were to leave, we were greeted with a heavy snowstorm. That meant the ground was pretty frozen and covered with snow. My Captain instructed me and another lowly Private to fill in the trench with earth. He commanded that we filled the trench in. He wanted it filled solid with earth and was packed down, so that all the deposits would be completely buried in the ground. The big problem was that the earth was so hard and frozen that it was impossible to get any earth to fill in the trench. The two of us were very innovative. We filled in the trench with nice fluffy snow and sprinkled enough earth on top of the snow to give the appearance that we did a magnificent job. I must say that our consciences bothered us, for about 2 seconds, when we thought of springtime. When the snow melts, some lucky person will accidentally find themselves at the bottom of that nasty trench. If you close your eyes and picture that scene, you will understand why I stayed a Private First Class.

We were fully packed and made our way back to our home base to recuperate. Life was back to normal at Camp Edwards for the next few weeks. One bright morning, we learned that we were being shipped out to Wellfleet, Massachusetts for anti-aircraft maneuvers. Pack up the duffel bag for the trip as soon as possible and then wait. Typical army routine was 'hurry up and wait'. Finally, all the trucks arrived that were going to transport us to Wellfleet. We were all jammed into the back of the trucks, which formed a neat line behind the Jeep with the Colonel in the lead. The time came for us to get on our way. The Colonel stood up in his Jeep, one hand swinging in a circle around his head, and pointed forward. This simple gesture got the whole convoy roaring down the roadway.

It seemed like eternity until we arrived at the isolated beach where we were to live for the next few days. We set up our pup tents in neat rows and settled down. For the next few days, we were going to practice firing a number of anti-aircraft weapons at a target that was being towed behind an airplane over the ocean. The anti-aircraft weapons were lined up on the beach facing the ocean, ready for action. The first weapon that I was assigned to was a 90-mm anti-aircraft cannon. As I remember, it took a crew of five to operate that instrument of death. I was assigned to sit on the seat at the left side of the weapon, just behind a wheel that controlled the gun to go up or down to find at its target on a vertical line. Located on the seat on the other side of this weapon was another GI with a similar wheel, however his control went from left to right in a horizontal line. The other three GIs' jobs were to load the 90-mm shell into the breach and then fire the weapon. They very quickly reloaded for the next firing. You can imagine the confusion between me operating the unit vertically, and my partner operating the unit horizontally, trying to zero in on the target for an accurate shot. I don't remember how many rounds we were able to fire, but I doubt if any of them hit the target. That maneuver took up the entire first day of our stay on that beach.

The next day we had a new weapon. This time, I saw a whole line of turrets on the beach facing the ocean. Each turret had two 50-mm machine guns on each side, for a total of four weapons, that when fired, all four went into action at the same time. When it was my turn, I hopped into the turret. In front of me was a control stick that would move the turret from right to left and up & down. On top of the control stick was a button that when pressed would fire all four guns. On the side, was a toggle switch with a string around the top of the unit going back to a safety officer behind the turret. This toggle switch, when pushed up, put the turret into a firing position; when pulled down, went into a safe position. In order to fire this weapon, I had to flip the toggle switch to the ON position, aim at the target, and press the trigger button. Then All Hell Breaks Loose!!! If for any reason I lost control, the safety officer would pull the string, which would shut off the unit, and immediately stop the gun from firing. I should note at this time that we were not issued any ear protection, not even cotton to muffle the horrible sound.

If you stood back and looked at the entire situation, you would have seen all these turrets lined up along the beach about 20 feet apart. We were told that in order to prevent any turret from shooting to the extreme left or right, which would annihilate the GIs in those turrets, we should not start firing until the target flying out over the ocean had passed the marker just after the turret on the left . When the target passed that marker, I started shooting. There was another marker on the right indicating when I should stop shooting so I that would not hit the turret on my right. This all seemed so nice and organized to prevent accidents and to give us practice of firing this weapon. I should note again that we did not have any ear protection to protect our eardrums from the tremendously loud noise of all four of those guns firing at once. There I was, sitting in this turret, aiming to my left, but not so far that I would go past the marker and annihilate my buddy on the left, waiting for the plane towing the target to come into my range. The plane started off all the way at the head of the beach and slowly worked his way across the entire row of turrets. One-by-one, as the target came into the range of each turret, they started firing and then shut down so that the next turret could pick up and start firing.

That was my first time in this turret and I had no experience as to what would happen when I pressed that button. There I was, waiting and watching that target getting closer to my range and when it passed the marker, I diligently sited in on that target and pressed the button. In an instant, all hell broke loose. The noise, the vibration, the smoke, and the entire experience was so unexpected and violent that I lost control of the weapon. The safety officer behind me pulled the string and shut the gun down and everything stopped dead in its tracks. When my ears stopped ringing, my body stopped vibrating, and the smoke cleared away, I looked straight ahead. To my amazement, I was facing all the way to the right, aiming at all the turrets down the beach. The safety officer was shouting out to me, "You almost shot the plane pulling the target!!" "Oh my God," I thought, "This is no way to conduct a war." Needless to say, I never fired this weapon in combat. After everybody got a chance at firing both these weapons, we packed up our tents and went back to our home base.

Finally, good fortune came to me when I was notified that I was being sent to Wheel Vehicle Mechanic School in Fort Dix, New Jersey, just a short ride from Brooklyn. I had mixed emotions. Since my profession was that of a photographer, why were they going to re-train me as mechanic? I was told by my Captain, "That's the way the army works and that's what you will do", and that's what I did. Classes started and I decided to do the best I can in this stupid situation. All seemed to be going well. I made a number of friends and we helped one another with our studies.

To my glee, the calendar said it was the Christmas and New Year's season. To celebrate the holidays, we were informed that half the base would be off for Christmas and the other half for New Year's. In that way, there was always somebody at the base and everyone would be able to celebrate some time at home. The notice came down and I was on leave for the Christmas vacation. On the given day, I put on my class A uniform and went off to visit Harriet and her home, where I was able to feel like a human being again. When time was up, after hugs and kisses, I returned to the Army.

Back at the barracks, when looked around, I saw no one. What happened to the rest of the GIs that were supposed to be back from the Christmas vacation? The New Year's group was leaving for vacation and when they were gone I found myself sitting in the barracks all alone. Why am I the only good soldier that came back to the base when I was told to be back? I turned around, went back home, and spent New Year's with Harriet and family.

Upon returning to the base for the second time, I found everyone had returned and things were going back to normal. Two days passed and I was summoned to the Captain's office. There, I found about 10 other GIs waiting for the Captain. He walked in, looked at us, and said, "You were all AWOL. You now have a choice to either plead guilty and get 10 days hard labor, which would be only on this outfit's records. When you go back to your normal outfit, the records will be expunged. Or, you can plead not guilty and go through a court martial, which will be on your personal record forever. If found guilty, which I am sure you will be, you will be sent to prison. Gentleman what's your choice." All 11 of us pled guilty. The Captain then turned to me, I do not know why, and said, "You're in charge. The 10 days hard labor starts now. I want you to take your men and post them each in a barracks boiler room. They are to completely clean out each boiler room and make it shine." Since I was in charge, I marched the men over to the barracks and assigned each man a boiler room to clean it up. I assigned one boiler room for myself, and upon entering it, I found a nice comfortable corner and went to sleep. I guess the rebel in me started to shine.

About two hours passed when I heard someone yelling, "Who's in charge here?" That woke me up. I went out and saw the Captain standing there in a very angry stance. He said to me, "I want to show you something" and we went from boiler room to boiler room. There was no one there. He then said, "Where are all your men that are supposed to be cleaning out these boiler rooms?" I said, "I don't know sir, I posted them and then I started the cleanup my own boiler room." He then said, "I will show you where they are. Come with me", and off we went to the PX, where to my astonishment, were the 10 GIs having a party and enjoying life. For some reason, they all decided to take this route and did not tell me since I was the authority. At that point, one of the men, who I did not know since we all came from different outfits, said that Private Efron posted them as he was told, and they, on their own, decided to go to the PX. I did not know why this fellow put in the good word for me. The Captain turned to me and said, "Return to your barracks and I will deal with you later." I sat in my barracks for two days and nothing happened. I went back to school. Everything was forgotten and I was completely off the hook. I do not know what happened to the other 10 guys and I was not going to try to find out.

While learning to be mechanics, we also learned how to have fun in stupid ways. We discovered that if you took a spark plug and mounted it on the exhaust pipe in the back of the car, with the spark section in the path of the exhausting gas, and then wired it to the battery, and added button on the dashboard, fun was about to start. When you pressed the button, the spark plug would fire. So, just for laughs, we drove into the local town of Wrightstown, and drove down to the middle of Main Street on top of the hill. In the evening, when it's nice and dark, we shut the engine off so some raw gas would run through the exhaust system. We pressed the button. The spark plug fired and a blast of flames flew out the back of the vehicle. What a great way to shock a bunch of civilians. I think about that now and I realize we were acting stupid.

Another thing we learned, that if you didn't like someone, a good way to get satisfaction was to take a potato and jam it in the exhaust pipe, in a way so it could not be seen. When that individual started to drive the car, the exhaust gases couldn't exit and it would blow up the muffler. What fun! To my amazement, the things we were doing were very minor compared to some of the stupid pranks that other guys in the class were doing. I am thankful no one got hurt or was ever accused of any wrongdoing.

Our studies finally came to an end and we were to receive our final test. When it was my turn, they took me into the garage, pointed to a Jeep, and said, "Your test is to drive the Jeep out of the garage". I got in the Jeep and turned on the ignition.. There was actually no sound. To me, that meant something was wrong with the battery. I opened the hood, looked at the battery, and noticed that card board was sticking out from under the clamp around the terminal of the positive side of the battery. I removed the clamp and card board. I put the clamp back on, started the Jeep, and drove it out of the garage. The Captain came up to me and said, "Congratulations! You're now a full-fledged licensed wheel vehicle mechanic".

The first thought I had was that if I was in combat, which did seem very likely, and the enemy was attacking and forcing us to get out of there fast, we would jump into the truck and try to zoom away to safety. I imagined that the truck would not start, and since I am the mechanic, everyone would look to me to get that vehicle working. I would, of course, not know what to do. That was my biggest fear. Thank goodness that scenario never happened.

Upon returning to Camp Edwards, I found out that on July 26, 1948, President Truman signed order number 9981 ending segregation in the Army. It took three years for that order to filter down to the troops and my level. I was told that I was being put in an outfit that was being integrated. I figured, what could be worse than the Alabama boys? I reported for duty to my new outfit. I entered the day room and met a pleasant looking black clerk who welcomed me and asked my name. I said, "I am Al Efron, your new recruit." He then called the Captain, who was also black, who gave me a very warm welcome to the outfit. I checked into the barracks to meet the rest of the fellows that I would be working with. All of the GIs in this outfit were black. I figured I would take things slowly and see what happened. To my amazement, I met the nicest bunch of human beings that I had ever seen before. I was welcomed and there was no talk of "you're white" and "we are black" or any discrimination. "We're all GIs in the same army and we have to look after one another." What a fantastic relief. Under my breath, I thanked President Truman for his courage. I spent about three weeks with these men.

Since I was a wheel vehicle mechanic, I was transferred to the motor pool and met my new Captain, who was white. Through the grapevine, I learned that the camp photographer was being discharged since he had put in his two years. The Captain in charge of the photography division was looking for a replacement. The minute I learned that news, I thought, "That's for me!" Fixing vehicles was not my idea of a job I would enjoy. I found out the name of the captain who was in charge, and contacted him. He invited me down for an interview. We worked in the dark room for a while and then went out on a photo shoot so he could evaluate my abilities to handle the work that he needed. After about a two hour session, the Captain said, "You're the guy for me. You can do it all. I will contact your Captain and have him transfer you to my outfit. You will spend your entire Army career here at Camp Edwards."

I was all charged up and waited to get the transfer. The next day, I was in the barracks and was notified that my motor pool Captain wanted to see me. I thought, "This is great. I'm going to get my transfer". I walked in with a smile, as ordered. The Captain looked at me but did not have a smile on his face and he said, "Efron, who the hell do you think you are? You went to see that Captain without getting my permission first?" "I'm sorry, sir", I said, "I'm new to this army business and did not know the protocol. I sincerely apologize." He then ordered me back to the barracks to wait for his orders. After about an hour in the barracks, an orderly came down with orders that he handed me and said, "Lots of luck". I only had to read the first paragraph, when I realized I was on my way to Korea to kill Chinese that were storming over the border at that time. What a terrible situation I put myself in.

    The next thing I knew, I was on a plane to Seattle to be put on a ship to Japan, and then to Korea and combat. In Seattle, while I was waiting for the ship, we sat around to kill time. One day, an officer came into the barracks and said he was looking for volunteers to paint barracks. I thought that it was a great opportunity to stay off the ship that was going into war, so I volunteered along with a number of GIs. They set us up in the barracks to paint ceilings. We climbed up on the scaffold. Being stupid young kids, we started to paint by playing tic-tac-toe, painting pictures of women and getting a good laugh. Then, we covered the whole ceiling with a coat of paint to hide our art. When we left to let the paint dry, we looked at the ceiling and thought it looked great. The next day, we were waiting to go back to work as painters when the officer in charge said, "Gentlemen, follow me". We entered the barracks, looked at the ceiling, and turned white. Everything we first painted had telegraphed through the finish coat. I guess you could suspect what happened next. You are correct; we were on the next ship to Korea.

    Getting on the troop ship was a new experience for me. We had to go down to the sleeping quarters, which seemed like climbing down ladders of a 10-story building. Finally, we got to this big open space with hammocks two or three high. That was to be our sleeping quarters for the next week to two. I was assigned the bottom hammock and I started to get in it. "There must be some trick to this", I thought, because I just couldn't get in without falling out. Finally, after about six tries, I was able to manage the situation. Another GI was assigned to the hammock above me. He tried to get into his hammock. After falling out a half dozen times and colliding with me, he finally made it. However, his body ended up about an inch and a half above my body, which did not stand very well with me because I have a slight case of claustrophobia. I said to myself, "I've got to get out of here". Then to my luck I heard a voice saying, "I'm looking for a volunteer". Within a split second, my hand went up and I yelled out, "I am your volunteer, sir." What I was volunteering for, I didn't know and I didn't care. I had to get out of that place.

The Sergeant took me upside, all the way up to where the sun was shining through all the windows. He took me into a room. It was a real room with a real bed and dresser and chair and a lamp and a reading light. It looked like heaven and he said, "This is your quarters." I wondered, what am I supposed to do in this paradise? The Sergeant told me that we were in the hospital section and my job was to sit up at night, and when any of the patients needed help, I was to call the doctor. That's it. I was given books and movies to help pass the time. I would eat all my meals with the officers and their families, upside. The food that was served included things that I had never seen before, such as avocados, being a poor kid from Brooklyn. This was one of the blessings that I referred to the beginning of this book; that everything I did was wrong, but it turned out in my favor.

Our ship finally landed in Tokyo, Japan. We all boarded buses that were waiting for us and took us to Tokyo General Station. We were there for a while, waiting to be transported to our final destination. While waiting, nature tapped me on the shoulder, notifying me that I needed the bathroom. I started looking around for some symbol indicating of a men's room. Then, one of my fellow GIs told me that the bathroom was straight ahead from where we were standing. I slowly walked in that direction and saw a large trimmed opening, about 20 foot wide, that was the entrance to what I thought was the men's room. When I was got close enough, what I saw shocked me. There was a row of water closets in full view of everyone in that huge waiting room. Sitting on one water closet was a lovely Japanese middle-aged woman doing what you naturally do while sitting on a water closet. About three water closets to the right was a man standing and urinating, as natural as could be. I stood there, staring at the situation for a minute or two. I'd been told that was the custom there, so I'd better get used to it. I stood at a water closet and did what I needed to do. At that time, it felt pretty natural, as I walked away with a smile on my face. Welcome to Japan. Remember, this was 1951 and the U.S. Army soldiers were still occupation troops. The Japanese customs were the same as before the Americans arrived.

I was transported to an Army base and set up in a standard army barracks. When everything settled down, my outfit was set up in classroom-sized lectures, for brainwashing as we called it, on how to handle ourselves in combat. I must say that they were did a great job, because I felt no fear or anxiety about the fact that we would soon be in combat, killing or be killed. The one statement I will never forget was when the instructor said, "Remember, when you are in combat, 'don't get sick'." My first question was, "How do you 'don't get sick'?" I never got that answer.

When these classes were finished, we had to wait for a ship to take us from Japan to Korea. There were thousands of GIs waiting for the ships, so there were a great number of days that we had nothing to do. One of the soldiers got a bright idea and said, "Let's all get tattoos. Next week we might be dead, so let's enjoy things now". Everyone thought that was a great idea. One of the fellows did some checking and found a tattoo artist not too far from the base. "Okay guys, tomorrow morning we are all going to go and get tattooed". I started to think that I really didn't want a tattoo, but maybe it would be a new adventure. I started to conjure up what type of tattoo I wanted and where would I put it. Maybe I'd get something small on my finger, or maybe on my ankle. Then the realization came to me that I did not want a tattoo. When the guys started to pile into the Jeeps to leave, I stood in the barracks. I heard the melodic voice of one of the soldiers, "Al, where are you? We are getting ready to leave". "No, I can't go now. I really don't feel well. Maybe next time". "Okay", and off they went. There was no next trip because I really did not want a tattoo.

The next bright idea that the guys had was, "Let's get drunk". Everybody had to chip in for the booze. The huge sum of 50 cents was all that was needed from each of us to get as much booze as we wanted. I was not an alcohol drinker, so I sat and chatted with the guys as they were drinking and I was not partaking. Then one of the guy said, "Al, you're not drinking". "No", I said, "I usually don't care for alcohol". "You chipped in, so you must drink." Then everybody joined in, "Al must drink". So, I guessed I had no choice and I took one or two drinks. At that point, everybody was happy, as they were all guzzling the stuff down. About 15 to 20 minutes after the drink, I felt nauseous. I felt for sure I was going to throw up. I did not want any of my guys seeing me do that. I quietly went to the other end of the barracks where my cot was and I laid down. All of a sudden, up it came, and I vomited all over myself. I quickly got up try to clean myself up before anybody noticed. After that, I got a little dizzy. I got back onto the cot and fell asleep. But an hour or two later, I woke up and my head was pounding. I felt like I was going to die before combat did it to me. I said to myself, "If that's the way you feel when you get drunk, why does anyone get drunk?" The answer came to me, don't get drunk. That was my first and last experience in getting drunk. To this day, I have never been drunk again.

In the Army, when you have nothing to do, an officer that sees you idle will get you a job, like peeling potatoes or cleaning out the grease trap. These jobs were not pleasant. So to avoid this situation, I signed up for the Army lecture course on spoken Japanese. My aim was not to learn to speak Japanese, but just stay out of some terrible project. As I remember, my classes lasted for about a week and a half, and then our ship was ready. I learned to speak some Japanese and was able to be understood and get around, but not really a Japanese speaker. Later on in this book I will refer back to my ability to speak Japanese proving to me that the human brain is a magnificently fantastic organ.

Finally our ship arrived. We were all transported down to the dock to get ready to board the ship that would take us to Korea. We must've stood there for about a half hour before it was our time to move up the gangplank and onto the ship. But, just a few minutes before it was my turn to march up the gangplank, an officer came by and identified five men to step forward. To my amazement, I was one of five and did not know what it was all about. I asked the officer, "What's happening, sir?" He asked, "What is your name". I said, "Private Efron, sir". He looked at his papers and said, "You're the mechanic?" "Yes Sir, I am". "Well, get in the truck because we are short a mechanic in Japan and that is where you're going to be stationed". Unbelievable!! Without thinking, due to the indoctrination I went through, I actually said, "No, I want to go with my guys". The officer looked at me and said, "Get into the God damn truck", and so I did. I realized what I had said and thought to myself, "Gee, I really don't want to go, this is great!" Since it was not my choice anyway, off we went, back to the base. To this day, I'm still shocked that I was so brainwashed that initially I wanted to get on that ship to Korea and I wanted to go into combat.

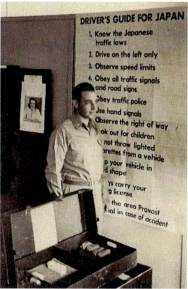

Ready for inspection.

We were transported to Johnson Air Force Base where I was to be stationed. After the induction interview, I was taken to the motor pool, where I would spend the rest of my required time in the Army. I arrived at the end of the day and all the trucks were being brought in to the gated enclosure for the evening. A Sergeant looked at me and said,

"Soldier, get in that truck and drive it into the enclosure". I hopped in behind the steering wheel without looking at what was behind me, started the truck up, and made a left turn through the gate of the enclosure. At that point I heard the ripping of metal and yelling of people to stop the truck. Unbeknownst to me, I was towing a huge 90mm anti-air craft canon that was attached to the truck. Not knowing that it was there when I made the turn, the truck cleared the fence but that 90mm anti-air craft canon did not. I had a very unpleasant welcome to my new outfit.

After my first unpleasant encounter had passed, I was shown to my quarters and told about the duties that I was to perform. To my great surprise, I was given a very pleasant assignment and lucked out once again, as I did on the troopship getting here. There were three of us mechanics that were part of the motor pool. We were assigned to a large room behind the motor pool, which would be our quarters. We were given a list of the Japanese mechanics, hired by the Army to do all the work. Our job was to make sure that all the vehicles were always in action. The three of us were in charge of this entire operation. That meant that I worked one day and had two days off, around the clock. On the days that I worked, I was in charge. We were called Second Echelon Maintenance. First Echelon meant that if a vehicle broke down bad enough while in action, it was junked. Second Echelon received all the repairable vehicles from the First Echelon, fixed them fast, and got them back out and running. This usually meant that whatever was wrong with the vehicle, don't bother to fix it, just replace parts. And that's what we did. The vehicles that needed more in-depth repair than we could handle with replacement parts went to Third Echelon. As long as we kept those vehicles in action, everyone left us alone. Seeing a sergeant or any officer was a rare occasion. This was a great duty in the Army.

For the next year and a half, I had a great time using my so-called Japanese speaking knowledge and traveling around on my time off. I got to know the Japanese culture at that time. My time on duty was also very pleasant. All I had to do as the vehicles arrived, and the necessary paperwork was given to me, was to evaluate the problem the vehicle was having. I then assigned the project to one of the Japanese mechanics to get it fixed. Those Japanese mechanics were not only excellent mechanics; I found them to be great people too. It was hard to believe that I was speaking with these Japanese people without a problem, considering the Second World War was not very far in the past. That situation was so different. There is something wrong with this world if a situation can be so horrible and so good with the same people and the horrible part cannot be eliminated.

Honey bucket man

In Japan at that time, all farming was fertilized with human waste. Human waste was collected by the honey bucket man. The toilet in each home sat above a basket that was underneath the building. All human waste was dropped into this basket and picked up by the honey bucket man through an access door from outside the building. You can imagine the odor that permeated throughout Japan in those days. However, the Japanese people were immune to all the ingredients that were in the food fertilized with human waste. On the other hand, the GIs coming from the United States were not able to handle this food. If we ate it, we would get drastically sick. So, the Army labeled restaurants with a large letter 'A' to designate those restaurants that did not use any products that were fertilized with human waste. If a restaurant was labeled with any other letter, that meant GI's should not eat there. My problem was that all restaurants labeled with an 'A' had the same food that we ate in the states.

Here I was, in Japan, and I could not experience the complete flavor of the Japanese palate. This feeling got the better of me. One day,

I spoke to one of my mechanics and I asked him if he would take me to a restaurant that served food that is typical of Japan. He was more than happy to make the arrangements. When the time came, we went to the small town of Inerema. We went to a local restaurant, which was very small. There were just four tables, a dirt floor, and everything was written in Japanese. My Japanese buddy translated and we ordered. I got what was called Omu-Rice. The food was served on a lovely plate, consisting of rice with a red sauce, rolled up in a Fried egg and surrounded by lovely looking vegetables. I started to eat and found it very tasty, with a nice spicy kick. When I got to the center of this rolled up piece of culinary art, to my horror, I spotted what looked like a large cockroach-type bug, right in the middle of the rice. I knew and witnessed the Japanese eating all sorts of bugs and insects, but I did not know if this one belonged there or had gotten there by mistake. Whatever the case, I was not going to eat it. Not to be rude, I told my friend that I was full and could not eat another bite of this delicious food. We finished with some tea and off we went back to the base. It did not take long for me to feel my stomach start to explode. To make a long story short, I spent two weeks in the hospital with dysentery from that experience. I guess you realize that whenever I went into town to eat, I always looked for restaurant with the large 'A' on the outside. I learned my lesson the hard way.

    Other dishes that I observed that were typical of the Japanese diet included snakes. In the US, if you go to a fish restaurant, you might see a tank with lobsters gently crawling around in a tank. A chef would take a lobster out of the tank, cook it, and serve it to the customer. In Japan they had a similar practice, but they didn't have lobster, they had snakes. It was the custom at that time to cut the head off and let the blood run into a glass. They served the glass of snake blood to the customer, while the chef took the snake to be cooked and served. Needless to say, my response was, 'to each his own'. These old practices I do not think exist anymore. I found that in 1970, when I was on the trip with a group of architects to Japan, Bangkok and Hong Kong, I did not see these items being practiced any more.

    I succeeded in satisfactorily putting in my two years of active duty with the U.S. Army. The time came when I was nearing my discharge. At that time, the army was short of its full complement and made every effort to re-up all manpower that it could. A recruiting Sergeant came to me about three days before my official active duty was coming to an end. The Sergeant worked very hard for about two hours to explain to me that the cost of living in the Army was very efficient. It only cost, if I remember correctly, 25 cents for a haircut and 10 cents for a pack of cigarettes, which I did not smoke. He said a haircut in New York was about two dollars and a pack of cigarettes was out of my economic range. So the solution was to re-up in the army. Needless to say, the poor guy left our meeting very downhearted because I was going home. The army experience was the best thing that had happened to me in my life up to that time. I received a tremendous education in life, dealing with people, and had a much better understanding of the world that we lived in. In those two years, I grew about 10 years, easily. And the best thing, overall, in getting this experience, I was going home, mentally and physically in one piece, with an honorable discharge.

Glad to be going home!

My New Civilian Life

I arrived home in March of 1953 to a fantastic reunion with all of Harriet's and my families, as well as a group of my friends. Within four days, Harriet and I had planned our wedding. Harriet had been teaching in Brooklyn while I was in the Army. I was not earning any money at that point, so we decided to have a small, family affair. That was what Harriet wanted and that was what I wanted, but that was not what my mother wanted. My mother, being an extreme extrovert, wanted a huge affair so that she could entertain the guests. Since the groom, bride, and her parents were in harmony, a small wedding it was going to be.

Our Wedding

My father had a friend who was a Cantor and we agreed to have the ceremony in his small chapel in Brooklyn. We would only have about 20 guests, all whom were relatives. We booked the back room of a local restaurant for the after-wedding feast. The wedding was set for March 15, 1953. Everything went smoothly except for one minor problem. The Cantor notified me that a witness has to sign the wedding agreement.

The person signing, however, could not be a relative; he or she must be unrelated. Since all the guests were family, related on my side or Harriet's side, there was no one to sign as the witness. Harriet's uncle went out onto the street and grabbed the first individual who was willing to sign the document. The payment we gave him was a good, stiff drink. He accepted and after about three of those drinks, he staggered out. All ended well.

Since we didn't have much money, and Harriet, being a teacher, was not able to get time off for a honeymoon, we had just Saturday and Sunday to celebrate our honeymoon. We ended up at the Taft Hotel in Manhattan with tickets to a Broadway show for Saturday night, and a good dinner for Sunday afternoon. After the Sunday dinner, we went back home. Thinking back over all those years, I know that being poor at the beginning was not a handicap, since we were very happy.

Money was tight, but we had enough to get by. Harriet's teaching job in Brooklyn paid a salary of $3,000 a year. I was able to earn some money on the side. We were able to rent a small, one-bedroom apartment on the second floor of a six-story walk-up building in Brooklyn, across the street from Prospect Park. Harriet's parents also had an apartment in that same building on the sixth floor. Our apartment faced the rear courtyard which was the only view we had. At least we could see if it was raining or sunny out.

In those days, peddlers used to come around the neighborhood and go into the courtyards, calling out in as a loud voice as possible, "I cash close". They were looking to buy or sell used clothes or other items. Another great amenity of this apartment house, was the use of the laundry room. This laundry room was located in a dingy, filthy room in the cellar. To get to this room that looked like an underground dungeon, you had to pass through a long, dark passageway from the sidewalk to the cellar. When going down to that laundry room, the main thought that every woman had was, "Will I be raped?" and for the men, "Will I be mugged?"

Another delight of living in that building, was trying to find a place to legally park your car on the street. They weren't any garages for rent in the area, so on-street parking was at a premium. To make matters worse, the city had a policy of alternate street parking. That meant that on a given day, you were allowed to park only on the east side of the street and then only on the west side on the next day. In that way, one side of the street was always open for sanitation trucks or whatever else the city needed. It also meant that when you found a place to park, you had to remember to move your car to the opposite side of the street on the next day.

Even if you found a spot, the next day, you'll be back parking again. Finding a parking spot was hard. There were times when the only parking I could find was 5 to 10 blocks away from our apartment. Talk about adding strife to your life; living in Brooklyn at that time had plenty of it. We managed to survive because we had each other and life was great.

In order to add a little joy to our daily existence, we managed to go to a neighborhood Italian restaurant on Friday nights. We chose this restaurant because they had a special every Friday night of lasagna for one dollar. And there we were, every Friday night, eating delicious lasagna. To end the meal with a cup of coffee, which I feel is a necessity, we did not want to spend the extra 5 cents for the coffee. We waited until we got back to our apartment and brewed up a fresh cup to end the meal.

Harriet being a very good housekeeper wanted everything to be clean and in its place. She tried to break me in to that type of lifestyle. One day, she told me that the bathroom needed cleaning. "Do you think you can handle that job", she asked? I thought for a second and remembered my days in the Army. When we had a clean the barracks, we called a GI party. I replicated what I did in my Army days for my civilian toilet-cleaning job. I first filled a bucket with soapy water. I poured it onto the floor of the bathroom, creating a small foamy flood, and then started to clean. It took maybe 3 or 4 minutes when there was a knocking on our apartment door. It was the tenant who lived below us. "What's happening up here? Do you have a broken pipe, because there is water dripping down the ceiling of my apartment?" "Oh no", I said, "Nothing is broken. I'm just cleaning the bathroom". The rest of this episode I will leave up to your imagination because it is too embarrassing for me to put in words.

During the summer, living in that apartment was very difficult, because of the heat that built up during the day. To cool the apartment down, I came up with a brilliant idea of making my own air conditioning unit. It only worked in one room at a time. I chose the bedroom to install my homemade air conditioning unit. I started by putting a large fan in the window. I attached a broom handle to the fan, facing into the room. At the end of the broom handle, I tied a pair of Harriet's underpants, which were very sheer. I took ice cubes from the refrigerator and put them into Harriet's underpants, suspended in front of the fan. With great expectations, I put the fan on and wow!!! It worked for about a minute and a half before all the ice cubes melted and dripped into the bucket I had placed beneath them. I realized that the only problem with this air conditioning unit was supplying it with a limitless amount of ice cubes. Oh well, that was a minor flaw, time to find another invention. It was a wonderful time to be alive. We were allowed to be young and stupid and still smile.

It was the time we all settled in to make an income. Shortly after our wedding, Alan Friedman, my old partner in photography was discharged from his Army career. He had married before he was inducted in the Army. Fortune was with them. As a US soldier, he was sent to Germany with his wife after he finished basic training. He spent his entire tour of duty living off-base with his wife and enjoying the entire experience. However, something went wrong. After his discharge, we had a meeting to see if we could get back into photography together. I was anxious to renew our partnership because it worked so well. He said he was not ready mentally to go back into business. I did not understand what he meant at that time. I was able to find out what was wrong. His drive, that had been so strong before his Army career, was gone. Every time he went on an interview for a new job, he would stop at the entrance door and feel very nauseous. He'd go to the nearest men's room and vomit. He would leave the men's room and go home without having interview. I was on my own.

I lost track of Alan Friedman for a number of years and then discovered that he was working as a salesman in a photography store. I also learned that he was divorced and never found out what happened to the little girl that they had together. I tried a number of times over the years to find his contact information on the computer. However the name Alan Friedman is too common and I found it impossible to find him.

My First Job, Building My Career

I went back in business on my own, photographing weddings, high school graduation pictures, and portraits. I started to shoot weddings for a local studio, named Dahill Studies, owned by Lew Bienstock, as a fill in. Since I never wanted to have a job and work for someone else, I always looked for ways to build a career in my own business. I got the bright idea to do more professional photography than the wedding and portrait business offered me. I came up with the idea, and made an offer to Lew, the owner of the studio I was shooting weddings for. I wanted to go to Manhattan and knock on the doors of all advertising agencies that I could find and do high-fashion and product photography. That's where I thought all the action was. The deal I proposed was that I will bring in the work, he provides the studio, and we share the profits from the work that I bring in. All the profits from his wedding business he would keep, and I would have nothing to do with that. He jumped at the deal. I was off and running.

Lew Bienstock and I, camp convention display.

I knocked on the doors of all the advertising agencies I could find, and as expected, got a lot of rejections at the beginning. It didn't take long and I was able to convince an agency to give me a chance. The art director wanted to see the photographs that I had taken in reference to fashion and products. Since I had none, I had to start my portfolio quickly for the next meeting with that agency.

My first problem was that I needed models to photograph. The high-fashion models are an expensive operation. I came up with the idea of visiting the Barbizon Modeling Agency. They were the biggest fashion agency in the business of modeling. This agency also had the Barbizon School of Modeling with the possibility for their student models to move up and work for the agency. I spoke to the Director of the school and said, "I know your students need modeling experience and have to build their own portfolio. I have to create my own portfolio. If you'll let me, I would like to put up a notice on your bulletin board. I'll photograph any model who wants photos for their portfolio and give them several prints. I'll do this for them, in exchange for the rights to the photographs as well. I could use their photographs for my portfolio too. It worked. In no time I had my portfolio. Several models had photos for their portfolio.

I got a job at my first agency. It opened up our business to other agencies as well. My business was starting to grow. We were off to a great start. I could see the possibility of building this business up and becoming a major fashion and product photographer.

The Mafia Changed My Career Direction

One day, Lew, his wife and I were in the studio, preparing to photograph the graduating class of the local school. She was our secretary and ran the secretarial part of the office. In walked two gentlemen and asked to see the boss. I use the word 'gentlemen' sparingly because they did not look very gentle. They looked a little scary, with permanent non-smiles on their faces. Lew told them, "We are all bosses." The taller of the two stocky men said, "We are here to notify you that we are starting a union of all photographers in New York City". We told them that we were a small operation and didn't have any photographers as employees. The two of us did all our own photography and the woman at the desk is Lew's wife. A union basically has employees as their members, not the owners of the studios. The tall gentleman with the growling face said, "Everyone joins our union".

It didn't take long before we realized that this was the Mafia, trying to get control of the photography industry. They said they would be back in a few days and out they went. I was not a very happy camper. I thought a while and concluded that I wanted nothing to do with the Mafia. Once they come in, they will suck you dry. "Let's think about it", Lew said. "We have a few days". In the next few days, those gentlemen approached another photography studio similar to ours about 2 miles away. The owner of that studio threw them out. That evening, a firebomb was thrown through their window and destroyed the entire building. These boys play rough. I decided that I would never get into a situation where I was not completely in control. No way would I accept outside forces, like the Mafia, getting involved in my life.

In the days in the 1950's the Mafia ran this country. Our esteemed FBI Director, J Edger Hoover, kept publicly saying there was no such thing as the Mafia or organized crime. Director Hoover's main emphasis was on the Communists. "That's where the danger lies". With that attitude, the Mafia had a strong overall influence in every facet of commercial life in this country. My mind was made up. I told Lew that I was out. Whatever business I brought in so far, I would give to him. He could keep all profits and do whatever he wanted with what I had started. "It's all yours. I am going to look for another profession."

The next weekend, a friend of Harriet's invited us their house party. That Saturday, we attended the party to forget my problems. At this party, I met a fellow who was a draftsman working for a kitchen cabinet manufacturer. His job was to draw the layout for kitchens and cabinets for approval by the clients. His drawings were then turned over for manufacture. He told me it was a great job because draftsmen were always in demand and the pay was very good. After hearing my story about being forced to look for another profession, he told me to come over to his house on the weekends. He would teach me how to become a draftsman so I could get a good job. I thanked him for the offer; however I was not the type of person who was looking for a job.

I was looking for a career, one where I would be the boss and in control of my life. I was not interested in a job working for someone else. Where do we go from here? It did not take long for me to figure out, that I had to research what professions are out there, that I could possibly pursue. Monday morning, I was off to the library. At that time, there were no such things as computers or calculators. The 'word processor' did not exist yet and could not even be found in the dictionary. 'Research' was very different then. In the library, I went through all types of publications, magazines & books. I looked up everything I could find about different professions and businesses. After a few hours, I came across an article about an architect. After reading that article and finding out what an architect did, it blew me away. An architect is an artist, technician, scientist and businessman all wrapped up in one and is in control of the entire construction process. Wow, that was for me. I figured there was no sense in looking any further. I would come back the next day, fresh and ready to research what I would have to do to become an architect.

That evening, I met with a group of my friends that were free for the evening. We met in the local diner for a pleasant guys-only dinner. Our wives were out that night playing mahjong. I made the announcement that, "I'm giving up photography and going to become an architect." They looked at me and laughed. Innocently I asked, "What's the problem?" They all answered me in the same manner, saying that it was impossible for a person like me to become an architect because I had never spent 1 minute in a college classroom. They explained that if you want to be a doctor, you have to go to college. If you want to be an engineer, you have to go to college. If you want to be a lawyer, you have to go to college and the same holds true for architecture. I looked them square in the eye and said, "Just because that's what you say, doesn't mean there is no other way that I can pursue the architectural profession." Again they laughed and said, "You can research everything you want and you will never find another way, because that's a fact of life. To become a professional person, requires a college degree or you're out."

The next day, bright and early, I was in the library again and spoke to a nice young lady behind the counter. I asked her where I could find all the state regulations for becoming an architect. "No problem", she said and took me to the area where that document was. I sat down at the table, opened it up, and started to read. At first, I found that a five-year college degree in architecture was required for the first step. Then, three years of practical experience working for a registered architect was required to round out your qualification of 8 years. Once qualified, you're able to take the state board exams. Upon passing the exams, you receive your license. The state board exams contained seven parts that were given over a four-day exam period. You must pass all seven parts to earn a license. You must pass a minimum of four parts in one session and then you could take the other three parts in the next session. If you passed three or fewer parts, you got no credit and would have to start all over again at the next session.

I was not deterred. I had just started reading and there are a lot of pages to go through in that publication. On I went and kept reading. About five or six pages later, I found my answer. I carefully read every word. It said, "In lieu of a five-year degree in architecture and three years practical experience, for a total of eight years to take the state board exams, you can work for an architect and get practical experience for a total of 12 years which also qualifies you to take the state board exams". After passing the exams, you got the same license as the person who had the five-year college degree.

The next day, when I showed it to my friends, they were dumbfounded. "That cannot be correct, we never heard of such a thing." I told my friends about the rules that I live by. Never, ever, under any circumstances, say "No, You Can't Do That". What you are actually saying is, "You do not want to do that". What you must do in a situation that seems impossible, is to you look for a solution. If you look for a solution, you will find it. If you don't look, you won't find it, and then you can't do it.

My Architectural Education

Now that I knew how I could become an architect, my next problem was to figure out how to get 12 years of experience working for an architect. I'm not qualified to work for architect. Back to the library I went to research schools where I could learn to become an architectural draftsman. Remember, this was late 1955. Today, schools that award all kinds of certificates and degrees in any endeavor of education can be found on almost any street, in any city, in this country. In my day, that type of education was hard to find. After my due diligence, I found the Institute of Design and Construction. It was a small school that taught architectural drafting and was located in an office building in downtown Brooklyn.

The next morning, I paid a visit to the school and met the director and owner, Vito Battista. It was a small operation. The school had four classrooms and an administration office. The director explained that his was the only school in this area that taught architectural drafting, as well as other types of engineering courses related to the construction and architectural professions. Since I was a veteran, the United States Army would pay my tuition. All I had to do was to put in one year, full-time, and that would qualify me to work for an architect. He also told me that since his was the only school in the area, he could guarantee me a job at the end of my year. All the large architectural firms that needed draftsmen came to him to fill their needs.

Once working as a draftsman, if I wanted to get a license, I could come back to the school in the evening and take any of the engineering, history of architecture, strength of materials, and city planning courses I needed. He did not give any degrees or certificates, all he provided was knowledge. And all I needed was knowledge. I signed up and started my one-year schooling. I was on my way to a profession of my choosing, where I would be the boss, not the employee.

My First Job as an Architectural Junior Draftsman

Upon completing my first year of studying the architectural profession with Mr. Vito Battista, I was ready for my first job as an architectural draftsman. As promised, Mr. Battista called me into his office and gave me the name of one of the largest architectural firms in the area, Eggers and Higgins. He said he recommended me for a job as a junior draftsman. I had an appointment the next day at 10 o'clock at their offices in Manhattan. I was very excited, full of spit and vinegar, ready to face the world and start getting rich.

The next morning, with my suit and tie, I showed up at the office at the proper time and was given an interview. I felt very comfortable and self-insured when I finished the interview. The interviewer then said the magic words, "Can you start tomorrow morning? We will pay you $50 a week." "I will be there with bells on", I stated. I was elated because this was the first step in building the professional career that I craved. I anxiously waited for Harriet to get out of school so I could tell her the good news.

I started working at Eggers and Higgins and learned the vital knowledge from inside the profession. The type of education you can never get in a college classroom. The stuff I was doing was for real, not theory or experimental. There were about 200 architects working at this firm, with a combined knowledge of the profession that provided me valuable insight and knowledge. I was assigned to the school department that specialized in elementary, high school, as well as college level buildings. I loved my job and was learning a lot. Everyone there were great people and very helpful to get me up to speed. I also made a lot of contacts with construction companies, other architects, engineers, and an array of other people related to the construction industry. I felt that this was the office that would give me the education and experience that I needed to build my future.

Long Range Planning

Some long-range planning was due on my part. I had 12 years to get all the additional educational requirements I needed to pass the state board exams and become a professional architect. Once that was achieved, I would open my own practice and be on my way to a great future. The only thing that I would need in order to open an office, would be clients. How to you find clients that want to hire an architect for major work and to build large structures? I was not interested in designing one-family homes because that would be too limiting and on a smaller scale. I reasoned that I had 12 years to mingle with the makers and shakers of our society. The makers and shakers that I was looking for were those people who owned businesses or were CEOs, presidents of banks, owners of large insurance companies, and anybody who was in the business world, on an ownership or high management level. Those were the makers and shakers that I wanted to break bread with. How was I going to find them? Since this type of thinking is not rocket science, but common sense. I soon discovered that these makers and shakers could be found on every non-profit board of directors; for hospitals, zoos, colleges, Chambers of Commerce, and organizations associated with illnesses such as the Heart Foundation, ALS etc. Politics would also be a great place to meet the right people.

I kept myself very busy as an architectural draftsman in the daytime hours and going to school at night. In addition, I was able to get a job as an architectural draftsman for a one-man architectural office that did inspections of boiler rooms in one-family homes for the City of New York. My job was to go into one-family homes, eyeball their boiler rooms and create drawings that my boss could put together with the paperwork to file with the city and get the boiler rooms approved. This work can be done in the evening hours. The money came in handy, plus the experience was fabulous. I enjoyed working those nights with that architect.

In an effort it to earn some additional money, I photographed weddings for a couple of photography studios in Brooklyn. Since photographing weddings was always on the weekend, Harriet usually accompanied me. That made working to earn some money and a night out with my wife possible. In order to be able to photograph a wedding, I had to have my own car. It would not have been possible to pack up all of my equipment, get to the bride or groom's house for family shots, then to the catering hall for the entire wedding, unless I had my own car. Since money was very scarce, I looked around for a second-hand car that would fit the bill.

When I did my research, I came across an ad for the sale of a "Henry J". When I read the ad, I wondered, "What is a Henry J"? I soon discovered that Henry J Kaiser was a prime contractor, building what were called 'liberty ships' during the Second World War. These ships were huge vessels with large cargo areas and open space for transporting troops and war material to Europe. Henry J Kaiser was a master of turning out the ships in record numbers. I don't remember the exact number, however five ships per day pop into my mind. At the end of the war, since ships were no longer needed, Henry J Kaiser converted his factories to build automobiles.

New automobiles, at that time, were very scarce, since none of the car companies were building cars for the public. They had all been converted to build jeeps, trucks, and other vehicles for the military. When the war was over and all those GIs were coming home, there was a great need for automobiles. So, Henry J Kaiser started to fill the need. The first car he put out was the Henry J. It was the first mini-car that we had ever seen in this country. It was a small, pardon the expression, hunk of junk! Henry J Kaiser also built an upscale full-sized car that he called the Kaiser Frazer.

This is what a new 1954 Henry J looked like.

Since car manufacturers did not have the ability to acquire the proper material for making bumpers, all Kaiser automobiles had a 2" x 6" wood plank mounted on the front as bumpers. It did not matter how bad these cars were because they ran, and that was all that mattered. I answered an ad for a Henry J that was for sale by a private party, making it a second-hand car. To the best of my knowledge, the car was for sale with a price tag of approximately $300. Thanks to my in-laws for helping us, we were able to raise the three hundred dollars to purchase the car. As I mentioned before, all I needed was a car that ran, sometimes. The Henry J's power left a lot to be desired and comfort was nonexistent. Shifting gears worked most of the time. When starting off from a green traffic light, you would try to shift from first into second gear. If you were lucky, the gears would slip into the place. However there were times, and many of them, when the gears would not slip in the place. I had to pull over to the curb, lift the hood, take out the wire hanger I had fashioned into the proper shape, hook it around a rod at the bottom of the engine, and pull up. It would snap into second gear. What fun, but it worked! We had that car for about two years.

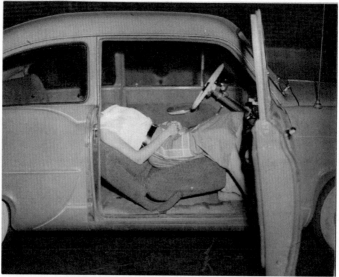

Harriet, at the scene of the accident.

One Saturday night, Harriet and I were driving to a catering Hall in the Henry J to photograph a wedding. I had all of my equipment in the trunk of the car. We were waiting at a red light, when all of a sudden, the car behind us did not stop and slammed into the back of our car. I looked at Harriet and saw that the back of her seat was completely broken down and she was in a horizontal position. I guess when the seat broke, it absorbed the shock. Thankfully Harriet was not hurt, which was a great relief. What about all my equipment in the trunk? I went around to the back of the car and found that the trunk hood was up in the air, and to my delight, all of my equipment was in great shape. That was another great relief of this incident. The driver of the other car and I did the necessary exchange of information and off we went to shoot the wedding. It was hard driving the car while Harriet was in a completely prone position, as if she was sleeping, and the trunk hood tied down so I could see out the back window. I was able to photograph the wedding, get us back home, and get the car fixed the next day. I was able to find a small garage that was able to fix the seat and the hood of the trunk, so we were back in operation.

In the meantime in order to round out my long term plan I started joining every and any organization I can to mingle with the makers and shakers. Politics seem to be a great start and so I joined the young Democrats on Staten Island. They were a great group to learn the workings and advancement in politics. Eventually, jumping ahead of my story, I became a zone leader in the Democratic Party on Staten Island. As zone leader I sat on the executive committee that control the entire workings of the Democratic Party on Staten Island. I eventually opened an office on a retail street in new Dorp Staten Island and had 300 County committeeman under my control. I had acquired great acquaintances with the makers and shakers in the political arena of the New York State.

Now back to the beginning. I started slowly but quickly advanced and joining all those organizations where the makers and shakers can be found. I was on a board of the hospital, nursing home, zoo, historic site, regional arts center, the blind, the deaf, Chamber of Commerce, New York City builders Association, borough president's advisory Council, and a number of other minor organizations throughout the city of New York.

At the end of my 12 year qualifying time, and then acquiring my architects license I will be well suited to build an architectural practice.

A Real Car

    Time went by, and with some of the money that Harriet and I saved from her salary and my small earnings, we could afford to buy a real car. The car that we bought was a new Buick Special.

Stock image of a new 1956 Buick Special.

    The Buick Company put out this model car in competition with the low-end Chevrolet. To us, driving in this car was like being in a Rolls-Royce. What to do with the Henry J? I could not use it as a trade-in because I was told it was worthless. Then one day, I noticed an ad from this company that bought cars that were past their prime and ready for the junkyard. I called the gentleman up and told him that I had a Henry J for sale. "How much is it worth?" He quoted me a price of $35. I said, "That's all you going to give me?" And then he proudly said, "No, that's what I am charging you for me to pick up the car and haul it away". Well, at least I had some use of the car when it was alive. I decided not to pay him to take it away. I donated the car to my father-in-law, who did not own a car and was great at fixing things.

    My father-in-law was an optometrist and had a practice on the street level of an apartment house his parents owned and lived in, not too far from where they lived. I gave the car to him, including the custom-shaped wire hanger, so he could drive it. When my mother-in-law was in the car as a passenger, she was on the nervous side. She was always saying, "Mac, blow the horn, that guy is in your way" or something to that effect. To make my mother-in-law feel more comfortable in the car and to stop her from bothering him every 15 seconds to blow the horn, he installed a button on the passenger side, wired to the horn, so she could press the button to her heart's content. That worked beautifully and kept love in the family.

About two years after I gave my father-in-law the car, I received a notice from the Department of Motor Vehicles. It stated that I needed to pay sales tax on the sale of the car that they said that I sold to my father-in-law. Oh, the wonderful nature of bureaucracy! It took quite some time to prepare an official legal document that stated that the transfer of the car was a gift, and therefore there was no sales tax due. Finally, the Department of Motor Vehicles accepted the document. Peace and harmony were back in the family.

Sad Events in Life

A few years later, my father-in-law, Mac, was diagnosed with cancer. His brother, who I referred to as Uncle Dave, was a doctor and did everything medically he could for Mac. However, cancer treatment was in its early stages at that time and Mac eventually passed away. His passing hit me very hard. Mac and I bonded the first moment we met. He was like a father to me. I spent many hours with him, working on various woodworking-type projects. His passing left a deep void in my life.

It wasn't too many years later that Mac's mother passed away. She was a widow and ran a candy store on the street level of a small apartment house she lived in and owned. It was where Mac also had his optometry practice. Since my father-in-law and his mother had passed away, the apartment house and both stores were willed to my mother-in-law. She asked me if I would help her collect the rents from the four tenants that lived in that building, as well as convert Mac's optometry store and the candy store to obtain new tenants for that space. The two of us managed to convert the entire retail space into a new type of restaurant called a pizza joint. Just as a side note, most of the pizza restaurants in that day were backed by the Mafia.

Once the store was completely rented and my mother-in-law was getting an income, it was my job to collect the rent from the tenants. My first adventure in rent collecting was a nerve wracking, body shaking, horrible experience. However, I told myself, this was going to be a monthly event, so I'd better get used to it. The building was very old and in terrible condition. The tenants were also very old, in addition to being very poor. So, collecting the rent was a humongous effort. I met the super, whose job it was to take care of the daily maintenance of the building in return for living there rent-free. I suppose, once in a while, when he wasn't drunk, he did something to fix an item that should have been taken care of months before. One of the first tenants that I met was a widow. She invited me to enter her apartment. I slowly entered and scanned the room. It looked like a scene from the movie Rosemary's Baby (horror movie). She said to me, "Would you like to meet my husband?" I was little baffled because I knew she was a widow. She took me over to a shelf, removed a large urn, and said, "Say hello to Jack".

What was I to do? I politely said, "Hello Jack". I turned to the widow and asked her if she had the rent. She looked at me with tears in her eyes and said, "Can you please come back in a couple of days? I should have some money then". There wasn't much I could do except to dread reappearing in that horrible building. But, since I was doing this as a favor to my fantastic mother-in-law, I continued for about two years. Finally, a real estate broker offered my mother-in-law a good price for the building. She sold it. Happy days were here again.

Al Efron, The Hero

One day, I was in my mother-in-law's apartment to install an electrical extension outlet on another wall so she could plug in a television set. This was a no-brainer. I purchased a simple surface-mounted outlet with an extension cord that I plugged into an existing outlet on the adjoining wall. I bought staples that were made for electrical cable to be attached to a baseboard. As I was gently tapping the staples into the baseboard, we heard a bang, and the wall in front of me developed a huge crack running from the floor up to the ceiling. My mother-in-law yelled, "What did you do?" "Nothing", I said.

However, based on my limited experience in construction, I concluded that the building was failing and there might be a major structural problem. I quickly notified all of the tenants to get out of their apartments and out on the street. I called the police and fire departments to save the world. There we were, everyone from that apartment house, standing on the street, as emergency vehicles parked with their red lights flashing. The emergency responders started climbing all over the building.

It so happens that the building was not in danger of collapsing, but there was a major problem. There had been an explosion in the building's boiler that had sent the crack up the chimney and throughout the building. So, it wasn't anything that I did. I was praised for the fast action. It was the right thing to do, even not knowing what the exact problem was. So there it is, I was the hero of the day. I felt vindicated with this action, especially considering my past bathroom-cleaning adventure.

Becoming a Military Civilian

At lunch with a friend one sunny afternoon, he told me about an organization he was a member of; The American Society of Military Engineers. That sounded like a good organization for me to get into to expand my network. He said that if I wanted to join, he would sponsor me and it would be no problem. A week later, I was notified that I had been accepted as a member of the American Society of Military Engineers. I went to my first meeting and was amazed at the caliber of people that were in this organization. Remember, I had been just a Private 1st Class, with one simple stripe on my uniform. The first gentleman I met was a retired General. A number of Colonels and Lieutenant Colonels were also members of the group. During all the conversations that day, I made sure to stay away from anybody who asked what ranks I had been in the Army.

The General, whose name I don't remember, approached me to join his committee. This committee was responsible for giving scholarships to colleges around the country for students studying engineering. I accepted his invitation, knowing that this would be a great way to meet people. At the first meeting of the General's committee, we discussed the process of approaching the colleges throughout the country and how to select the winners of the scholarships. Each member of this committee was given about eight colleges to contact in an effort to select the scholarship winners. It was a simple task. All I had to do was contact the Deans of Engineering at the colleges and ask them to select a top student in need of financing to receive a scholarship. That next week, I was able to contact all the colleges given to me. I had my secretary type the list of colleges and students, which I presented to the General. This was an easy task and I quickly made many friends. I was on this committee, making the phone calls, for about three years.

Around the fourth year, one college Dean did not return my call. I kept calling him, to no avail. I tried to find another person in that department to help me out. When I made my report, I made note that I had been unable to make contact at that college. At that point, the General was retired. Without his past power, he no longer had authority over guys like me, who had been just a private and now a civilian. In a commanding voice, he wanted to know why I did not drive out to the college and see that Dean. My friend, who was sitting next to me, saw the expression on my face and knew that I would probably say the wrong thing in anger. He grabbed me by the hand and said, "Al, don't argue with the General". I turned to my friend and said, "F--- him". My friend did not let go of my hand until the moment passed peacefully.

An interesting learning experience I had with the military engineers involved dredging New York Harbor. Silt and other types of materials at the bottom of the Atlantic Ocean get washed into the bay around the City of New York. This creates a problem with the depth of the bay for the entry of large cargo ships. So, the military engineers were assigned the project of cleaning out the bottom of the bay as needed, so that all shipping vessels could enter New York Harbor. I was invited to witness this procedure of taking the bottom of the bay out into the deep ocean in order to maintain the proper water depth of the harbor.

One bright and sunny morning, I was driven down to the bay and escorted on a dredging ship called *The Esseance*. We were served coffee and snacks and given a tour of the ship. The whistle blew and the ship started to gently leave the dock. The ship then maneuvered to get into the proper position to start sucking up the bottom of the bay. To my amazement, there were these huge arms on each side of the ship, with large vacuum cleaner-type arrangements at their outer tips. At the command, those vacuum cleaners were positioned to allow them to travel all the way down to contact the bottom of the bay. I was standing on the top, outside deck, looking down into a cavernous area inside the ship. I heard those vacuum cleaners switch on and tons of sea bottom were sucked up and dumped into the bottom of the ship. The ship gently moved up the harbor until it was completely full of dirt, debris, and anything else that happened to be on the bottom of the bay. These huge vacuum cleaners were then brought up and attached to the side of the ship. While the ship traveled out to sea, we were escorted into the cabin for a great lunch. When we reached a point in the deep ocean, the bottom of the ship was opened and all that material that had been vacuumed up from the bottom of the bay was dropped into the open ocean. When all the debris was gone, the bottom doors were closed, and the ship headed back to its docking location. After a couple of discussions with the membership, I learned that everything we had dumped in the open ocean would return to the harbor and the entire procedure would need to be done over again. I am not an oceanographer, but it seems that a better system should be found.

Discovering Jackson Heights, Meryl

A lot was going on in our lives that made every day very exciting. The Principal at Harriet's school in Brooklyn was transferred to a school on Staten Island. He asked Harriet to transfer to Staten Island with him. She agreed and started working on Staten Island. Those days, Harriet was teaching second grade and I was working as a draftsman. In the evenings, I went off to school or board meetings, three or four nights a week. On the weekends, Harriet and I spent time together and visited a number of great friends that we both had. We were still poor, but our finances were getting better. Life was good.

My first job as a junior draftsman.

With Harriet's $3,000 a year and my $2,600 a year salaries, we felt that we could afford a better apartment. After searching the apartment market, we found a very nice two-bedroom apartment in Jackson Heights, Queens, New York. It had a good-sized master bedroom and a smaller second bedroom for a new arrival that we were contemplating. It had an adequately sized living room, full eat-in kitchen and a small nook in the passage way to the bed rooms that they called the dining area. The building was privately owned, but was under rent control by the FHA. That meant that the owner could not raise our rents unless it was approved by the FHA. The cost of the rent we felt was workable with our income, so we moved in.

It was a lovely area consisting mostly of young married people, in a safe and clean neighborhood, with lots of activity for young children. It did not take long for Harriet to notify me that I was to be a father! That was great because we were ready to build the family and grow on all fronts.

One day we were sitting around the apartment when Harriet was in about her eighth month of pregnancy. The doorbell rang and I answered the call. It was our neighbor. "Why are the two of you sitting and moping instead of doing something interesting? Come on over to our apartment and let's play bridge." I announced that "I do not play bridge, I do not want to play bridge, and card games do not turn me on." Harriet, on the other hand, was a bridge player and love to play. My law for keeping and maintaining a great marriage was to say just two words, "Yes Dear".

We went to our neighbor's apartment, where they had the bridge table set up with a deck of cards, paper and a pencil. They served some snacks, which were mandatory for bridge playing. They started to teach me how to play the game. We went slowly at first, until they felt that I had enough information to be able to play. We were ready to play for real. I never knew that bridge players are like golfers; either you win or you get aggravated. Harriet and I played as partners against the other couple. They were doing pretty well. After about 20-30 minutes, I started to catch on and things changed. Harriet and I forged ahead and the friends were woefully behind. Their facial expressions slowly changed from smiles to grins to horrible angry looks. Then the vocal expressions started. I don't remember the exact words, but the wife started with some negative statements about her husband's playing style, at which he came back with stronger terms. She came back with much more stronger terms. He was about to come back with even more stronger terms, when all of a sudden, all of the woman's cards flew through the air right at her husband. I looked at Harriet, and she looked at me, and we both agreed the game was over. We excused ourselves, went to our apartment, and after we stopped laughing, we had a great snack and enjoyed the rest of the evening. That was the end of my bridge playing career forever.

Another month or so passed, then Harriet informed me that she was ready to give birth. It was time to go to the hospital. We were living in Jackson Heights, Queens but the hospital was in Brooklyn where

Harriet's uncle, our doctor, had privileges. It was about an hour ride, so I added a little speed to the car as I drove. We got there in time, notified Uncle Dave, who came down to the hospital. He told us that she was really not ready, that it would take some time. He suggested that I go home and leave her in the hospital and he would notify me if there was any change. Two days went by and there was no change. Finally, Uncle Dave told me to take Harriet home because it would be awhile. About three days later, we started it all over again and went back to the hospital. I was told it could be any time, but one never knows.

Meryl the baby, Harriet and I.

Since there was a very important chore I had to do while Harriet was stalling in the hospital, off I went to the camera store to get my 8mm Bell & Howell movie camera that had been repaired. While I was on this important mission, Harriet decided to give birth. Lo and behold, unbeknownst to me, I was a father and had a daughter. When I got back to the hospital, Uncle Dave took me under his arm and escorted me to the maternity ward. There, I found Harriet and Meryl, both in good condition. I am so glad that I had the time to fix my camera. Harriet never let me forget that I thought my camera was more important than the life event that was unfolding. The minute that Harriet and Meryl came home, my movie camera never seemed to stop running. I had taken a series of movies before Harriet gave birth, with her large pregnant stomach, walking from the corridor into the bedroom of our apartment. When Harriet came home with Meryl, I took some more movies of Harriet coming out of the bedroom and holding Meryl. When I spliced them together, the viewer was able to see the entire event. It was a nice effect. I kept taking movies of Meryl every month for the first year was so. I spent hours creating animated titles on all the movies for posterity. Jumping quickly forward to the birth of Paul, some four years later, I don't remember taking many movies. Does that make me a bad father? (Al, you are forgiven. Love, Paul)

A Bad Change In Career Path With A Fabulous End

One morning, I was at my office drawing up plans for a school auditorium project, when my phone rang. Upon answering the phone, I heard the voice of a good friend of mine, who was also an architectural draftsman. He was working for a small architectural firm that specialized in building six-story apartment houses on the Grand Concourse in the Bronx, New York. The Grand Concourse was the Bronx version of Manhattan's Fifth Avenue. In those days, this area was an expensive, upscale location for those who could afford that lifestyle. After the usual greetings, he asked me to have lunch with him. He wanted to discuss an opportunity for me that his boss was offering. We arranged to have a lunch meeting the next day so that I could find out just what this opportunity was.

The next day, we met as planned, at a small quiet restaurant where we could have lunch and a quiet conversation. My friend told me that his boss had just been commissioned to design a large high school out on Long Island. Since he did not have the necessary experience in designing school buildings, he was looking for someone with that ability to join his office. After hearing more of the details, my friend said, "Let me set up a meeting with you and my boss and let him convince you that this is a good move for you".

Two days later I found myself in the office of H. I. Feldman, Architect. Mr. Feldman had a reputation for the luxury apartment houses that he had designed along the Grand Concourse. At that meeting, Mr. Feldman proposed that I recruit the necessary additional staff to bring with me to his office to take over the design of this project.

The school was a large high school in a new area of Long Island, New York with a rapidly growing population. The building was to be located on a large site that provided space for future additional buildings as well as the requirements for a future addition to the height of this building. He offered me a salary of $100 per week to be the leader of this design team. When he said $100 per week, which would double my salary, my body started to shake. To sweeten his proposal, he said that I was like a little bird in a nest. I must grow and learn how to fly out of the nest into the future. Working in his office on the school project would give me that opportunity that was like that little bird in the nest. This seemed like a great opportunity that I did not want to lose.

The next day, I spoke to the team I was working with on the school at Eggers and Higgins about this offer. This team consisted of four draftsmen. I described the offer. I was able to convince them to quit our current jobs and join me to work on the school for H. I. Feldman's architecture office, with me as the team's leader. The following Monday we all showed up at our new office ready to design a great school with that client. The five of us little birds, as Mr. Feldman explained, started working with much enthusiasm. We all worked many hours, doing whatever was necessary to make sure that we completed this project within the contract completion date. This project gave me great experience, not only in designing the school, but in the capacity as team leader. When the project was 100% completed, packaged up with all the necessary documentation, it was then delivered to the school board to be sent out for the bidding process. My team and I sat back and took a deep breath of relief. We were proud to have done a good job. We worked extra hard and felt that we proved ourselves to our new employer.

We delivered the project on Wednesday, the day before Thanksgiving. We congratulated ourselves and were ready to enjoy a great Thanksgiving. Mr. Feldman called the team into his office. He thanked us for doing a great job, and then to our horror, notified us that we were being fired. I looked at Mr. Feldman with an uneasy feeling and wondered what happened to that little bird in the nest. We were supposed to stay in this office until we felt we could fly on our own. Mr. Feldman just stood up and walked out of the office.

Panic set in. Not working and earning money was something new to me. I was married with obligations. I could not be unemployed. The five of us left and looked for the closest phone to see if we could make some contacts before the end of the day. If we couldn't do anything that day, we'd have to wait for the Thanksgiving weekend to pass. The only thing that I was able to find, as far as employment, was work at what was known as a 'job shop'. This is an office that provides drafting services for architects who do not have the staff to produce the work. The problem with working for a job shop was that time working there would not count towards the 12 years necessary to take the state board exams. At least starting Monday, I would be earning some money. Needless to say, that was one horrible Thanksgiving weekend.

Early Monday morning, I received a phone call from a friend of mine who also worked with Mr. Feldman in the capacity of a building department expediter. A building department expediter files all the necessary drawings and obtains the approval of the department of buildings to obtain a construction permit. He told me of another company that he worked for that was looking for somebody with my experience. He set up a meeting for me that morning. I showed up on time at the office of Shuman and Lichtenstein Architects. They offered me a job as Senior Draftsman in their office at the same $100 a week salary. Their office consisted of two other draftsmen and a secretary/Girl Friday who ran the administration of the office. I quickly agreed to join their firm, since working for an architect would count towards my 12 years necessary for me to be able to take the state board exams.

With a song in my heart, I called the job shop and notified them that I would not be able to accept the position. That afternoon, just for curiosity, I picked up the New York Times and looked at the want-ads to see what other opportunities were out there. Looking over the list of offers, I came upon one ad that made the hair on the back of my neck stand at attention. It read that the office of H.I. Feldman had five openings for junior, intermediate, and senior draftsmen. Why did Mr. Feldman tell the five of us that we had done such a great job and then fired us, only to put in ad in the New York Times looking to hire five draftsmen a few days later? I had to find out what the truth was in this matter. When I was working with Mr. Feldman, I got friendly with his son, Jeffrey, who was also a draftsman in that office. I called Jeffrey and asked him what had happened, why he fired us and was looking for new people? "You don't know? That's the way my father operates. He hires everyone for one job and when the job is finished he fires them. He hires new people to take their place. That way, everybody in his office is always at entry-level. He does not have to give his employees raises at the end of the year and this keeps his payroll down." Wow!! Did I learn something about human nature?

It just so happens that Mr. Feldman's firing of me was the best thing to have happened in the long term. By the next Monday, I had a job with the firm of Schuman & Lichtenstein Architects. It was where I would find my 40+ year architectural career. I worked with that firm for many years, until I qualified to take my state board exams. After I passed the state board exams, I became a registered architect. By that time, the firm had grown to Shuman, Lichtenstein & Claman Architects and was later changed to Shuman, Lichtenstein, Claman and Efron Architects.

When I became a partner in the firm, it was still a relatively small to medium-sized architectural practice. As time went by, we were able to build it up into a major architectural firm, building in many U.S. states and overseas. Years later, when Mr. Feldman retired, he did not want to sit at home. He approached us and asked if we have space in our office for him to use to keep busy and out of the house. As a favor to him, even though we did not need him, we gave him access to an empty office that we had at that time. After about two years, we needed that office and asked him to leave. What a chain of events that was for me over those years!

Back to My Life & Staten Island

Times were great for our family of three. I tried to spent most of the evenings during the week with Harriet and Meryl, except for the nights I was at school, taking various engineering, history of architecture, and other such courses to round out my knowledge. The weekends were spent with family outings and chores. Every year, the landlord would present us with a new one-year lease for us to sign. Much to our surprise, the rent was higher than the year before. I spoke to the landlord and told him that since this was an FHA rent-controlled building, he could not raise the rents. With a self-assured smile on his face, he pulled out the FHA approval document. By our third year, the rent was getting quite high. Our budget was being stretched to an uncomfortable position.

Since Harriet was teaching on Staten Island and had a number of friends who lived there, we felt that a move to Staten Island would be great for us and Meryl. It would be a good place for other children we intended to have too. At that time, Staten Island was not crowded and still had a huge amount of open space and undeveloped land. Her friends told her of a number of new developments that were being built on Staten Island that were very affordable. The next weekend, we took a drive down to the Staten Island Ferry and took the boat ride. It felt as if we were on a cruise overseas. It was a delightful half-hour trip across the bay.

On the Staten Island side, waiting for us was a real estate agent that our friends recommended, to show us new homes that were being built. The builder had a small office on the construction site where he had drawings and floor plans of the buildings for us to examine. Looking out of the window of the sales office, we saw a beautiful wooded area. A light breeze was blowing as the trees were swaying. Harriet and I watched this view and felt that it would be a great place to live. Each home was a one-story ranch-style building with a full un-finished basement.

The home consisted of two small bedrooms and one slightly large master bedroom. There was a full eat-in kitchen, and L-shaped living room/dining room combination. There was one fair-sized bathroom that the family would have to share. The front door had a small entry area.

There was a side entrance door that had access to the first floor and to the basement. The basement was completely unfinished, however they did put the plumbing rough-in for future installation of a second bathroom. There was no garage, only two concrete strips on the side of the front yard to park a car. The building was completely freestanding, giving an open feeling, even though the side yards were quite small. The rear yard was 30 foot deep by 45 foot wide, which looked tremendous to us.

Our first ticky-tacky house.

We felt that this house would fit our needs. It was in such a lovely area which gave you the feeling of being in the country. After discussing the cost of the house and the financing, including my veterans entitlements, the mortgage plus any other carrying charges looked like this would work for us. In fact, our monthly mortgage payment would be less for this house than what we were paying in rent for the apartment in Queens; plus that rent would keep rising. This arrangement qualified us to purchase this house, in keeping with my earlier law of never going into debt. We then took a deep breath and with the generosity of Harriet's mother, we were able to put down a $2000 deposit on an $18,000 house including all of the extras. We were able to get a 5½%, 30-year fixed, VA mortgage. My first subconscious concern was, "Will I ever be able to pay off the mortgage?" Little did I know that in 25 years, I would sell this house for $109,000.

Back at our apartment, we notified the landlord that we would be leaving when our current lease expired. The next four or five months were a busy time until the house was ready for us to move into. Planning the move, planning the decoration, and taking trips around Staten Island to find out what was available in the surrounding area took time. The only shock we had, occurred one day on a trip to Staten Island. We stopped off to see how the construction was going on our house. When we had originally picked out the lot, the builder said our lot would be "between this tree and that tree". Now that the construction was in full blast, we stood in front of all of the lots, but could not find any trees, anyplace in the area. The builder had leveled the entire area and started to build the homes. It was a little disappointing, but not a tragedy. We spent 25 glorious years in that little house, raising two children who we were always extremely proud of.

Harriet's mother, Ida, Harriet, Meryl, and Paul.

When construction of the development was approximately 75% complete, a majority of those houses were sold. Every day you would see a number of moving vans unloading furniture into the completed homes. It seemed like overnight that many homes were occupied and the community was being formed. Harriet, Meryl, and I were one of those new move-ins. There were a lot of introductions and greetings of new neighbors. Almost all of the new residents were married couples with one child and a number on the way, just as we were planning. It was a very happy time and everyone on our block were very nice and we formed a number of great friendships.

Things now calmed down and normal life started. When Meryl started kindergarten, Harriet was able to get a job teaching 2nd grade in the same neighborhood school, which was about four blocks away. Both Meryl and Harriet went to school every day together and returned home together.

After a while, two problems that were caused by the builder became evident. One problem was not only in our development, but also across a major portion of developments on the South Shore of Staten Island. The terrain on this section of the island was very hilly. Therefore, on almost every block, there was a house on the high side of the hill, houses on the slope of the hill, and a house at the bottom of the hill. If you close your eyes and imagine the situation on a rainy day, you will see that the rain that falls on the rear yard of the house at the top of the hill gently runs down the hill, flowing over all the yards until it comes to the bottom of the hill, with that poor homeowner now having an unwanted swimming area in his backyard. To alleviate the problem, the people with the unwanted swimming pools simply installed a low, concrete block wall along their property line to prevent the water from entering the property. So, what happens then? That second house was now lucky enough to acquire the unwanted swimming pool. So, what does that resident do? You guessed it. He builds a wall. And so it goes up the block. Both before and during the construction of these concrete block walls, there was quite a bit of heated conversation amongst neighbors. This was happening all throughout the South Shore. The residents realized that fighting amongst themselves was not the solution. The answer was to get the government involved. Homeowner associations started to form, which produced protests, letters to the editor, and phone calls to the elected officials, with many meetings to find the solution to this problem.

Meryl on the rock we were unable to remove.

Since this problem occurred about 60 years ago and I do not own that property anymore, nor do I live on Staten Island or New York State anymore, I will now admit my solution that worked beautifully. How proper or legal my solution was, is immaterial. All I know is that it worked. I simply dug a deep pit at the low point near the wall that my neighbor installed on his property. I put a stainless steel bucket in the pit, attached it to a drain pipe that ran underground and into my basement, then ran the pipe along the basement wall and hooked it up to the house trap. I then finished the basement with a furred out partition along the wall concealing the drain pipe. So, the rain came merrily down the mountain, approached my neighbor's wall, and then went into the bucket. It flowed through the drain pipe into the house, along the basement wall, into the house trap, then out into the city sewer. Problem solved. I just sat back and let all the other angry neighbors fight it out.

The second problem developed after a number of years of living in the neighborhood. After a while, almost everyone living in that neighborhood, including Harriet and I, had a second child. A number of neighbors were more productive and added a third child. As the children grew and reached driving age, they obtained driving licenses. What good is a driving license without a car? So, now the families bought a second car, and in some cases, a third or fourth as the need became evident. Since these homes were built providing space for one car that was parked on concrete ribbons in the front yard, what to do with those additional cars? The only solution was to park the additional cars in front of their houses, and in most cases, extending in front of their neighbor's house. If there was a third or fourth car, then neighbor watch out!

The worst was when it snowed. A homeowner will diligently shovel out the snow in front of their house to park their extra cars. Lo and behold, before he got a chance to move his cars into the newly cleared space, another neighbor would quickly park in that space. Holy hell broke loose! I'll leave the situation to the imagination of the reader.

At that time, I had completed one year of education to become a registered architect and was working as a draftsman. I felt it was time that I got some practical experience by finishing our basement all by myself. I worked at this chore for one solid year, every Saturday and Sunday. During the week, I found going to work was difficult due to all the aches and pains that I developed over the weekend. By Wednesday, I felt fine and couldn't wait for the next weekend.

Furring out a concrete wall with 2 x 3's on paper is very easy. But actually doing it was quite difficult, I quickly learned. I installed the base and header 2 x 3s, and then installed each vertical 2 x 3, 16 inches on center, making sure they were completely plumb. When I finished the first wall, I proudly looked to make sure all the 2x3s lined up. To my horror, I discovered that every 2 x 3 had a natural curve, and when installing, you should look down the face to find which way each piece is curving and make them all curve in the same direction. When I examined my construction, they were curved every which way and I felt like crying. I decided to leave it the way it was and somehow I would get the paneling installed and no one would know the difference. It took some doing but eventually when everything was finished and the furniture put in the room, we really could not tell that the wall was a little wavy.

I also discovered the physical problem of putting in a ceiling with acoustic tiles that are stapled to the framework. After installing about 20 acoustic tiles, I felt all of the muscles between my wrists and elbows start to lock up. Knowing that I had a long way to go to complete the ceiling, I decided to do it in small sections at a time, since my muscles were not used to this type of work. I found the same problem installing the tile flooring. I thought my knees and back would never heal when the job was completed. After that year of work, I learned my lesson and used the telephone to hire the proper people.

In the long run, it was a great room to have. There had many political cocktail parties in that room. I would invite our neighbors to attend in order to meet the candidates running for various offices like Congress, District Attorney, Borough President, etc. We also had many great celebrations down there because we could accommodate about 50 people and make a mess without worrying.

Our second child arrived on March 23, 1961. The bundle of joy was a boy who we named Paul David Efron. Meryl, our first child being four years old was delighted to have the baby brother. She kept looking at him bundled up in the crib and kept touching him to see if he was real. The only problem with Paul's birth was trying to obtain an official ruling of where he was a born resident of. Staten Island is very provincial and the people look at things in a very narrow field. I was having lunch with a friend of mine who was the editor of a local newspaper, the Staten Island Advance. I thought to myself, that he would be the perfect person to make a decision whether Paul is an official Staten Islander or not. As we sat and ate lunch, I gently said, "Lester, can I ask you an important question?" "Sure, what is your problem?" "My wife, Harriet, conceived our son while living on Staten Island. She then carried the full nine months on Staten Island. Our doctor is Harriet's uncle. Uncle Dave lives and practices medicine in Brooklyn. The hospital he has privileges is in Brooklyn. That March, we had a snowstorm on Staten Island. In order to not be delayed going to the hospital because of the snow we left Staten Island a little early. We arrived at the hospital in time for Harriet to check-in and get comfortable. A few hours later, she gave birth to our beautiful son. Three days later, Harriet and Paul were back on Staten Island to begin our lives. In my opinion my son is originally from Staten Island". "Oh, No, No, No!", said my friend Lester. "He is formally of Brooklyn". About 80 or 90 years from now, that's what his obituary will read. Now you know why I call Staten Island provincial.

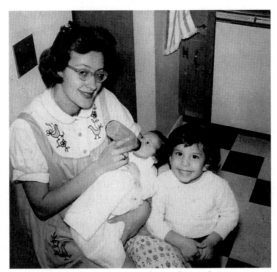
Harriet, Meryl, and Paul

My Family.

Always Listen To Your Children

One Sunday afternoon when Paul was about 8 years old, I was mowing the postage stamp-sized front lawn of our ticky-tacky first house, my neighbor came to inform me about some terrible thing that my son Paul had done. When he finished telling me his tale of woe, I told him I would speak to my son.

Later on, when Paul came home, I brought up the subject of this action that troubled me. After I finished expressing my opinion of the situation that I learned from my neighbor, my son, very quietly and intelligently said, "You can't make a decision of this incident because you never asked me about my side of the story". He stopped me, dead in my tracks. I hesitated for a moment. Then I realized that he was one hundred percent correct. How could I make a judgment, not knowing both sides of the story? Paul then went into great detail of the situation and what had actually happened. After hearing his side, I realized that my neighbor was off base, and I apologized to Paul. I never forgot this incident, and always made sure before coming to any conclusion, that I got all the facts from all sides of any situation.

My Children; Meryl and Paul

Welcome to the Democratic Party

Now that we were settled in on Staten Island, it was time to push my career, by building up my personal network and joining as many organizations as I could. A good starting point, I thought, would be politics. The next day, I was off to the Democratic headquarters on Staten Island to join up. I quickly learned that you could not just join a political party. You had to be elected, in a primary election, to a position in the party. However, to get started, I was told that since I was a young man, I should join the Young Democrats of Staten Island. I was told to contact John Carney, the President of the Young Democrats Staten Island chapter. I made the phone call and was invited to attend their next meeting. I attended the meeting and was off and running.

At that first meeting, I was warmly greeted as a new member. This chapter of the Young Democrats totaled about 20 members. It was a group of lovely young men and women looking to create careers in politics. The Democratic Party at that time was gearing up for the general election. We were given the usual political tasks necessary for an election, such as distributing literature, installing front yard signs at private homes, preparing meeting rooms where candidates would be conducting debates, etc. All of this activity was new and exciting for me. I was meeting Congressmen, City Councilmen, Borough Presidents, and other elected dignitaries. I was learning the entire political process that makes politics work. When the election was over, I had the opportunity to go to the victory parties of those Democratic candidates who won their elections. Also included were those Democrats who were not elected. Harriet and I enjoyed every minute of the entire experience.

Once the election was over and there was not much political activity, there wasn't much that the Young Democrats could do. At our next meeting, we contemplated what actions we could take. We decided that we would have to make a name for ourselves. We would do something spectacular and create the condition where the Democratic Party felt that they needed us. After much brain storming, we came up with a fantastic idea. At that time, the much of the South Shore of Staten Island was undeveloped. Driving through, you would see mostly forests and meadows and lakes. It was beautiful to behold. However, there was talk about building a bridge connecting Brooklyn and Staten Island. This bridge was to open Staten Island to the rest of the city.

At the time, the only transit between Staten Island and the rest of the city was by a ferry system that carried passengers and automobiles. It was a pleasant half-hour ride across the bay. Unfortunately, because of the huge line of cars waiting to get on a ferry, the majority of the time it could take anywhere from an hour to three hours to get on a boat. The home-grown Staten Island lifetime residents were against building the bridge. They liked their private little world 'as is'.

The newcomers, like me, saw the bridge as growth. We realized that this bridge was inevitable and would be built. This new connection with the city would create a huge increase in our population. That meant that eventually, the city of New York would have to build new police stations, fire stations, schools, and other facilities that are required for a smooth running community. So, we reasoned, why wait for the developers to buy the land and start building all those new homes, shopping centers, and other commercial buildings. We, the Young Democrats, would start a movement to get the City Planning Commission of the City of New York to create a master plan for the development of the entire South Shore. Once we had that master plan, the city would know where the future police stations, fire stations, schools, etc. would be located. Then, the city could create a land bank for the future facilities before the land was bought up by private developers. This land bank would eliminate the need for the city to obtain the land in the future by eminent domain.

We had a plan, but how were we going to put it into action? We reasoned that the best way to put pressure on elected officials to move in that direction, was to create a large movement of local residents that would be in favor of this endeavor. We concluded that to get these residents organized on our side, we would have to meet with all the homeowner associations throughout the South Shore to get them on board. The best way of accomplishing this would be to divide up all the homeowner associations. One of our members would be a guest speaker at as many meetings as we could, to sell this idea. That way we hoped to get all the homeowner associations on our side. We Young Democrats would then lead this coalition onto Borough Hall and City Hall.

At the conclusion of this momentous discussion, was dead silence. Then one member spoke up and said, "I'm not going to get up and speak before group. I never did public speaking". Another fellow said, "I'm with him. Count me out." The heavy discussions started. As far as I was concerned, I never had the opportunity of public speaking either. I was concerned that I wouldn't be able to get up and sell the idea to an audience while shaking in my boots. I remember turning to one of the fellows who said they didn't want to do public speaking. I looked at him and said, "You are on your way to become a lawyer. When you pass the bar, you will have to do public speaking at trials and everywhere else that's required of the law profession." "When that happens", he said, "I'll worry about it then". We all agreed to continue this discussion at our next meeting.

At home that evening, I was thinking about me doing public speaking. I realized that is an essential part of being a professional in whatever field you choose. After some deep thought, and remembering my impressions when some of our candidates gave their presentations, I realized that all I had to do was create a system that worked for me, so that I would be in complete control of the situation. You must remember that this was around 1955 and there was no such thing as computers; the word 'computer' was not even in the dictionary. PowerPoint wasn't even a consideration in anybody's mind. Even though I knew nothing about these future tools that would make life easier for public speakers, I came up with a system. I created a presentation and broke it down into sections. I got a large, white piece of cardboard, and with rub on letters that architects use for their renderings, I put down what looked like the title of each of the sections that I going to speak on. This is similar to the future PowerPoint which I never knew would exist. I felt that this cardboard, hanging up behind me, would inform the audience of what I was talking about. But it really was to remind me of what I was going to speak about. I could see each thought up there, which would keep my presentation in the proper order. It really worked for me.

I took close notice while watching television, about how those people presented themselves while trying to win an audience. I noticed some of the body language that the speakers were using. At our next meeting of the Young Democrats, I said, "I'm ready to go. What's the worst that can happen? Will they boo me off the stage?" After more discussion, we were all on board and the program was ready to put into action. We contacted the presidents of all the homeowners associations and scheduled speaking engagements. When it was my turn to speak, I asked a friend of mine, who was an attorney and was used to public speaking, to come down with me as an observer. He agreed and we were off to my first public speaking adventure.

The meeting was held in a large meeting room at the local school. About 60 members of the homeowners association were in attendance. I was introduced. I put my chart up on the wall with some scotch tape to hold it in place, and started my talk. After about one minute, I felt so at ease as I was talking. The more I spoke, the easier it was, and I found myself using the body language I had seen on television. I kept checking my chart and my talk ran smoothly. I felt my talk was very successful. When I finished, my friend said, "Al, you're a natural. There is nothing I can tell you for you to correct." The president asked for a vote on adopting the program that I had spelled out. It was unanimous. We had our first homeowners association on board and were anxious to move forward. That experience was a turning point in my entire future life. That one talk gave me so much self-confidence and I will never forget it.

The other members of the Young Democrats were making their talks and we eventually had the vast majority of the homeowners on our side. We set up a meeting with the Borough President to present this program. If the Borough President went along with our idea, it would be a major accomplishment. At that time, the City of New York was run by the five Borough Presidents. These Borough Presidents made up the Board of Estimate, which controlled all the money that was collected and spent in the City of New York. The Mayor, in those days, was pretty much a figurehead. When a Borough President wanted to spend money for something, they would negotiate with the other Borough Presidents to make sure they got want they wanted. Everybody was happy since they voted for each other's needs. They were all winners. Now that the young Democrats of Staten Island had the community behind us, we were ready to make a presentation to the Borough President of Staten Island.

With such a strong backing, we were the leading force with this proposal and succeeded in making a name for ourselves. This was what got the City Planning Commission to start working on a master plan for Staten Island. Although the city did not follow our entire plan, they did create, what was called the Greenbelt, to keep open space and not fill every inch of land with buildings. They created a blue belt that allowed some construction that would be limited to certain conditions and other zoning requirements, making for an orderly development of the South Shore. What a great way to start my activity in politics.

After some time as Young Democrats, we found ourselves growing up and becoming real Democrats. I acquired good relationships with many elected officials, commissioners, and other people who were the makers and shakers in government. A lot of the young people who were buying the new homes that were being built all over Staten Island were running into many technical problems created by not so honorable developers. One of the biggest problems we found, was when a developer builds a large-scale development, they were required to build all the streets and sidewalks throughout the project to meet New York

City requirements. To ensure that this requirement would be complied with, the builder was not issued a Certificate of Occupancy which was necessary before the buyers could take possession and move into the homes. The banks were required to hold a portion of the money that was due to the developer until all of the streets and sidewalks were installed, before the Certificate of Occupancy was issued.

However, the banks were lenient with this requirement of holding back the final payment. Once certain developers received their final payments, they notified the people that they could move in. This was completely illegal because the streets and sidewalks had not been built and the Certificates of Occupancy were never issued. The innocent homeowners, having no knowledge of this problem, moved into their homes thinking everything was in order. The developers disbanded their organizations, created new construction companies, and started to build houses in other areas under new company names. Soon after the poor homeowners moved in, they were notified that they had to leave their homes. Without a Certificate of Occupancy, they did not have the legal right to live in their houses. In order to get a Certificate of Occupancy, the homeowners had to install the roadway and sidewalks in front of their houses at their expense. This was a shock to those young families who did not have the finances to pay for the construction of the roadway and sidewalk and had no place to go.

A couple of friends of mine found themselves in one of these homes and were heartbroken. They contacted me to see if I could help them work out some arrangement with the Department of Buildings to legalize staying in their new homes. This situation, it seemed to me, to be a good opportunity to help these people, as well as work with elected officials and commissioners, etc. I met with the government officials to discuss what options we had to legalize the situation. The first concession that I was able to get the city to make was to allow the people to stay in their homes while a solution was being discussed. The building department inspectors then made sure that all of the houses in question were safe and complete, with all city requirements, with the exception of the roadways and sidewalks. Then, as I search my memory of this event that happened over 50 years ago, we worked with the banks, various city agencies and elected officials, to establish a fund to construct the roadways and sidewalks. The city also created new requirements for the builders and banks to ensure that this situation would never occur again.

One day, our County Leader, who was a retired judge, and a friend of his, another retired judge, decided to go fishing. One of them owned a good-sized power fishing boat that they used for the day. Sometime during the middle of the day, their engine died and they couldn't get the boat moving. The only alternative they had was to call the Coast Guard. The Coast Guard sent out a patrol boat to help the stranded judges. Our local newspaper, finding out about the situation, sent their eye in the sky, as they called their traffic helicopter, to see what the situation was and if there was a story for the next day's newspaper. When the helicopter passed over the stranded ship, they got a beautiful photograph of the two judges standing with their mistresses. This situation and photo made a fantastic story for the next day's edition. To make a long story short, the huge outcry from the Democratic Party of this calamity forced the County Leader to not run for re-election.

Our Congressman declared his candidacy for County Leader. We, the Young Democrats, who now were regular Democrats, had no love for this Congressman. We questioned whether his interest in the community was above his personal interests. Just as a note, a number of years later, this Congressman was convicted of taking bribes and went to jail for 18 months. Since we were no longer Young Democrats, but real Democrats, we decided to take action. We were going to get our own candidate to become County Leader and take over the Democratic Party on Staten Island.

The political organization consisted of County Committeemen who were elected by the people in the primary election. County Committeemen represented an election district, which was the area around the voting location where they lived. Each election district had four County Committeemen. That meant that there were many hundreds of County Committeemen in the organization at the end of the primary election. All the County Committeemen met in a convention to elect a County Leader. That was the position that our Congressman wanted. He felt that he could not lose since a lot of the County Committeemen got jobs or received favors from the Congressman. The 20 of us Young Democrats, now real Democrats, decided to run our own candidate against our Congressman.

Al with Governor Hugh Carey and Congressman Jack Murphy

We called a meeting to plan our strategy. What mattered was the number of votes of all the County Committee people who would be attending this convention. We obtained a list of the existing elected County Committee people. When we scrutinized the list, we were shocked to find out that there were approximately 60% vacancies on the County Committee. No one seemed to realize that those positions were never filled. We reasoned, if we could quietly recruit enough people to run in the next primary to fill those vacant positions, we would have enough votes to elect our candidate as County Leader. Once that was established, we could control the executive committee and therefore the Democratic Party on Staten Island. That would be our ace in the hole. Not only did we fill those seats, but we also aligned with other groups in the Democratic organization to make sure the candidate we chose became the County Leader. To make a long story short, we found the perfect candidate, put all the votes in order, and waited for the next County Committee convention.

That evening, as the hall filled with the County Committee, our Congressman stood on the side by the stairs leading up to the stage. In his hand he had his acceptance speech that he was sure he would get to read. The first item that came up was our request for a secret vote. We felt that with the secret vote, some of the Congressman's voters would be on our side. The Congressman forced the issue and wanted a voice vote.

He wanted to see everybody stand up and be counted. He won that round. A number of the Congressman's voters were on our side but did not want to vote against him. These people held jobs that they had gotten from the Congressman and did not have the courage to stand up to vote against him. They quietly got up and left the room, supposedly to go to the bathroom. However they never returned. The voting started and the secretary called out each name to cast a vote. When all the names had been called and the voting was done and calculated, the announcement was made that our candidate won. Our Congressman stood there for a couple of seconds, not believing what had just happened. And then, when it really set in, he crushed that paper containing his speech and stormed off.

Our group was now in control of the Democratic Party on Staten Island. As result, my close friend, who was a Zone Leader, was eventually appointed to become President of the Board of Education for the City of New York. That opened the seat for a new Zone Leader. A Zone Leader is the so-called boss of all the County Committeemen for one third of Staten Island. Hence, there are three Zone Leaders on Staten Island. Zone Leaders also sit on the Executive Committee. The Executive Committee was a powerful group. They decided the Democrat who was going to run for any elected position, as well as controlled the entire voting procedure in his zone. I got my little army together and prepared to put my hat in the ring. The Congressman and his forces, not being on the winning side, did not have any love for me. They put up a candidate against me.

From out of the woodwork, more people put their hats in the ring. By this time, I had acquired enough political skill to start maneuvering the situation. I quietly made alliances with two of my opponents, since they didn't have the number of votes that I had and neither of them could win, they joined with me. We kept this maneuver quiet and started to make sure that my voters were all on board. The Congressman's forces felt that they could defeat me if they held this special election on a Saturday morning. I am Jewish and an election being held on a Saturday morning might keep a lot of the Orthodox Jewish voters at home because they are not allowed to drive on the Sabbath. That dirty trick didn't work and I was elected Zone Leader. Now that I had some political power, the fun and games began.

The first thing I wanted to do was organize the County Committee into a well-oiled political machine. For some reason, when an election was over, the party officials felt that it was time to rest and wait for two months before getting busy and working once again to get Democrats elected. My vision of a political organization is that it should work 12 months a year. The downtime, when there is no election and no reason to contact the voting public, is the time to contact the voting public. The great advantage of contacting them when there is no election, is because they are not being harassed with phone calls, visited at home, or pounded by radio and television ads at that time. None of that is going on so they are more receptive to listening to your message in a positive manner.

I have a theory that I have lived by my entire professional life. I do not ask someone for a favor unless I have done a favor for them first. Doing a favor for someone puts them in the mood that they feel they owe you a payback. Another theory that I live by is to always look professional. By that, I mean, it's show business. Act professionally. Dress like a professional. Speak like a professional. People will treat you like a professional and you will be a winner all the time. Just suppose you have a community association meeting and the subject of selecting someone for a project comes up. Let's say you are very much interested in getting that position because it would help you with the contacts you can make and on your resume. Another fellow at this meeting has the same desire that you have and also wants to get that position. However, before you went to that meeting, you took the time to put on a nice suit & tie. You look and act professionally when you show up to the meeting. Your competition didn't bother to take the time to dress up and wears blue jeans with a T-shirt to the meeting. When the time comes to select the person for that position, who do you think has the upper hand? Me. It works all the time.

It was time to start organizing as Zone Leader. My first chore was to set up a professional organization that was run in a professional manner and commanded respect. To start, I needed an office. He who has an office looks professional. He who operates out of his home doesn't. Remember, I was still an architectural draftsman and did not have a professional architectural license yet. That meant that I was working for an architect at that time. My boss saw the way I operated and was impressed. After working with a number of organizations, I was able to bring an architectural commission into the office from one of my contacts. A few months later I submitted the names of the architectural firm I was working for in the bidding process to build an elementary school on Staten Island for the Board of Education. After a number of interviews I was successful in winning the competition and the firm was officially awarded the contract to build that elementary school. When I told my boss I was getting involved in politics as an elected Democratic Party official, my boss was again, very impressed. He was a long-range thinker and saw a potential in me. He told me that he would back me up with any finances that I might need.

About a week later, I spoke to my boss about my need to open a political office that was available on the second floor of a local shopping area on Staten Island. The cost was small because the office was on the second floor of a shopping center and was very hard to rent. My boss agreed that he would help with the monthly rent and take care of any other expenses that I was unable to obtain. We both agreed, shook hands, and I was off and running.

As a point of information, firemen working for the City of New York had a lot of time off. As I remember they worked three days and then had three days off. In their time off, many of them ran small home-repair construction businesses. I had about 10 close fireman friends who were also interested in politics and they volunteered to help me fix up the office. They did all the necessary construction and got everything working in beautiful condition.

Another friend of mine said that he could get me furniture that would not cost me anything, but we needed a truck to pick it up. I asked him how he found such a great deal. He told me he had a friend who worked on the loading dock of a large office building in Manhattan. One of the tenants moved out and left quite a bit of furniture that they did not want. It was there for the taking because it was all going to be thrown away. "Great", I said. "I have another friend who owns a large truck and I'll see if I can get him to drive us to the city to pick up the furniture." My friend with the truck said he had no problem with helping me out and would be glad to drive us there and help load the truck with the furniture. We set a date.

The driver, two other friends, and I took off to pick up that furniture. When we got to the office building, the friend who arranged this whole thing got out first. He said, "Let me talk to my friend at the loading dock". He came back and said, "Okay, you can back the truck up to the loading dock in this slot". We were all set. We went up to, as I remember, the 22nd floor, and found a huge amount of furniture. We selected what we needed, loaded everything into the elevator, and took it down to the loading dock. We loaded it all in the truck. We had just about everything we needed, except for a few incidental items. At that time, the friend who set up this great find said, "We'd better get out of here fast because my friend is going off duty". "What's the rush", I asked. "Al", my friend said. "Trust me. Let's get out of here." It seemed odd to me, so I asked if this furniture was really being thrown away. My friend said, "What do you want to do now? Unload the truck and put it back, or keep it? Let's get the hell out of here fast". We jumped in the truck and took off, as my heart beat like chattering teeth and my hands trembled. I couldn't wait to get back to Staten Island and safety. Had I known that the furniture was not being thrown away, I would have never agreed to such a deal. However, since that's the way it worked out, we furnished that office beautifully and professionally. That furniture was there throughout all of the years that I was the Zone Leader. The lesson I learned was to make sure you really know all the facts before you get into anything.

The real organizing began. Staten Island was divided into three zones. Each zone had approximately an equal number of Democratic voters and was run by a Zone Leader elected during a Primary Election. The County organization consisted of a County Chairman, Vice Chairman, Secretary, Treasurer and the three Zone Leaders. This was the group that formed the Executive Committee. The Executive Committee was the decision-making committee for the entire county. One of its primary responsibilities was to nominate candidates wanting to run for elected office on the Democratic ticket. However, the County Chairman acquired his position by a vote of the entire elected County Committee. This set-up put me in a very important position. I oversaw and had, somewhat, control over one third of the County Committee on Staten Island, who votes for the County Chairman, and in turn, all the other Democratic candidates running for office. So, to strengthen my position, I needed a strong organization behind me.

My first job was to make sure that every position on the County Committee was filled. If my memory serves me right, there were about 75 election districts. Each election district had four County Committeemen. When you add it all up, that meant that I had approximately 300 elected County Committee people in the Democratic Party that made up my political army. One of the four County Committeemen in each district was appointed Captain of that district. To back up my organization, I'd need another, non-political army under my control. So, I established the Zone Leaders Association. This new group was a civic group that unofficially organized to help the Zone Leader. This non-political organization was extremely important because they could raise funds for incidental, non-political reasons in a legal manner. As an example, when election time came around, they could organize a community barbecue. Everyone in the community would be invited, including all candidates running for office. This little army of mine was also very helpful with filling many vacancies on the County Committee. As I previously said, my organization had to work 12 months of the year and do favors for the Democratic voters in their neighborhoods.

I called a meeting with all the Captains, to be held in my office. When we were all assembled, I laid out the plan of how "each County Committeeman shall operate". Notice, I used the words 'shall operate' in lieu of 'will operate'. In my training as an architect, learning to write specifications was part of the agenda. I learned quickly that 'shall' is mandatory and 'will' is permissive. It means that when I say you shall do something, you have no other choice. If I say that you will do something, it means you will do it if you want to and I am only giving you permission to do it. It's a minor clarification, but it can have drastically different legal consequences.

The huge strength of this organization was built up by the following operation: I notified all my Captains and the County Committeemen on how this organization would operate. The month of April and May will be the kickoff for building an organization for the next election in the fall. I chose April and May because Christmas, New Year's holiday festivities are over. The snow and freezing of winter are on their way out. The heat of summer and vacations would not have started yet. April and May is a very quiet time with lovely weather and everybody in a good mood. The people would be rested up from the excitement of the past season.

Since each County Committeeman was elected in the neighborhood where they lived, all of the people living in that area were friends, neighbors, and acquaintances, not strangers. They knew one another from church on Sunday, synagogue on Saturday or mosque on Friday. They met in the supermarkets and their children played with one another, so everyone was interacting with everyone else. I told my Captains that on April 1st, they and their Committeemen shall have a meeting to review the list of registered Democrats in their district, obtained from the Board of Elections. They shall identify every registered Democrat in that area that they personally knew. They were to make sure that every listed Democrat was paired to a friendly County Committeeman, without duplication.

Earlier in the year, I had business cards printed up with space on them for each Committeeman to write their name, address, and phone number. I also had printed up a list of all the emergency phone numbers for the area, such as police, fire and sanitation etc. Remember, this was before the emergency phone number 911 was established. In New York, now there is also the number 311 for non-emergency problems that are the responsibility of the City. Every Saturday in April and May, from 10 to 12 in the morning, every committeeman was to visit all the registered Democrats that they knew. They were to give out their cards and the list of emergency contacts. When they greeted their neighbors, they were to inform them that they are their officially elected connection to help them with any government problems that they may have. Examples of problems could range from potholes in the roadway near their home or problems with official government documents. At that time, calling a NYC government agency for anything could be a nightmare. Trying to find the right person to help was almost impossible. There was no Google. Phone books were updated only once per year. This group committee people was formed to help.

The Committeemen were to tell the voters to not be shy and to not hesitate to call for help. If the voter had a problem, they were to set up meetings with me, the Zone Leader. The people would be asked to bring their friends to the meeting, to review the problem, and work to get it solved. We would try our best to get it done. The Committeemen were to tell them that their Zone Leader would be in his office every Wednesday evening from 7 to 10pm, in an effort to help any citizen with a problem related to the government. This procedure fell in with my doctrine of never asking a favor of anyone until I had done a favor for them. With these visits, the Committeemen was meeting the voter on a personal, friendly basis, offering to help them with whatever they needed and not asking for anything from them in return. In the fall, when the political system started, when a Committeeman rang a bell, he would be greeted with a smile from people who were receptive to listen. In most cases, they would vote as suggested by the Committeeman.

I 'held court' in my office every Wednesday night. I do not know how the term held court was established however it became the norm. I do not remember any time that I was not able to legally fulfill the wishes or correct the problems that were given to me.

I should mention that in those days, there was a lot of pressure against discrimination of minorities and women. The State Democratic Party set a policy that all Committeeman positions were open to all ethnic groups and that all leadership shall consist of two people. One must be a male and the other must be a female. When this order came into effect, I was directed to appoint a female as my co-leader until the next election. At the next election, we will both ran for election as co-leaders. My co-leader's name was Barbara Kett. She was very helpful to fill in for me on the few Wednesday nights that I could not make those meetings.

Here is one quick example of the many problems that were given to me over the years: A couple booked a cruise to Europe about eight months before. They submitted applications for a passport for each of them. When they came to me, it was less than a week before they were to board the ship for the cruise and they still didn't have their passports. They made numerous calls to the bureaucrats who were supposed to help, to no avail. When they gave me the problem, I called our Congressman's Chief of Staff, to do me a favor and get these people their passports within a few days. A couple of days later, the doorbell rang at this couple's house. When they opened the door, they were handed the two passports. We then had two solid Democratic votes.

Another interesting problem was brought to me by a couple whose son was arrested in Brooklyn. It seemed that the young man was driving his car at night and passed a stop sign. Just his luck, there was a cop in the area who stopped him. The cop noticed one marijuana cigarette in the car. In those days Nelson Rockefeller was Governor of New York State. He wanted to stamp out the use of drugs, so he came up with very tough legislation. If you were caught with one marijuana cigarette, you went to jail, no second chance. So the young man was arrested and locked up in Brooklyn. The couple came to me to explain their problem. Since they lived on Staten Island, it was an issue to go to Brooklyn with their attorney to take care of their son's arrest. The trip from Staten Island to Brooklyn, where their son was locked up, was about a 2-hour drive. It meant driving over the Verrazano Narrows Bridge, which, incidentally, cost seven dollars at that time, which was quite a bit of money. The bottom line was that it was a 4-hour trip, plus time meeting with their son, being billed by their attorney and the authorities. It was quite a problem. They asked me if it was possible to have their son transferred to Staten Island. Being closer to home would substantially reduce their time-consuming burden. I said, "Give me all the facts and I will look into it". The next day, I called the District Attorney and asked him if he could have the young man transferred to his domain and jailed on Staten Island. "No problem", he said, and it was done. There were at least two more happy Democrats in our camp.

Throughout the years, I took care of many hundreds of such problems as a service to our community. Every request that I received and took action on was always 100% legal and ethical.

Time passed, the election campaign started, and the County Committee swung into action. When our Committeemen, who took care of people's problems, rang those people's doorbells, they were greeted with a smile. When they were asked to vote for the Democratic candidate, the answer was always yes. What I do not understand is why political organizations today, hire and pay bright, young college students to ring bells at strangers' homes. Voters are sick and tired of all of the political phone calls and mailings that they have been receiving. How can you expect to have a positive outcome when speaking to a stranger, who means nothing to them and are a just a bother to their busy lives?

It seems to me that the reason most people get active in politics is they want a political job. No way was I interested in making a career in some job that I would need to be appointed to in government. When the powers that got me the job were not reelected, I would have to struggle to find a new position. That was not for me. My aim was still to be in my own architectural practice. I wanted to use politics for my mental stimulation, to do some good for the voting public, and build up a huge network of contacts. This would be of great help to me in the future. However, the local Democratic organization looked at me as an elected party leader without a job. I think I was the only leader with that designation. Throughout the years, I was offered many jobs, including member of the New York City Planning Commission, Commissioner of the Board of Standards and Appeals, member of the Health and Hospitals Corporation for the City of New York, Architect for the State of New York and others. I always turned the job offers down. My goal remained to become a member of the architectural profession. I found that being on any government commission would create conflicts of interest, since I often testified before various commissions in reference to projects that I worked on for my clients.

Joining Organizations & Networking

Once I was active in the political arena, it was time to branch out into other organizations to build up my private network. As I went through my daily routine of interacting with as many people as I could, I was introduced to a member of the Board of Directors for Wagner College. Wagner College had a large campus located on Staten Island. It was lunchtime, which gave me an opportunity to invite this gentleman to lunch so that we could get better acquainted. During that conversation, I learned that there was an opening on the Board of Directors. As subtle as I could be, I let it be known that I was interested in that position. By the time the lunch was over, he had invited me to attend a board meeting as his guest. After a little verbal maneuvering, I was asked to join the Board of Directors of Wagner College.

That evening, I wondered if I was stepping out of my background. Since I never spent 1 minute in a college classroom, and had no college degree, was it proper for me to occupy a seat on the board of a college? That thought lasted about 20 seconds, leaving me feeling very comfortable in that position.

By the third board meeting, everything began to gel. I learned a lot and began to contribute. My life experience elevated me to the chairmanship of a committee whose mission was to provide a complete energy conservation program for the campus. The problem facing society and the United States at that time was the embargo by the Arabs on all Arab oil. Remember OPEC? For the readers who lived through those days, they will remember the chaos of not being able to get gasoline for your car or other equipment due to the embargo. The lines at gas stations were blocks-long and very heated at times with angry people trying to get enough gas to run their autos. They used a rationing system for a while, where you could only get gas on even or odd days, based on the last number on your license plate.

After a few meetings of the board, I met a professor at the college who designed a new concept of solar energy. Any new source of energy that did not use gasoline was on top of everyone's agenda, including the federal government's. I arranged a working session with the professor to get me up to speed with this new technology. His system was a complete new concept. He designed a glass tube inside an outer glass tube. The final unit was about 4 feet long and about 4 inches in diameter. The air would be taken out of the space between the tubes, creating a vacuum, which allowed the suns rays to heat the water within the glass tubes more efficiently An array of these tubes would be plugged into a manifold. A group of manifolds would then be assembled together on a large roof or field that would be facing the sun. It would be connected to a water source. Water would circulate through the outer tubes and heated by the sun, then travel through the inner tube to the boiler room. There, the water would go through heat exchangers to be used for heating and/or air-conditioning the campus. The glass manufacturer was Libby Owens Ford, who felt there was a great future in this technology. They started to manufacture these glass tubes that we used in this demonstration model.

With the permission of the college President, we were given the authority to build a platform over a large parking lot located on campus. The professor then designed all of the controllers and other appointments that were needed to make this whole thing work. There was only one more problem left to solve. Where to get the required money to construct this demonstration project? The college felt that they did not have the funds for this project, so we were on our own to raise the money. Due to my political activity, I contacted our State Senator. I invited him down for lunch at the college to explain this exciting new project we were working on. At the end of the lunch and all the salesmanship that I was able to deliver to the State Senator, he asked me how much money we needed. I sheepishly told him $1,500,000. He then said, "Give me a couple of weeks and I'll see what I can do". To make a long story short, a check in the proper amount was presented to the college, ear-marked for the construction of the experimental solar energy project.

I started to design the platform and all accessory items needed in conjunction with the professor's requirements. I 'put the arm' on a couple of contractors to make sure everything was built within our allotted money. The day came when everything was complete and I was ready to throw the switch. We held our breaths and started up the system. And much to our surprise, it really worked! We kept the system going for a number of months without any problems at all. This whole concept was to prove that we could use solar energy on a large scale, eliminating other energy sources, like gasoline. Libby Owens Ford started a publicity campaign to sell this system to other organizations. And then, disaster struck. The Arab embargo was lifted, so oil and gasoline was flowing again. Now, nobody was interested in solar energy anymore. No one had the foresight to look into the future and see how valuable this system could be. So, bringing this adventure to an end, Libby Owens Ford stopped production on the glass tubes because they felt the market had disappeared. The entire demonstration project sat on the campus working beautifully for a few years. Then the problem arose requiring replacement tubes to keep the system going. However no one was manufactory those tubes and the entire system started rotting away, until it was finally demolished. It was not only a great adventure for me; it was a fabulous learning experience.

      This Wagner College experience was reported on in our local newspaper. It led to me being invited to join the Board of Directors of Staten Island University Hospital. As time went on and I was interacting with new appointments, I was asked to join other Boards of Directors. After a while, I was on the boards of Eger Nursing Home and Staten Island Zoological Society. I was Chairman of the Architectural Design Award Program sponsored by the Staten Island Chamber of Commerce and the Staten Island Advance, our local newspaper. I also started to get involved with the Blind and Deaf Society on Staten Island. Then, the Borough President asked me to serve on his Community Board. Later on, when I had my architect's license, I became active with the American Institute of Architects and became Treasure and then President of the New York State Association of Architects. This was the American Institute of Architects' state component. Eventually, I became a Fellow of the American Institute of Architects. There were many other organizations that I got involved with in the other boroughs of New York City, as well. The main reason for describing all these memberships, as I previously stated, is that I wanted to build up my own private network of people. It was the most important thing for my career, to build this network for future connections, for after I received my architectural license.

      Going to school at night, working during the day, and getting involved in all these organizations took a lot of my time. My wife Harriet never once said, "You're never home." Or, "We don't have nice things." She knew I was working my tail off to build a career. She gave me the complete freedom to pursue these dreams. In the end, it all paid off for both of us, thanks to Harriet, the love of my life.

Our House On Todt Hill

In the early 1980's, I had progressed in the architectural profession, which had allowed me to earn much more than just a decent living wage. We now were able to join Richmond County country club, learn to play golf, and rub shoulders with the makers and shakers of Staten Island. In real estate development, the money the developer needs at the beginning, before a project is funded with a construction loan, is 'hard money'. There are expenses and fees that come first, out of the developer's pocket, including architectural fees. You can't get a construction loan without a building design. To ease our client's burden, on some projects we would take a percentage of ownership in the project. My partners and I would each provide a personal check in the amount of our ownership. All these investments we made were very profitable in the long run. We were able to acquire enough money from distribution of the existing projects we owned to finance additional projects as well as increasing my personal bank account. Hence joining the country club on the hill.

Harriet and I decided to upgrade our living conditions by buying a bigger house, again as they say, up on the hill. In this case, the hill was Todt Hill on Staten Island. It just so happens that this hill is 400 feet above sea level. Because of that height, it makes Todt Hill the highest point on the eastern coastline of the United States from Maine to Florida. We spoke to the real estate agent about finding us the next house of our dreams. One day, Harriet and I were getting ready to go to the Richmond County Country Club for a day of golf, when the phone rang. Our real estate agent said that she had a great house for us to see that was within walking distance of our country club. I told her that when we finished golf, we would meet her there so that we could see the house.

After golf, I drove up the street looking for the house and almost passed it. This house happened to be set back about 100 feet from the road with a beautiful wall of evergreen trees at the street line. This gave the house a huge amount of privacy. I drove the car into the circular driveway and stared at it in amazement. I said to Harriet, "We can park about 15 cars on this driveway". What a relief from the fight for parking we lived within that little ticky-tacky house. Just looking at the size of this house from the driveway, I felt we had found it. Our real estate agent drove up and parked right next to our car. She got out and said, "Let's go inside so you can see what a great house this is." I turned to her and said, "I want this house and will give you a check now as a binder to lock this house up for us". "But you didn't see the inside yet", she said. I told her, "Whatever is inside that we don't like, we will fix and change." I gave her a check for one hundred dollars and we went inside to examine the house. It didn't take long for us to make an agreement to buy the house. We were going to live on top of the hill.

The next evening, Harriet and I were having dinner with friends of ours who were makers and shakers of Staten Island. The husband was Chairman of the Board, President, and CEO of a local bank. His wife was very active in just about every non-profit organization on Staten Island. At dinner, I told him that we were in the process of buying this house. They knew the house and the area. He asked me where we were getting our mortgage. I told him that I didn't believe in mortgages and was planning on paying cash. If I couldn't afford it, I wouldn't buy it. He asked me how much the house was and I told him $360,000. Just an aside to note, that was a large sum of money at that time. About 20 years later, I was offered $2 million for that house.

Getting back to the story, my friend, President of the bank, told me that it was a stupid thing to do. He said that he could give me a mortgage for $200,000 at 16% for 15 years. If I put the $200,000 cash in a savings account, his bank would pay me 18% interest. All I would have to do is pay $160,000 cash for the house. You have to remember that at that time, Jimmy Carter was President of the United States and interest rates rose above 20%. If I took this mortgage, I would be making 2% on my money. It would not really be like a mortgage because I had the cash in his bank that I could always use to pay it off. He did a good job of selling me on it and I took the deal. After about a year, I was not happy with the thought that I had this mortgage even though I did not have a financial problem. I just didn't feel right. So, I went to visit my friend at the bank and told him that I wanted to pay off the mortgage and end the deal. He then informed me that he did not have my mortgage. I looked at him, puzzled. He said that he had bundled my mortgage with other mortgages and sold them on Wall Street. I tried not to get too excited and asked him, "What gave you the right to sell a contract between you and I to a third-party without my permission?" He told me that the law allowed it. I found out who had my mortgage, paid it off, and breathed a sigh of relief. At that point, I realized that the home mortgage industry was based on manipulation that could crash in the future. And so it did and that is what we call the housing crisis of 2008.

Guns As A Sport

In keeping with my law of learning how to do everything there is in this world that I needed for self-preservation that I mentioned in the beginning of this book, I had the opportunity to get involved with the proper use and safety of firearms. I had a friend who belonged to a neighborhood gun club. He took me to a meeting to meet the guys and gals who handled guns as a hobby and the sport that it offered. I found the membership to be a great group of people who enjoy the sport. Needless to say, I was hooked and became a member. The first couple months as a member, I learned the safe use of all types of firearms. There were a number of safety rules that could never be broken. They informed me that if anyone violates any one of those safety rules, they were automatically thrown out of the club.

The time came when one of the members whom I befriended told me it was time to get into my first competition. Since I did not own a gun at that particular time, the club provided me with the revolver necessary for that particular competition. The competition consisted of five metal targets mounted on hinges and placed, to the best of my remembrance, about 50 feet in front of the shooting line. Behind each contestant was a club member acting as a safety officer. They explained to me that the object of this competition was, when the buzzer sounded, to raise the revolver, aim at the targets, and try to shoot down all five targets. The catch was that I was only given, as I remember, 15 seconds from when the buzzer started to when it buzzed again, which meant stop firing. If I missed any targets, I would have to reload and keep firing until I ran out of time. My friend showed me how to load the revolver with six rounds of ammunition. He also showed me how to clear out the shell casings and install new rounds. I thought to myself that 15 seconds to do all that seemed impossible.

I diligently loaded the revolver with six rounds and had a box of additional ammunition on the chair next to me in case I had to reload. It should be noted that in competition, to cut down the expense of buying new ammunition, members reloaded the brass and made their own rounds of ammunition. Therefore, after you finished firing, you collected the brass to take home and create new ammunition. I loaded the revolver as I was taught, relaxed, and placed one hand in my back pocket. In competition, you are not allowed to use two hands to hold the gun. I held the revolver in my right hand, with the barrel pointing down and my left hand in my back pocket, as I waited for the buzzer to ring. When I heard the buzzer, I brought up my right hand that held the revolver, sighted in on the first target, pulled the trigger, and kept firing until I ran out of ammunition. All five targets were proudly standing up, direct and smiling at me. I quickly reloaded and started shooting again just when the second buzzer rang, I stopped firing.

The safety officer said to me, "When you reloaded, why did you stop shooting?" "I did not stop shooting", I said. "Well nothing happened once you reloaded". He then took my revolver, looked in the chamber and said, "You didn't reload. All these rounds have already been fired". After some time considering what happened, I realized that when I emptied the revolver and the brass fell to the ground, the safety officer, as they always did, put the spent casings on the left side of the ammunition box. There was my mistake. When I reloaded, instead of taking new ammunition from the right side of box, I pulled the empty casings from the left side of box and reloaded just empty cartridges. Needless to say, I was the talk of the town. It took about three or four meetings before everybody forgot my first folly. It's all part of education and experience.

In time, I had my own reloading equipment set up in the cellar of my house and was ready for business. After more than a year, because of the strict gun laws in New York City, I was able to purchase a 38-caliber revolver, a 22-caliber pistol, a 357-magnum pistol, and a 45-caliber pistol. For readers who are not familiar with the different types of guns, let me explain. A revolver is a gun that was used in the early days of the Wild West. It has a turret that spins or revolves that you load with a round of ammunition into each of six openings. When you pull the trigger, the round fires, and the turret revolves so the next round is ready to be fired. A pistol has a magazine that you preload with the rounds, depending on the manufacturer's design. When you fire the gun, the casing is automatically ejected and a new round is inserted into the firing chamber.

The club had many different kinds of tournaments. Each was very challenging. I tried them all and got better as time went on. However, at my best, I was no match for those sharpshooters who had been handling guns for many years. One day, I asked one of the members if he had any hints that he could give me so that I could improve my game. "Yes", he said, "I have two". His first suggestion was for me to become Italian, because he had never heard of a Jew who handled guns. HIs second one was for me to take about 20 years off my life because I was too old. Oh well, there was nothing I could do about that advice.

Since my handling of guns was for the purpose of self-preservation, I met the challenge very well. When shooting at targets in competition, you want to have all the rounds hit the target within a tight circle of about 1 inch diameter. When shooting at targets that have a human form printed on them, I am deadly because there is so much room in the human body to hit and I could stop an assailant to protect myself. However bad I was at hitting tight patterns on targets did not stop me from having a great time with a bunch of great guys who hosted many fabulous barbecues and parties.

After a while, I wanted to expand my experience and knowledge with firearms in a real setting. That meant hunting. Since I don't believe in killing a wild animal just for the sake of killing, that aspect of hunting was not for me. However, to kill a wild animal for food is nature's way and happens every day throughout the world. I felt I should know how to hunt in the wild, field dress an animal as to not taint the meat, and find my way out of the wilderness, and back to civilization in a safe manner. The gun club that I belonged to owned thousands of acres of virgin forest for hunting. It was far up north in New York State. The tools of this new experience were different. To get ready for my first hunting experience, I purchased a 12-gauge shotgun and a carbine rifle. After practice sessions with these new guns at the club, I was very comfortable with the safety and operation of both of them. The date was set for the next hunt.

I outfitted myself with a compass, flashlight, matches in a waterproof container, hunting knife, whistle, pouch for food, water canteen, and other necessary items for survival in the wild. There were 12 of us in four cars and off we went. After about a five-hour ride, we arrived at a small one-room shack right next to the forest. I looked around at these meager surroundings and said, "Guys, I saw a nice motel about 3 miles down the road. It's on me. I will pay for 12 rooms and we can live in style for the next few days." They looked at me as if I was either sick or crazy! Out came the sleeping bags and food that did not need cooking. Well, I guess I lost that round. 'When in Rome...', as they say. I prepared myself for the surroundings as well as I could.

I should mention, in that county, we were hunting in had laws that mandated the use of rifles illegal. You were only allowed to use shotguns. To shoot deer with a shotgun, you had to use what are called slugs. Instead of small pellets being installed in the cartridge, it was loaded with a solid lead slug. To be safe in the handling of a double barrel shotgun, you must carry the barrel opened and away from the stock without any ammunition loaded in the barrel. In your left hand, you put two cartridges between your fingers so you are ready, just in case you see a deer. Then it would be easy to quickly slip the two cartridges into the barrel, snap it closed, verify the target as one you want to hit, aim, and fire the weapon.

The next day we were ready for the adventure. Off we went into the woods. The guys showed me how to read all the signs that animals leave. After about half an hour or so, the experienced hunters found a flyway. This is a path that deer use every day. If you position yourself along the flyway, you're bound to see a deer using that path. And so to prevent us from shooting one another, we all posted ourselves were we could see the flyway and would not endanger any of us from a missed shot. There we sat. Each of us was alone, quietly enjoying nature at its best. That day we saw nothing. The second day, we went through the same routine and saw nothing. I was convinced that the deer must've seen the latest newspaper that said hunting season was now open, so they all disappeared. The third day was pretty much the same.

Late that third afternoon, we discussed the situation and wondered if we should call this trip over and go home. The guys were sitting on a low stone wall facing the forest with their backs to a large open field. I was resting with my back on a tree facing my buddies and the large open field behind them. My shotgun was cocked open and two rounds of ammunition were in my fingers. I was talking to a guy sitting on the stone wall. As we talked, I was aware of, but not really thinking about two large dogs that were running across the open field. When the two large dogs got close to us, I realized that they were not dogs. They were deer and one was a buck! I did not notice whether the other one was a buck or a doe. The minute that those deer spotted us, they swung to the left to get away from us. At that point, I spun in the same direction, made sure my buddies were out of the line of fire, quickly inserted the two cartridges, and snapped the shotgun closed. Ready to fire, I focused on the buck. I fired one round. I got a clean shot and that deer was dead before it hit the ground. I made sure not to hit the other deer because I didn't know whether it was a doe or a buck and I did not have a license to hunt doe. The other deer kept on running and disappeared into the forest.

My buddies looked at me and their body language told me that they were both amazed and angered that they, the experience hunters, did not fire a shot. There I was, my first time hunting, the first time ever pulling the trigger of a shotgun on my first hunting experience, and I got a clean kill. In fact, I stood there in an amazed shock of what I had just done. When everything calmed down, I was told, "You shot it. You have to field dress it." For those of you, who are not familiar with field dressing a wild animal that has just been shot, brace yourself. There I stood as my buddies gave me all the gory details.

They said, "Number one, take out your hunting knife, cut around the deer's scrotum, then hold the blade of your knife so that just about an inch or so of the tip of the blade is exposed, and make one slice from the scrotum all the way up to the deer's neck. By using only a small part of the tip of the knife, you prevent cutting of any internal organs. Cutting the wrong organ could taint the meat. Next, open the chest of the animal, again holding the knife with the tip exposed, putting your hand up the deer's gullet, to cut the windpipe and free all of the eternal parts so they can be carefully removed them without any damage that might taint the meat."

People who knew me at that stage of my life would have a hard time believing that I could do such a thing. It was not easy and I felt horrible as my blood-soaked hand made the necessary cuts and I cleaned out the entire entrails of the deer. We packed some snow into the deer and hung it up with its head down from the tree to drain out any blood that was remaining. After this entire horror was over, they forgave me for being the inexperienced one who was the only one to bring home the meat. We celebrated with a slug of water and celebrated again with either a late lunch or an early dinner, whatever you want to call it. We finished eating the delicious, dried-out sandwiches that we pulled out of our backpacks, put our gear together, and headed home. We tied the deer to the car roof and had our deer-hunting licenses ready in case the authorities stopped us. When we got back to civilization, we went directly to the home of one of our buddies that had the facilities to butcher this deer. Our driving through the streets of New York created many onlookers. People were pointing and shouting at us, both bad and good. After we pulled into my friend's driveway, the neighbors soon surrounded us. The story of my magnificent ability was described in detail. All the neighbors' thoughts did not bother me in the least. The only thing that I enjoyed was having my two kids look at me with smiles on their faces, knowing that their father was the hero for a day.

The guys quickly strung the deer up from the basketball hoop that was in their backyard, took a chain saw, and started to butcher the animal. I was amazed at that fellow's talent as a butcher. He separated the meat into chops, ribs, and other parts that could be used as they were cut. He took the rest of the meat and set it aside to be ground up into hamburgers. We divided all of the meat equally between us for future good eating. My son, being an avid Boy Scout, said he wanted the skin so that he could tan it and use the leather. My buddies put the skin in a large plastic bag and handed it to my son.

Let's start with the first fiasco. My son took that skin, put it in the slop sink in the cellar, and tried to clean it up. Not knowing what he was doing, he tried to pull the meat and fascia off of the back of the skin. It was much too hard to do it that way. He didn't have the right knives or tools or knowledge to even clean the back of the leather, let alone the many other steps involved with the rest of the tanning process. The skin sat and then started to rot. A horrible odor started to fill the house and this ugly looking skin, lying in the slop sink, turned all our stomachs. I said to Paul, "Get rid of it". And so he did. After cleaning up the mess and airing out the house, we continued our usual Sunday afternoon.

That evening, my wife prepared some of the deer meat for dinner. We all sat down at the table and Harriet put a plate with the deer meat in the center of the table. Everyone was supposed to help themselves to what we hoped would be a great dinner. The first voice of dissidence came from my daughter, Meryl. Looking at the meat, she said, "Oh my, I can see Bambi's eyes". And then my son piped up, "Yes, you're right, Meryl. I see them also and he is saying 'please let me go'". Slowly, my two lovely children pushed their plates away from them. Harriet looked at me, and I looked at her, and guess what? We disposed of the meat and went out to a restaurant for dinner. Arriving home from a real dinner in a restaurant, we packed up the remaining meat that was in the freezer and sent word out to our neighbors that free deer meat was available. It did not take long for all of the meat to go with people who did not see Bambi's eyes.

 The next hunting season, I went upstate with the guys to our property for another hunt. As I mentioned earlier, I do not believe in killing an animal for the sake of killing. However, it is acceptable to kill an animal for food, known as self-preservation, so I went hunting. The beginning was the same scenario as the last season. We positioned everybody out on the flyway and waited. It didn't take long before I spotted a deer crossing in front of me. I raised my shotgun, took aim, held the gun sighted on the deer for a second or two, and then put the gun down. I had my thrill and the deer was still alive. However, I knew that deer would not see the light of day after today. The deer was walking through the woods, heading right towards one of my buddies posted about 1000 feet from where I was sitting. And sure enough, as I sat there listening quietly, I heard the shot, and knew that my buddy was there, and possibly got a kill. That was, I thought, the last hunting experience that I ever would have for the rest of my life. When we all got together, my buddy who made the shot said to me, "Didn't you see the deer that walked right past you?" "Yes", I said, "I saw the deer, but I didn't want to kill it". Everyone looked at me as if I was crazy. "Then why are you out here?" "I like being in the woods", I said as my friends shook their heads.

 One day, I was having lunch with a friend of mine who was an avid hunter. He was telling me about this fabulous place in Pennsylvania where they had hundreds of acres that were stocked with more kinds of wildlife than could be imagined. They had deer, wild boar, turkeys, and other similar wildlife for hunting. They also had elephants, giraffes, and many other exotic animals that are not wild in this country. They had cabins where hunters could stay for the night before the big hunt. Hunters were given a schedule of the animals that roam wild over their property and the cost you would be charged for each type of animal shot. I looked at my friend as if he was crazy. Who wants to shoot an elephant or giraffe? However, after much talk, I was convinced that this might be another great adventure in my life. Two weeks later, we made arrangements to spend three days at this hunter's paradise.

When we arrived, we were escorted to our cabin to get comfortable before dinner. At dinner, we met a number of other hunters who were excited about the next day's activity. I slept well that night, and in the morning, after breakfast, we left with all our gear for the day's hunt. The first hour, we did nothing but walk through the dense forest. We did not see any wildlife or any other hunters. After about another hour, my friend spotted some wild boar. He said that since this was my first time, I could take the first shot. I took the safety off my rifle, leaned up against the tree to stabilize my stance, took careful aim, pulled the trigger, and hit one of the wild boars.

My friend told me that I only wounded the animal and that I should quickly take another shot to finish the job. I quickly sighted in, pulled the trigger, and fired the weapon. The boar went down. I said, "That boar is now dead". My friend said, "Yes, you're right. However, the boar you just killed was the second boar. The first boar that you wounded took off running through the woods." I said, "Let's go after it and shoot it so it does not suffer". My friend reminded me that if I shot the second boar, I would have to pay for two boars, and that would be $75 for each one. He said, "Let me handle this and I'll show you how it's done. The Rangers are always patrolling these woods. They will see the wounded boar and they will shoot it. In that way, the animal will not suffer, and you won't have to pay for the second boar".

About a minute and a half later, we heard a shot. My friend said, "That boar is out of its misery now." A couple of minutes later, the Ranger came up to where we were standing and asked whether either of us had shot the boar that was wounded. My friend then proudly said, "No, not us. This is the boar that we shot". He pointed to the boar that was on the ground. The Ranger left us to continue our hunting. My friend said, "Do you know what they're going to be serving for dinner tonight?" "No", I said. He said, "Wild boar, that first one that you wounded". At that point, I'd had enough of killing and was not interested in any more hunting.

We still had an awful lot of daylight left. We kept walking through the woods and then spotted a bunch of large turkeys. My friend took aim, fired, and that turkey went down. Finally, the day came to an end. I dragged the wild boar and my friend carried out the turkey.

Back at the camp, I was told I could have a butcher cut the animal up into steaks, chops, and packed on ice to bring home. That was a great idea, so I went to the butcher who he did his job. All the wild boar meat was neatly packed on ice and kept in the freezer until it was time to go home. My friend gave the butcher the large wild turkey, which to me look like a tremendous bird. We watched as the butcher removed all the feathers and stripped the bird down to the bare meat. When I looked at the bird, it was tiny. My friend said, "It's enough meat for my wife and I". The next morning, we packed up the car and drove back to Staten Island.

Since I am the world's worst chef, the task of cooking the boar fell onto Harriet. She called one of her friends, whose husband was also an avid hunter, and was told to wrap the boar with bacon. Since the boar was a wild animal and was constantly running through the woods, it had tough muscles and the meat would be dry. The bacon added juice and acted as a tenderizer to the meat. Our family sat down at our dinner table, and just like pioneers, we devoured the wild boar. That was the last time that I ever went hunting to shoot an animal.

The next year, when hunting season came around again, my guys said, "Let's get a license and go out into the woods again". Since I had fulfilled my desire to learn how to kill and field-dress deer, and I had no desire to kill another animal, I hesitated. I did like getting out into the woods, so I agreed to join the group. We drove up to a house that one of our friends owned in the area and settled in for a quiet evening of dinner, relaxation, and good-night sleep. In the morning, we all got up, had breakfast, got into one car, and went off to the area where we would be hunting. We staked ourselves out so that we all knew where everybody was located, to avoid an accidental shooting of one another. I sat, all by myself, and enjoyed the solitude and beauty of the area. All of a sudden, I saw a dear coming along the flyway. The deer crossed in front of me, did not know I was there, and slowly kept walking. I picked up my gun, took aim, and said quietly to myself, 'bang', and did not pull the trigger. Since I did not need the food, I did not feel that I had to shoot it. That animal was heading down the flyway and I knew it was going to pass in front of my friends. And sure enough, a little while later, I heard the firing of a rifle, and knew that deer was on its way to heaven.

By now, it was getting late, so I left my comfortable little hideaway and went to my buddy, who shot the dear. When he saw me, he asked, "Didn't you see that dear? It walked right past you." "Yes", I said, "I did see it, but I had no reason to kill it". "Well I got it", he said. He had finished field dressing it and was ready to haul it out of the woods. I asked, "Can I help you?" He said, "No, I can handle it. I have about 10 minutes of clean up around here. I will drag it out by myself. You go ahead and meet the other guys and get ready to go home."

Off I went, to walk back to the staging area, where the rest of our guys and the cars were. I walked through the woods and walked and walked and walked. Then it dawned upon me that I had walked too far. I looked around and realized that I must have made a wrong turn someplace, because I was lost. But, not to worry, I had everything I needed to survive in the woods. I had matches in a waterproof container on my belt. I had food, water, my gun, ammunition, a compass, flashlight etc. So, I said to myself, "Since I am in upstate New York and not out in Africa someplace, if I walk in a straight line, I must hit a road or a farmhouse or some other form of civilization and find my way out of the woods."

By now, it was getting dark, so I took out my flashlight and compass, set a course, and started to walk in a straight line. I walked about 15 to 20 minutes, and sure enough, I came out of the woods on a road. It was pitch black on that road and I did not see any sign of people or houses anywhere in the vicinity. I decided to walk along the road. I picked a direction at random and started to walk. After about 10 minutes, I saw two headlights, way up the road, coming in my direction. I stood there until the car got close and then I flagged it down. I stood next to the driver's side as the window went down and I looked in. I saw a beautiful, young woman who was about 19 to 20 years old, sitting in the car all by herself. She asked, "What's the problem, sir". I told her that I had lost my way and would she help me get back to civilization. She asked the winning question, "Where do you want to go". "Oh my", I thought to myself, "I don't know". I did not take notice of the address of the house where we are staying because we came as a group. But, I did remember the gas station that was within walking distance of the house. I described the gas station and she said, "I know exactly where that is. Hop in". I hesitated for a minute, and wondered, "Here I am, dirty, carrying a gun on a lonely road, and she's inviting me into her car. Oh well, since I mean no harm, and she is my salvation to get out of here." I got in the car.

She took me straight to that gas station. I thanked her and started to walk to the house. When I got to the house, there was no one there. I entered, took a shower and got dressed. I waited for the rest of my guys. After waiting awhile, I wondered why they hadn't returned. So, I went out, got into one of the cars, and drove to our staging area. All of them were there. I said, "Guys, why didn't you return to the house?" They looked at me with both astonished and angry faces. "Where the hell were you", they asked. "Well, I got lost. I was able to find a road, stopped a car, and a beautiful girl brought me back to the house." "Did you know that we were going to call the police to get a search party to start looking for you?" Oh. My. God. It never dawned on me that anyone would think I couldn't take care of myself out in the woods. After my humble apologies, we became friends again, and went out to dinner.

Don't Let Your Ego Gain Control

One day, I learned that the New York City Tax Commissioner from Staten Island was resigning for a bigger and better advancement. For some unknown reason, the Tax Commissioner from Staten Island had always been Jewish. There was no regulation, law, or anything with that as a requirement. In keeping with the tradition, the County Leader asked me if I would be willing accept the appointment as the new Tax Commissioner. Since I knew nothing about the office of the Tax Commission, I was hesitant to accept this proposal. But, as I kept thinking of it, my huge ego got the better of me. After checking with the ethics commission to make sure there were no conflicts of interest, I accepted the challenge.

The Tax Commission of New York City is made up of five Commissioners. Each borough had its own Commissioner. The job of the Tax Commissioner was a simple one. At the end of each year, the tax assessors went through the communities of Staten Island to check the value of the homes. If they saw any improvements from the previous year, the improved condition was noted and the taxes were raised accordingly. After all of the new tax assessments were in place, they were made public. At that time, homeowners could see whether their taxes had gone up or stayed the same. If any homeowner felt that the tax did not truly reflect the value of their home, they could protest. That was when the Commissioner got involved. In February, when everything had settled down, the Commissioner would open court and hear all the complaints, one by one, from each homeowner. If the Commissioner felt the homeowner was correct, then he could lower the tax. If he felt the assessment was correct, he could leave the tax the way it was.

If any property owner did not like the Commissioner's decision they could appeal and ask for a rehearing by the entire commission. At that time, all five commissioners would get together and hear all of those cases.

This seemed like a fairly easy and interesting assignment. It didn't pay much, but the prestige was great. I was to receive an official badge and parking space near Borough Hall on Staten Island. My name was submitted to the Mayor for his approval. Without any delay, the

Mayor approved my nomination and my case went before the City Council for confirmation. During the confirmation hearing, one of the city Council Members asked me, "What does your background as an architect have to do with running the job of Tax Commissioner?" I told him my background did not qualify me to be Tax Commissioner, however that I learn very fast and would be up to speed in no time at all. The vote was unanimous and I became the Tax Commissioner.

Being sworn in by Mayor Abraham Beame.

The next day, in all the local newspapers, there were small articles about my appointment. All appointments to government were always reported in the newspaper for everyone to know who their Commissioners were. It didn't take long for some of my clients to call and congratulate me, knowing that it was good to have a friend who's a Commissioner in the City of New York. At that time, I was working on a housing project for Catholic Charities that was being funded with federal funds. The attorney who I was working with was also the County Leader of the Bronx and the supreme political boss, of the Bronx. It didn't take long for him to call me about my appointment and he wanted to have lunch with me.

At lunch, he talked about a number of scenarios that I would be involved in as a Tax Commissioner. He wanted to make sure that I understood the conflict of interest problems. I told him that before I accepted the position, I checked with the Ethics Commission and asked if there was a conflict of interest. They had done their investigation and found that there was no conflict of interest with my role in the construction industry. My luncheon partner then spun a tale for me. "Your client is Catholic Charities. One day, Catholic Charities owns a piece of property that they claim is a church and therefore exempt from taxes. The assessor, after visiting the property, decides it does not fall under the category of a church, and therefore must pay taxes. Catholic Charities then asks for a hearing by the full Commission. There you are, the Commissioner, being asked to make a decision in reference to your client." I told him that I would do what is customary, recuse myself, step aside, and not take part in those hearings or decision. The other four Commissioners would be the only ones making the final decisions. Then he went on. "The remaining four Commissioners find in favor of Catholic Charities. The case is over. All is well. A little time goes by and some wild, do-gooder citizen comes up with an accusation that Al Efron, the Tax Commissioner, used his influence with the four tax Commissioners to obtain a favorable outcome. Now you are in the spotlight." I said, "It is not true." "You're right, young man", he said. "It is not true, but you will swing by the neck anyway. Is it worth it?" The next day, I called the mayor's office and notified them that I was resigning. No way did I need that type of aggravation in order to satisfy my BIG EGO. Case closed.

Learning The Art Of Presentation

Through one of my connections, I was introduced to a non-profit group that was going to build a senior citizens housing project under a new federal program. After some discussion, I was selected to become their architect. I was notified that I would have to get the approval of the Borough President's Community Board. I designed the building and prepared the preliminary drawings that I would need in my presentation to the Community Board. Since this was my first experience making such a presentation, I came up with a new plan for the presentation that I thought would be the proper way to get the approval of the Board. I mounted all of my preliminary drawings onto foam core boards that could be displayed. That way, the members of the Board would understand exactly what I was proposing. I got down to the meeting room very early so that I could mount all my drawings on the walls. Then, when the Board members arrived, they could review the drawings at their leisure before the meeting started.

Having little experience, I had no idea what 'NIMBY' was. After the meeting, I found out that it meant 'not in my back yard'. By hanging my drawings so that the board could see them close up and understand what I was doing, I gave them all the ammunition that they needed to cut me to pieces. I got up there, full of confidence, and proudly described the wonderful building that I was going to be putting up in their community. Then the first shock came. "Mr. Architect," one of the members said. "I'm looking at your drawings and see that you have only 20 parking spaces. This building has 100 apartments." And then, with a strong voice, he continued, "Without enough parking, they'll have to be parking on the street. All the additional street parking will create traffic jams around our area. You will be killing our children as they play and cross the street. You will be blocking all traffic and creating a horrible situation." I stood there dumbfounded with my inexperience shining through. After many other outbursts of this nature, the Board voted and turned down the project. With my tail between my legs, as they say, I left that meeting hall. The next day, I sat down to figure out what I had done wrong and how to prevent it in the future. After much soul-searching and observing of other public speakers, I realized the errors of my ways.

The next opportunity I received to go before the Community Board was for another project proposed by Catholic Charities under the same program. This program was a federal program and as such, spelled out all of the requirements that had to be met to get the funding. As far as for the parking, the federal government thought that senior citizens did not drive cars and did not own cars. Therefore, the requirement stated that adequate parking to satisfy the complete needs of the building shall be 20% of the number of apartments. Therefore, a senior citizen's building with 100 apartments only needed parking for 20 cars. That was considered ample parking for that building.

I was ready for the Community Board, once again, but this time with a little more experience. Just as before, I mounted all of my drawings onto foam core boards. But this time, I covered the drawings with butcher paper. I arranged the drawings in a specific order and marked the sides so that I could select the appropriate drawing as required. I put all of these foam-core boards with the drawings on them into a large leather carrying case. It stayed by my side while I sat up on the stage, waiting to be called.

When it was my turn to speak, I got up with a smile, and pulled all the drawings out. I placed the first drawing, covered by the butcher paper, on an easel that faced the audience. I described to the audience what they were going to see. I told them just what I wanted them to know and no more. And since all they could see was butcher paper, they had no time to gather any ammunition to use against me. At the right time, with a little bit of flare, I flipped the butcher paper up, exposing the drawing. I walked to the other end of the stage. By this action, I gave the audience a choice. They could either look at my drawing or follow me to the other end of the stage. The audience's eyes automatically followed me. They did not look at the drawing. However, if they had looked at the drawing, they would not have seen very much. They were quite a distance away from the drawing. What they would see is what I wanted them to see as I made my presentation.

When it came time to discuss the parking, I said in a loud, commanding voice, "This project has ample parking to cover the entire requirements of this project". I did not tell them that the requirements were only 20 cars, and I did not lie. As I was speaking, I kept reading the body language of my audience. I felt that I had this audience in a positive mood and if I finished at that moment, they would approve the project. I quickly pulled out the drawing that was marked on the side, put it in the front again, with the butcher paper facing the audience, and informed them that this drawing was a rendering of a jewel of a building that was going to be built in their area. I told them, "When I remove the butcher paper, I want to hear everyone in the audience say 'Ooh' and 'Ahh'." That got the audience laughing and in a good mood. I removed the butcher paper and turned to the audience, "Let's hear it!" And sure enough, they were all laughing, with 'Ooh's and 'Ahh's, and not really paying attention to the building that I was proposing. Then, I quickly put all of the drawings back in the leather case, thanked them, and left the stage. At that point, the chairman asked for a vote. Since they were all in a very good mood, I received unanimous approval. I quickly learned the facts about public speaking and controlling your audience. I did a huge number of presentations during my career using these and other tactics.

When we were ready to start construction on that project, the community NIMBY took legal action, trying to stop the construction. In court, during the testimony, the community Executive Director stated that the architect had lied by telling them that there was ample parking when it only provided for 20 cars in a project that had 100 apartments. The judge turned to me for my response. I stated that I had told them that this project had ample parking to satisfy the residents of this building. I took out the federal guidelines that stated exactly the words that had I used. I then asked the judge if we could listen to the audio tapes that were made during my presentation. After the judge heard the tapes and saw the federal guidelines, he gently said, "The architect did not lie. Therefore, case dismissed." The building was built.

Raise The Flag! I Have My 12 Years of Experience

At this time of my life, I had put in the full 12 years of experience working for an architect. I could apply to take the State Board exams. I assembled all the required documentation and filed with the State Education Department. After about two weeks, I received notice that I was qualified to take the State Board exams. The next exam session would be in about four months.

To make sure that I would have the proper knowledge to pass the exam, I enrolled in a school that instructed people like me in the proper way to take and pass the architectural exam. Those instructions covered all aspects of the seven parts of the exam. The only information that the State Department of Education would release, was the categories the exam would cover. The architectural design portion of the exam was designated for a full 12-hour session.

For the architectural design section, the instructor informed us that the exam would be to design a boys' school. Based on past experience, he felt that the requirements we would be given would be for a large campus-type situation with separate classrooms and housing buildings etc. We worked on various scenarios around this campus concept. After studying for all of the other aspects of the exam, I felt I was ready to conquer it.

The time arrived for me to take on this momentous challenge. The night before I was to take the design portion of the exam, I assembled my drafting board, scales, pencils, and other equipment that I would need for this 12-hour experience. Since the exam was to be given in a typical classroom, the students had to bring their own drafting equipment necessary to produce the design in the session. In addition to all the equipment, I had to make sure I had my breakfast, lunch, and snacks to keep me going for the full 12 hours.

The day of the exam, I packed the car and took off to Columbia University, where the exam was given. I left myself plenty of time to make sure I would not be late. Upon arriving at Columbia University, I looked for a parking spot near the entrance of the building. Not finding one, I slowly started to circumnavigate the building, looking for that parking spot. The entire area was a sea of cars, completely filling every parking space available. I kept circling the building, taking in a larger area. I realized that I was running out of time. If I didn't park soon and get into the classroom before the bell rang to start the session, I would not be allowed to take the exam. I was in a state of fear, shock, deep concern, and bewilderment. At that moment in time, I was about 10 blocks from the school and time was ticking. I spotted a gas station, and in a state of desperation, I pulled into the rear of it. I jumped out of my car and ran into the office, completely out of breath. I whipped out a $10 bill and asked the owner if he would please let me keep my car there for the day so that I could take that exam. The owner saw the horrible condition I was in. I was holding all my equipment, including drafting board, tools, and lunch. I was sweating like a pig. He told me, "Get going kid, and take that exam".

I ran back to the school at full blast. I found the classroom and went through the door, with about 2 seconds left before the buzzer sounded. The door was locked behind me. I had barely made it. However, I was in no condition, mentally or physically, to take this exam. Since there was no other option, I sat down. I got my drafting board in place and everything in order.

I opened the exam booklet. To my shock and horror, the boys' school design was that of a high-rise in an urban setting, not the campus-type that I had studied for. All of the instruction that I received at the prep school was out the window. A lot of the requirements that were part of the exam were not part of my experience in the profession. Hands trembling, with sweat dripping down from my forehead, I took a deep breath and started to draw. I thought that day would never end with me still being alive. I did survive, but I was not a happy camper.

I finished the other three days and six parts of the exam. I went back to my normal daily routine and waited anxiously for the results of the entire experience. Please note that the requirements of this exam were that you must pass all seven sections to get your architectural license. If you passed a minimum of four parts, then you could keep those four and retake the other three. If you passed only three or fewer parts, you got no credit and had to retake all seven parts.

The day finally came when the results of the exam were announced. It was with a huge sigh of relief that I learned that I had passed five of the seven parts of the exam! I failed the architectural design part of the exam, but I felt that it was inevitable. Also, I just barely failed the structural design portion. I only had to concentrate on those two parts of the exam for the next time. Pass them and I could nail this episode in my life shut.

For the design section, I did not bother to go to another prep school. I decided to do my own research. The state released the subject of the design portion of the exam. The building that we were to design was to be the main building on a golf course. Since, at that time, I was not a golfer yet and had no idea what was required to design that building, I started my research. I went to the library and found every book that I could about golf courses. After examining many articles and pictures of that type of building, I felt I had a good understanding of what had to be done.

On the night before the exam, I loaded my car with all the equipment I needed, plus breakfast, lunch, dinner, and snacks that would cover the 12-hour session. In addition, I took a wind-up alarm clock and a large thermos of coffee. At 2am on the morning of the exam, I drove to the school where the exam was being given. I found a great parking spot right in front of the entrance. I set my alarm clock with the proper time, snuggled down, and went to sleep.

In the morning, the alarm clock rang and awakened me. I was well rested and in full control. I had my coffee and breakfast in the car with a smile on my face. At the proper time, I gathered all my equipment, quietly entered the classroom, sat down, prepared my drafting table, and patiently waited for the exam to begin.

When the exam began, I opened the booklet. The architectural design requirements for that building were in keeping with my research and felt I could nail this one.

The other section that I still needed to pass was structural design. There, I felt I could go to a different prep school to make sure I had all the knowledge I needed to pass this section. I quickly found another school that had the classes I needed. The instructor took portions from previous exams that covered the design of all types of buildings, from reinforced concrete, to steel frame, to wood design. We practiced endless conditions of designing columns, beams, cantilevers, and every other combination that you could ever come across when designing a building.

When it was time to take the structural exam, I brought the workbook that we had created at school when we reviewed past exams. Since the nature of the subject required the endless use of catalogs and other publications, we were allowed to bring in any material that we wanted to the exam. A good friend of mine took the prep course with me and was taking the exam at the same time. In the classroom, I sat about four seats to the right of him. The door closed, the bell rang, and the exam started. I opened the booklet and examined all the requirements. There were four problems. Each problem was equally worth 25 points towards the total 100%. I read the first problem and wasn't sure what I was reading. I said to myself, "This looks awfully familiar". Referring to my notes, I discovered that this problem was from a previous examination that we worked on at the prep school. Through an impossible coincidence, the instructor at my prep school selected the exact same exam for us to practice on. I looked at my friend, and he looked at me, and we both realized what was in front of us. It took me about 5 minutes to finish the first problem of the exam, which would give me 25%, right off the bat.

This is an unbelievable situation! I hunkered down for the second question. Oh My God, again, the designer of the exam selected a problem from another old exam that our instructor used for us to practice. Again looking at my friend and he looked at me and was very difficult to keep from shouting out loud!! It took only another 5 minutes to answer this problem. Now I had 50% of this exam nailed.

All I needed was a minimum of 20% more to get a final score of 70, which was passing. So, I went to third question and did not believe my own eyes. This was not possible. A chance of something like this happening was one in a trillion. The third problem, again, matched the exam that my instructor had given us at the school. All I needed was another 5 minutes to solve this problem. I would have 75% of the test completed. I was confident that I had passed and could go home.

But, the door was locked, and I had to sit there for the entire time allocated for the exam. In a cavalier movement, I checked the fourth and final question. This time, it did not match. So, I put all my skills together and worked out the final problem. When that was done, I had to sit there for a number of hours until the bell rang and we were done.

We had nothing to do but wait for all the exams to be graded and to get the final announcement. The day finally came. On my architectural design, I passed with an extremely high grade. Sorry, I don't remember the exact score, but was up in the 90% range. I checked the structural design and my mark was 98%. For some reason, I lost two points on the fourth question.

All joy rang out. I did not feel guilty about the gift of the first 3 problems, since I did so well on the last problem. I knew I would've done well on the other three, even if I didn't have the answers. I would've passed anyway. That experience was great to have gone through. It gave me the story to write about it here that you are now reading.

The exact day that I received the official notification that I was a Registered Architect in the State of New York, I swung into action. Up until that time, I was not a Registered Architect and therefore, could not legally be a partner. I had the title of Associate and I could share in the profits. Since I was now licensed to practice architecture, I could be a partner in an architectural firm.

I met with my firm's bosses Sam Lichtenstein, Sid Shuman, and Peter Claman, who were all Registered Architects. We got together and the architectural firm of Shuman, Lichtenstein, Claman, Efron was formed, known as SLCE for short. It was the start of an era of growth and expansion for me. I finally had accomplished what everybody said could not be done. I proudly became a member of the American Institute of Architects, Staten Island Chapter. Here's SLCE's brochure:

SCHUMAN LICHTENSTEIN CLAMAN EFRON · ARCHITECTS

841 Broadway, New York, N.Y. 10003 (212) 979-8400 Fax (212) 979-8387

Metropolitan Tower
67 - story luxury apartment tower

30 East 85th Street
98 luxury condominium units

Established in 1941, Schuman Lichtenstein Claman Efron (SLCE) is an architectural and interior design firm with a history of design excellence built on the successful completion of numerous diverse projects.

The 60-person firm's versatility and attention to detail stems from the combined talent of its managing principals, who carefully guide each project from inception to completion. This ensures that every assignment meets the most stringent planning and design standards.

Working with both public, private and non-profit organizations, SLCE demonstrates a commitment to the highest level of architectural service - always with sensitivity to design aesthetics, cost and schedule.

The firm's comprehensive range of services includes:

- Site and Master Planning;
- Feasibility, Cost and Zoning Studies;
- Programming and Project Design;
- Contract Documents;
- Professional Services during all phases of construction;
- Facilities Management and Interior Design.

This breadth of capability is supported by an experienced staff of specialists at SLCE, whose managing principals include:

Peter Claman, AIA
Albert Efron, FAIA
Jerrold Clarke, AIA
Enzo DePol, AIA

Dedicated to client satisfaction, SLCE continues to earn critical recognition and - more important - praise from its impressive roster of repeat clients.

NY Hospital Helmsley Tower
Medical facilities

Two Grand Central Tower
43 - story office building

ARCHITECTURE · INTERIOR DESIGN · PLANNING

SCHUMAN LICHTENSTEIN CLAMAN EFRON · ARCHITECTS

Port Imperial, Weehawken, NJ
New waterfront development

100 United Nations Plaza
51 - story luxury apartment tower

Fannie Lou Hamer Apartments, Bronx
75 senior citizen units - 202 program

PROJECT TYPES

SLCE's talented professionals and extensive building experience enables the firm not only to meet the unique challenges of virtually any type of project but distinguishes it from other firms that confine their skills to a limited number of project types.

MEDICAL AND HEALTHCARE FACILITIES

SLCE has planned and designed through phased development hospitals, laboratories, staff residences, geriatric-care centers, nursing homes, and other health facilities. Public and private clients include New York Hospital - Cornell University Medical Center, New York University Medical Center, Brookdale Medical Center, Kingsbrook Medical Center, Montefiore Hospital, Peninsula Hospital, and the Albert Einstein College of Medicine.

RESIDENTIAL PROJECTS

The firm's award-winning designs include tens of thousands of housing units ranging from luxury and middle-income high-rise residential towers to low-rise low-income residences for public housing and nonprofit groups. Clients include the Brodsky Organization, Zeckendorf Properties, Millenium Partners, Sterling Equities, the Durst Organization, Catholic Charities, Presbyterian Senior Services, the Yonkers Housing Authority, B'nai B'rith, the Jewish Association for Service to the Aged, and the Mid-Bronx Senior Citizens Council.

The Ronald McDonald House
11 - story patient / family residence

Kingsbrook Medical Center, Brooklyn
140 - bed acute care wing / ICI-CCU

Fifth Avenue Place
150 affordable housing units

EDUCATIONAL BUILDINGS

SLCE has extensive experience in new school construction and campus master planning as well as building alterations. Successfully designed projects include Fordham and Cardozo Schools of Law, St. John's University, La Guardia College, Pace University, Yeshiva University, Albert Einstein College of Medicine, and Stern College, as well as primary - and high school-level projects for New York City's Board of Education and School Construction Authority.

Erasmus Hall High School, Brooklyn
400,000 sf restoration / addition

Port Richmond HS, Staten Island, NY
225,000 sf addition / modernization

SCHUMAN LICHTENSTEIN CLAMAN EFRON · ARCHITECTS

Mercy S.R.O., Brooklyn, NY
78 units for homeless women

Residential Care Center for Adults
57 - bed rehabilitation center

Unified Court System of NY State
Courtrooms and ancillary facilities

Yeshiva University / Gottesman Pool
NCAA competition pool facility

ADAPTIVE RE-USE/REHABILITATION

Analyzing current layout and building conditions, SLCE undertakes gut and moderate-renovation assignments, as well as adaptive re-use projects for commercial, health, educational, industrial and residential facilities. These include projects completed for New York City's Vacant Buildings Program with HPD/LISC, New York City Department of General Services, the United States Department of Housing and Urban Development, and Enzo Biochem, Inc. Research Laboratories.

OFFICE/ RETAIL/ HOTEL AND INDUSTRIAL FACILITIES

SLCE has completed numerous commercial and industrial developments including high-rise office structures, site development, design of industrial parks, strip and regional shopping centers, and parking garages. TIAA-CREF's recently completed 20 story expansion of its corporate headquarters which includes a conference center and dining facilities demonstrates SLCE's abilities in handling complex program assignments.

CRIMINAL AND CIVIL JUSTICE FACILITIES

Some of the criminal justice works in which SLCE has participated include grand-injury and civil-trial courtrooms, courtrooms for the New York State Supreme Court, as well as district attorney facilities.

ENTERTAINMENT/ RECREATIONAL FACILITIES

Significant leisure and sports facilities to SLCE's credit include health clubs for the New York Health and Racquet Club totaling more than 100,000 square feet, Sports Club L.A.'s 140,000 square foot Lincoln Square facility, a nine-theatre cinema complex for Cineplex Odeon Theatres and a multi theatre complex with 600 seat IMAX for Sony Pictures. The firm also has completed gymnasium facilities for St. Joseph by the Sea and Stern Athletic Center at Yeshiva University.

The Royal Elizabeth
81 - unit condominium atop retail

Roosevelt Mall, Philadelphia
Shopping center

127 East 30th Street
Entrance lobby

The Belz School of Music
Student Theatre

SCHUMAN LICHTENSTEIN CLAMAN EFRON · ARCHITECTS

SLCE Offices, 841 Broadway, NYC
Administrative area

INTERIORS AND SPACE PLANNING

SLCE's interior design approach starts with determination of the users' programatic needs, as well as developing distinctive and efficiently designed spaces. These include 150,000 square feet of medical offices for New York Hospital, corporate headquarters for Krasdale Foods, interior and space planning for Montefiore and New York University Hospitals, a master space-plan for Brookdale and Peninsula Hospitals, and interior planning for Deutsche Telekom, TIAA-CREF, and other legal and corporate clients.

Deutsche Telekom
Corporate interiors

The Gerard Avenue Apartments
121 pre-fab affordable housing units

FACTORY-BUILT CONSTRUCTION

SLCE is accomplished in designing with modular units, cellular systems and panelized construction. The speed and efficiency of prefabricated, site-assembled construction has been successfully employed for the Yonkers Housing Authority, the Gerard Avenue Apartments, and Fort Hamilton and Midwood High Schools.

American Express Center, Beijing
Mixed use 5-building complex

Fordham University at Lincoln Center
20 - story student dormitory

INTERNATIONAL ASSIGNMENTS

As a member of an international architectural consortium, SLCE offers American businesses the advantage of a presence throughout Europe. Each local European affiliate is experienced in commercial, industrial, residential or corporate design, and has extensive knowledge of local conditions and approval requirements. SLCE has also worked in the Soviet Union and the Far East.

SLCE combines an unwavering commitment to meeting scheduling and cost requirements with the highest standards of technical responsibility to achieve an unparalleled record of excellence for providing creative solutions to clients' needs.

The Coronado
122 luxury apartments atop retail

ARCHITECTURE · INTERIOR DESIGN · PLANNING

Richmond County Country Club

At that point in my career, I pulled out my huge network ledger and started to convert all the appropriate contacts that I made over the years into my clients. I was taking the first step on a wild ride in my professional standing as an architect. I was delighted to shed the title of Draftsman or Associate. In addition, I joined the Richmond County Country Club and started to learn the game of golf. Everyone in the construction industry knew that if you didn't play golf, you could not survive. With my club membership and my architect's license, the world was mine.

Golfing with clients

Eventually, I was appointed to the Board of Directors of Richmond County Country Club. This position gave me the opportunity to rub shoulders with many makers and shakers on Staten Island. Each board member was giving a standing job for one of the needs in the operation of the country club. My job was that of House Chairman. As House Chairman, I was to oversee the general operation of the clubhouse, kitchen, and dining facilities, as well as to create entertaining programs and party events. Harriet and I took the party events seriously. We contacted an engineer friend of mine who also had a theater group that produced Neil Simons plays. We booked him for a complete series to be held on Friday nights. Those plays were so successful that we included Saturday nights as well. One weekend a month, we filled the place for all the shows.

One day, I got the bright idea of getting actors to volunteer and put on shows. I made contact with a local supplier of theater costumes. I proposed that since he was in contact with a lot of young up-and-coming actors looking for experience for their resumes, that we create various shows using these actors. The actors would not be paid since they were getting experience for their resumes. All costumes would be rented by the Country Club from the costume supplier. The owner of the costume store agreed and we were off and running.

Our first show was of a pirate theme. We decorated the Country Club to look like we were on old wooden pirate ships. After the party started, for about a half-hour, all of the actors were dressed as pirates and attacked the ship, swinging large rubber sabers. They took us prisoner, then forced us to do a conga line and other line dances, creating a fun-filled, exciting evening for all in attendance. Club members spoke of that evening for many weeks after. We put on a number of other themed shows and we were very successful.

The one that stands out most in my mind was the Western night that we put together. The club was decorated in a complete Western theme and all attendees were encouraged to dress in Western attire. I got the bright idea to get live animals to use as part of the decorations. At that time, I was on the board of the Staten Island Zoological Society. I spoke to our Executive Director and asked him if it would be possible to get some of the live animals to decorate our facilities. He agreed to provide some small horses and goats with handlers.

I got the bright idea that we should get live chickens to raffle off at the end of evening. We would have the chickens sent to a butcher to prepare them to be given to the winners. However, I was informed by a attorney on our board that it was completely illegal to slaughter chickens in the City of New York. That canceled that adventure.

I was aware that the zoo had exotic chickens that ran around their enclosure. The children who visited the zoo loved to see them. I asked our Executive Director if we could have some of those chickens in cages, placed around the place. He agreed that he would bring the chickens in cages to the club. He would give me the necessary food and water for the chickens, since they would have to spend the night at the club. In the morning, he would send his crew down to pick up the chickens. All was agreed.

The event went on and we all had a ball. The zoo's horse and goat handlers took their animals back to the zoo that evening. The chickens were left in my care overnight. Before leaving the club that evening, I left the food and water for each of the chickens. It was a nice summer night, so I felt there was no problem with them being left out on the patio for the evening. At about two o'clock in the morning, I awoke in a sweat, realizing that we had many roving raccoons and possums that could attack these exotic chickens. I frantically got up, dressed, and dashed over to the club. To my relief, the chickens were fine. I made myself comfortable and sat there until the morning, when the zoo truck arrived to take the chickens back.

That evening was a fantastic success. We had many other such successes at the club. Eventually, Harriet and I decided to become snowbirds, to spend six months in New York in the summer and six months in Tucson in the winter. I resigned as a board director to make room for someone else who could spend the full year at the club.

The Firm of Shuman, Lichtenstein, Claman, Efron Architects

The way our architectural firm seemed to evolve was that each of the four partners mostly handled our own clients. Once a week, we met to discuss all the conditions and problems of the business, such as hiring/firing, collecting fees, paying bills, etc. We did very little firing, mostly hiring. That time in my career led to a vast new learning experience of being a boss and no longer a worker. One of the very first projects I worked on was for New Plan Realty. Their main business was to buy losing shopping centers and turn them into fantastic winners. All of the little things I encountered made learning seem like magic. I remember working on the design of a large regional shopping center in Northern Philadelphia. I was working with new government bureaucrats and their procedures, which in many ways was far from what we did in New York. I made great contacts with the local building department and the elected officials who had jurisdiction over my project.

That new experience gave me a great advantage when dealing with other state organizations in the following years. Two very minor details opened my eyes and changed my thinking of how to design buildings. The shopping center had a huge parking lot, required by building code, to satisfy the parking needs of all the stores in this development. One of the main buildings was approximately 800 feet long. When I was establishing the size of the sidewalk in front of this store, I made it 25 feet wide. I felt that since the length of the building was so large and would attract such a large shopping population, we would need the extra width on the sidewalk so that people could get around easily. When my client reviewed the drawings and noticed the sidewalk was 25 feet wide, he gently and politely asked me to cut it down to 10 feet, maximum. I explained that in my opinion, it was too narrow to accommodate the numbers of shoppers that would be using this sidewalk. He informed me that the main street, opposite the sidewalk, was about 500 feet away on the opposite end of the parking lot. If I made the sidewalk 25 feet wide, then people 500 feet away would see this building and get the feeling that there weren't too many people, so there'd be no sense in going there to shop. But if I made it 10 feet wide, it would force the pedestrians to crowd together, making them look like a crowd. This would attract more shoppers from the opposite end of the parking lot. That was lesson number one; don't always think as an architect and get some practical thinking in your design.

Another change my client requested was to get rid of all the benches, tables, and convenient sitting areas. He wanted people go into the shops and start buying, not to rest outside. Wow, this practical merchandising approach to shopping centers blew my mind.

In order to jazz up some of the architecture, I designed a fountain, strategically located where it would not interfere with the merchandising. It was a beautiful work of art, with water gently spraying up and dripping down the sides. When the shopping center opened, on the very first day, to my horror, my client said, "I think it's time to remove that beautiful fountain because as a gentle wind blows, you cannot control the spray, and we are spraying the people with water, forcing them away from the stores near the fountain". Boy, was I learning!

Eventually, all construction was completed and the shopping center was in full operation.

As time went on, I got more involved in larger and more exciting projects. It got to the point where I felt pretty comfortable in the position of a practicing architect. Since I am always dreaming up crazy ideas, being an architect could not stop me. A number of times, I would bring up some of my ideas to my partners. We tried some with success, and once in a while, not so successful. But the law of averages was on my side.

One day, I was watching a television documentary on Africa. They were showing the lives that some tribes lived, out in the deserts away from all civilization. It was a very difficult way of life because they had to live off the land without the aid of modern society. I began to wonder what happened when they cut their finger and needed a Band-Aid or had a headache and need an aspirin. Those minor things were not available to those people. That also meant that the major items, such as hospitals or first-aid stations, were also not part of their lives. There I go again; there must be a better way.

After much thought, I came up with the bright idea of designing a small, self-standing, self-contained first-aid building that would be factory-manufactured in the United States. These buildings, that I called 'pods', could be dropped into any location to provide the necessary minimum health support for those people. As need grew, additional pods could be added to provide other functions, such as minor operating rooms, etc. As time went on, and more and more pods were added, they would eventually end up with a full hospital to service the needs of the growing community. I got the idea of factory-built pods for medical use from a similar project I worked on, where we used factory-built housing. I discussed my ideas with my partners, who said, "Al, do what you want". I guess they were tired of all my harebrained ideas.

    I started to push this idea into reality, if possible. My first challenge was to find a way to contact the responsible government officials in the African communities. Into my network I went. I was lucky enough to find a woman in the public relations profession whose father was a ranking member in the United Nations. I contacted her to explore the possibility of getting me invited to meet with the various ambassadors from the African countries. She told me that it would not be a problem. However, she wanted an upfront payment of $18,000 for one year, to provide me with all the services I needed in setting up these meetings. Since my partners had said I could do what I wanted, and I knew I was working within reason, I hired her.

    She promptly went to work and set up breakfast meetings at a local hotel near the United Nations with a string of these diplomats. At every breakfast meeting, I described my ideas for getting medical attention to the people living out in the desert of their countries. Each diplomat was very excited and positive that what I was proposing would definitely help his people. After about the fifth or sixth successful breakfast, I waited for the diplomats to get back to me, after discussing the proposal with their delegation. Time went on and I heard nothing. To make a long story short, I met a member of the American delegation to the United Nations and discussed my experience. He enlightened me of the real facts in relation to diplomats at the UN. He told me that these diplomats were living in New York in upscale, expensive apartments in Manhattan. They had chauffeur-driven luxury cars. They ate in the finest restaurants and life was just fantastic. The thought of going back to Africa and living under those horrible conditions was always on their minds. So, to protect their positions, they would not do anything to jeopardize them. In conclusion, he said, they did not want to get involved with projects that might not work. It could be a black mark on their careers and send them back to their country. No way would they let that happen. These diplomats wouldn't do anything that had any potential to ruin their cushy lives.

As a follow-up to my pod concept, someone else had the same idea. But they did not go to Africa to build medical facilities. They stayed in the United States and built prisons. They designed a pod jail cell and an administration pod. They sold these pods to small towns across the country to fill the need of housing prisoners. With this system, the company would be responsible for the prison system of that community. They would add or subtract the number of pods required at any given time. No need to build a large prison. I remember reading about this company using my idea. I am sure they had the same idea on their own, but it made me feel that my idea was not that crazy.

Every day that I went to the office, I never knew what great adventure or terrible condition would come my way. One day, I was in my office when the phone rang. It was a friend of mine, a developer, who was trying to put a deal together in Detroit, Michigan. The problem that he had was that the government of Detroit was on the verge of bankruptcy and the entire area was a disaster. He asked if I would accompany him to Detroit to meet the mayor and other political personnel. They were trying to avoid bankruptcy by getting some major projects moving. He felt that my experience in New York politics, as well as architecture, would be of great help. We were doing the type of development that he was interested in.

I should note that it was the middle of January. That meant it would be frigid-cold off Lake Michigan in Detroit. I packed up my attaché case, put on some warm clothes, and was off to Detroit. When we arrived at City Hall, we were escorted into a large meeting room. We met the mayor and a number of his top aides, as well as other elected officials. We had an in-depth discussion of the political, financial, and physical condition of Detroit. The first thing that I noticed, which was very obvious, was that the entire political leadership was inexperienced and uninformed about running a city. It was quite evident that the qualified leadership of the city had either quit or had been forced out. The group that took over was completely out of their league.

There was one major, large, upscale development that was being built in the area. It cost huge amounts of money but sat empty. It was draining massive resources of money. That one building, as far as I could see, was the only decent structure in the entire area. Their automobile manufacturing companies had left. This hit other industries that provided material or products to the automobile industry.

The main push for the day was to find some way for my friend, the developer, to take over a rubber manufacturing plant that he had identified. He wanted to build a project on that site that could help revitalize Detroit. They took us to the site so that we could get a good understanding of the existing conditions. The thing that I remember the most was looking at a building that was about to collapse. I stood on the driveway that was covered with ice and the howling winds coming off the lake were so cold that I just couldn't think straight. After going into some detailed thinking of the rubber plant, my friend and I agreed it was too risky a project to be successful.

It was quite obvious that the top qualified leadership of Detroit read the writing on the wall and ran before everything fell apart.

At this point, I would like to talk about my theory on how to run an architectural practice, or for that matter, any business or corporation. There are two basic items that any business, corporation, or other type of business organization must have in order to be successful. I am not talking about the CEO, Board of Directors, investors, etc. Those people come later on. The first thing that is mandatory for success of any type business is to have a customer, client, patient, or any other type of person who's going to spend their money to buy your product or service.

The second thing that is also essential for the success of any business is a loyal, dedicated, happy staff. Without great staff to provide the product or service, you're out of business. When you have these two entities, the rest can fall into place. In the practice of architecture, my partners and I had the obligation of acquiring the client to satisfy the first requirement of a successful practice. The second part was to hire a staff of bright, energetic, and loyal people. In order to ensure that your staff will do the best job they can for you, you must make sure you provide the best working conditions and pay each employee the best living wage that you can. Never nickel and dime your employees and always make sure they get their piece of the pie. They produce the pie that the client is willing to pay for. One should keep those two entities happy for your architectural practice or any business to thrive.

In keeping with these thoughts, we never nickel and dimed our clients for any additional cost for work that had to be done. All of our energy went into providing the best service, to obtain the best outcome of the construction process, to keep a client happy. As far as our staff went, we had a profit-sharing plan and a bonus plan to cover all of our employees, so they would get their piece of the pie. The more money we made, the more money they took home. The combination always provided a dedicated, loyal staff.

An example of keeping our staff happy, was when an employee had a problem, we would try to help them out. One day, one of our senior employees had an accident and broke his leg. He was out with this condition for about 24 days. Our Office Manual stated that every employee got 10 days sick leave per year. As we usually did, we ignored our Office Manual and paid that employee for every day that he was out on sick leave.

When his doctor told him he could return to work with the use crutches, he thought his troubles were over. He arrived at the office on his first day back, looking like death warmed over. "What happened?" I asked. He said, "You should try to go down a long flight of stairs, into the subway with two crutches. Then enter the crowded train hanging onto the crutches. Then maneuver out of the crowded train and up the stairs. Walk two blocks and take the elevator up to the office. You do it with crutches and you will look the way I look". After a quick discussion with my partners, we agreed that we would have a car service pick him up at his house and drive to the office for the day. At the end of the day, the car service would pick him up at the office and take the home. The office would pay all expenses and last for as long as he needed to be on crutches. This type of thinking makes for a loyal staff.

Once the word got out that we cared about our staff and wanted to do the best for them, they became concerned about us and wanted to do the best they could for us. It's the staff that produced all the profits. At our year-end holiday party, we noticed that this same fellow was dancing his heart out as the band played. I told my partner, "I hope his car service was ended".

My partners and I celebrated many birthdays, anniversaries, children births, and weddings etc. with all the members of our staff. I cannot tell you how many days each month that our receptionist announced through the loudspeaker that someone was having a birthday, or other event, and everybody was invited into our dining room for coffee and a piece of cake. The office just stopped. Everyone went into the dining room and was given the goodies. We all sang 'Happy Birthday' with great melodic voices. Everyone returned to work refreshed and smiling.

There were also a number of great employee weddings that we attended. I remember one wedding in particular. One of our senior draftsmen became engaged to one of our senior draftswomen. Both the bride and groom were from the Philippines and had been working for us for many years. My partners and I, with our wives, were invited to this joyous traditional Filipino wedding.

We arrived at the catering hall, checked our hats and coats, and entered the ballroom. We were each given a straight pin. Men attached them to their jacket collars and women put them on the top of their dresses. We all looked at these pins and wondered, why? We were told that we would need them later, after the ceremony, during a customary event. When the wedding services were over, the official husband and wife entered the main ballroom. We were told it was customary for the entertainment to begin. This was always arranged by relatives. One by one, each of the relatives got up on the stage and did a fantastic job of telling stories or singing or providing other types of entertainment. It was very professional.

The band played and the bride and groom had their first dance. The couple entered the floor and started to dance. Much to my surprise, a gentleman in the audience walked up to the dancing couple, took the bride, pinned a $5 or $10 bill onto her dress, and then had a short dance with her. At the same time, a woman from the audience went up to the groom, with the same arrangement, and had a short dance with him. This continued with different members of the wedding party, one after the other, pinning money onto the bride's dress or groom's tuxedo. After about 10 to 15 minutes, the bride and groom were each covered from head to toe with US currency. When there wasn't any more room on their clothing, the money was attached to long tails of bills. What a great way to send a couple off into married life.

The Donald

A friend asked me if I would do him a favor and help Mr. Fred Trump, who was building midrise apartment houses in Brooklyn, Queens, and Staten Island. He was having some construction problems. He was involved in a new building construction, as well as putting in improvements for existing rent-controlled apartments that he owned. Since my friend used the four magic words, 'do me a favor', I agreed.

There was a program that was being proposed by the City of New York, which involved the updating of existing apartments to prevent them from becoming slums. The owners of the buildings would provide updated improvements as outlined in the program, and in return, the City would allow the owners to raise the rents.

At my first meeting with Fred Trump, he discussed the construction problems he was having. The problems were broken down into two categories. The first category concerned many minor problems with maintenance. The second problem involved Building Department coordination on alterations for a huge number of rent-controlled apartments that he owned and were fully occupied. This type of small-scale alteration work was not in keeping with the new construction, that our office was geared to do. However, as a favor to my friend and Mr. Trump, I agreed to help him out with these problems.

I found Fred Trump to be a hard-working, hands-on-type developer. Our meeting lasted close to two hours. Most of the time was spent talking about his architectural problems. After quite a bit of time, Fred, as I called him, told me about his career as a developer. He also talked about his community activity in the boroughs of New York City where he was building. At the end of the meeting, we agreed to meet early the next morning at one of his existing buildings to review the problems. We met bright and early and proceeded to the roof of the building. We discussed the problems and how to solve them. Fred also noted a number of minor conditions that the superintendent of the building could handle. We proceeded to other parts of the building.

When we were done, it was still quite early. Fred said, "Before we leave, I want to talk to the superintendent." We went down to the apartment that was occupied by the superintendent and Fred rang the bell. The superintendent opened the door, and with a surprised look on his face, noticed his boss, Fred Trump, standing there. "Good morning", Fred said. The super greeted Fred and said, "I did not expect to see you this morning". Fred handed him the pad, which contained the problems that he'd identified for the superintendent to take care of. What impressed me about Mr. Trump was that he politely handed over the pad, with a smile on his face, and said, "Please take care of these items." This gentle approach with an employee was not the interaction I usually noted with other developers.

I was able to clear up all the Building Department coordination problems very quickly. We began the alteration work of the apartments, so Fred could raise the rents. At that time, Fred introduced me to his son, Donald, who had just graduated from college and was working for his father. Fred asked me to work with Donald and show him the ropes, to bring him up to speed with the alteration work we were doing. Fred said that any decisions Donald made were not final, until Fred reviewed them and approved or adjusted them. Donald and I, in coordination the contractors that Fred hired, worked for about one year to upgrade these apartments.

It was not too long before Donald stopped working for his father and started on his own. In no time at all, Donald Trump became "The Donald". He was building a major career of putting together all sorts of big money deals with various investors and banks.

I remember one time when my partner, Peter Claman, and I were in Donald Trump's office. We were to negotiate a contract for him to hire us to be the architects on one of his projects. We were deeply involved in the details of the agreement, when Donald, all of a sudden, said something to the effect of "I was playing golf at my West Chester Club and had a fabulous round. Have you guys ever played there?" "No", we said. We then got back to negotiations. A short time later, Donald again interrupted with something about his holdings overseas. This kept on for the full time that we were in his office. These minor interruptions popped up a number of times during the negotiation. When the negotiations were complete, we left the office and went to the elevator. Peter and I both had puzzled looks on our faces. After sharing our feelings, we realized that Donald, with all his interruptions, created a situation where he was in command and was able to get a more favorable contract, because of the psychological effect of all those interruptions. That was a fabulous lesson that I learned in the art of negotiating. However, that project never materialized.

Quite some years later, Donald Trump was in our office to negotiate the construction of a group of luxury apartment buildings on the west side of Manhattan, on land that he had purchased from the railroad. Since travel by railroad had pretty much disappeared with the advent of automobiles and airplanes, all that property containing the railroad tracks was completely deserted. Negotiations were finished, a deal was made, and we were under contract for architectural services to design the apartment buildings. Our office started to gear up for this project. Donald Trump then went to another architectural firm that was doing the same type of work that we were doing, and tried to try to get a better deal. He showed our competitor our contract, and asked the other architect if they would quote him a lower fee than the one that Donald had already agreed to with us. The other architect gladly quoted him a lower fee. At that point, Donald returned to our office and stated that he could get the other architect to work for lower fee. This type of negotiation is highly unprofessional. You shop the fee before you arrive at an agreement with any architect, not after an agreement is reached and we had spent time and money to gear up for your job. Based on Donald Trump's unethical reputation, we told him, as politely as we could, that we were not interested in doing business with him anymore. As it so happened, Donald ran into major financial problems and lost control of this huge project. The Chinese developers who got control of the project returned to our office to discuss becoming the architects. These Chinese developers seemed like honorable people, so we agreed. The only item in this entire project that Donald Trump was able to acquire was that his name would be cut into the stone at the front of each building.

In my personal dealings with Donald Trump, either businesswise or in the few social events that we both attended, I found, not being qualified in the field of human psychology, that there must be something about him I just do not understand. That's all I choose to say in writing.

My partner, Peter Claman, decided to have a party to be held at Madame Tussaud's Wax Museum in Manhattan. When Peter was going through the building to arrange for the party, he noticed a wax figure of Donald Trump standing in a prominent location. At that point, Peter said, "If Donald Trump is standing there, then we cannot have the party at this facility". The owner then gently picked up the wax figure of Donald Trump and placed him in a closet. The party was held at the Wax Museum and was very successful. After everyone left, the staff gently removed Donald Trump from the closet and put him back on display for the public.

More Donald Trump Stories

A close friend of mine, Tony Gliedman, was the Commissioner of the New York City Department of Housing Preservation and Development. Tony was offered a job by Donald Trump to leave the City and work in a senior position in the Trump organization. My friend accepted the position, quit his job with the City, and started a new career with Donald Trump. About six months after he started working for the Trump organization, I asked him to join me and two other friends for a day of golf. He gladly accepted and said he would meet us at my country club for a great day.

My two friends and I arrived at the golf club and were waiting for Tony. We waited for about a half-hour and Tony still had not shown up. So, I told the starter that we were going to tee off, and asked that when Tony arrived, for him to bring Tony out to the hole we would then playing. By the time we reached the fourth hole, the starter drove up in a golf cart with my good friend Tony. He apologized for being late and explained what had happened.

Donald Trump owned a rent-controlled apartment house that he wanted to demolish to make room for a new luxury high-rise building. The problem was that the existing apartment house was fully rented. All of the tenants in this building refused to move. Under New York City law, you cannot evict a tenant in a rent-controlled building. In order to force the tenants to move, Donald proceeded with unethical conditions, such as shutting off the water, shutting off heat, and other harassments of the tenants. The tenants called a strike and marched outside the building with large signs, and created an incident. The press and police arrived to keep order. In order to calm the situation, Tony rushed out to the area, where he spoke to the police and the tenants and was able to get it under control, and everyone left. However, there was a reporter there from the New York Times who witnessed the entire event. Before the reporter left, he had a quick interview with Tony. That's why Tony said he was late for golf.

We finished playing that day, had at a great dinner, and enjoyed the evening. The next day, in my office, I got a call from Tony. He told me that he had just quit working for Donald Trump. In his words, he said,

"The man is crazy. Working here is very stressful and you never know, from moment to moment, when a horrible situation will occur." He then said that he had been sitting in his office when the door was angrily thrown open by Donald Trump. Donald Trump then yelled, "You don't get your name in the paper. You get my name in the paper", and slammed the door closed. That interview with the New York Times had been just a very short explanation of the situation at the apartment building. Tony had no idea that the reporter was going to use his name. However, working in the Trump organization was like that every day of the week. This incident clearly shows the type of person that Donald Trump is.

I personally did not have any connection or involvement with Donald Trump's investments or his dealings with the banks or any of his partners. However, I knew most of the major developers in New York City who did have financial knowledge or connections with, as they called him, "The Donald". Many stories of his investment strategies circulated throughout the New York City construction industry. Some of the strategies that I heard about Donald Trump were, 'Never use your own money', and 'Obtain the largest loan you can from the bank'. If a project goes bad, you are in control, because the bank does not want to take the property and manage it. They will always work out a deal for you to stay in control. I assume other developers used the same strategy.

One story I remember about Donald, was that he took a large loan from a bank to purchase two helicopters. Sometime after this helicopter purchase, there was a slump in the construction industry. Donald was having trouble paying back the loan. So, he told the bank that they could take the helicopters. What was a bank going to do with two helicopters? The bank told Donald to keep the helicopters and extended the loan.

Another major story that went around, explained Trump's strategy in financing projects. Donald Trump would manage to get the highest amount of financing from the banks and partners for new project that he was starting. He then took the largest management fee right off the top. Getting a management fee for this type of project was perfectly legal and acceptable. It was the amount of the fee and when the fee was taken that could be questionable. For example, if finances got tight due to a downturn in the economy, the project would have a hard time paying off the mortgage. It was due to the structure of the deal, since a large amount of the money went for Donald's management fee. So, Donald would take a second mortgage, giving a personal guarantee to cover the first mortgage. Again, he took another large management fee off the top of the second mortgage. When money got tight again and he was unable to cover the payment on the second mortgage, he would turn the finances into junk bonds and sell them on Wall Street. I was told that this wiped out his personal guarantee which transferred to the investors that bought those mortgages from Wall Street.

What I find more mind-boggling, was how the Trump organization was able to keep track of all the twists and turns with the tremendous amount of projects that he was doing around the world.

My Freeport Adventure On The Island Of Grand Bahama

It was fund-raising time for the Democratic Party on Staten Island, New York. They started with breakfast at Richmond County Country Club. They had a day of golf, followed by a cocktail party and big dinner where they announced all the awards and winners of the day. At dinner, Harriet and I were at a table sitting next to a good friend of mine, New York City Councilman Edward Curry. He told me that he was intending to call me, in reference to a friend of his who was looking for an architect. He said his friend represented a group that was putting together a huge project in the Freeport area on Grand Bahama Island. He said if I'm interested, I should call him and set up a meeting. His name is (For the use in this writing I will use the name)Tom Cupo. I told Ed that I am always interested in a business opportunity and I would be very happy to call Tom. I took his phone number down and said, "The first thing Monday morning, I will be in touch with your friend". The rest of the evening was delightful, with great food and many awards and gifts, which was the usual fair at these events.

When I arrived in my office on Monday morning, I poured myself a cup of coffee, sat down at my desk and called Eddy Curry's friend, Tom Cupo. I informed him that I was the architect that Ed was talking about and I'm interested to hear what he's offering. He informed me that the German Government passed a law stating that in lieu of paying income taxes to the German Government, any individual can invest that exact same amount of money in any venture that would help the economic growth of the country. However, the German Government did not specify that the money had to be invested in Germany. Therefore, many Germans were looking to invest money around the world in an area that would benefit them the most. Because of this law, a large percentage of the German population was looking to invest their money in Freeport on the Grand Bahama Island. The investment by the individual German citizen in a condominium hotel located in Freeport would qualify as an investment in keeping with the German law.

He informed me that the area of Freeport was exactly what its name implied. It was a free port that allows any amount of money to be brought into the country and taken out of the country. Taxes were very low too. No taxes on any new businesses. He went on to tell me that he made connections with the government officials in reference to building a large condominium hotel complex on land that will be donated by the government. One portion of the property contained a large beach front on the ocean connected to a deep river running along the entire side property line. He then informed me that he has a group of investors and they are ready to put this project together. They're looking for an architect to design this entire project and if the architect wishes they can be an investor also. He said in three weeks he was going down to visit the government officials, view the property and close the deal. If I'm interested, I could go with him. He'll bring the survey of the property. I told him I was interested in being the architect, as well as investing my fee for architectural services in trade for a portion of the project. He said he would accept my fee as an investment. I told him I would like to discuss it with my partners and I would let him know shortly.

I discussed this project with Sam Lichtenstein, who was the SLCE partner who handled all of our investments. Sam was not that excited about this project because it sounded too good to be true. However, since I came up with all sorts of deals, which in the vast majority of cases were very successful, he said, "Al, do it and have some fun. Since our investment is only staff time, there wasn't really much to lose." I made the phone call to Tom to notify him that we were in and to get the process going.

He came to my office with the survey and other documentation. I sketched up the necessary schematic plan. Judging from the survey it was a fantastic piece of property. Any developer of a luxury hotel would grab this opportunity. I met with my design team and came up with a 30 story luxury high-rise condominium with all the usual amenities for such a project. We also designed a group of about 50 one-family luxury homes along the river, each containing their own dock to anchor a pleasure boat and provide swimming facilities. Arrangements were made for the two of us to fly down to the Grand Bahama Island and meet with the government officials. We arranged for him to first meet in my office the morning that we would be leaving for the airport.

On the designated morning he arrived at my reception area and was escorted to my office. I innocently said, "You can leave your attaché case in my office and come into the drafting room. I will show you what we created." He said, "Oh no. I cannot leave my attaché case unprotected." He quietly put his attaché case on my desk and opened it. To my shock and amazement it was packed solid with $100 US currency bills. They must've been more than a half million dollars neatly stacked in that case. He told me when entering or leaving Freeport, luggage is never inspected and you are allowed to legally bring in and/or take out as much money as your heart desires. This country is truly a free port. All money that is brought into this country can be deposited in a numbered account that will be perfectly secure for your use only. He lifted his pants leg to show me a 38 revolver strapped to his ankle. He said, "Al, if you ever have money you want sheltered, bring it down. I quietly informed him that my practice does not handle cash. All our financial transactions arose through checks and are heavily documented.

I showed him our drawings of the proposed complex. He was very pleased and felt that we designed a winner. We went to the airport and were on our way to Grand Bahama Island. Just as he described, going through customs on the island was a breeze. It was just about a matter of picking up your luggage and walking out. We drove to our hotel and got comfortable for the rest of the day.

The next morning a large military-type jeep and driver were in front of our hotel to take us for a meeting with the government officials. The government officials that we met were typical British. They were wearing army type uniforms, spit and polish, with shorts for pants, short sleeve shirts, and a lot of military type ornaments. We spent about two hours discussing the project and reviewing my drawings and came to the conclusion that this project was a go. The next step was for the lawyers who draw up all the legal documents.

We went on a guided tour of the property and surrounding area to get completely familiarized with the entire situation. This huge piece of property that was bounded by the beach and ocean on one side and the river on the other side was spectacular. If this project is actually built as planned, it could be a fantastic winner. We were driven back to our hotel to prepare for the evening festivities.

I was told that our government contact made arrangements for us to see the show at the casino. That evening we were joined by three gentlemen who were investors in this project. We all had a fabulous dinner and someone picking up the tab. I assumed we were guests of the government. After dinner it was still too early for the show, so all my companions started gambling. Since I am not a gambler and do not enjoy the games, I stood by and watched. My four companions each took out a large wad of hundred dollar bills and started rolling dice. I looked around the casino and noticed a large wheel that was spun until it stopped on a number. If you placed any denomination of coin or bill on that number, you would be the winner. 'That's for me.' I played that game for about a half-hour.

The doors opened indicating the show was about to begin. I collected my money, counted it and discovered that I made 75 cents. I am ahead! That's great! How my companions made out, I never found out. I never asked. We enjoyed a great show to round out the evening.

The next day we toured the island so I could see the type of architectural design that was indigenous to this area. I made some quick sketches and took notes and enjoying the entire tour. That night we had a quiet dinner in a local restaurant. The next day we boarded the plane and went back to civilization.

Two days later, Tom and I had a meeting in his office on Staten Island (he was a resident of Staten Island). We discussed the fine details, so I could go full steam ahead with all the documents and drawings that were needed to build this project. When leaving, he went to his garage to get his car. He called me over and said, "I'd like to show you something. You have to be very careful with money." He then pointed to a floor drain in the garage. He bent down remove the grading on the so-called 'drain' and said, "Look down the drain". As I looked down, I saw a large metal box with a heavy combination lock on top. He proudly said that is where he stores his money and it's all his. You would think at this time I would wonder what I'm getting into. He had the attaché case stacked full of hundred dollar bills. He had a 38 revolver on his ankle. He was transferring money back and forth to Freeport. And now he shows me this hidden safe. I guess he doesn't like to pay income tax. I started to wonder where he is getting all this cash from. We left and I went back to my office.

We completed all the design work for the models. Construction could begin and the sales apparatus could be put together. Furniture for the model apartments was being purchased and kept in a storehouse in Florida ready to be shipped to Freeport. Things were moving along very smoothly and I felt comfortable with the situation. One day Tom came to my office to give me the stock certificates in the sum that my architectural fee would normally be. Everything was falling into place. The next weekend, I was sitting at home reading the Sunday Times, when I noticed an article that turned me white. 'Tom Cupo of Staten Island was arrested and accused of fraud in many Workmen's Compensation cases.'

It seems that my good friend Tom made all this money by getting people to act as if they are sick, paying doctors to testify that they were sick. He also paid off various political officials to help with this scheme. Since Tom was the point man in our Freeport project, upon this news everything stopped. To make a long story short, he was brought to trial, convicted and placed behind bars for good number of years. Now our fantastic project completely fell apart. All construction on the models stopped. I do not know what happened to furniture in Florida. And I had no idea who paid any bills or if there was any money left over. None of this affected me since I did not invest any money other than my office time so my losses were negligible. Sam Lichtenstein read that same article that Sunday morning. When he came into the office Monday he looked at me with a smile and said, "You can't win them all." This project ended in a disaster, but on the positive side, I had a great trip down to Grand Bahama Island. It was not a total loss.

Sailors Snug Harbor

Sailor's snug harbor, located on Staten Island, New York, was one of first Continued Care Retirement Communities that we know of. This community was very special. It was built in 1801 for the sole occupancy of, as noted on the stained-glass window in building 'A', 'Haven for aged decrepit and worn out sailors'. This institution was built on 85 acres and contained 50 mostly four-story brick faced concrete buildings to accommodate 900 residents. This entire complex was financed and built by Admiral Robert Richard Randall. Admiral Randall was the Steve Jobs of his day in the shipping business. He owned a vast fleet of wooden hull sailing ships. Being a sailor on those vessels was a very dangerous occupation. The vast majority of them retired young and as Admiral Randall described, they were decrepit and worn out. He felt that those poor souls, who are responsible for him acquiring a life with health & wealth, deserved some gratitude and help. The Admiral also set up a legal financial vehicle that will provide the necessary funds for the complete maintenance and operation of the institution for its entire life.

As the years went by and steel steam ships started to replace the old wooden sailing ships, there was a decline of aged, decrepit and worn out sailors. By the time the 1950s arrived, the resident population had slowly dwindled down. As a result, many buildings were abandoned and started to decay in a dangerous condition. A number of buildings had to be demolished. By 1960s, there were less than a handful of sailors still in residence. The management at that time decided to relocate to North Carolina where they were able to acquire smaller facilities to better fit their needs.

Meanwhile, Sailors Snug Harbor and grounds, that were in a terrible a state of decay and a danger to the community, was sold to a developer. This developer proposed to build a luxury residential apartment complex. The community was up in arms at the thought of losing those 85 still beautiful wooded acres from their community. Pressure was put on the City to acquire that property from the private developer by the use of eminent domain. The City, due to community pressure, got control of the entire property. The City of New York set up a non-profit board for the purpose of designing, building and financing a regional educational and art center on the site. This non-profit board was given ownership of all the buildings existing and new. The City obtained ownership of the land and was responsible for the building and maintenance of sidewalks, roadways, parking lots and cutting the grass.

I was recruited as an architect to serve on this non-profit board. This new board's membership was made up of about 20 men and women from various professions and businesses on Staten Island. The board members were an excellent mix of knowledge and involvement in many areas of the City that was vital to our success. I, as the architect, was elected chairman of the architectural committee. This committee was responsible for the rehabilitation of all existing buildings and the design of all new buildings on the entire project. I formed a committee and the work began.

The first problem was to obtain financing to stop the deterioration from getting any worse in all the existing buildings. That meant new roofs, windows, doors and whatever else was needed to keep the weather out. Once that was achieved, the interior demolition of walls and any equipment that was beyond repair was to be removed and replaced. Once that was achieved, the board was to provide a plan for the new use including the renovation and construction of new buildings.

To obtain the first amount the seed money, we approach our State Senator to provide the necessary funds from the State of New York. We were successful and received the necessary financing. The board then proceeded and raised all the required financing for the maintenance and operation of the entire site through fund raising events and foundation funding. To make a long story short, over the next 10 years, the entire board put in a tremendous amount of time and effort and was able to refurbish the buildings for use by various organizations as well as building new buildings and other attractions within the educational and art fields.

All this activity kept my committee very busy. As of this writing, Sailors Snug Harbor has been, and is still, running the full operation as an educational and arts center. It contains many buildings and attractions such as a children's museum, art galleries and art teaching facilities. It includes all forms of art from painting, sketching, photography, jewelry making etc. It includes a theater for music and shows, huge botanical gardens, restaurants, and a complete Chinese Scholars' Garden. It included a large fish pond surrounded by a fantastic walk way and numerous buildings where Chinese scholars used to work. This project was completely built in China and shipped over from China with an architect and construction crew to assemble this fabulous educational exhibit.

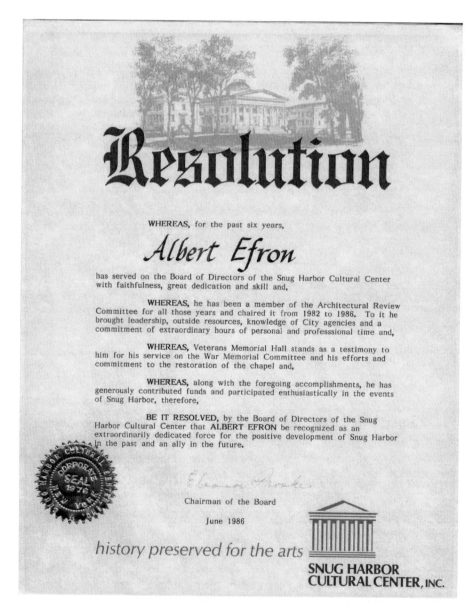

My AIA Fellowship

To become a Fellow of the American Institute of Architects, you must do something special in the form of a new architectural design or system, outstanding community service in relation to the architectural profession or a number of other achievements as specified by the AIA. It took me about a year to put together an application for Fellowship that contained a narrative of my community service in the 10 year project at Sailors' Snug Harbor. It included all the documentation that had to be approved and signed by either supervisors or coworkers. This substantiated my material and photographs. A number of other forms were also required. I finally completed everything and had it bound into book form. I submitted the package and waited anxiously for a response. It should be noted that if an applicant's first submission is turned down, he or she has the opportunity of redoing it and re-submitting it a second time. To the best of my knowledge, if you were turned down a second time, you could not resubmit for five years.

After about three months, I was notified that my submission was accepted and that at our next national convention , I would be sworn in as a Fellow in the American Institute of Architects. This was a fabulous achievement for me, especially considering my background and lack of any formal college education. At that next convention, I wore a cap and gown and proudly went up on that stage to receive the sash and Fellowship medal. I am supposed to wear this around my neck at formal AIA events. I also received as a small version of the metal that was made into a ring.

My Testimony Before A Congressional Committee

The United States Congress was looking into regulations in reference to professional organizations being allowed to advertise. Most professional organizations such as the American Institute of Architects, American Medical Association, and many other professional organizations considered advertising their services as being unprofessional. A United States congressional committee was formed to conduct hearings to acquire pros and cons of the subject by the various professional organizations across the country. This congressional committee then set up hearings in New York City for the architects to testify.

Early one morning, I received an urgent call from the President of the New York Society of Architects, an organization that I was a member of. I was informed that this congressional committee has scheduled them to testify that afternoon at two o'clock. Then the shocker came over the phone. "Al, we all agreed that you should be the one to testify." The first thought that came out of my mouth was 'are you kidding'. I have no idea what all the facts are, pro or con on the subject, because I never thought about it. How could I testify if I had not prepared with all the necessary information to make my point. Besides, is our organization for or against advertising? We are definitely against advertising and are in agreement with all the other architectural organizations such as the AIA.

After quite a bit of conversation, I agreed to make the attempt, the best I could, to defend our position. I had about three hours to do some quick research and prepare for my testimony. I arrived at the hearing site and signed in. I diligently listened to the various testimonies before my time, to get a feel of just how the conversation would go. It did not take me long to ascertain that the congressman who was chairman of this committee was totally in favor of advertising by all professional organizations and their members. I now knew the task I had before me. Not having enough time to properly prepare for this testimony put me at a great disadvantage.

When it was my turn to testify, I was sworn in and faced that hostel congressional committee staring down at me. I started my presentation by describing all the conditions why the architectural profession felt that advertising was unprofessional. I backed it up with as much information that I was able to ascertain in the three hour period before the hearing. For some reason, the chairman was in a very angry mood. He then started to lecture me in more of a yell than a speech, why his opinion on advertising must be made mandatory. He picked up a manual that our organization printed every year with the approval and in coordination with the New York City Department of Buildings. This publication contained the entire building code plus other information that is helpful for architects in working with the New York City Department of Buildings. It also contained one page that gave suggestions for architects trying to establish what a fair fee would be for both the architect and the client. The chairman started to swing the publication around and yelling at me "restraint of trade" and "price fixing". I try to explain that list was clearly stated as just 'guidelines'. At this point I realized it did not matter what I said or what I did, this chairman was not interested in an architect's opinion. He had made up his mind clearly before these hearing started. I very quickly concluded and sat down. To make a long story short, advertising for all professions is now legal.

Yonkers And The Law

One day, my partners and I were notified that a developer friend of ours recommended us to be the architects for the Yonkers Housing Authority. The Town of Yonkers is a small town located in Westchester County just north of New York City. It seems that the National Association for the Advancement of Colored People (NAACP) was suing the town because the schools were segregated. All the black students went to a black school and the white students went to a white school. No one would accept busing as a solution to the problem. A solution that the courts were seeking was to build low income housing for the colored students in the white residential community. The larger all white upscale community would not under any circumstances accept this solution. The Housing Authority needed an architect to try to work out some way to build housing in the all-white area and to work with the courts to make this approach legally binding by the white community. Being the youngest member of SLCE, I was given the privilege to take on this client.

I met the Chairman of the Yonkers Housing Authority and their senior staff. We were to design an approach that would end with the construction of this new housing in the all-white area. In order that this book does not run into hundreds and hundreds of pages, I ask the reader to imagine the number of meetings that were held, with the local political leaders, with the state political leaders, with the federal attorney's office, and the community. The best I can say is that it was a very ugly negotiating time. The federal judge handling this case came down with the ruling that the situation must be corrected. Any solution needed approvals by the local Yonkers elected officials. In order to express their views, the white community began mailing packages containing 45 caliber bullets to the elected officials as a gentle reminder how the white community felt. Need I say more?

The federal judge in this case was fully committed to the housing solution. In order to finalize the months of fruitless meetings, he convened a meeting with the federal attorneys, Yonkers government attorneys and the Yonkers Housing Authority. This meeting was to finalize the legal requirements to get this project moving. The Chairman of the Yonkers Housing Authority directed me to attend that meeting on his behalf and to represent Yonkers Housing Authority. I very politely objected, since I am an architect, not an attorney, nor did I have any involvement in the legal situation as it now stands. The Chairman politely convinced me to take on this assignment. He gave me the terms that he would accept and would not accept. As long as I stick to these guidelines everything would be fine.

There I was, sitting in a large conference room in Federal Court with a large group of attorneys from the Federal, State and local governments. The judge outlined exactly what he wanted to do and how he was planning to rule and then demanded that all the attorneys get on board and agree to the solution. The judge wanted unanimous consent and for this to move ahead. However, there were a number of items that the judge was proposing that were not in keeping with the terms that I was directed to accept from my client, the Chairman of the Yonkers Housing Authority. When the judge finished his very angry display of what he wanted, he received approval from everyone in the room except me. I quietly raised my voice and said, "Your honor, on behalf of the Yonkers Housing Authority, I cannot accept the following conditions". I outlined them.

At that point the judge stood up with the very angry face and started to yell on the top of his lungs, that I had no right to screw up his whole proposal, that all the federal attorneys and other attorneys that were in the room were accepting, and how dare I refuse to accept this proposal. If I don't approve his proposal he will take whatever legal action against me and it would not be very pleasant. I was thinking what to do, as perspiration was running off my brow and I was trying to stop my hands from shaking. I quietly said, "You win your honor, I accept those conditions".

Now my problem was to tell the Chairman of the Yonkers Housing Authority that I caved. When I finish telling him the whole gruesome story, he gently said, "Oh, I kind of figured that would happen. I did not want to go through that. Thank you very much. You did a great job". Some thoughts start going through my head. Do I accept my client's thank you? The client pays the money that creates my reputation which I'll need for the future. Or do I kick him in the groin? I accept it with a smile.

You can just imagine the uproar from the white community to this court ruling. We will be creating low income housing for the black community to be built in their nice neighborhood. The marching, yelling and threatening groups of gangs encircled the Housing Authority. It was a very very nasty time. Part of the settlement that the judge had arranged was for the Yonkers Housing Authority to take over an abandoned school that was close to the white community and to rehab it as a new school for the community that would be totally integrated. This was rubbing salt into the wound.

My chore was to design one-family homes in an area where the local population had threatened to shoot anyone trying to construct these buildings and blow up whatever they could. It did not take long for me to realize that we could not build housing in the normal construction manner. After much research, I found a construction company in Pennsylvania that built one-family homes in a factory on an assembly line. The only construction on the site was to install the foundation and bring in all the utilities. Once that is done, these factory-built homes could be installed at the rate of three homes a day. Each home would be fully completed and the people can move in right then and there. It takes the entire construction project out of control of the community. They only have a very short window to create trouble. It could be more easily contained by the local authorities. All the buildings were designed and I was able to get local building department approval. I turned the drawings over to the factory to construct the entire project.

My next chore was to rehab the school. The first thing I needed was some accurate dimensions and conditions of the existing building. I made arrangements for my crew to go down to the building to measure and photograph the existing conditions. Since this was a hostile area, I insisted that the Town give my people police protection while they are doing their work in the building. That was all arranged and agreed to by all parties. The police were to meet my people at nine o'clock in the morning and stay with them for the entire time while they were in the building. They were to make sure that my guys were safe until they were gone from the area.

The problem that occurred is at my people got there about 8:45am. They were sitting on the steps of the school waiting for the police protection to arrive. In the meantime the community noticed my crew there and an ugly incident popped up. My staff was quickly surrounded by people, as was explained to me later on, by the biggest, strongest, menacing men they had ever seen, holding all sorts of nasty equipment that could be disastrous if put into action. My crew chief tried to calm down the crowd and explain they are just here from the architect's office and have nothing to do with any decisions that were made. They just kept talking, until finally the police arrived to save the day.

My crew got all the information that was needed with that one visit, because they told me that they would never visit that school again. To make a long story short we rehabilitated the school and it was put in operation. All the one-family homes were built for the low economic black people as well as the existing white people. Eventually all the new factory built one-family homes were installed and completely occupied. Eventually everything settled down and they were no further incidents of violence. Life went on and the two groups managed to live together as far as I can see in a peaceful manner.

After this project was over, the Yonkers Housing Authority gave me a number of other projects to work on with them. One day I found out that the Town of Yonkers was very upset with the Chairman of the Yonkers Housing Authority. They could not understand why he hired an architect from New York City to work for the local Housing Authority. There were a number of qualified local architects in Yonkers. I later found out that the pressure and threats were made against the Chairman of the Housing Authority. He was threatened to not be reappointed unless he replaced me with a local architect. That went on for close to a year. Since I had a great relationship with the Chairman and he felt safe with me as the architect, as I demonstrated throughout those difficult days, he refused to give in to pressure that was put on him. I remained their architect for many years, until the Chairman had to step down for health reasons and was moved into a nursing home. That was one great adventure in my professional life.

Gay Rights

On a bright sunny Tuesday afternoon in Manhattan, my partners and I were having a quick lunch in our conference room. We were discussing some organizational items that we were putting into place. My secretary notified me that I had a very important call. I picked up the phone and it was a friend of mine. He started a conversation with the four magic words that I always live by. He said "Al, do me a favor". I immediately answered, "You got it. What's the problem?" My friend went into detail about a problem one of his clients was having. His client owned a health club in an office building located in Midtown Manhattan. The existing facilities were too small for his growing business as well as his lease was running out. The client found a new location that would be perfect for his business in another office building. He needed someone to go before the New York City Community Board to get the necessary approvals. The Board would be hearing his case that Friday. He desperately needed someone with experience and was familiar with the Community Board's procedures to present the case. If the client does not get the approvals, he would find himself out of business because his current lease was running out. I told him to give my secretary his client's name, address & phone number and I would speak to him.

I called my friend's client. I made an appointment to meet him that afternoon because we only had three days to prepare. I arrived at his office on time. I entered the office building and rode the elevator up to his floor. I walked from the elevator to the entrance of his health club and entered the facilities. I found myself standing in a very small vestibule, with two chairs on one wall that were occupied by two men. There was a receptionist sitting behind a caged enclosure in front of me. As I stood there, a little uncomfortable, I noticed the two gentlemen sitting in those chairs eyeing me up and down. I approached the receptionist and told her who I was and that I was there to see the owner. The owner promptly came out and greeted me. While escorting me into his office, he explained that his operation is a complete health club in full compliance with all New York City building codes. As required, he provides all the health instructions and classrooms, exercise facilities and massage treatment. He took me on a tour of the facility.

We passed a row of 4' x 4' rooms with doors for privacy. I looked into one of the rooms and noticed a hole in the wall about 5-foot above the floor. I looked through the hole and I was able to see whatever was going on in the adjacent room. I looked at the owner and said, "What are these rooms?" He said that some of his customers like to observe other people and the people in the other room also like to be observed. It was pretty clear to me that this was a gay house of prostitution. I told this gentleman that this facility is going to be a tough sell to the Community Board. He told me that all the services that he offered were 100% within the law as required. In addition, there were no laws outlawing what his patrons were doing. He went on to tell me that this is a first-class upscale facility. "My clients happen to be the writer Truman Capote, the actor Rock Hudson and many others. We never had any complaints from anyone in this building." I told him to give me all the literature that he has as well as any advertising that he does so I get a good understanding of his operation. He put together a package for me to take, plus all the information that I needed in reference to the Community Board hearing. I asked him for his personal phone number, so I could call that evening after I put together what I intend to do. I might feel that I could not get the approvals that he's looking for and would need to talk with him.

At home that evening I went through all the material and started to think about this entire situation. Whether they are gay or not, they should have rights and privileges as anyone else. The new facility they are seeking approval for is on the 15th floor of an office building in the middle of Manhattan. There were no children or schools or families anywhere near this facility. They will not be bothering anyone or causing any kind of disruption. I felt that they deserved the human right to follow life as they see fit. I decided that I will do my best to try to get this approval. Friday evening arrived and I entered the hearing room with plenty of time before my case was called.

As always, at these hearings, were many attorneys representing their clients. New York City is a big place, however these hearings are small and all the attorneys and architects making these presentations know each other. I entered and greeted my attorney friends. I sat down and waited for the hearing to start. One of the attorneys asked me, "What case do you have?" When I told him which case I will be presenting, he looked at me for about a split second and started to laugh. You will never get that approved. It is a male whore house. The word spread with the other so-called friends of mine with the same response. I told him that I felt these people have a right to live their life as they see fit, as long as it does not interfere with anyone else. They shook their heads and said, "You're going to be a loser whether you like it or not". I used my usual phrase, 'never tell me what I cannot do'. I always find a way and I will get these approvals.

When it was my time to make my presentation, I used every emotion, public speaking trick and tactic that I knew and went all out with a legitimate detailed human appeal. When I finished, the Chairperson called for the usual vote. I held my breath. "All in favor?" Much to my surprise every Board Members hand went up. "All opposed?" Not one hand went up. I thanked the Board, turned to my buddies and smiled. I felt very good after that adventure because I feel there is no room for bigotry in this country.

A Prominent Elected Official & Suicide

Another adventure I had as an architect, had a very sad ending for a leading prominent member of the political community. I designed a building under Section 8-202 Federal Program for low income senior citizens to be built by Presbyterian Senior Services. This project was located in the Borough of Queens, New York. One of the approvals that I needed was that of the Borough President's Community Board. I felt if I get the Borough President's approval first, it would be easier to get the Community Board approval. I knew the Borough President Donald Manes from various Democratic events we both were involved in. I spoke to Donald and explained the details of the project. He told me that he would approve the project.

On the way out of his office, one of his top lieutenants stopped me in the corridor. He asked, "Do you know if the Borough President is going to approve your project?" I said, "Yes, he told me he would". "Well you have to take care of us." I said, "Tell me when your next fundraiser will be held and I would be happy to buy a table or two". The gentleman said, "You don't understand. We need cash." I politely told him I do not pay cash or get involved in any other arrangement that is not 100% legal. He notified me that the Borough President will not approve the project. I said, "Then I will have to find another way to get the approval."

I attended the Community Board meeting and made my presentation. The Community Board voted. I receive a large majority of the yes vote and the project was approved. About six months later, the Attorney General indicted the Borough President and a large group of lawyers, architects and engineers that got involved in the transfer of illegal money. After the indictment, the Borough President tried to commit suicide and failed. About three months later he tried again and this time succeeded. A great number of the other people involved were convicted and sentenced to prison time. With a sigh of relief, I am glad that I did not get involved in that or any other type of illegal operation.

Staten Island Blind Society

On a happier note, I got involved with the Staten Island Blind Society. The Blind Society was operated by a group of very dedicated citizens trying to make life better for people who lost their sight. We ran a number of fundraisers in order to acquire the money to open up a school to teach the blind people how to use a cane. The cane can act like eyes for some of the handicapped people. Through the cane, they can feel change in surface & elevation and feel for obstacles.

We were not able to raise enough money to rent the needed space. Through my political activities, I had good contacts and friends in the New York City Health and Hospital Corporation. The Health and Hospital Corporation owned a huge piece of property on Staten Island called Seaview. Back in the days when tuberculosis was rampant throughout this country, the United States Government decided to build the research hospital to find a cure for tuberculosis. This hospital was built on Staten Island which was then deep forests. As time went by and a cure for tuberculosis was achieved, the hospital was not needed and therefore went abandoned. As time went by, the New York City Health and Hospitals Corporation got control of the land and built a nursing home on the upper portion of this property. The original tuberculosis hospital was in ruins, as were a large number of cottages that were built for the employees of the hospital. I was involved with a group that wanted to rehab the hospital and the cottages.

None of these proposals were approved. I got the bright idea that if the City would give us one of those cottages rent free, we could use it as a school to teach the blind caning that would solve our problem. I spoke to the Commissioner of Health and Hospitals Corporation, who lived on Staten Island and was a good friend of mine, to see if we could work out some deal for the Blind Society to get control of one of those cottages. The Commissioner told me that he would be glad to let the Blind Society use one building rent-free, however that organization does not have the financial power to handle any problems that could happen while they are using the building. He told me if I, Al Efron, signs a document to take full responsibility and personal liability, they will get their building. If it takes him off the hook for any future problems, he's on board. Being a glutton for punishment, I signed on the dotted line, and we got control of one of the buildings.

Now the problem was to clean up the building. All the plaster on the walls had rotted away and had to be removed before the start of any alteration. So we went to work bringing in as many community business volunteers as possible. I was going to provide the architectural design and working drawings plus the department approvals as required. We recruited a major lumberyard that supplied us with a truck and two helpers to demolish the plaster, load the truck and disposed of the debris. We started Phase 1.

The truck arrived, but because of all the trees, the truck could not get close to the building. We needed manpower to fill wheelbarrows with the plaster and bring it to the truck for disposal. The blind people got together and came up with a plan. They will man the wheelbarrows from the building to the truck and back to the building as long as there are helpers to fill the wheelbarrows and empty them into the truck. The next day, to my amazement, they put down wooden plank walkways running between the trees from the truck to the building. They placed radios playing music at every change in direction of the walkways. I stood there and watched in amazement. The blind people walked down the planks pushing the wheelbarrows and navigating with the use of the music. The lumberyard helpers filled the wheelbarrows with the plaster they ripped off of the walls. The blind people walked the wheelbarrows to the truck, down the plank walkways listening to the music. More helpers unloaded the wheelbarrows. This went on until the job was completed. It was beauty to behold. To make a long story short, we were able to enlist a number of members of the community to do the rest of the work. We raised enough money to buy fixtures and what else was needed. We were in business. The Blind Society used that building for five or six years before they were able to get funds to move in to better facilities. When that happened I gladly met with my friend the Commissioner of Health and Hospitals and tore up the agreement I signed at the beginning of this project. I was off the hook.

"I Will Not Play Golf With Them", Harriet Told Me.

Every time I meet a new potential client, the first thing I try to do is arrange is a golf game. Since this person is new to me, we are really not yet in a comfortable friendly relationship. However after one round of 18 holes of golf and dinner, we will be buddy buddy. I followed this philosophy through my entire career very successfully. I was introduced to the Ambassador from Australia who was serving at United Nations in New York City. The Ambassador was not familiar with New York City at that time. He asked some friends if they could recommend an architect to speak to. It so happened that the Ambassador's friend was also my friend and the introduction was made. After some talk, I felt comfortable enough with him for me to ask, "Do you play golf?" "Oh Yes, I love golf". I asked, "Does your wife play golf?" "Oh Yes, We always play together". "Great", I said, "Why don't you and your wife, joined me and my wife at my country club on Staten Island for a round golf and dinner?" "We would love to", he said and we set a date. We continued with the conversation based on his architectural needs for the rest of that lunch.

When we were getting ready to leave, I wanted to find out how good of a golfer he and his wife were, so I asked him, "What is your handicap?" He said, that sent shockwaves through me, "I'm a one handicap and my wife is a three handicap." Oh my goodness what have I done? My wife and I were fair golfers at best. We were nowhere near the professional 'one and three handicap' golfers they were.

That evening when I came home, I was really concerned as to how I am going to break this news to Harriet. Finally I got my courage up and I told Harriet the position I put us in. She said, "No problem from my end because I will not show up to play." What do I do now? The next day the Ambassador called and said, "Al, I just received word that I am needed back in Australia immediately. So please don't hate me for not being able to play with you and your wife." With a sigh of relief I said, "Maybe sometime in the future", hoping that 'sometime in the future' would never happen.

Another Dangerous Golf Adventure

A large number of our employees were from the Philippines. They are terrific, honorable, hard-working people. A few of them had great connections with politicians and other important people in the Philippines. The Philippine Embassy was having a special social event honoring quite a few Philippine survivors of the Japanese occupation of the Philippines during the Second World War. One of my Filipino employees had the connection to invited Harriet and I to the festivities. At this event I was introduced to President Fernando Marcos by his Ambassador, close friend and advisor. We were at the same table during dinner and engaged in a very informative mutual conversation.

During the ceremony honoring the survivors of the Second World War, we heard some heartbreaking horror stories of what those people went through. Not too many managed to survive those horrible days. In keeping with my philosophy of playing golf to make friends and influence people, I asked the Ambassador if he would join me for golf some afternoon. With a great smile he said he would be honored. We set the date to meet for a great round of golf and dinner.

The day before we were to enjoy this golf game, Fernando Marcos' opposition candidate for the presidency of the Philippines, Benigno Ninoy Aquino, was returning to the Philippines from the United States. As he was leaving the plane at the airport in the Philippines, he was assassinated. Upon hearing that news, I became a little concerned. These people play rough. I could imagine myself on the golf course with the President's Ambassador when a shot rings out from the woods missing the Ambassador and hitting me. Far-fetched, but who knows? The phone rang and it was the Ambassador informing me that he has to rush back to the Philippines because of this crisis. I wished him well as I sipped on my Canadian Club neat.

Imelda Marcos and My Neighbor

A number of years after that assassination and the overthrow of Fernando Marcos slowly disappearing from the newspapers, my neighbor called to invite me to a special dinner at his house with his good friend, Imelda Marcos. "How do you know Imelda Marcos I asked?" He informed me that his wife's father was an ammunition manufacturer in the Philippines. His biggest customer was Fernando Marcos. Their families have been very close over many years. He told me that Mrs. Marcos called him to arrange her to visit their family. They have not seen one another for a good number of years.

My friend invited a few of the neighbors to meet her. The night of this event, 15 of our neighbors assembled in his house awaiting her guest of honor. After about a half-hour, an entourage of about 10 large Lincoln limos and town cars arrived on the narrow streets of our quiet upscale community. I never saw so many uniformed personnel. They wore Filipino and United States uniforms and accompanied Mrs. Marcos. My wife and I were pretty surprised to see this tall beautiful woman entered the room with such grace. I don't know why, but that was not the image that we had of Imelda Marcos.

    While we were sitting at the kitchen table, I told her that a large portion of my staff were from the Philippines. She got excited and called over an aid to bring her a stack of her photographs. The aid gave her the photographs and she signed each one and handed them to me to distribute to my Filipino employees. After a while, as things calmed down, my friend set up a group of chairs to form an audience area. Mrs. Marcos got up in front of us and put on a fantastic show. She had a great voice and sang all types of songs. She told stories and was the entertainer of the evening. That event was the talk of the town.

    The next day in my office, I distributed the signed photographs to all my Filipino employees. The combination of joy and excitement of getting an autographed photograph for them to keep was overwhelming. They all had a hard time getting back to work after that.

New Philippine Government

Mrs. Aquino, the wife of the assassinated candidate opposing Fernando Marcos, managed to overthrow the government of Fernando Marcos and became the President of the Philippines. She sent a delegation to New York to seize all the property from the previous administration that belonged to the Philippine Government. The new Ambassador, upon arriving in New York, called me asking for my help. He said my name popped up in their government circles. They felt I would be a good contact to help the new government get settled in New York. He set up a meeting for me to meet him at the Embassy which also doubled as the home of the Marcos family when they were in New York.

I arrived at the Fifth Avenue address to meet the new Ambassador. He wanted me to see the entire building and help in their determination of just what to do with this huge, fabulous building in the highest rent district of New York City. Going through the building, I was amazed at the lifestyle the Marcos lived. In the basement was a complete disco with loads of space for dancing, a great bandstand, large bar, tables and chairs plus a large mirrored ball suspended from the ceiling to create the disco feeling. I can imagine the parties that must've gone on there.

The main entrance on the street, brought you to a large vestibule, similar that used to be shown in the old movies of the way the rich people live. There was a monumental circular stair going to the upper floors. Starting at the bottom of the stair, going all the way to the top on the wall were mounted the photographs of Fernando Marcos, Imelda Marcos and other dignitaries that I did not recognize. We went through all of the rooms in this building. It could accommodate anything and everything that the occupants needed. When we came to the top floor, we went through two multi-room suites. One was for Fernando, and the other was for Imelda. Going through Mrs. Marcos' suite, I noticed the huge shoe closet that everyone was talking about. Many of the closets held great luxury throughout. We went into the bathroom. It was magnificent. There was a large round glass enclosed shower, plus other custom-designed fixtures and finishes.

I noticed in the back of the bathroom was a door. I asked where that door lead to. He walked me to the door, opened it so I could see what looks like a secret passage to another door at the other end. I said, "Where does the door at the other end lead to?" With a straight face, he said that is the door to actor George Hamilton's suite. Whenever Mrs. Marcos was in her suite, George Hamilton, her lover, occupied that suite. That passage was very convenient for them to meet. When I got home that evening, I said to Harriet, "You not going to believe what I learned." I told her that George Hamilton was Imelda Marcos' lover. Harriet said, "I know. That's been around for a long time." Since I am behind the times, I just sat down and watched television.

Other Famous People

At this time I would like to take a literary break with two stories that proves that everyone has flaws. One afternoon I was on my way to a business luncheon given by some organization. I arrived at the hotel, went up to the ball room and started my usual networking procedure. The announcement was made that the luncheon was being served, and would everyone please find their table. I looked at my ticket and noticed that I was at table 15. I glanced around the room, spotted my table, and took my seat.

Since I did not know anyone at the table, we started the introductions. I turned to the young man sitting on my left and said, "Hi, I'm Al Efron." He told me his name. I asked him, "What do you do?" He said, "I play tennis". I said, "Nice to meet you. I am an architect." We had a very pleasant lunch with a lot of great conversation until the meal was over. On the way out, a friend of mine said to me, "It must've been an exciting lunch you had. How was it talking to Arthur Ashe?" "Oh my", I said, "Was that Arthur Ashe?" When he told me his name, and said he plays tennis, it just never registered with me.

About a month later, I was attending another such event. I arrived at the hotel and saw a sign indicating that our luncheon was on the second floor. I went up the staircase going to the second floor to the entrance of the ballroom. I noticed at the top of the stairs was a man greeting people as they passed. That man looked very familiar to me. As I was climbing the stairs, I wondered how I knew him; as an architect or through politics. When I reached him, I introduce myself and said, "You look familiar to me. Where do I know you from?" He then looked me right in the eyes and said, "Everybody approaches me, looks me square in the face and tells me they know me but don't know from where. Did you see the movie Stalag 17? Remember the character they call the animal? I've been in couple dozen other great movies too." I kept looking at him and then it hit me. Yes I recognize him but have no idea what his name is. I lucked out and he told me that his name is Robert Strauss. I smiled and shook his hand and told him I was honored to meet him. I turned and started to go into the luncheon. He said to me, "You're like everybody else. They all come up to me, say I look familiar and then walk away. Do me a favor, talk to me for a few minutes." So I did and we had a lovely conversation.

While I'm talking about famous people, my partner Sam Lichtenstein's nephew is Sandy Koufax. Those of you old enough to remember, Sandy Koufax was a famous baseball pitcher for the Brooklyn Dodgers which later became the Los Angeles Dodgers. His reign as a baseball player was from 1955 to 1966. Sandy used to come up to our office for lunch visits. He was a very bright but shy individual. He had a great talent of controlling the baseball. He was also an excellent golfer. We had many discussions in the technique of the golf game.

I remember at one of our lunches, I said that I hated when my ball ended up the sand trap, because it is so hard to control the ball lying in the sand. He disagreed with me and said he can control the ball better in the sand than in the grass. He gave me a demonstration of how he does it, while standing in a conference room of our office. I watched him closely. The next Saturday on a golf course, I put the ball in the sand. I tried out the Koufax special. Much to my surprise, I could not get the ball out of the sand no matter how hard I tried. I guess that is why I am not a scratch golfer or good pitcher.

Many times when Sandy had lunch with us, we would send one of our delivery boys down to the sports store to buy a couple dozen baseballs. Sandy would autograph the balls and we would distribute them to our staff. Everyone was so excited to get one of those baseballs. For some stupid reason, since I considered Sandy more over friend, I never took one of those balls. When my kids found out about the signed balls, they had a fit that I never took one. They kept reminding me that those balls now are worth big dollars. Sandy, for those of you who remember, was married to Anne Widmark, the daughter of famous actor Richard Widmark. While talking about famous people, Sandy's neighbor and best friend was the famous actor Buddy Hackett. Sandy used to tell us all the times he and Buddy were together. He told us that Buddy was always on. It was laughter from the minute they got together until they parted for the day. Yes I know this does not make me famous at all, but it makes for a good story.

Paul's Famous Golf Ball

I mentioned golf above. It reminds me of the time that my son Paul sent me a very special golf ball. He said that his friend is a chemical engineer who came up with new material that can be used in the construction of golf balls. The great thing about golf balls, made with this new material, is that it allows you to hit the ball with your normal swing, but the ball goes much further than standard balls. I put this golf ball in my golf bag to try out the next time I played golf. The following Saturday, I was on the course with my buddies. I got to the ninth-hole and remembered that I had that special ball. I explained to the rest of my foursome about the wonderful things this ball was supposed to do. I teed the ball up as the four of us waited with excited anticipation of what we were about to see. I took out my driver and with great diligence made a perfect swing. My golf club came smoothly down to make contact with the new wonder ball, to send on its way. My club head came square in contact with the wonder ball and to our surprise, horror, and amazement, it exploded into this fine dust that slowly drifted down, covering my head with what was left of this fabulous new discovery wonder ball. I stood there for a few seconds in the state of shock as my buddies were hysterical. The moral of the story is that there is none.

The Handicapped Law

Getting back to business, I am a member of the American Institute of Architects and I started to get active. I was a member of the Staten Island chapter. This was a group of nice Staten Island architects who met once a month at a local restaurant and had dinner. They all had a local Staten Island practice. They did one-family homes and local retail businesses, such as banks etc. It was enough to make a good respectable living. Being a member of the Staten Island Chapter gave me access to the NY State AIA organization.

One day, I was asked if I would serve on a committee to be established by the New York State office of the American Institute of Architects. This committee was assigned the task to write legislation for the handicapped which was becoming a big concern and push by the federal government. This committee became part of the national committee in Washington. This was a great experience for me. We had many meetings to figure out just what the handicapped needs are since none of us were handicapped. It amazed me when I realized the simple fact that a person in a wheelchair could not cross a street by themselves if they could not maneuver the wheelchair off a curb. This obstacle could be easily eliminated with a simple curb cut. With that simple problem solution and the rest of the problems in the equation, this was a big deal that needed to be addressed. Something had to be done, because of the huge number of handicapped people who are out there and hurting. I was reminded that someday I will become a senior citizen and it is quite common for senior citizen to have some form of handicap. I put my entire effort into that committee. There was a lot of homework and research that we did in order to get a complete understanding of the entire problem and find practical solutions that made sense for everyone. I forget how many months the committee worked on this problem, and how many trips I made to Washington, and back to New York, but we did it and we presented it to the powers that be. Our preliminary work was turned over to the government, so they could use all of our research to create a handicapped law. When completed, the law would be part of federal legislation covering the entire country.

The amazing twist of faith that came knocking on my door, came about a year after the legislation was passed and became the law of the land. The law started to trickle down to the local building departments and was included in their building codes. At that time, I had filed a complete set of drawings to the building department for approval of a luxury high-rise in Manhattan. I got a call from the Building Department Commissioner notifying me that my project is the first project to be built in New York City using the new handicapped law. He also stated that his staff was trying to get up to speed with the new legislation. Since I was involved in writing the preliminary document with the AIA, he wanted me to work with his staff and figure out just what has to be done to get a full project through the building plan review process. There I was, working on my project under the handicapped code to iron out all the details. There will be issues that will need correcting or adjusting, as is always the case with any new legislation. As we started to work on this, lo and behold all of the little problems popped up that were completely and understandably unforeseen.

One such problem was that in Manhattan, all luxury high-rises apartments must, according to the real estate agents, have balconies. These balconies were small and no one ever sat out on them. The balconies seem to be more of a show item. The apartment residents were nervous standing on the balconies of the high floors at these high elevations. In addition, there were strong winds encountered high up. All the sales agents told us we must have balconies because it's easy to sell apartments with a balcony even though nobody uses them. In a high-rise building the wind pressures at the upper floors get very high. In order to prevent any rain from blowing in under the doors leading out to the balcony, we had to provide a small 3 inches high step up to keep the apartment dry. You can't get a wheelchair out on the balcony because of that three-inch step up. That little detail took hours of negotiations and discussions with various construction manufacturers to come up with a solution. We did finally work out a saddle detail with the manufacturers, that was able to accommodate a wheelchair and also keep the rainwater out. This gives you an idea of the problems that we had in the beginning. There were literally hundreds of little details that had to be taken care of to conform to the building code that were practical for all parties. This was one of the toughest challenges we ever faced.

Efron For President

The story of how I was elected President of the State component of the American Institute of Architects is another lesson in not listening to those who say 'you can't do that'. The organization of the American Institute of Architects starts with the national organization based in Washington DC. This is the main governing body for the entire organization. It breaks down to a component established at each State in the Union. The State organization is involved with the day-to-day operations on a State level. These operations include lobbying on the State level for architects interests, in reference to all laws, directives and other conditions. The organization breaks down to local chapters in each county throughout the State. These local chapters in some areas contain just a few members because of their rural location. Local chapters vary in size from small rural ones all the way to chapters like the New York chapter, AKA, Manhattan chapter. There are 13 chapters of the New York State AIA.

I was a member of the Staten Island chapter because I wanted to be with my local friends. Staten Island is one of the five boroughs of New York City, along with Brooklyn, Queens, Bronx & Manhattan. Manhattan is what most people think when they refer to 'New York', and New Yorkers refer to Manhattan as 'The City'. It's mostly what you see when watching movies filmed in NY. The Staten Island chapter is a small chapter with about 20 local architects that did mostly one-family homes and small retail business type construction. My partner, Peter Claman, was a member of the Long Island chapter. Their membership was somewhat larger than the average chapter but nowhere near the number of members in the Manhattan chapter. Due to this large variance in size of the number of members in each chapter, the voting power was in the hands of the Manhattan chapter which controlled approximately 50% of the total vote of the entire state organization. As a result, if you wanted to run for a State office you always wanted the Manhattan chapter as a sponsor. Through the history of the State organization, it is hard to find anyone who was elected to a State office position without the Manhattan chapter's backing.

The first State position that I was elected to was that of Treasurer. No one seemed much concerned with the position of

Treasurer, so I was easily elected. As time went on, I decided to run for President. Everyone sat up, at attention, and took notice. The problem I had was being a member of the Staten Island chapter and my partner, Peter, being a member of the Long Island chapter. That made us outcasts by the Manhattan chapter. They were after us for years, saying since we were one the major architectural firms in the City and had our offices in the City, we should be members of the Manhattan chapter. Peter and I did not want to join the Manhattan chapter, because their membership was so large they could not have monthly meetings. Instead, the membership had to join a committee and not get involved with the running of the organization. The organization was run by the 4 or 5 members of the executive committee. All the other chapters throughout the State have monthly meetings and all the members were involved with all the decisions that had to be made.

The minute the word got out that I was seeking the office of New York State President, the Manhattan chapter swung into action. They had friends of mine who were members of the Chapter call me and try to convince me to join their Chapter if I want their backing. I declined the appeal from all calls. It was made very clear to me that if I ran without their backing, they would put up a candidate against me. It would make it impossible for me to win since they control about 50% of the vote of the entire State organization. In essence they were saying 'you can't do that'. Since I never accept the concept that 'you can't do that', I told the powers that be in the Manhattan chapter that I will remain a member of the Staten Island chapter, I would be running for President without their support, and they should select a potential candidate to run against me. Let the games begin.

The fight was now on. I quietly started to think of the strategy I would use to win this election. Assuming I will get none of the votes from anyone in the Manhattan chapter, and since the Manhattan chapter controls roughly 50% of the total vote, I must receive all of the non-Manhattan votes in order to win. I must receive 100% of the votes from the other 12 chapters around the State of New York plus a few renegades from the New York City chapter in order to win. This was to be a monumental chore, however monumental chores never bothered me, since I believe strongly in the fact that you can always find a way, if you look for it.

I waited patiently for the Manhattan chapter to announce the name of the architect that would be running against me. After about two weeks, the announcement came down with the name of my competitor. I knew this architect. He was a sweet and very honorable guy. He also had a large practice similar to mine and did some fine work. There was one thing about the candidate against me that made me jump for joy, he was a terrible speaker. Whenever he got up to speak, inevitably the audience would fall asleep. I just found my way around 'you can't do this'.

My strategy now set, I challenged him to a series of debates to be held in every chapter throughout the State of New York. Since the process for electing a President allowed us one year before the actual voting to campaign, we had time to carry out my challenge. To my delight, he accepted and we set up a schedule of dates to speak at every chapter in New York State, from Niagara Falls to the tip of Staten Island. Part one of my attack for the Presidency was in operation.

At the first chapter meeting we would speak at, the President of the local chapter said he would flip a coin to see who speaks first. I quickly put part two of my attack into action. I said, "I bow to my opponent. He can go first." To my amazement my opponent accepted. Anybody who is familiar with public speaking and debates knows that you never want to be the first speaker because it puts you at a great disadvantage. The first speaker reveals his entire thinking and strategy to the audience and the second speaker. The first speaker now knows nothing about the second speaker, but the second speaker knows all about the first speaker. The second up can knock down all the first speaker's addenda.

In addition since there are only two speakers, the audience always remembers what is last said, wiping out the first speakers remarks from their memory. My 'you can't do that' attack is now underway. We continued to the second and third and all the other speaking engagements throughout the State. At every speaking engagement, to my utter amazement, my opponent accepted my stepping aside so he could be the first speaker. As true to form, my opponent spoke in a monotone boring manner and lost his audience. I used all the tricks and skills that I have learned over the years in winning over an audience. I went into detail of the problems and solutions and inserted jokes that were appropriate to the situation. I used all the body language and other public speaking approaches that I knew.

The day after every debate, the President of that chapter would call and inform me that when we left, the chapter voted unanimous in my favor and the entire chapter was in my corner. This scenario played out at every chapter that we visited and had this debate. The only problem we had was not being able to arrange a debate date with the Buffalo chapter. Time ran out and it was time for the convention. At that point, I had 11 chapters, 100% of all the chapters except Buffalo. I did not know where they stood. My opponent had, at the start, 100% of the New York chapter which was 50% of the total State vote. I must get the Buffalo chapter in my corner.

The moment I arrived at the convention, I contacted the President of the Buffalo chapter and requested that we have a debate just before the convention starts. The President said that the chapter had voted in favor of my opponent, however to be fair he, will arrange for us to debate. To make a long story short, after that debate, just before the convention was to start, the President called me and said, "Al, you blew us away. We are now 100% of your corner". If you add up the votes I had 50% of the entire State and my opponent had 50% of the entire State just from the New York chapter. My hope is that a few friends of mine who are in the New York chapter would support me and vote for me. The voting was a secret ballet.

The election crew set up all the voting machines. At the proper moment, the gates were opened and the voting started. It usually took about three hours for the entire vote to be complete because some members always left the convention for early round of golf. At our luncheon meeting, we all waited for the announcement of the results of the voting. Nothing happened. Nothing was announced. Everybody was wondering what happened. No explanation was given as lunch was over and we continued with the convention. Usually the voting results were announced at the luncheon. Time kept ticking and ticking and ticking and no results were being announced.

What was going on? I was getting concerned but there was nothing I could do it that time. At dinnertime we all assembled in the ballroom for another great meal. And from the dais, the Chairman of the voting committee got up and stated that the winner of the election is Al Efron and sat down. Wow! I did what they said it couldn't be done. I did it. One of our members from the audience asked what the final count was. The Chairman of the voting committee said that the committee voted unanimously not to announce the final vote count since it had no effect on the outcome of the voting. This was very unusual. The total vote was always announced, year after year, usually at the luncheon.

I sent my spies out to find out what was going on. They reported back to me that I received 100% of all the New York State chapters, plus a large percent of votes from the Manhattan chapter. The Manhatant chapter was so embarrassed by the results of losing such a large percent of their members to me that they refused to release the results. End of story. Never ever say 'you can't do that'.

During my term as President of the New York State Association of Architects, we geared up for the annual convention. It has always been customary to hold these conventions in an upscale resort hotel in the Catskill Mountains of New York State. These hotels provided everything that a convention needs including all the sports, theaters, restaurants etc., all on-site. At these conventions, we always invited the corporations and companies who provide material and services in the construction industry for the architects to meet. These companies would purchase space and set up booths and display the material or services for the architects to see. These booths were a way of raising money for the operation of our organization.

At a meeting with the Manhattan chapter, a request was made that the next convention be held in Manhattan. The reason for this, was that the majority of architects were located in Manhattan. Therefore a great number of architectural draftsmen working for these architects would have the opportunity of attending the convention. These draftsmen did not have the funds or time to attend a convention in the Catskills Mountains. Through a united campaign of these architects and draftsmen, a message for change was loud and clear. I held an executive meeting with the leadership of the organization to address this request. After much discussion the change was approved and we made arrangements to have the convention at a hotel in Manhattan.

The committee that I appointed to run this convention proceeded with all the details necessary for a successful convention. Contracts were signed by the various companies purchasing booths for their display as has been done in the past. Finally all arrangements were complete and the day before the convention was to begin, all the vendors drove up to the hotel with the trucks to unload their displays. At that point, an official of the hotel notified each truck driver that they are not allowed to unload the truck. Unloading the truck must be done by a union crew provided by the hotel and paid for by the vendor. This was a new shock that was not expected.

Once the truck was unloaded on the loading dock the workman were notified that they could not take all the material up to the convention floor. All the material must be carried up by another union crew. This group also had to be paid for by the vendor.

Once on the floor, the vendor was notified that they cannot assemble the display with their crew but must use another union crew.

The final shocker came when the vendor wanted to plug-in their equipment. They were notified that all equipment to be plugged into an electric outlet must be done by a union electrician.

Once all that was paid for and everything was set up, the vendor asked for a picture of water and some cups. They would be notified this will be supplied at a cost.

This entire procedure seemed like we were sitting in the middle of an earthquake. When we held the conventions in the Catskills, everything was included with the hotel and the vendors handled their own stuff without any additional cost. All the vendors notified us that the situation is in violation of the contract. After the convention, we had to discuss this issue in detail. Since this convention was held in Manhattan, the attendance was extremely larger due to the attendance of the draftsmen and other architectural firm employees that were never able to attend conventions held upstate New York. After a number of sleepless nights, we came to the bottom line of dollars and cents. Most of the additional earnings from the greater attendance were lost reimbursing the vendors for the additional costs due to the union requirements. Needless to say, from that day on, all conventions went back to the Catskills.

In order to create income and provide a service for all member architects, I hired a publishing house to create a desk calendar and directory. This directory contained a listing of all the architects within the State of New York and their contact information. It also contained a list of all elected officials and department heads on the State level with all their contact information. This publication also was a desk calendar arranged on a daily basis. In order to create income, we sold advertisement space to companies that provided services to the construction industry. We distributed these calendar directories at no cost to all of our members and elected officials throughout the State of New York, as well as to advertisers. This publication was a major success. Everyone loved having access to this information in one publication – list of contact information for the architects, State officials and advertising companies. The money that this directory produced was a major help in running our Albany New York office (Albany is the capitol of NY State).

The Law &/or Codes Are Not Always in the Public Interest

The practice of architecture can be a very rewarding profession as well as having very aggravating moments that in most cases have nothing to do in relation to the design of buildings. Such an incident I lived through was when we receive the commission to change and rehab the complete use of the existing seven story RCA recording studios, into classrooms for Baruch College. The building that was to be completely renovated was located on E. 24th St. in Manhattan just a block away from the main college buildings of Baruch College.

At that time, the State of New York had a law that required any project being funded with State money, comes under the jurisdiction of the Wicks Law. Wicks Law states that all trades working on the project shall be prime contractors. Construction projects not under the Wicks Law have one prime contractor that is responsible for the complete construction of the project. That prime contractor is usually the general construction contractor who then hires all other subcontractors such as the plumbing contractor, the electrical contractor, the heating, ventilating and air-conditioning contractor etc. The general construction contractor is then responsible for all coordination and operation of the entire project. Under the Wicks Law, all the contractors are prime contractors. They are paid directly by the owner and not under the supervision of a general contractor. They become the only ones responsible for the coordination an operation of their trade. Under the Wicks Law, there is no one boss coordinating the entire construction effort. These projects are a nightmare for the architects and the owners.

There is another stipulation that governs these projects that are required by the architectural specifications. That stipulation is called 'Liquidated Damages'. Liquidated damages states that the project must be completely finished with all government approvals for occupancy by the owner on a specific date that is included in the specifications. It is also specified, that if the contractor fails to meet that completion date, he shall be charged a fee for 'Liquidated Damages' every day until the project is finished. This could be $1000 per day, or whatever number is agreed to in the contract, until the building is turned over to the client. In addition, if the contractor completed the building and turned it over to the client before the approval completion date, then the contractor is entitled to a bonus of $1000, whatever number is agreed to, per day.

Under these conditions, the aggravating ploys and construction maneuvers are practiced by all the prime contractors. They find ways to extend the final completion date to lessen the chance of paying the liquidated damages. It also gives them an opportunity to complete the project before the date of liquidated damages so they can receive a bonus.

Back to the construction of the Baruch project: Construction contracts were awarded and the games began. The first thing that had to be done was to demolish all walls, partitions and all of the facilities within the building. This process was in the second or third day when I get my first aggravating phone call. All the prime contractors put an official notice that construction has stopped and therefore the completion date had to be adjusted. I rushed down to the site to find out what the crisis was.

There I see in the middle of the floor, a huge pile of construction debris from the ripped down walls, ductwork, plumbing fixtures, electrical cables and the rest. All this debris was piled in one nice huge package in the middle of the floor. What's the problem I asked? I was then notified that all debris has to be removed from the site so they can continue their work. I then quoted my specifications that stated that the contractors are responsible to remove and dispose of all building debris off-site in a proper legal manner. All the contractors agreed that's what they have to do.

The plumbing contractor said he could not remove this debris because a general contractor put all the sheet rock on top of his plumbing waste. The electrical contractor said he could not dispose of his material because the plumbing contractor had all his waste mixed in with the electrical contractor's waste. And so on. It was clear to see that this was a concerted effort by all the contractors to be able to stop work and therefore extend the completion date. This was almost mutiny. I stated that I will get a waste management contractor to remove all the waste material and back charge each contractor 25% of the cost since all contractors waste was involved. I heard a loud 'NO' from the electrical contractor first. I will not pay 25%. I only have about 5% of that debris bundle. There were more games and distraction to waste time. Now you can see the aggravating situation that that exists. After many negotiations, it was finally agreed by all parties that a new completion date be established and all the prime contractors will coordinate amongst themselves to remove and dispose of all debris off the site. The building went full blast ahead with the cooperation of all contractors, so they could beat the new construction date and get the bonuses. The practice of architecture is more than drawing pretty pictures.

Once the building construction was 100% completed and all required conditions were met by all the contractors, the building was turned over to the State of New York and Baruch College moved in. Furniture began arriving and was distributed throughout the building by use of a large fright elevator. The elevator was part of the original building and was rehabilitated for the new occupants to use. A number of the college staff started to outfit all their equipment and furniture throughout the building. All went well by the coming weekend, when everybody took a break.

On Monday morning, I received a frantic phone call from one of the Deans that was moving into the building. He informed me of the unbelievable happenings that took place over the weekend. It seems that a truck was driven onto the freight elevator and taken to the top floor of the building. The thieves involved methodically loading up all the new furniture and other items onto the truck floor by floor, and then left an empty building. The police were called. I made my way down to the building. Sure enough the building was void of any furniture, filing cabinets and all the goodies that should be in the building. I was standing in the freight elevator talking to the Lieutenant of the Police Department. I noticed that on the floor of the freight elevator there were tire tracks that were etched into some mud on the floor of the elevator. I brought this to the Lieutenants attention and asked him if they could use this evidence in locating the truck and the people who conducted this robbery. The Lieutenant looked at me with a smile on his face and firmly said, "Do you know how many of the situations I see in a day? Do you think we have time to get into all those details?" He then walked away, got into his car and drove off. I shrugged my shoulders and went back to my office. You must realize that this is the City of New York and not a Hollywood movie.

I tell the authorities at the College to call their insurance company and start the process going. In time, new furniture and all other items were delivered, the interior decoration was completed and the staff moved in. I never found out who paid to replace all be furniture and equipment. About two weeks after everyone had moved in and the building was in full operation, I got a disturbing call from one of the Deans. It seems that while he was sitting at his desk in his office, a large 40 pound light fixture fell from the ceiling and was swinging by the electrical BX cable. It just missed hitting him in his head. I rushed down to the building to inspect this horrible condition. The superintendent of the building was able to get me a ladder, so I could climb up to the ceiling and determine what happened.

It took me about a minute and a half to fully understand this latest crisis. The ceiling construction was a standard hung ceiling that consistent of metal T-shaped bars suspended from the slab above. Acoustic tiles (2 x 4 foot) were installed in the T-shaped suspended grid. Standard 2 x 4 foot ceiling light fixture were installed in lieu of ceiling tiles where required. This light fixture was supplied with four anchors that are attached to the light fixture and clipped onto the T-shaped suspension system. Once these anchors are in place they lock the T-bars and light fixtures together to prevent the light fixture from falling out of the ceiling. As I inspected the light fixtures, it was plain to see that the contractor never installed the anchors as called for in my specifications.

I instructed my field inspectors to check out the entire building to make sure that these anchors are in place. After the entire building was inspected the final report stated that none of the fixtures had anchors installed as required. Now it is clear, that every light fixture throughout the entire building installed in the hung ceiling is in danger of falling. An emergency meeting was held with representatives from the electrical contractor, New York State Dormitory Authority, the College and I. It was clear to me that the contractor was not in compliance with the contract documents and has created a dangerous situation. I stated that the contractor has full responsibility to install all those anchors throughout the building and create a safe condition in conformance with the contract documents.

The contractor agreed to do the work, if he were paid eight dollars a fixture to cover his costs. I refuse to approve any payment to the contractor to perform this work. After much heated conversation, the meeting ended with a disagreement between the Dormitory Authority and me. The Dormitory Authority was willing to pay the contractor to do the work. I felt this was an injustice and the contractor should not be paid for work that was called for in the contract. He shouldn't be paid for work done incorrectly. In my opinion, he deliberately did not install the clips to save money. Therefore I refuse to approve the payment. The Dormitory Authority stated that without my signature of approval they could not make any payments. The contractor took me aside and suggested that if I approve the eight dollars per fixture he would pay me two dollars per fixture. I don't remember how many hundreds of fixtures were in this building but that can add up to quite a bit of money. As calmly as I could, I turned down his offer and directed him to start installing all those anchors immediately without any payment. The meeting broke up and I went back to my office.

About 20 minutes after I arrived at my office, my phone rang. On the other end was a very prominent influential New York State Senator who was an acquaintance of mine. He said, "Al, what are you doing to my boy?" I was taken back by the phone call. He was trying to influence me to approve the payment. I said nothing for a few seconds. Then with a little anger in my voice I said, "Senator are you part of this payoff?" The phone then slammed down on his end and I gently hung up the phone on my end. A few minutes later I got a call from the Commissioner of the New York State Dormitory Authority informing me that he received authorization to override my position and paid the contractor. If there were any repercussions because of this payment, that would be the Dormitory Authority's problem. The contractor finished all the work, took the money and as they say, smiled all the way to the bank.

   This project was funded by the New York State Dormitory Authority. The Commissioner of the Dormitory Authority has the last word in all decisions in relation to the design and construction of this project under State law and codes. A major disagreement occurred between the Commissioner and me in reference to a number of items in relation to the design of this project. The Commissioner insisted that I design a monumental stair going through the entire building. I objected to this design because it was not legal under the New York City building code. A monumental stair that would be open on all floors creates a chimney like effect. If there was a fire within the building, the fire can rush up the staircase and spread the fire throughout the building very quickly. New York City building code states that all such stairs shall be completely protected as a three-hour enclosure.

The Commissioner stated that this project falls under New York State laws and requirements. New York State, as well as Federal projects, are exempt from complying with local building codes. Based on that stipulation, the Commissioner could direct me to create that open staircase. I still objected, because while the open stair might qualify under the State requirements, it is still a dangerous situation that could endanger the safety of all occupants of the building. The Commissioner insisted that I follow his demand. To solve this problem, I stated that I will design the project with the open staircase, if the Commissioner will sign a document that I will prepare. It would state that this is a dangerous situation, even though it is legal, I am designing it under protest as directed by the Commissioner, and I accept no responsibility for any future mishap. The Commissioner agreed. I prepared the document, and he signed it. I designed the building with the open staircase.

The building was finally completed; the State of New York took control and Baruch College moved-in. About four years later I got a call from City University. A very angry voice notified me that I design a dangerous illegal building that does not meet the New York City Building Code. We scheduled a meeting. At that point I found out the problem. The State of New York sold the building to the City of New York. Once the building was transferred, the building came under the jurisdiction of the New York City Building Code and was completely illegal. I simply took out my signed document and turned it over to the powers that be. To try to enclose that staircase and create a legal situation at this time was close to impossible. I just sat there, with a confident smile on my face and said, "Gentlemen, you have a problem." And at that point, I left. I never heard anything after that and do not know what was actually done.

Times Change

On the lighter side of the practice of architecture, I remember when the New York City Board of Education changed their entire construction philosophy. In the 1950's to the 1970's, there were a lot of developers building large scale one-family home communities all over the City. Every time one of these communities was built, they sold out mostly to young parents starting families. In no time there was a huge demand for a school in those neighborhoods. Bowing to a local pressure, the Board of Education was building new schools in all those developments. As time went by, those children grew up, and went off to college or joined the work force. Lo and behold, all those schools were empty. The Board of Education was faced with the problem of spending huge amounts of money to build schools that in a number of years would be completely empty. Those schools had to be either sold or demolished or whatever else was necessary from an economic standpoint. To solve the problem of building schools that would become obsolete, the Board of Education decided to rent large spaces such as catering halls or other such facilities to be converted for school use. When the need for the schools has gone, the Board of Education simply does not renew the lease on the building and they are home free.

At that time, the Board of Education rented a large catering facility in the Bronx and I was selected to be the architect to convert that space into an elementary school. I went through the entire process of design and construction and turned the facilities over the Board of Education in time for the beginning of the school year. Everybody was happy with this very successful new school facility. The only item that was left was a final inspection.

There I am, with members of the Board of Education, representatives of the construction company, and the school Principal. The school was in full use and every classroom had a class in session. Our group went through the building, starting on the roof and went down room by room, going through checklists to sign off of everything that had to be done. We came into one classroom that was in session. We quietly walked along the side wall to a closet that we wanted to inspect. On the door of the closet was a large lock that prevented us from opened the door. The superintendent of the building, who was with us, had a large key ring on his belt with many keys to open any lock in any door in the building. We stood there as the superintendent struggled to find the right key to open the door. After about 5 minutes or so, one of the students tapped me on the shoulder and proclaimed in a confident voice, "Do you want me to open that door for you?" I looked at the teacher. She shook her head giving consent. I said to the young man, "Go for it." He walked up to the door, turned his back so we couldn't see what he was doing, and before you count to three, we heard the click. He stepped back and we saw an open door. My next question was, "Why are we spending money putting locks on all those doors, when the kids can open them, but the authorized people can't." That question was never answered.

As I keep writing this book, events that were part of my everyday activities keep popping into my mind. If someone asked me to tell them some of my personal adventures, I would be at a loss. After just finishing the incident I described above with the Board of Education, another chapter in my life comes to my recollection.

To the best of my memory, in the late 1960s or early 1970s, every school building within the entire City of New York was in complete disrepair. Complaints by the various Parent Teacher Associations stated that some of the classrooms could not be used because of unsafe conditions. They had a host of complaints, including water damage in the classrooms and other dangerous physical condition of the schools. The bottom line of the complaints stressed that the schools were unsafe for human occupancy.

There were many serious articles in newspapers and on television that criticized the administration for not taking any action to ensure that all the school buildings in the City of New York were safe. They were to provide a decent environment for learning and living while in school. The political powers started to take notice. In an effort for the administration to obtain a complete unbiased evaluation of the school conditions, a commission was formed and charged to provide a complete study of the existing conditions, the reason for the deterioration and a solution to each problem. The commission was made up of architects, engineers, attorneys, members of large construction companies and educators.

Because I was active with the American Institute of Architects and have designed school buildings, I was appointed to the commission. The commission was formed and gathered to create a program and methodology to meet and surpass all the requirements of the study. With the cooperation of the Board of Education, a schedule was created with times and dates for the full commission to visit the schools and truly understand the problems. The Principals of each school were directed to give us full entry into all areas of the school, to meet and interview teachers and other staff. Once everything was in place, the study began.

On the day we visited the first school, we were greeted by the Principal and her staff at the entrance of the building. We started with a walk around the exterior of the building to get familiar with the grounds. The first thing we noticed were many broken windows, missing glass, the parapets around the roof area showed signs of brickwork that was cracking. As we walked around the building, each of us took notes for later discussion. We were invited into the building and assigned a teacher that was to be our guide to take us through the building and visit any area that we wished to see. As we approached the first classroom, the teacher escorting us around said, "The first thing I'd like you to see is the wall behind the door when the door is completely open." As we approached the classroom the teacher opened the door a full 90° and we looked behind the door. What we saw was the door knob had punched a hole into the plaster wall. The reason for this condition was that a simple doorstop installed on the bottom of the door was missing. If the doorstop would have been replaced, this problem would have been solved.

The teacher proclaimed she put in a number of work orders to have this very inexpensive item installed to no avail. This condition runs throughout the school. The teacher stated that she was willing to buy these doorstops and install them herself. She was told that she was not allowed to do it. That work had to be done by the superintendent in conformance with his contract with the Board of Education. Therefore you can only put in a work order and then it's up to the superintendent to carry it out. She showed us this condition so we could understand the process that was ruining the schools throughout the City. This is a very minor condition, however the system continued throughout including major problems. There are leaks in the roof, cracking parapet, flooring buckling and dangerous conditions to walk on because of water damage. They put in work orders but nothing was ever fixed. We continued walking through the school and were shown many classrooms that were empty because the staff felt it was too dangerous for the students to occupy those rooms. As we inspected each dangerous room, we agreed with the teacher's conclusion.

We went down to the auditorium. There we saw about 40 or 50 children sitting in seats and reading comic books. Some kids were drawing or listening to radios without a teacher in sight. We spoke to a number of students to find out what they were doing in the auditorium at that time. They told us that there was no classroom for them to use. They were told to sit quietly in this auditorium until a teacher and a space can be found for them. They said some days they never find a teacher or classroom, so we were just told to go home.

At that point, the teacher that was guiding us around, looked at us firmly, and in a half cry said, "Give me some decent facilities to teach these kids in. We are ruining these children's lives and all the teachers that I know in this school are very upset. Because of the conditions, we want to teach but we can't".

We continued examining other rooms throughout the school and found exactly what the teacher was talking about. There were buckling floors to such an extent that was impossible to walk on. There were missing windows making the room cold. The wind would be coming in. On a rainy day these rooms would be impossible to use. There were broken tiles all over the place.

We went on the roof. There in the corner, was a pile of dirt that had accumulated from the wind that blew over the roof. It seems that some seeds must've fallen in that pile of dirt and start to grow. There was this 4 foot high tree growing on the roof in the corner of the building. In an effort to find water, the roots were creeping down into the mortar and brick. They were getting any water that was absorbed into the masonry when it rains. Now I know why I saw that cracking and spalling of the brick when we did the walk around the exterior of the building.

I know that the superintendent had not been up on the roof in years to inspect its condition. To make a long story short, we visited many schools in all parts of the City of New York and found the same as well as some other horrible conditions. After checking some the rules and regulations and contracts that the Board of Education had put out, we found the major problem. The Board of Education did not have any superintendent or maintenance people on the staff of the Board of Education or at any school. All the maintenance work was to be the responsibility of an independent contractor superintendent. The Board of Education signed a contract with all the independent contractor superintendents stating that they had full authority for the maintenance of the building and were answerable only to the Chancellor of the Board of Education and not the Principal of the school. This independent contractor was given a fixed amount of dollars that were mutually agreed upon to cover all maintenance work within the building as well as fees and salaries for the maintenance staff.

Since this independent contractor was completely isolated from the executive staff of the school, they made all the decisions as to how and what should be maintained. After our commission examined some of the paperwork and operation of these independent contractors we found that a huge portion of the money that the Board of Education paid them as part of their contract was used for their salaries. The money that was supposed to go for maintenance instead went into the superintendent's pocket. They did very little, if any, maintenance and ruled supreme with full confidence of getting paid but not doing anything for the schools. These findings turned out to be quite a scandal. After our report, it did not take long for this entire system to be changed. The future superintendents were on the payroll of the Board of Education and were answerable to the Principal of the school. Once this was in place, things rapidly started to change and the horrors of the recent past slowly faded away. Although I describe this event in a few paragraphs, the work of the commission ran close to a year before the final report was issued to the Board of Education.

Gentrification Of Manhattan

The practice of architecture at times can drastically change a community and living style for all the residents. My firm received the commission to build a luxury high-rise apartment house on the East side of Manhattan near Cooper Union College. The existing community consisted of 3 to 6 story residential buildings that were constructed many years ago. The inhabitants of this community were in the middle to lower economic strata of society. All the commercial stores in the area were located on the street floor of those buildings. The merchants were all small mom & pop business operations such as carpenter, shoemaker, pharmacy, grocery store, vegetable store, etc. My client had an option to purchase a number of those buildings. His intent was to build a luxury high-rise building like the ones being built in other areas of Manhattan. This proposed project would completely destroy the existing culture of that community. This change which was going on in many areas of Manhattan was called Gentrification.

Before my client actually purchased the land, he was given an option to buy, which gave him time to obtain the necessary approvals from the City needed for him to proceed. The first hurdle was to obtain approval from the Community Board. As the architect, part of my responsibility is to make a presentation to the Community Board, in an effort to gain their approval. Since this proposed project would have a drastic effect on the community, the attendance by the residents living in the area was tremendous. That Community Board meeting overflowed the auditorium.

The members of the audience could be broken down into two groups. One group contained the residents, who were renting their apartments at a cost that they could afford. The other group was made up of the property owners, who stood to receive large payments for the sale of their property. The entire auditorium was hot; in both reference to the temperature of the room and the attitude of the attendees. The Chairman of the Community Board made his introductory remarks and then introduced me as the architect to make this presentation.

Within a few minutes of my opening remarks, I heard screams and noticed a number of people in the audience yelling and screaming, as fists were flying. The police quickly sought to restore order so that I could continue with my presentation. The fighting in the room started to escalate. I, as the architect, who was going to create this complete economic change of the community, was to blame, and became the center of their attention. The next thing I saw, were angry faces heading in my direction. Three police officers came up on the stage and physically protected me from the mob while they got me to an exit. The police officers escorted me to my car and watched me drive away with the sigh of relief. As an end to this saga, the residents of the community won the dispute and the building was never built.

AIA Symposium To Expo 70, Osaka Japan

On the lighter side of my life, experiencing travel comes to mind. In 1970, Japan was a host to a World's Fair called Expo 70. It was a gigantic international event that attracted people from all over the world. The American Institute of Architects, of which I now was a member, decided to have a seminar which would take place in Japan, Hong Kong and Bangkok. Since this was a seminar, it was tax deductible. The American Institute of Architects arranged to have our own 747 to accommodate the 200 architects and their wives on this trip. We started the trip in Japan to visit Expo 70. After a long plane ride to Japan, we checked into the hotel to relax for half a day. After our rest period, we were off to see the town. Our first adventure was to go to Expo 70 itself and visit the American Pavilion. We loaded the buses, with smiles in anticipation.

Arriving at the Expo, we were able to get into the gate. We noticed the hundreds and thousands of people that were on these grounds, visiting all the different exhibits from around the world. Our group proceeded to the American Pavilion. We were out of our element and even had to figure out which side was up on the map. We knew we were somewhere in Asia. That accomplished, we finally located the proper direction and off we went.

Arriving at the American Pavilion, we saw that the line of people waiting to get in was miles long. We could not see the end of the line. One of the architects with us was a U.S. Army Colonel in the reserves. He announced, "Get me to a telephone. I'll pull rank and we will get in". As we were standing around the phone, we heard him say, "This is Colonel Arbite. I am outside the US Pavilion and I want to speak to somebody to get me and my group into the exhibit hall." We were all standing around the phone, listening to him try to convince somebody to do something, since he is the Colonel.

I noticed a back door to the Pavilion. I walked up to the door and gently knocked on it to see what happened. The door opened and the uniformed guard said to me, "Can I help you sir." "Yes", I said, "I am with the American Institute of Architects. Our group is trying to find our representative with the paperwork, so we can enter without standing on the large line". I continued, "I don't know what happened to our representative, so we are stranded out here". He said, "No problem. Get your people and come on in". I went over to the phone. I said, "Everybody keep your mouth closed and follow me." Everyone followed me into the pavilion!!

We walked into the Pavilion and were guided down the corridor to the balcony. Little did we know, but this was the VIP entrance. It seems that the Japanese visitors knew this was the VIP entrance. Since we had just entered through the VIP entrance, they assumed we were VIPs and rushed us for autographs. We all stood and signed autographs. We chuckled when someone said, "Let's sign Mickey Mouse". Poor Colonel Arnold Arbite. He wasn't laughing and didn't say much. We had a wonderful visit to the American Pavilion. When we were all done with sightseeing at the fair, we loaded our buses and went back to the hotel. The bus approached the hotel and came to a stop behind a number of other buses. These were from other tours that were in front of us. Little by little we inched forward, getting closer to the hotel.

On these tours, every bus had a guide. The guide was usually a young lady with the flag at the end of the stick. The flag had a color, our flag was red. If you're ever moving with the group, you have to make sure that you follow that red flag or whatever flag represents your group. If you get mixing in another group, you could end up in another hotel in another country and you will not be smiling.

The bus got close enough, so the bus driver felt he could back into an open space. We all got out of the bus and stood on the side as our little Japanese girl guide with the red flag directed the bus driver to back up into his very tight parking space. I was standing towards the back of the bus and I could see the other end of the bus that our little girl with the flag could not see. She kept telling the driver to back up. I was just standing there, sort of aware of the situation, but not really paying attention. All of a sudden, I don't know how this ever happened, I opened my mouth and I yelled out, "Jeda Mati Cudisai". I don't know how you would spell Japanese word sounds into English. What I said was, "Please stop the bus". The bus driver hearing me, slammed on the brakes and stopped the bus, inches before he would have mashed into the parked car. Everybody looked at me and said, "You speak Japanese?" I said, "No." If you asked me at that time to tell a bus driver in Japanese to stop the bus, I would not have the slightest idea what to say. Evidently that phrase was buried in my mind from the Spoken Japanese lesson I took when I was in the Army 20 years ago. That phrase just stayed hidden in my brain and came out all by itself at the proper moment. The human brain is some magnificent organ!

My friend Arnold Arbeit was also a professor at NYU. He had a student whose parents lived in Hong Kong. He looked up his student's parents. We met them and embarked on a private, behind the scenes, tour of the places and scenes in Hong Kong that tourists never see. It was a real eye-opener. This trip Included meeting various government officials from the Hong Kong Housing Authority. They took us on a tour of different housing that they were building for poor families. The first building they took us to was a very nice piece of architecture and was done very tastefully. We went inside to see one of the apartments. Our host was very proud. He opened the door and showed us his home saying, "This is an apartment for a family of four people." It was one 10' x 20' room with a small balcony about 3 feet deep. He explained that at night, they move the table to one side, open up the sleeping blankets, and spend the night lying on the floor. In the morning they roll up the sleeping blankets and move the table to the middle of the room for the day's use.

On the balcony was a small toilet. There was also a special fitting on the railing for the resident to insert a pole that would project out of the building where the tenant could hang their laundry to dry. This apartment, he explained, was an extreme upscale facility compared to the previous living conditions for these people. We all stood there quietly and politely and did not criticize. Each culture has their own standards. The other thing that blew my mind, was when they took us so a new construction site. The workmen were busy installing a brick curtain wall on which seemed to be a 10 story building. The thing that amazed me was the bamboo poles tied together as scaffolding, going up the complete side of the building. I noticed about 30 middle-aged women with wicker baskets on their backs that an attendant filled with bricks. Once their basket was full, these women would climb up that scaffolding to deliver the bricks to the bricklayers. This method of construction was extremely dangerous! It would never be allowed in the United States. Why dozens of people would be willing to do this type of construction is beyond me. But again, each culture has their own standards.

The thing that stood out in my mind the most in Bangkok was our trip up the river. We were put in large canoe-type boats that were powered by outboard motors. We were warned to not eat anything that you couldn't peel the skin off of without touching the interior edible portion. That set the stage for a hungry afternoon. The thing that stood out in my mind as we traveled up the river, were the people that lived on the river. They drove poles into the ground under the water and built platforms on top as a living base. They had some form of roof on top which created a home. The river was used for bathing, soaping up anything freely, washing vegetables and any other food. Washing your laundry and everything else was done right in the river at your feet. All of the water was contaminated, yet this is where they washed their food and clothes. How people survive that way of living without dying of some sort of disease is beyond me. Again, everybody has their own standards.

Name In The Newspaper Competition

Back home on Staten Island, all was going well. Meryl was involved in a bowling league. She traveled to other parts of the City in bowling competitions and seemed to be pretty good at the sport. At the end of each game, the results were printed in our local newspaper, The Staten Island Advance. Inevitably, they would screw up the spelling of her name. That did not fit very well with my daughter. It was a constant fight with the newspaper to make sure that they got it correct.

My named appeared enough times that eventually the spelling was right on the mark. At the same time, I was getting deeply involved in politics and my activities started to appear in the paper. Please note that this local paper, The Staten Island Advance, was published daily and was only distributed on Staten Island. Being a small town, if you sneezed three times, that was a headline. They were always looking for things to write about, making it very easy to get your name in the paper. There were a number of articles and reports on my political doings, as well as some of the other organizations I was involved with.

The situation grew into a loving but fierce competition between my daughter, Meryl, and me. In the early days of this competition, she couldn't come near me. She tried hard. Little by little, she became involved in as many organizations as I did. She became a leader in these organizations, and little by little, the number of times her name was in the paper crept up to mine. It got to a point where she buried me. One day I raised a white flag and surrendered. She had the biggest smile that warmed my heart. Just to give you an idea how popular she was on Staten Island, because of all of her activities in those many organizations, they named a street after her after she passed away, 'Dr. Meryl J. Efron Way'.

She unfortunately passed away at the age of 55. We never did find out why she passed away so young. When I was in my prime in politics, our Borough President passed away. His wife approached me to get a street named after Tony. I tried very hard. I spoke to the mayor. I spoke to Counsel people. I spoke to the Commissioners. I could not get a street named in honor of a past Borough President. To my delight, Meryl's friends had no problem getting a street on Staten Island named in her honor. If you go on the South Shore of Staten Island today, near Richmondtown, you will find a section of Richmond Road near Arthur Kill Road has been renamed, 'Dr. Meryl J. Efron Way'.

Marybeth (on right) and Lizzy with City official at sign mounting ceremony

Meryl's dearest friend, Adrian

The Adventures Of Boy Scouting

On the other hand, my loving son Paul took another route. He became a Cub Scout and then a Boy Scout. When he moved from Cub Scouts to Boy Scouts, I started to get a little involved with the Boy Scouts. The Scoutmaster resigned, to this day I don't remember why, but I found myself as Scoutmaster. As Scoutmaster, I decided that one weekend every month of the year we will go out camping. And we did. We were out there in the freezing winter, the burning summer, and the delightful fall & spring. We were out there and all had a great time.

At times when we were at our meeting hall on Staten Island, we would reminisce on some of our camping experiences. The best times that we remembered were those when we had some of the worst conditions, like when the temperature was close to the freezing point or our tents blew way in the wind. We learned how to thaw out frozen water in cardboard containers over a fire, while keeping the cardboard from burning. The stories we told had us laughing so hard. They were great adventures and we had great times.

I remember very clearly, taking my troop to Ten Mile River Boy Scout Summer Camp. We all looked forward to the day of arrival at the camp. We found our campsite, got ourselves unpacked, and ready to start a great week in the woods. The first chore was to bring the Troops down to the waterfront to be instructed on all safety procedures while in and around the lake. The waterfront Scout Leader assigned each camper to a buddy – The Buddy System. That way there always was somebody looking after someone else in case of a problem.

One of the campers said he forgot something that was back in his tent. He asked me for permission to run back to the tent, which was about 25 yards from the waterfront. I could see him the entire time. As he approached the tents, he yelled out in pain and fell to the ground. I yelled to the waterfront counselor to watch the rest of my boys and ran up to see what happened to the boy lying on the dirt. He told me he thought he was bitten by a snake! I looked at his foot and saw two fang marks with blood coming out. At that point, I was only wearing my bathing suit which was soaking wet because I was in the water with the boys. I picked up my injured Scout, notified the waterfront counselor that I'm going to the first aid station.

Arriving at the first aid station, I announced that I have a scout that was bitten by a snake. To my horror I was told that they were not equipped to handle that situation and was told to go to the local doctor. They gave me the doctor's name and address and I was on my way. I quickly put the boy in my car and drove to the doctor's office at top speed.

When I arrived at his office, I quickly ran through the crowded waiting room. Since I felt this was an emergency, I banged on the doctor's door and he quickly opened it. I explained my situation and told him to please do whatever has to be done to save this boy. Much to my surprise, the doctor informed me that he had a general practice on Staten Island and just moved to this location. He told me he had no idea what to do for a snake bite. He directed me to the nearest hospital where they would be able to take care of him.

I hopped in my car, still just dressed in a wet bathing suit, and went speeding down the highway until I found the hospital. I ran in and said, "I have an emergency!" We got to see the doctor immediately. I made sure that my voice was strong enough that the bureaucrat standing behind the desk would be intimidated and get a doctor. It worked. The doctor took the kid into an exam room. He informed me that he was not allowed to take care of the boy, unless he has the parent's permission. I noticed a phone on the wall. I quickly picked up the receiver, and just like in the movies, I pretended to dial a phone number, while one on my fingers was on the lever that disconnected the line. The doctor believed that I was talking to the mother. I told the doctor that we have the mother's permission and hung up. The doctor told me to wait outside and they would take care of the boy.

I sat in the air conditioned waiting room, in a wet bathing suit, and shivered from head to toe anxiously awaiting the outcome. All of a sudden another panicky person came into the doctor's office holding a boy with a fish hook in his cheek, just below the eye. The bureaucrat sitting behind the desk said, "You have to sit down and wait until I can get to you". I just couldn't believe that any human could act as this bureaucrat did. I was going to tell the fellow holding the kid with the fish hook, to be more forceful. But I decided to mind my own business and let the doctor concentrate on my patient.

After about 15 minutes, the doctor came out and notified me that my boy is okay. I can take him back and have a great time at the camp. I guess the bite wasn't from a dangerous snake. This episode gave me not only mental stimulation, but much physical stimulation. When I got back to the camp, I realized that no one at the hospital asked me for money or insurance information. I guess I must've really scared those bureaucrats.

One day, at a scout meeting on Staten Island, we decided to take a trip to upstate New York and shoot the rapids in canoes. This sounded like a great adventure and we started to plan. One of the other Scoutmasters that I knew was an expert in shooting the rapids in a canoe. I asked him if he could work with us to give my troop some practical experience before going on this trip. I made arrangements with the Jewish Community Center to use the pool one evening, to give the boys practical experience with a canoe in water.

We assembled all the boys at the pool. My expert brought in a canoe and placed it in the pool. He took two boys at a time and put them in the canoe and instructed them on the proper handling of that vessel. He deliberately turned over the canoe so they fell in the pool, to teach them how to right the canoe and get back in after capsizing. After that, all the boys felt they were experts and ready for the trip. I asked my expert if he would join us on the trip to make sure we had no problems. He agreed. One Friday evening, we packed up the cars and were ready to make an early start in the morning.

After about a four and a half-hour ride, we arrived at the Riverfront and parked our vehicles. We loaded our gear onto their bus and they drove us to the starting point on the river. There we rented canoes to accommodate two boys per canoe. We loaded up the canoes and off we went.

Just before we came to the first set of rapids, our expert advisor instructed all the boys to line up on the river bank. They were going to demonstrate how to negotiate the first set of rapids. Our expert did not realize that his canoe, which he brought with him, had a very shallow depth. On his demonstration run, water was splashing into the canoe over the sides, and little by little, his canoe filled with water. They never capsized their canoe, but were swamped. They kept going down the rapids until all we could see were their heads and shoulders above the water. I looked at my young, inexperienced scouts, and saw a little concern on their faces.

I took control and told all the boys to get in their canoes. I took the youngest boy in my canoe and I would be stationed behind the group. That way I could keep an eye on everybody and make sure nobody got lost, ran into trouble or fell behind. I instructed them to keep paddling because the minute you stop paddling, the water takes over and you are lost. The other quick instruction was, when you see the water splashing over the rocks, beware because the rocks are about 2 - 3 feet closer to you than the splashing water, so steer the canoe accordingly.

"Okay guys. Let's go." And off we went. Those boys paddled like there was no tomorrow and we went full speed through the rapids. This scene was a thing of beauty. We kept going without any mishap to the end of the rapids. The canoes that we rented had higher walls than our expert's canoe and took much less water over the sides from splashing.

Later, the water was calm and we had to paddle for quite a long distance until we reached the beach where the bus was parked to pick us up. There, the owner of the canoes would retrieve the canoes. We paddled and paddled and paddled. It started to rain, just a light drizzle slowly coming down. We kept going and I kept counting 10 canoes make sure we didn't lose anybody. About an hour and a half later, we were getting near our final destination. I counted 10 canoes. At that point there was a turn in the river. We made the turn in the river to our landing area where our vehicles were. We beached the canoes. Just to make sure, I gave one more count and to my horror I only counted nine canoes. One canoe was missing! That means two scouts are out there, maybe on the river or maybe IN THE RIVER.

There were three parents with me. Their boys had made it to the beach. I was not aware of who was missing. I jumped in the canoe and was going to paddle upstream. One of the fathers was yelled at me said, "No way can you paddled upstream. You'll never get there." "So what am I supposed to do? Let the boys drown?" I started paddling as fast as I could, when all of a sudden there I see the 10th canoe coming around the corner. Who do you think was in it? It was my son and his friend. In a very thankful and angry voice at the same time I said, "What happened?" They said they got tired and stopped for a few minutes. They didn't realize the end was just beyond the next curve in the river. I do not know how I missed that canoe leaving the group.

I sat down on a rock to let my whole body calm down and get ready for a trip back to Staten Island. All the boys packed their gear into the cars. I had four boys in my car and off we went. By this time the rain was coming down very heavy.

About halfway home, to make matters worse, which I thought could not get any worse, I got a flat tire. The rain was coming down very heavy, so I told the boys to stay in the car. I was able to jack up the car enough to get the tire off of the ground. However, the tire iron wrench that goes around the nuts to remove the tire must have been stripped. I couldn't get the nuts off. I told the boys to sit tight and keep the doors locked and I was going to walk back about 1 mile where there was a gas station. I was able to reach the gas station and asked the attendant to borrow a wrench. He said I could, but I had to leave a $20 deposit, which I gratefully did and went back to the car. I was able to change the tire and get the car moving again.

We arrived home and all the boys met their parents with great smiles and said they had a wonderful time. In the future, when we discussed some of our adventures, we always mention this one, because of all the problems that happened that made it very interesting. Again, mental and physical stimulation.

Paul was very active with the Boy Scouts and became an Eagle Scout. That was a great achievement if you are familiar with the Boy Scouts. And I remained Scoutmaster. By this time, Paul made a great discovery of life. He found a thing called girls. I guess he grew up. Once girls started coming to his life, he disappeared from scouting, but I was still Scoutmaster. I was in so many organizations and so busy with my architectural practice, that being the Scoutmaster and my son is not even in the troop was getting to be too much. However, none of the other parents would touch the job and take over for me. I struggled on as Scoutmaster for I guess for 3 or 4 years. Finally some young friend who just turned 18, decided to be nice to get involved in scouting. Before he knew what he was in for, he became the new Scoutmaster. I was free. Paul in the meantime stuck with his girls and also managed to be on the swimming team in high school and all was well.

Sometimes all was not well. I remember one incident with Paul, a student of New Dorp High School, who decided to take a day off and go visit friends that went to Tottenville High School. In my political organization, I had a number of school teachers that were like my private spies. So any time Paul moved around in a manner that was not typical, I got the word. I remember that evening when Paul came home I asked, "How was school?" He said, "Fine." Then I asked, "Which school?" He knew I had him. He was a fantastic son that Harriet and I were always proud of him. He was always a joy.

Heimlich Maneuver

The area that we live in on Staten Island had a homeowners association. One day, an election was being conducted to vote in all the offices that were to run the organization for the next year. My name was put in nomination for President of the organization. Since no other person was nominated against me, I was unanimously elected.

At that time I also served on the board of Staten Island University Hospital. I learned that the hospital had a team of volunteers that conducted classes on how to give first aid to people suffering from drowning, choking, and similar problems. After about two months into my term as President of a homeowner's association, I arranged for the hospital to give our full membership a series of classes. At the conclusion of those teaching sessions, we all receive certificates noting that we were capable of providing emergency care for those conditions. When the last meeting was over, Harriet and I went to a local restaurant for dinner. We proudly carried our certificates of graduation.

We ordered our food and drinks and were discussing the valuable information we learned from our class. One of the items that we learned was that if someone is choking, they would put their hands on their throat to indicate the problem since they were not able to speak. The waiter brought our food and we began to eat. All of a sudden Harriet was making a strange sound from the mouth and her hands were on her throat. I quietly inquired, "Are you okay Harriet?" She stamped her feet as I quietly looked on. With a heavy cough, she was able to clear her throat and the crisis was over. Harriet, in a not so pleasant voice, said, "I was choking and couldn't breathe. Didn't you see my hands on my throat?" I realized what had happened. I deserve to completely flunk the course. I surrendered my certificate, the one we just worked so hard for, that certified my ability to be able to do what was necessary under the circumstances, to Harriet. Through the years, I was never allowed to forget my brilliant action that day.

My Invitation To The White House

At this time, my co-leader, Barbara, and I were becoming well-known for the work in the Democratic Party. We were referred to as the Dynamic Duo. Jimmy Carter had just completed his first term as President of the United States. As was expected, Jimmy Carter ran for a second term. The problem he had was that the economy was in turmoil. Interest rates were about 18% to 20%. Inflation was hurting the average American citizen and they were angry.

In addition, the Shah of Iran was deposed and the religious right of that country took control. The new leadership of Iran was not friendly to the US. Trouble was brewing. A group of Iranian students broke into the United States Embassy and took a number of employees of the embassy as hostage. We saw horrible scenes on TV of what was going on in Iran at the time. Just about every news program on television was covering this event. There was a lot of pressure on Jimmy Carter to do something to free those hostages. He was so consumed with the day-to-day operation of the hostage situation that he was unable to campaign for re-election.

Jimmy Carter tried hard to find a way to free the hostages and came up with a solution that was a disaster. He had Special Forces try to fly secretly into Iran an attempt to rescue the hostages. The whole operation was a fiasco because the plane's propellers kicked up the sand, which then clogged the engines and the planes would crash. Carter had to send in another force to rescue the rescuers. In the meantime, Jimmy Carter's opponent, Ronald Reagan was running a tough campaign and had complete control of the situation. Jimmy Carter felt that he had to do something to get his campaign going. Since he did not have the time to campaign nationwide, he came up with a solution. He told the Secret Service to invite approximately 10 Democratic leaders from each State to have lunch with him at the White House, one State at a time. His though was to get these leaders to stimulate the campain.

When the Secret Service went over the list of who the hotshot Democrats in the State of New York were, to my amazement and delight, I was one chosen to have lunch at the White House with the President. Unfortunately the schedule that was set for me to attend this luncheon was the same time I was going to be overseas in China preparing for new project. I had to decline the invitation. I guess I missed out on a great adventure of having my photograph taken at the White House with the President. However, just knowing that I was selected as part of this group, from all of the Democrats throughout New York State was very gratifying.

Your Girlfriend, Not Your Wife!!!

On a lighter note, one day I was home in our kitchen with Harriet listening to the radio while doing our household chores. We heard an ad about a restaurant in Manhattan not too far from my office called 'A Little Table In The Corner'. The commercial sounded very interesting and struck our interest. I told Harriet that we should try that place the next time she comes into the City. "Great Idea", she said, "I was looking for a new restaurant." We made a reservation for dinner on a day that Harriet came to the City.

That afternoon in my office, the phone rang. It was a friend of mine that I was deeply involved with in the Democratic Party from Staten Island. We were discussed political business when I happened to mention that I was going to have dinner at 'A Little Table In The Corner'. My friend asked, "Who are you going with?" I told him that Harriet was coming up to the City and she and I are going to dinner there. I heard a little chuckle from my telephone companion and I asked, "What's the problem?" He told me, in a strong voice, that you do not take your wife to that restaurant. When you are married, that where you take your girlfriend. I told him that I am happily married and I do not have a girlfriend and was just going to a restaurant for dinner. Since it is a restaurant in Manhattan, and had an ad on radio, it must be a legitimate business. He said, "Al, when you get there you will know what I'm talking about." At this point I didn't know whether to become concerned or just interested.

We kept our reservation. I met Harriet at my office and we walked down to his questionable restaurant. At the entrance of the restaurant, there was just a plain simple door with a doorbell right in the middle of the door. I rang the doorbell and the door opened. There stood a nicely dress man with a smile on his face standing at the entrance. He was holding a reservations book. "The name on the reservation", he asked. I told him, "Efron." "Oh yes", he said after checking. "This way", he said as we entered. He took us down a corridor, guiding us with a flashlight because the space was in total darkness. I could not see a single light in any direction. There was no doubt about it. You could not take one step without a flashlight to walk safely in the entire area. We heard very low muffled voices as we entered the restaurant. He took us to an area. All we could see was a wood beaded curtain hanging in front of us. He opened the curtain and there was a table for two people. There was a very small light that looked like a doorbell mounted on the wall. Harriet and I sat down and the gentleman said, "No one will come to this table once I close the curtains. If you want a waiter, press that lit button. If you do not press that button no one will bother you."

We sat there in the dark, chuckling and realizing that my friend was right. This place is where you bring your girlfriend. We quickly pressed the button and sure enough a waiter approached. We picked out something from the menu that we could hardly read and placed our order. What we ordered, we did not know because was too dark to actually read the menu. We sat there, trying to hold in laughter as not to disturb the rest of the people. They were all hidden away in each little table in all the many corners in this establishment. I would leave what they were doing up to your imagination. The food came, was placed on the table, and the curtain closed. We tried to eat some of it. It just felt like this is really not the place for people like us. We quietly opened the curtain, got up, spotted the waiter, asked him to put his flashlight on so we could pay our bill and please lead us out of the place.

Just a follow up on this story, the fellow I spoke to on the phone that told me that 'you do not bring your wife to this place', was caught a few years later in the following story.

Stupid Elected Officials

My friend changed political parties from Democrat to Republican and ran for Congress. He was elected as a Congressman from Staten Island and started his political career. If my memory is correct, I think he was in his second term as Congressman. One day, he and a number of friends who live on Staten Island, went to a party that was held in Washington DC. On the way home, his friend said, "Let me drive you home because you've had too much to drink, and I don't think you are in the proper condition to drive." "No", he insisted, "I am okay and in full control." He took off by himself. Sure enough, having bad luck, an office of the law stopped him and he was arrested for driving under the influence of alcohol. When an elected official on the federal level finds himself in this type of situation, the first thing he always does his calls his Chief Of Staff. The Chief Of Staff is the person who has all the connections to take control of the situation and make it all go away. But the Congressman did not do that.

Instead he called this woman who then rushed down to the Police Station where he was held. When the press found out that a Congressman was arrested on drunk driving charges, they sent their reporter down to check out the situation. This is a normal situation. When the press got down there, they saw this woman trying to get everything squared away with the police officer behind the desk. What the press usually does, they start looking into the situation. Who was this woman? What they found was, to say it gently, a bombshell. It seems that this woman was his lover. He also had a daughter with this woman and he was the father. They also found out that this woman set up housekeeping and was living as if they were married.

It turned out that my friend, the Congressman, was going back and forth between his family on Staten Island and his family in Washington, DC. He should've stayed at 'A Little Table In The Corner'. It would've been safer. To make a long story short, everything got out of hand and was so bad that he was forced to resign his seat in Congress. It was about this time when I was spending more time in Tucson, Arizona and lost track of what happened to him.

In Keeping With Bad Political Stories, Here Is Another One

Before the incident with the Republican Congressman that I described above, we had a Congressman who was a Democrat as well as a West Point graduate and decorated combat Captain in the U.S. Army that was retired. He and I were civil to one another but did not see eye to eye on the art of working with people. The problem was that he was 'gung ho' on his background in the army. I was a Private who deliberately stayed at that low rank and put in my two years to get out alive and in one piece. The Army life was not for me. My friend, the Congressman, felt he was still an officer in the Army and everybody he interacts with would be subject to his command. That just doesn't work in civilian life. Anyway, it is a juicy story.

When the Congressman was in college, he was classmates with a fellow who became President of Panama a number of years later. At that time, Jimmy Carter was President. Carter was trying to stop the drugs coming in from Panama. It seems that the President of Panama at that time was a driving force in the drug business in Panama. He was sending their drug products to the United States. Carter instructed the State Department to set up a meeting with the President of Panama, to try to convince him to stop the narcotics trade to the United States.

When the delegation arrived to meet the President, to their surprise and horror, this Congressman was sitting next to the President of Panama and was taking Panama's position. This is not what makes the President of the United States very happy. This episode was burnt into the minds of the people involved.

Sometime later, in an effort to stop the corruption in government, the FBI set up a sting operation. This operation was called Abscam. Just as an aside, this operation made huge headlines and later was made into a very successful movie, American Hustle. It involved a number of politicians from New Jersey, New York and Staten Island. The FBI set up a room in a hotel that was completely outfitted with hidden cameras and microphones to record everything that went on. They dressed the FBI operators as Arabs coming to this country and wanting to do business in the United States. One by one they invited Mayors,

Congressmen and Senators into this well-documenting room. They offered them bribes for favors in reference to any construction that they wanted to do in this country. To make a long story short, it was an extremely successful operation and I forget exactly how many, but several elected officials went to jail.

As far as this Congressman is concerned, because of the incident with the President of Panama, he was not a friend of the White House. He was one of those who were invited in and offered a bribe. He accepted the deal and was handed an attaché case that contained $10,000. The FBI arrested him. At the trial, the Congressman's defense was that he never took the money. The money was taken by his aide that was with him. This was quite a lame defense and based on all the video from that room, he was convicted and spent 18 months in prison. I remember meeting him when he just got out of prison. I found it very uncomfortable and did not know what to you say to a disgraced ex-Congressman in that situation. We struggled through some small talk and then parted. I haven't seen him since.

Unfair Legal Decisions

In keeping with the stories that I experienced in my professional career that happened on the negative side of life, this next installment is a doozy. One morning I was in my office when the phone rang. Upon answering, I heard the voice of the New York City Building Department Commissioner. This Commissioner was a friend of mine and we played golf together a number of times. He informed me that we might have a problem with a project that my office designed that had just completed construction. The contractor made an application to receive a Certificate of Occupancy. All C of Os are issued by the Building Department when their inspectors determined that the project has been fully completed and is in compliance with the approved drawings and all zoning and building code conditions. Once a Certificate Of Occupancy is issued, the owners could close on their sales and start moving people into the building.

He told me that Civitas, a neighborhood Civic Association on the upper West side of Manhattan, was taking legal action, stating that the building that just has been completed is not in conformance with the zoning resolution and that 12 stories of the building must be removed. It should be noted that the members of this Civic Association included Norman Lear (television producer), Jackie Onassis (wife of the deceased President John F Kennedy), and other notables. The Commissioner asked me to check out the situation and see what they're talking about. I checked with my partner who was the architect in our office that designed the building. We checked all the records. I checked all zoning requirements and found that everything was in order. I also found a copy of the building permit that was issued by the New York City Department of Buildings which gave us the legal right to commence with construction. Everything was in order, and for the life of me I couldn't figure out why any Civic Association would file such a claim.

I contacted my friend the Commissioner, and told them everything was in order. The Commissioner agreed with me saying all his investigations showed that his department reviewed all our drawings and documents and issued a building permit. Since we found nothing wrong, we decided to wait until we got more information. A few days past, the

City did more investigation into the situation when they discovered the problem.

Civitas felt that the existing zoning resolution allowing the buildings to be built to the height that was specified in the zoning documents was in their opinion 12 stories to high. This Civic Association took action to change the zoning resolution to require all construction in that neighborhood to be lowered by 12 stories. After the necessary public hearings the City granted them the approval and directed the City Planning Commission to update the zoning maps. From then on, all buildings built in that area would be 12 stories lower.

However, when the City Planning Commission prepared the updated zoning drawings, they created an error in drawing the lines determining all the sites that were to be part of this new regulation. The lines that indicated which areas were part of the new zoning, did not include site that my client owned. According to the updated zoning maps, the site that my client owned, which we designed and received approvals from the Building Department, was not governed by this revised new zoning and could be full height. Nobody at the City Planning Commission noticed the error. They issued their maps as legal documents for all architects to follow. The building was 12 stories too tall according to the new law, but not according to the official zoning maps. The Building Department Commissioner told me that we had not made a mistake and the Building Department had not made a mistake in issuing all approvals for constructing the building. It was the City Planning Commission's error. Therefore the Mayor and his attorneys have to do something to resolve this problem. But the building was built and was 12 stories too tall.

In an effort to find the solution for this problem and avoid the horror and humongous expense of removing 12 stories of a high-rise building in Manhattan, I had a meeting with my partners and my client to see what we could propose. My client notified us that he owned a piece of property about two blocks away. After much discussion, we came up with a solution. My client offered to donate the property to the City of New York. My firm would design, without fee, a senior citizen's housing building containing 150 apartments under the federal housing and urban development program known as Section 8, 202. This program was designed to provide housing for low income people who worked all their lives and retired with Social Security as their only income. Living with an income from Social Security would not allow you to acquire any housing in the high cost areas of New York City or any other major urban area in the United States. With this program, the federal government would provide a grant to a legitimate non-profit organization to build the apartment house. The City would then subsidize the cost of the rent that was above 30% of the tenant's income.

I designed a large number of apartment houses under this program with four or five legitimate non-profit organizations. I called the Deputy Mayor of the City of New York, who also happened to be a friend of mine, to arrange a meeting with the Mayor, so we could make this proposal. The meeting was arranged, we made the proposal, it was agreed upon by all parties and we felt the solution should solve the problem. However Civitas turned our proposal down and started legal action. To make a long story short, after about a year of litigation the judge reasoned that the City of New York was the people of New York, and the people of New York are not responsible for errors. He then reasoned through investigation by entities other than the City, that we should have discovered the City's error. This reasoning in my opinion was ridiculous. However, I am not the judge so that decision became law. At a meeting with the Mayor again it was decided that this case should now be turned over to the City's Board of Standards and Appeals for approval of our compromise to build and donate the senior citizens housing project that would be owned by the City and managed by Catholic Charities.

The Board of Standards and Appeals was created by the City to handle community and zoning problems like ours. After about a year of testimony from all parties involved, the Board was ready to announce their decision. Before this decision became public, the Deputy Mayor called me and with a shaken voice said, "Al, I do not know why Mayor Ed Koch did what he just did. I offer you my humble apologies." I asked him what Koch did. The Chairperson of the Board of Standards and Appeals asked the Mayor just what decision does the Mayor want the Board to come up with. At that point, instead of the Mayor stressing the point that we have a proposal that was approved by all parties, he said, "Do what you feel you have to do." That released the Chairperson from approving our proposal and avoiding the wrath of Civitas and their high-powered members. That is what happened.

Now we were informed that we had to remove 12 stories of the building because the City of New York made a mistake but we suffer the damages. We met with our client, worked out all the costs involved and came up with a solution. My office will contribute $6 million dollars, and the developer agreed to contribute the rest of the money that was needed to remove the 12 stories of the building and build additional apartments on some of the remaining land.

My office had professional liability insurance that covered us for situations like this with the maximum of $3 million dollars. My insurance company paid the first $3 million. My partners and I came to an agreement with the developer; we would pay $1 million dollars, the developer would pay $2 million dollars and we would reimburse him the $2 million, with that much worth in professional services over the next eight years. All was agreed, the money was paid and we were on the hook for the next eight years to provide $2 million dollars of free architectural services to my client.

I agreed with my partners that I would be the partner to handle this situation for the next eight years. That meant I could not retire for these entire eight years until all commitments were met. During the next eight years, I provided all the architectural services that my client requested and treated the situation as if it was a normal condition, the same as if we were receiving a full fee. My attitude is that a commitment, no matter how bad, must be honored and treated in the proper manner.

One of the projects that I got involved with in relations to my eight-year obligation to provide architectural work, involved Roseland, a property owned by my client. To those readers of this biography who are not familiar with Roseland, I must bring you up to speed. In the 1940s and 50s Roseland was a very famous dance hall in Manhattan. They used to have the top bands of those days, such as Tommy Dorsey or Harry James, perform at dances held on the weekends. My friends and I used to go to many of these dances to meet girls in a safe environment and dance to these famous orchestras. As I remember attending the dances during those early days at Roseland, the dance floor was huge. There was plenty of room to provide tables where we could sit at and enjoy the conversation with old and new friends. We use to look forward to those great days and time spent at Roseland.

My client spoke to me about the possibility of building a high-rise luxury apartment house on that site. He did not want to demolish Roseland, because it was a moneymaker. It attracted young people who wanted to dance to the music of the day. He asked if it was possible to build this high-rise on top of a one story dance hall. "To create such a structure would be very difficult and expensive. However, let me see what I can do." I made arrangements to visit the dance hall to check out the existing conditions.

On the day of my inspection, I entered through the main entrance and walked into the lobby. I was very disappointed, seeing a dirty, dilapidated lobby that looked nothing like that grand entrance in the days when I used to attend dances. I went to the main dance hall. Another shock! What I saw was a stage, a large dancing area and two huge bars on each side of the room. I said to my client who was accompanying me on this inspection, "Why does the place look so dirty and dilapidated?" He informed me that there was no need to spend the money to fix it up and make it look good. The dances always took place in the evening and the lights were always very very low. You really could not see the condition of the room.

I said, "I do not see any room for table and chairs where the people can congregate and enjoy a drink & conversation. I was informed that nobody sits at the tables at the dances. The band performs on the stage and the huge crowds jam in, body to body, in front of the stage and fill up the entire dance floor. Everyone starts shaking and screaming in place and time with the music. The types of dances in the old days were more personal and romantic.

The people who were not dancing were standing at the bar drinking. Looking around at this facility and listening to my client, as he explained how things worked, I felt like crying. I returned to my office and started to design a system of construction that would accommodate a high-rise on top of the dance hall without affecting the continued use of Roseland for dances. I came up with the system and obtained some preliminary prices and presented it to my client. After much discussion, my client felt that he's making too much money from the dance hall as is and decided not to build the high-rise above.

I remember talking to Harriet about this whole episode. She felt just as I, because we both used to enjoy those great dances with music provided by those famous bands.

The day that the eight years was completed and all commitments had been met, I had a meeting with my client to sign off on this situation. My client looking at me and said, "Al, you were a gentleman and treated us so well and honorably, as if we were a paying client." He continued, "You left me with the feeling of high respect for you and this office." That statement meant more to me than the million dollars that my partners and I had written checks for and the eight years of work that we did without a fee. My reputation means more than any money. Because of that attitude, I'm sure we made up for any losses with all the new work that we were able to get. In addition, this episode in my life did not change my style of living or have any impact on my future success. So in the end all was well.

Bloomingdale's

Another mind-boggling adventure I lived through involved Bloomingdale, the famous department store which was one of our clients. I worked with their design team for number of years doing major renovations throughout the Manhattan store as well as their other stores located in Westchester, New York. I had just finished the design and construction of a completely new restaurant located on the roof of the Manhattan store. We created an entrance from the top floor through the roof to this restaurant, so they could take advantage of the great views. The restaurant was called La Train Bleu. The design of the restaurant was that of an elegant dining car from a height of the railroad era.

At a meeting with the Store's Director of Design to discuss the next project, I was informed that Federated Department Stores just took control of Bloomingdale's. A new CEO was to take charge of Bloomingdale's and was arriving the next day. We agreed to set up a meeting in two weeks to let the new CEO get settled in.

Two weeks later, a meeting was set so that can meet the new CEO and discuss the future construction projects. I was ushered into the conference room and greeted with the existing design team that had just arrived. After a couple of minutes, in walked the new CEO with his design team. At that time I was sitting with the existing design team to my right and the new design team to my left. This arrangement just happened without any forethought. It did not take me long to feel the tension in the air and the rivalry between the two design teams. The new CEO introduced himself and his members, which were followed by introductions from the existing team. The conversation started by the existing team listing the projects that identified should be worked on. I could feel the tension between the two teams as the discussion proceeded. The tension grew and grew and grew to a point where I felt very uncomfortable sitting in between these two unhappy factions. The conversation got even little louder. One member of the new team got up, walked around the table and swung his fist, which landed square on the jaw of one of the members of the existing team, projecting him across the room.

After the commotion died down, the meeting was jarred. Back in my office I told my partner, Peter Claman, about my harrowing experience. I said, "They are too crazy. I'm giving up Bloomingdale's as a client." Peter said that I'm overreacting and if it's okay, he will take over Bloomingdale's. "Peter", I said, "It's all yours."

Sometime later another meeting was called and this time Peter attended. Later that afternoon I was in my office when Peter returned from that morning's meeting at Bloomingdale's. Peter informed me that he was thoroughly convinced that, "Yes. They are crazy and we are officially dropping them as a client." We had no further contact with Bloomingdale's.

The Story Of An Horrible Architectural Blunder
Thank Goodness I Was Not The Architect

In the early 1960s, the Port Authority of New York and New Jersey started the planning process for the construction of the World Trade Center located in lower Manhattan of New York City. In August of 1968, construction started on Tower One. A friend of mine and fellow architect worked for the Port Authority as the architect in charge of this project. He was the eyes and ears of the Port Authority during the entire construction process.

One afternoon he and I were having lunch to discuss an issue that was brewing within the American Institute of Architects. At that lunch, the topic of the construction of the World Trade Center became part of the discussion. He was telling me of this unique design of the building that allows construction to proceed much more rapidly than the standard design. He then invited me to take it a tour of Tower One with him. We set the date for my visit which I anxiously awaited.

On that day we met at the base of the tower. At that time the entire frame of the building was complete and the installation of the exterior walls were beginning. He took me on a tour, starting about three quarters of the way up the tower and walking down three or four floors so that I could get a good understanding of the construction. After seeing the design of the structural frame of the building and the architectural concept in the use of the building, I was horrified.

The concrete floors at each level were supported by bar joists. Bar joists are lightweight members consisting of steel bars bent to form a truss configuration welded to steel angles at the top and bottom. In order to make them fireproof a spray gun coats the bars with a foam-like fireproofing material. The entire floor plan was designed without the use of partitions in what is called an 'open floor plan'. The elevator and stairs running through the entire building were located in the center of the floor plan. I told my friend that this entire concept is illegal in New York City and they are creating a very dangerous building. New York City building code requires that each floor be subdivided in compartments. Each compartment shall have walls of either one hour or three hour fireproofing as called for in the building code. The reason for this compartmentalization is to prevent fire from spreading throughout the building. It gives the occupants time to seek safety from a fire in any location on each floor. This type of safety is vital because it is impossible for the fire department to get ladders up to those floors. Without those fireproof compartments, fire will spread through the floor very rapidly endangering the lives of everyone.

Secondly, if there was any explosion on a floor from some equipment that a tenant might be using, the vibration would loosen the fireproofing and it would fall from the bar joists exposing them to deform and fail from the heat of any fire that might develop.

My friend informed me, which I already knew, that the Port Authority is a State organization and therefore exempt from the requirements of the New York City building code. I told my friend, "I know that is true; however that does not mean you can build a dangerous condition." "Al", he said, "Your fears are so far-fetched that such a catastrophe would never happen."

The rest of the story, dear reader, you know.

My Life's Adventure Into Sports.

At this time, I would like to take a break and talk about my activities and abilities or lack of abilities in the field of sports. It should be noted that I never had a favorite team in any sport, never knew the names of any players of any team in any sport, or paid attention to that endeavor. I know that makes me an outcast, because everyone I knew was deeply involved and followed sports. I found that my lack of knowledge and interest in sports was somewhat of a handicap in my business life. It seems that when I would join a meeting in reference to my business activity, it was always customary, before the meeting started, to discuss the latest sport scores and activity of the day. In that situation I just sat there with a smile on my face and waited for the business meeting to begin. However, that does not mean that I did not try my talents at sports. So to you, Mr. and Mrs. Reader, sit back and listen to my tortured adventures in many sports.

Sport Number One: Football

When I entered high school I said to myself, "It is time that I learned at least one sport." On the first day I entered high school, I went down to the gym and signed up for the football team. My thinking was that since I am a beginner, the coach would teach me all the rules and regulations of the sport. I also assume they would teach me how to play the game. Weighing about 240 pounds at that time, I felt   that with some training, I could be a contributor to the team.

The coach in charge took me to a back room and outfitted me with an entire uniform. He told me to report at three o'clock the next Monday. That afternoon, a game between my team, Lincoln High School in Brooklyn, and the opposing team Curtis High School from Staten Island was scheduled.

I arrived as ordered, came down to the field, and patiently sat down on the bench as both teams entered the field. The whistle sounded and the games began. After about 10 or 15 minutes sitting on the bench, the coach yelled out, "Efron get in there. You are a Guard." I looked bewildered and had no idea what the coach was talking about. He grabbed my arm and escorted me to the field and said, "Get down at the end of this line. You are a guard." So I crouched down as my fellow players did and faced the opposing team just inches away.

There I was, in this crouched down position, looking at this monster a few inches from me with a menacing stare. Before I knew what happened, the center flipped the ball and the action began. It seem like a split second later, I felt some hands come up, catch me under the chin, snap my head back and flip me over, putting me in a dazed and confused position, flat on my back. I also felt the blood dripping out of my nose with all the accompanying pain. All kinds of action were running around me. When things calmed down, I was dragged off the field.

They tended to my wounds, as I tried to catch my breath and get back into control of my faculties. After resting a while and gaining my senses, I very politely took off my uniform, handed it to the coach, and told him with a jittery voice, "I quit". At that moment, I knew my football career was over.

Sport Number Two: Baseball

You would think I learned my lesson from sport Number One, however I did not. On Sunday mornings, anyone interested in playing baseball gathered on the baseball field at the local school. When people arrived, two teams were created with everyone who wanted to play. Even though I never played baseball, I figured out the only way to learn is to do it. So I was chosen for one of the teams. With a flip of the coin, the decision was made which team would be up at bat first. My team lost the toss and took the field. I was told to play right field.

There I was, standing in the hot sun, all the way out in right field. The game started. The pitcher was able to strike out the first two players. So far everything was great. The batter hit the next pitch. It was a low grounder between third base and shortstop. The ball got away from the shortstop and the batter was safe on first.

The next batter got up and hit the first pitch. It was a high flying ball coming straight at me in right field. I had my keen eye on the ball and my glove ready to grab it. The next thing I knew, I felt the ball hit my glove, bounce in the air, and slowly rolled to the right. I looked up in amazement and heard them yelling, "There's a hole in the outfield". I quickly recovered and threw the ball toward second base I learned that the runner was already past third base and was on his way home. I do not think at this time I have to describe my feelings & attitude, and that of my fellow ballplayers. I'm sure your imagination will do an accurate job.

I was suffering in the outfield until my team was able to get the third out. It seemed like an eternity. I stood with my head down as my team's first batter was up. He hit a great ball and was able to reach first base safely. As I remember, the fellow who was acting as manager of our team told me that I was the next one up. Being very angry at myself for looked like a fool in the outfield, I picked up a bat and said to myself, "If I can slam this ball for a home run, all will be forgiven." As I got in batting position, one of my teammates said the bat I picked up was cracked, and I should select another bat. My mind was really not thinking intelligently. Since my anger was showing and I felt unhinged, I said, "No I will keep this bat." The pitcher released the first ball. It was coming straight down the middle. I swung the bat and made contact with the ball. The bat cracked and flew across the field into pieces. That was disaster number two. I could not wait for that day to end and I'm sure my teammates felt the same way. As a result, my baseball future ended.

Sport Number Three: Boxing

One pleasant sunny day, I was reading an article about the art of boxing. At the bottom of that article was an ad for the local gym that trained professional boxers. Their ad stressed the fantastic features that boxing can do to build a strong muscular body and healthy physical condition. "That's for me", I foolishly thought and joined the gym. Since this was a professional boxing gym, everything that you did when you were in that facility was built around the body and boxing. All the mirrors that hung on the wall were deliberately placed at a very low position. That meant if you wanted to look in the mirror, you had to bend your knees and curl your torso, using muscles that you have never used before, so you could see yourself in the mirror. The entire physical environment of the gym was meant to keep every muscle in your body moving.

Once you were dressed and ready to work out, you would proceed onto the floor of the gym. Timewise, the gym was divided into two time sessions. When the bell rang you had 3 minutes, which is the normal time of a boxing round, to work on one of the punching bags or weightlifting or any other activity that was available. When the buzzer rang again you had 1 minute to rest. However, rest meant that you must keep moving and walking around until the next buzzer for the next activity.

They also had a boxing ring set up in the middle of the floor with the number of boxing gloves hanging off the corner of the post. When the 1 minute resting buzzer sounded, if it was your turn to go into the boxing ring for the next 3 minutes, you would put on a pair of boxing gloves. You did not have time to securely tie the gloves to your hands.

The three-minute buzzer rang and I entered the boxing ring. Another participant in this activity would also enter the ring with me and we would box for the 3 minute session. We would dance around and throw some punches. After couple swings, I saw an opening and took a hot swing. I missed my opponent's face by fractions of an inch, and my glove went flying off my hand. I tried to tell my opponent that I lost my glove. Either he didn't hear me or didn't care, **but the** cold leather of his glove bounced off my face three times. The only way to stop this onslaught was to get down on the floor and that I did. I guess that by now you have been able to figure out what my next move was. You're right. That was the end of my boxing career.

Sport Number Four: Basketball

Oh well, so far I'm a total failure at sports. But I am not smart enough to know when I had enough, so on I went. One day, I met a friend who played basketball every Sunday at the local school yard. He said that there were a great bunch of great guys there. He had a lot of fun and the exercise was wonderful. "Al", he said, "Why don't you come down and join us? These games are open to everyone who shows up." Being a glutton for punishment, I showed up one Sunday morning.

The game they play was full-court. That means my team's basket was on one end of the court and the opposing teams basket was on the complete opposite end. Okay, I thought there would be a lot of running, which is good for me to lose some weight and to get in better shape. The ball was put in action and we started.

The opposing team got the ball and was racing down the court with our team in hot pursuit trying to prevent him from making a basket. Then we got the ball and started racing down to the opposite end of the court to our basket. We did not make the basket. Then the opposing team got control of the ball and we were charging all the way back to the other end of the court. I quickly realized what was happening. We would charge back and forth across that large field. I was always at the back of the group trying to catch up. Then everybody start going back the other way.

There I was, on the opposite end of the group and again trying to catch up. This was a no-win situation. Finally, it must've been half-time or some other rule that allowed us all to sit down for a few minutes before the game started again. My friend gave me a hint on how to prevent the opposing player from stopping you from tossing the ball in the basket. He said, "When you start to rise to put the ball in the basket, bring your right knee up with you in a position to hit your opponent in the groin, if he tries to block you."

From running back and forth across the court, trying to catch up to everyone in both directions, and trying to prevent myself from having a knee smash into my groin, I decided basketball was another dead sport as far as I'm concerned.

Sport Number Five: Judo

During my Army days, when I was stationed in Japan and we were waiting for the ship to take us to Korea and into combat, I met a Japanese judo instructor. He told me all about the great advantages of learning the art of judo. It is not only good to keep the body in shape and flexible, it is also a great advantage in self-defense. He had me convinced and I signed up for judo lessons and was ready to go. I would meet him in the school gym located in a very small town near the Army base.

Learning to be thrown!

My instructor started the basic form and positions of the various moves. He taught me the art of falling, also known as being thrown to the ground without hurting yourself. He started with moves and positions for self-protection and getting control of your opponent. He gently threw me down so I could get the feel and technique of hitting the ground and getting up quickly. I started to learn how to get control and throw my opponent down.

Who's throwing who?

After about four or five sessions, I felt very confident in my ability to throw my opponent, and the proper technique of falling when my opponent flips me, and I land safely on the ground. We progressed into harder and more sophisticated movements. After a while, I realized that when I threw my instructor and performed the entire sequence perfectly, that my instructor was sort of throwing his body and making it easy for me to get him down. I told him not to make it easy for me, because I think I'm getting pretty good at this sport. He did not listen to me. I felt that he was still making it easy for me to perform the movement.

Tea after the match.

I guess I got under his skin for asking him not to make it easy for me, because I wanted to see how good I really was. I could see in his eyes that he got the message. I was going to give it full blast. We started again. Every time I got near him, I was flown in the air and slammed to the ground. I looked up at him with little smile. I got up quickly with an attack movement executed perfectly and to my amazement, I found myself flown in the air and slammed to the ground once again. At that point, I realized that it was time to see if there any more sports out there that I could excel in.

It so happened that I was saved from any further humiliation because the ship we were waiting for arrived to take us to Korea. There I would be able to kill as many Chinese that were pouring over the border with my handy rifle.

Sport Number Six: Golf
Thank Goodness! A Sport I Can Handle

I reached the point in my life when I became a Registered Architect and was starting to make some real money. I learned that in the construction industry, if you want to succeed in that industry, you must know how to play golf. Harriet I signed up for golf lessons at a local high school. Upon arriving the first evening for our first lesson, we assembled in our local high school auditorium. After some minor instruction on the proper way to grip the golf club and the proper swing, we were all escorted on the stage in front of the auditorium. We were issued small rubber tees and plastic whiffle golf balls. The instructor told us hit the whiffle balls into the empty audience seating area. This exercise was a lot of fun but did not teach anyone how to play golf.

For the next step, we joined the Richmond County Country Club and signed up for real lessons given by the club professional. Our goal was to learn the fundamentals to a point we would be able to go out on the golf course and be somewhat respectable at the game. We signed up for two-week golf course at a professional golf school in Florida. This put the finishing touches on our ability and we were now Country Club golfers. From that point forward, our entire recreational life was centered around golf and the Country Club. By this time Harriet had retired from teaching and immersed herself in golf. She and her friends played golf almost 7 days a week. It is customary at many Country Clubs that on Monday, the club is closed to members, so that normal maintenance can take place. The golf course is sometimes rented out on Mondays to organizations to have fundraising golf outings. Harriet and her friends would buy tickets to those outings to be able to play on Mondays too.

It is a known fact that the construction industry revolves around golf. It seems that every corporation, construction company, bank or any other entity in the industry has golf outings. These golf outings are fantastic tool for networking, meeting people and making friends.

These golf outings usually start out with a great breakfast and a very short formal introduction. All guests are given golf balls, hats, jackets and other swag with company's logos on them. We assemble in foursomes, each on the tee that they were assigned to. The games begin. About every three holes, you'll find a refreshment table. There you can help yourself to a drink, all sorts of snacks, and if you like, you can have some hard liquor. The game goes on. When you finish the round, you assemble for the cocktail party. There again is more food and hard liquor. Now the time comes for the formal dinner. Your foursome finds your table and a fantastic dinner commences. About halfway through the food, the fun begins with the announcements of the winners and their prizes. It seemed that almost everybody won something. In most cases there might also be some professional entertainment. Finally the evening comes to the conclusion. Everyone says goodbye to all our new friends and acquaintances. We hope these may be future business acquaintances. Everyone gathers their winnings, gifts and swag and heads home.

Finally, I found a successful sport that I can handle. It has lasted up until the writing of this book and onward. When I got home, Harriet would ask me if I had a good time. My answer was always the same; I was out there working the crowd to get new clients and to keep the old ones happy. Golf outings are not for fun, just the best part of the working day.

He's a word to clarify the serving of hard liquor at these golf outings. It was as a normal offering, as it was before an anti-liquor legislation was passed. Due to community pressure, it was felt that liquor being served at events like golf outings or even at bars causes many car accidents from those overzealous drinkers. So laws were passed. Basically, the organization or bar that serves liquor shall be held liable for those people that were served liquor and on the way home had an accident because of being intoxicated. After that law took effect, liquor was not served at the vast majority of these golf outings anymore.

It did not stop the many golf outings that were held and that I fully enjoyed. Golf, like all sports, is loaded with gadgets and gimmicks that claim to make you a professional golfer. Since I am a typical golfer, which really means I'm a gullible golfer, I looked for all those magic gadgets and gimmicks to turn me into a pro. One day I was thumbing through a typical golf catalog while resting on the outside deck of my Staten Island home. All of a sudden my eyes focused on a piece of equipment that guaranteed that you will be able to find a lost ball in the deep grass or wooded areas.

Since I spend much time on the golf course in the deep grass and wooded areas, this instrument looked like a real winner. If I hurried, I could get it while it was on sale for $80. I guess now you are thinking ahead of me and know that I'm going to hurry up and buy that gimmick. Well you are correct. I did make the purchase. About two weeks later this beautifully wrapped box was delivered by my local mailman. I quickly opened it up and examined it closely. It was the size of a small handheld radio and contained an antenna that could be extended out from the body of this unit. There were no knobs or buttons or windows or anything on the plastic case. The instructions simply said, "Point the antenna straight down the center of the fairway. Slowly walk forward and the antenna will automatically move to the right or left and point you towards the ball."

The next time I was on the golf course, I showed this fantastic instrument to a close friend of mine. He said, "Let's try it out right now." We went down to the first tee and I threw a ball about 10 feet in front of us all the away to the right. We then pointed the antenna straight down the center of the fairway and started to walk in that direction. Much to our amazement the antenna actually swung to the right at the location where I have thrown my golf ball. This was an amazing thing. By this time the rest of our foursome joined us on the first tee and were ready to play. We all teed off and did not lose sight of our golf balls. By the fourth hole, one member of our group hit a ball out of bounds and into the deep grass. With great flair, I pulled out my new instrument and as instructed went to find the ball. For some reason it did not seem to work at this time as it did at our first try.

A little disheartened, I put the gadget in my golf bag and went on to finish the day's golf. When I got home, I packaged this modern wonder and mailed it to my son Paul in Tucson, Arizona. Paul is noted as when acquiring a new instrument, the first thing he will do is to take it apart and re-engineer it. I felt that this instrument in Paul's hands would be thoroughly investigated and made to work. About a week later, I got a call from Paul to report his findings. He said that he was able to open the plastic case to study the mechanism on the interior. He said, "Do you know what I found inside that plastic case?" I said, "No. Fill me in." With a great laugh he said one word, "NOTHING". "You my dear father have been had."

Evidently, when we tried it out on the first hole, I must've held the unit and tilted my hand in the direction of the ball making the antenna swing over. This probably worked like the ouija boards that were sold years ago. When the next edition of that catalog came out, I flipped through the pages and could not find that miracle ball finder listed anywhere in that catalog. I guess the company that put out this phony gadget, collected as many $80 payments from suckers like me as they could and went to the bank with a great smile on their face. They probably said, "Let's not milk this anymore and quit while we are ahead."

Back To My Daily Adventures
This Little Tale Is An Incident In My Life That Is Just For Laughs

One of my clients was looking to purchase land in upstate New York. We schedule the date for the two of us to make the trip, so we could evaluate the project. I was to meet him in his house at eight o'clock in the morning, so that we have enough time to drive upstate and visit the site during daylight hours. Promptly at 8am, I arrived at his house and received a warm welcome. His wife brought me a cup of coffee and told me to sit in the den while she was getting the children ready for school and send them on their way. I was sitting in the den quietly drinking the coffee as my client, his wife and children ran back and forth trying to get their act together and get ready to leave.

As I sat there quietly, their dog, a strange looking bulldog, came walking up to me, stopped about 2 feet away and stared at me. What am I to do, I stared back. At that point, the dog got in position and relieved himself of a meaningful size stool. The dog glanced at me one more time and strolled away. There I sat, watching that freshly manufactured stool lying there. In the meantime, everyone was still rushing around, getting ready, and going back and forth but never seeing the wonderful package that the bulldog left.

Then my client said, "Al I'm ready to go." What do I do now? Do I tell him my adventure that morning or just let it go. I decided to be a coward and just ignore it. Off we went on a trip upstate. Nothing was ever said about that for the next 25 years that I've known that client. As far as I know that turd is probably still sitting there slowly drying away. What would you have done?

We All Get A Chance At Not Being Well

      I was in my office, working as usual on an average day. I felt the urge to go to the men's room. The men's room was located just out the entrance of my office in the public corridor. I entered the men's room and all of a sudden I didn't feel right. Within a few seconds I got these terrible pains just below my stomach. The pain was so bad that I fell to the floor. I crawled out the bathroom and managed to crawl to the front entrance to my office and bang on the glass door. The receptionist saw me, yelled for my partner, and they quickly got me onto a chair in one of the offices. It just so happened that my partner was having a meeting with members of a hospital. One of the members in the hospital meeting came rushing in and examined me. He proclaimed that I'm having a kidney stone attack. They called the hospital to be prepared because they're bringing me down there right away. A friend of mine that worked in the office took me down to his car and rushed me to the hospital. After being examined, they confirmed that I did have an attack of kidney stones. To make a long story short, the hospital gave me what I needed to kill the pain. After a couple days, I passed the stones and was back to normal.

      Upon coming back to work, I said to my partner, "Who was that doctor who examined me that day in the office?" He looked at me and said, "That was not a doctor. That was a plumbing contractor." I just stared him in a complete disbelief of the entire situation. I don't know what background that plumbing contractor had, but he did make the proper diagnosis. We did get a good laugh talking about that situation many times since.

      While we're on the subject of my health, the many episode saga of my right ear comes to mind. In the good old days in Brooklyn, New York, when fireworks were legal and young children were stupid, my brother and I managed to acquire firecrackers. I must've been about 11 years old and my brother was about two years old at that time. I guess because I was the older of the two, I should've known better, but did not. We opened the window of our small apartment that was facing an empty lot. We lit a firecracker and threw it out the window. When we heard that firecracker explode, there was nothing but a stupid smile on my face as we applauded this magnificent event. We lit another firecracker with the same enjoyment. Then a third and fourth, still smiling and applauding. You would think by now we would tire of this boring game. But no, we kept on going. One time I lit a firecracker and threw it out the window and tried to light a second firecracker and toss it out the window before the first one exploded. Much to my horror the last firecracker exploded a few inches from my right ear as it was leaving my hand to fly out the window.

After the first few seconds of shock, I got my senses back and realized there was a ringing in my ear and it did not feel right. That ringing in my ear lasted for hours. When my mother came home and found out what happened she took me to the doctor to check out my ear. Lo and behold, I ruptured my ear drum. I now ask the reader to remember this as Episode One.

My friend, Bernie Champagne, managed to acquire a snipe when we were about 16 years old. A snipe is a very small sailboat that's large enough to accommodate four people maximum. The sailboat had an outboard motor to help it along on those days when there was not adequate wind. One evening Bernie, I and my photography partner Alan decided to take the sailboat out to the open ocean at the mouth of the Hudson River. It was about 11pm on a lovely warm evening. To make the evening more interesting, we decided to go skinny-dipping. We stripped down nude. Alan got into the ocean first and splashed around and told us it feels very invigorating. Bernie dove off the boat and splashed in the water joining Alan. I stood up on the front deck, got ready to dive in the water, when this huge private yacht came by and put this very bright spotlight that illuminated my entire naked body. I quickly threw myself in the water to escape the views of everyone on the yacht. By throwing myself in the water, I managed to have my right ear hit the water first which ruptured my ear drum again. It was the same ear drum that had tangled with the firecrackers. I was knocked unconscious. My friends dragged me out of the ocean and into a boat. Again Reader, Please remember this as Episode Two.

I am now a grown man, married with two children, belonged to a Country Club and considered to be an adult. The District Attorney on Staten Island was a personal friend of mine. One day he called me to request a favor. He had a very close friend who never played golf at my Country Club. The District Attorney asked if it would be possible for him, his friend, and his driver/bodyguard to join me as a foursome for a round of golf at my Club. "No problem", I said, and we set a date. On the day we were to play golf, the skies were cloudy and there was a very light drizzle that came floating down from time to time. This was no problem and we teed off. On the first hole, the four of us did quite well in spite of the weather. We teed off at the second hole as a very light drizzle started to fall. The District Attorney's driver/bodyguard, a large strong individual, got ready to take his second shot. I was standing about 15 feet behind him and about a foot or so closer to the target.

For the life of me, I cannot figure out to this day, exactly how it could happen, but it did. He hit his ball aiming at the green ahead of him. Instead the ball shot all the way behind him, which seems like an impossible thing to happen. It hit me in the head, right behind that same right ear that had the ruptured ear drum!! It tore a part of the ear away from my scalp. The noise was unbelievable!! I was lying on the ground. I was quickly put in a golf cart and driven to the Pro Shop to get help. Due to the rainy weather I was wearing a yellow slicker jacket. Streams of red blood ran down the yellow jacket as my ear was dangling in the wind. I was holding my ear up against my head, so it should not rip itself loose. I came to my senses and realized that my ENT doctor who was a personal friend and golfing buddy, has his office 1 mile up the road from the golf course. I told my buddies to go finish the game, I will hop in the car and drive to my friend, the doctor, and all will be well. My friends agreed.

They put me in the car and I start going up the road. After about a quarter of a mile, there were a number of police cars and an ambulance, attending to a car accident. This was blocking my way to my destination during an emergency. I made a fast U-turn. I had to go quite a distance out of my way to get around that car accident. I finally got to my friend's office. He checked my ear. He said that I must first see a surgeon to re-attach the ear back onto my head before he can work on my ear.

I should note that Staten Island is like incest, because the surgeon is another friend of mine that I also play golf with who has an office about a mile away from where I was. My doctor called the surgeon who told me to come right down and he would take care of me. I did, and my friend, the surgeon, re-attached my ear. I went back to the ENT doctor who did whatever he could until the swelling went down. He told me to come back the next day and we will plan what has to be done.

The next day at the doctor's office, he was able to do a complete evaluation of the ear and said that I needed more surgery. But he could not operate on the ear until there is more healing. I returned to my office and waited for the ear to heal to a point where he could operate.

My partner, hearing my saga said, "You can't get an operation from a local Staten Island doctor. You have to go to the best doctor in Manhattan." Since we were the architects for New York University Hospital, my partner made contact with the administration to get the top doctor to look at my ear. An appointment was set. I saw this doctor that examined my ear and said, "Yes, You need microsurgery on that ear." The date and time was set for the surgery at this place in two days. Since this was microsurgery, I had to be strapped down to prevent me from moving. The nurse told that me since I was strapped down and could not move, I should notify her if anything itches and she will scratch it. The minute I was informed of the situation, everything on my body started to itch. I closed my eyes and tuned it all out. The nurse tried to open a special blanket that's required to put over me, with the sterile surface facing up. She was having some trouble and the doctor yelled at her in a very unprofessional manner. He also yelled at an attendant. Everything finally settled down and the surgery took place.

When the surgery was over, I asked the doctor if he was going to give me an antibiotic because before the surgery my ear was infected and dripping a liquid. This arrogant bum of a doctor said in an arrogant voice "I'm the doctor. You don't need an antibiotic." He instructed me to go home and come back in two days. While Harriet was driving me home, I felt the liquid dripping out of my ear and she saw that the bandages were being stained. When I returned to that arrogant so-called 'expert New York doctor', he said the ear was infected and he would have to re-operate. He told me to see the appointment nurse and she will schedule the re-surgery.

At that point, I went home to my little doctor on Staten Island and told him my tale of woe. My Staten Island doctor informed me that all the ENT doctors on Staten Island including himself studied under that New York doctor. He's an excellent teacher but a horrible surgeon. He teaches, but does not operate. After being examined by Staten Island doctor, he told me that the so-called expert operated from the outside in which was the wrong thing to do in my case. He said he would do the operation from the inside out and everything will be fine. And so he operated, and all was fine. This is Episode Three and the end of the stories of my right ear's travel through life.

Christmas For A Jewish Couple

On a brighter side, one December evening, Harriet & I were home watching television, as snow was falling and turning the neighborhood white. Our front door bell rang to announce a visitor. Upon opening the door, I found six of my very close Irish Catholic friends and neighbors, all dressed for the cold snowy evening. They proclaimed that we should put on our winter outer garments. We are all going throughout the neighborhood Christmas caroling. I stood there for a few seconds trying to absorb the situation. Six Irish Catholics and two Jews are going to walk through the neighborhood ringing doorbells and singing Christmas songs. My wife came to the door to join me. In hearing their request she said, "Let's try it." We got dressed and off we went. We went up and down the blocks, ringing doorbells and singing all those great songs that go with the season. At the end of the evening, I felt that I was an Irish Catholic. We had such a great time, with the feeling of joy and love for all the world, that I went out and bought a small Christmas ornament to hang on the door. As the song goes, all the halls were decked.

Great Wedding?

One bright sunny afternoon, I went to our mailbox at our Staten Island home to retrieve the days communications delivered by our lovely mail woman. I brought the mail in the house. Harriet and I sat down at the kitchen table to sift through the large collection of bills, junk mail and one or two pieces of important mail. We came upon a wedding invitation. The son of our good friends, the Winston's was getting married. The wedding was to take place on a farm that the Winston's owned in Bennington, Vermont. Harriet and I were delighted at the invitation, not only because it was the Winston's, who were very dear friends of ours, but also because the affair was at their farm that we visited a number of times. Every visit we had at their farm created great memories.

The farm had the atmosphere of New England. It was very picturesque, going back to the early days of this country. Their farm consisted of a great farmhouse, a large barn and two small lakes as well as a great mountain that was part of the entire property. The wedding ceremony, as noted on the invitation, was to take place at the very top of the mountain located on the farm. Arrangements were made for us to stay at a historic building. It was restored as a bed & breakfast to reflect the era in which it was built. Harriet and I were anxiously waiting for the day when we would be attending this romantic and exciting event that we would be sure to remember for a long time. Finally the day came.

We drove up to Bennington, Vermont and found the bed & breakfast that we would be staying at. We drove up to the parking area right near the entrance. The address of the building, as I remember, was 1820. We found out later that all addresses of all the buildings were the actually date that the buildings were constructed. Now we know we are going to stay in the building that was built in the early 1800s, during slavery, when James Monroe was in office as the 5th US President.

We entered the building, into a small vestibule that contained a simple desk. In the corner was the owner, standing behind the desk to greet us. It didn't take us more than a few seconds to get the feeling of the period when the building was constructed. After signing in, we walked up one flight of stairs to our room. I looked around and started to realize that staying in a historic building might not be the most joyous occasion that we thought it would be.

In the room, we found the bed located in the middle of the room. It was not very large. Besides taking up a good portion of the room, the bed was extremely high. On the floor, by the side of the bed, was a large step stool. We would have to get used to getting up to this high bed. I noticed an electric cord hanging from the ceiling with a simple 40 W bulb screwed into it. I started to browse around the rest of the room. I did not see any electric outlets. This was a concern, because of the electric toothbrush and shaver that might need to be recharged. I noticed these very heavy blankets neatly folded on a low piece of furniture. Later on, I found out that those heavy blankets were needed to keep you warm in the building, because it was very difficult to heat. I don't remember seeing any closets because I remember living out of our suitcases.

There were toilet facilities down the hall, which I suppose were very upscale in the 1800s, but would leave much to be desired in today's world. Oh well, the atmosphere was great, so we told ourselves. We spent the night struggling to keep the heavy blanket on ourselves to avoid the shivers, but my partner turned over and pulled some of the blanket off of me.

The next day they served a good breakfast of delicious food that was very fattening such as pancakes with eggs and sausage and other such delights of the early days. This was the day of the wedding!! We looked out and much to our horror it, was a dark, cold, heavily rainy day. This is not the weather you would want for a wedding on top of a mountain. When we got to the farm, we saw my friend, his son and his son's friend dragging 4' x 8' plywood sheets up the mountain. They were trying to build a walk way up the mountain to the top where this ceremony was to take place. We hoped the muddy water running down the mountain with this huge rain hadn't washed everything down. It would be terrible if the 4 x 8 walkway got washed away. A neighbor came with a small tractor that was able to transport the band up to the top of the mountain. They started to transport some of the guests up the mountain. Everyone was all dressed for the event but was now pretty much soaking wet.

Harriet looked at me as we stood near the farmhouse, waiting for our turn to get in the tractor and said, "I'm going into the farmhouse. I'm going to spend the day there. You are in charge of the wedding. When it is all over, report back to me on how it went up there, on the top of the rain soaked freezing mountain."

I grew impatient and did not want to wait for the tractor, so I started to walk, or should I say slide up the mountain. It did not take me long to realize that this was not a smart move. The rain water was gushing down the slope and washing all the mud with it. I was fighting my way up the slope trying to stay as dry as possible and not fall onto the muddy ground. I finally made it up the mountain. I was cold, shivering, tired & hungry and joined the rest of the wedding party, who were cold, shivering, tired & hungry. The band was trying to play the best they could which quite honestly was not very good. The Rabbi stood there under the Chuppah (Bridal Canopy), which looked like he was going to fly away at any moment. The groom stood next to the Rabbi quietly waiting for the bride to appear.

The original arrangements were for the bride to come up the back of the mountain to make a spectacular entrance. However, due to the rain, she was having a hard time getting up the slope. Finally, there she appeared, this beautiful white wedding gown, soaking wet and full of mud. Hanging loose was her hair which was dripping wet. In her hand she held a pair of shoes with high heels that used to be on her feet. When you looked down, you saw that her feet were bare. It was impossible for her to climb that mountain in high heels. Anyway, she was there and the ceremony started.

The Rabbi was determined to make sure nothing was missed so the service was not abbreviated. Finally at the conclusion of the ceremony, it is customary for the bride and groom break a glass by stomping on it. The Rabbi put the glass down by the bride's foot. She turned to the audience and asked, "Does anybody have a slip on sneaker that I can wear to break the glass by stepping on it?" After a good laugh was had by all, everyone started down the mountain.

I was going to say everyone started walking down the mountain but that wouldn't be accurate. What actually happened is that almost all the 2 x 4 sheets of wood got washed away. Everyone started sliding down the slope one way or another to the farmhouse. Everyone got a chance to get back to their hotel and change clothes. We all assembled at the catering hall where the dinner was to be served. Everyone in attendance was now in very good spirits. We were all saying this is the best wedding we ever went to, because we will remember it all our lives.

Thinking Outside The Box

When Harriet and I became members of Richmond County Country Club on Staten Island, our lifestyle changed. In no time at all, we became deeply involved, not only in golf, but the whole social structure of Country Club living. It was a new experience for us and we loved every minute of it. Since it was a very short walk from my house to the clubhouse, we found ourselves spending much time in a great variety of activities. We also enjoyed the great food that they served. It did not take long before I was asked to become a member of the Board of Directors. I agreed, and as all the other directors did, I spend quite a bit of time on all the issues that we would discuss.

Just for background, which is at the heart of this episode, the City of New York was trying to put us out of business. One of the reasons that the City did not like us was that this Club was formed in 1888. At that time it was customary for clubs of this nature to be completely restricted. No Catholics, Jews, Blacks, etc. were allowed to become members. However by the 1950s, this situation had changed. The Club was running into financial problems and desperately needed an influx of membership for monetary reasons. Therefore, the Club stopped being restricted and was open to anyone who made an application. The City of New York was still not happy. They kept raising our real estate taxes to a point where it was difficult to make ends meet. The City doubled our tax burden. At the next board meeting we discussed how to handle this new extremely large bill and stay in business. In my political travels, I remembered reading about Federal and State programs to save open space. The main concern of government was that too much land was being sold and overdeveloped. That included acres of farmland, as well as land within cities. I suggested that I be given the authority to work with the State or Federal Government, to see if we could come up with some program to save the Country Club. I was told to go for it.

I started on the State level and contacted my political connections. I wanted to identify the proper person that I could sit down with and discuss the situation. It did not take long before the State of New York was very anxious and wanting to work something out. The solution we came up with, was for the State to lease the property of the entire golf course. It would become open space permanently and under the control of the State of New York. Since the State does not pay real estate taxes, that would solve our financial problem. In discussing this with the City, to say the least they were not very happy. However they had no choice. The only controlling factor that they had was that if the State gave up its lease on the property, then the Country Club would have the pay all back taxes from beginning of this arrangement with the State. It was a good try but didn't work.

Next was to try the Federal Government. Again, through my contacts, I was able to find the proper agency and Commissioner to discuss our proposal. During my phone conversation with him, he sounded very interested in working something out. I invited him to spend the day at the Country Club so he could get a feel of the entire area and situation. He agreed and we set the date.

Upon his arrival, I took him on the tour of the facilities and the golf course. This was done in one of our golf carts that just happen to have some martinis available. We spoke for most of the afternoon and then had dinner together. At the conclusion of this meeting, I introduced him to the other members of the Board of Directors to inform them of the deal that we worked out. I wanted to make sure the entire Board was willing to go along with these arrangements.

The deal was simple. The Federal Government bought the entire golf course and paid the Club $6 million. The Federal Government then leased the golf course to Richmond County Country Club for 100 years without any fee or payment. At the conclusion of 100 years, the people in charge at that time could re-negotiate with the Federal Government for another 100 years. Now that the Country Club is owned by the Federal Government there was no City real estate tax. It did not take long for the Board to unanimously approve this proposal. The attorneys went to work to put this down on paper to be signed by all parties.

When everything was completed, the Club had $6 million in its treasury. Our accountants told us that if we spent the $6 million to rehabilitate the club, we would not have to pay income tax on that sum of money. If we do not spend that money altering the club, we would have a tax burden. So what did we do? We built a new larger catering hall, a great health club, and a number of other improvements. The club remains in business and is still a thriving Country Club as of the writing of this book.

South Bronx NY, Redevelopment

The next adventure in my life as an architect was a sad commentary on human nature. This took place around 1976–1977, when Jimmy Carter was President of the United States. The South Bronx in New York in those days was a horrible slum. Buildings stood empty and dilapidated. Crime was high. Employment was low and there was human outcry that something had to be done to fix the entire South Bronx. When Jimmy Carter was campaigning for President, he made a visit to the South Bronx and pledged he would do something to turn this horrible condition around.

In those days, it was customary for an urban renewal, like what the South Bronx desperately needed, all federal money would be given to the local government authority to carry out the work. However, there was so much waste due to the overbearing bureaucracy and corruption in the NY government at that time, that the Carter Administration decided not to give money to the local government to build this project. Instead they created Community Boards that consisted of 100% of the citizens living in each area. President Carter felt that by giving the money to the people themselves, they would use it appropriately and avoid the bureaucracy and corruption that they found in government. This procedure would allow the people that live in each neighborhood to do the planning to restore their own neighborhoods, as they feel it should be for them to live in. Large sums of money were made available to these Community Boards to start the re-development process.

I was notified by a Community Board that they are in the process of selecting an architect to design the entire urban renewal area for a huge section of the South Bronx. This was to be the first project under this new program. If I was interested in being considered as the architect, I was instructed to come down for an interview on a selected day and time. There were about five other architects that were asked if they were interested in being interviewed.

On the selected day and time I arrived for my interview. At the conclusion of my interview, I was told that they would notify me in about a week or so, if we were selected or not, after the entire interview process was complete. Two weeks later, I was called by the Chairman of the committee and congratulated that I was selected as the architect in charge of designing the entire project. They selected a date and time to meet in my office to discuss and work out our contract and the procedure for creating this urban renewal project.

There were four members of the Community Board at the meeting with my partner and me. In the middle of the discussion, one of the members said, "You know that you'll have to hire some of our people." At that point, I told him that the only person from the community that I would have to hire would be a representative that can speak for the community, so we have good coordination and agreement on all aspects of the project. I made it clear that this person would be on my payroll and go through the entire payroll process, as all my employees do. We would be filing with the IRS and the State with this person as an employee. "No", he said, "That would not do. You will be given a good fee as the architect and therefore we need cash to take care of our people. That money is not distributed as an employee. Do you get my drift?" "Yes, I do get your drift."

The whole point is that the Carter Administration wanted to avoid corruption of government by giving the money directly to the people, so they can help themselves. What are they doing? They are trying to start up new corruption. They wanted to take this money that wa there to help their people and instead put it in their own pockets.

At that point, I made it clear that in no way would I operate in that fashion. Everything has to be legitimate, on the books, in the proper manner. He then said, "That with your attitude, we cannot use you as our architect." I looked at my partner and we both agreed. I said, "Thank you very much. It's been a pleasure talking to you. I think this conversation is over." They left and I took a sigh of relief. I know they approached other architects. A lot of time went by and very little was done. How much money was wasted or spent I do not know. I never found out what ever happened to the money. All I know is that the entire urban renewal process never happened. It was broken down into small sections that were done with the New York City Government taking charge again.

Another Sad Commentary Of Human Nature

My office designed a high-rise office building on Lexington Avenue and 41st St. in Manhattan. The building was constructed and the tenants moved in. A few days after one of the tenants moved in they called my client with a complaint. The tenant was reporting an odd noise coming through the wall located in the toilet room of his office. My client and I then visited the building to investigate this problem. Sure enough there was a loud continuous whistling sound coming through the wall in their bathroom. We tried to isolate the sound and find the exact location where that sound was coming from. We were completely baffled by the situation, because there was no mechanical equipment of any kind behind that wall. I directed the contractor to gently break open the wall in the location of the sound. The contractor followed my orders, broke open the brick at that location so we could examine the interior of that area. We all stood there, staring at that wall with a gaping hole, in complete disbelief. It seems that some disgruntled mason that constructed this partition, created this noise as a prank or maybe he was angry at his boss. This portion of the wall was enclosing a ventilating shaft that exhausts air from the toilet rooms up to the roof where a fan was located that was exhausting the air. The mason cleverly took a Coke bottle, and built it into the wall with the mouth of the bottle facing the interior of this exhaust shaft. When the roof fan was on and the air was moving through the shaft up to the roof, it passed over the opening of a Coke bottle creating that whistling sound. I am sure during your lifetime you held a Coke bottle up to your lips and blew over the opening to create that same sound. Fun and games in the construction industry.

Another problem that we lived through on the same building occurred about two years after the completion of construction. One day I got an emergency call from my client stating that the brick façade of the building was falling off to the street below. The police and emergency crews closed off the street surrounding this building. A number of City agencies including the District Attorney were getting involved in investigating this crisis. My partner and I rushed down to the building. We met our client and saw this unusual and dangerous situation. A number of investigations into the situation were started by a number of City agencies, as well as my office.

My structural engineer, my partner and I revisited our construction drawings to see if there were any errors. If the building was constructed in strict conformance with our drawings, there should be no problem. The plans looked fine.

Construction crews started to remove all the bricks on the face of this building. In doing so, we discovered the problem. Our architectural and structural drawings called for the typical detail for supporting the brick face on a building, which was the standard construction method. One component of a steel anchor was to be embedded in the face of the concrete slab on all floors of the building. A steel angle was then attached to the face of the concrete slab with a special bolt into the steel anchor. The brick facade of the building would rest on the steel angle at every floor throughout the building. After close examination of the existing conditions, we found that the contractor never took the time to tighten the bolts as specified. After some time, the weight of the brick on the loose angles slowly tilted, forcing the bricks to slide off the angle and down to the street. It was clear to all the investigating teams that this was the problem.

This was pure malpractice on the part of the brick contractor. An in-depth investigation was then started to locate the brick contractor to start legal proceedings. However, it was discovered that the brick contractor dissolved his corporation and was not in business anymore, at least not under that corporate name. The sad part of human nature is that this contractor went back into business under a different name. He was not liable for any work that was done in his past. The owner of the building then, at his expense and whatever insurance he had, was obligated to tighten all those angles and replace all the brick face of this building.

Another Urban Renewal Project

On another urban renewal project I got involved with, I was able to gain control of the project as the developer and architect. It made for an entirely different story from my South Bronx adventure noted previously. On Staten Island we had an area called Jersey Street. This had been an upscale shopping area for many years. To the best of my knowledge, around 1960 -1965, the area had disintegrated. All the shops and stores had moved to other areas of Staten Island that were in better economic condition. Jersey Street went downhill and the area was infested with drug addicts, crime and everything else that goes with it. The area became completely abandoned. The City of New York declared Jersey Street as an Urban Renewal area. It was divided up into two sections. One section was to be commercial containing a large supermarket, drugstore and other type businesses to serve this new community. The other section was to be developed as housing for middle-class people which was desperately needed in that part of Staten Island. The City commenced with the process of selecting a developer that would design and construct the housing portion of this project.

I put together a team consisting of myself, as the architect and developer, a partner who was a major construction company that we had previously dealt with, plus a number of engineers to complete the team. I made this submission to the City as other teams did. Another proposal was made by an attorney who at one time was the Deputy Mayor of the City of New York. All of the negotiating and politicking took place in the usual manner.

As I previously noted earlier, I was elected as the Tax Commissioner for Staten Island for the City of New York. As I mentioned, I resigned after a very short stay because I felt there might be some conflict of interest. I mention this only because when the newspapers' reported on the proceedings for this project, it was noted that the past Tax Commissioner of the City of New York was bidding against the past Deputy Mayor of the City of New York to become the developers for this urban renewal project. This was a little embarrassing, but really had nothing to do with the entire process. It did make for some good newspaper reading.

After much deliberation by the City, I was finally selected and awarded the project. I started the process, beginning with the design of the individual buildings, as well as the site plan covering the entire six square city blocks that were involved. It was agreed that we would build two-story garden apartments. I designed the buildings and made my presentation to the Community Board for approval. Usually these two-story projects had an entrance to the building that led into a vestibule with the staircase going up to the second floor apartment. Off of the vestibule there was an entrance directly to the first floor apartment. I did not like that particular type of design. There is a problem that is created with the design where the apartment entrance and stairs to the second floor are off a public interior vestibule. It creates a condition where during the night, people can be attacked by people hiding in the vestibule. To avoid that, I designed this project so both apartments would enter directly from the street, just like in a one-family home. You come up the steps from the sidewalk to your front door, open the front door, and you're safely in your apartment of the first-floor units. You enter the second floor apartment the same way. You open a door directly from the sidewalk and go upstairs. You would be safely in your apartment at the bottom of the staircase.

This was part of the presentation I made to the Community Board and received their approval. I proceeded and received the approval from the Borough President and then the City Planning Commission. All was well. I was on my way. All the necessary documents for the construction of this entire project, coordination with all engineers, and the construction team were finalized. However, as always happened in dealing with communities, even though everyone felt that the project is good and needed, they would say, "Please don't build it in my backyard." These people are known as NIMBY. Not In My Back Yard. These NIMBYs filed a lawsuit, to try to prevent the final Building Department approval, in an effort to kill the project.

The trial started and the attorney for the community stated, "The architect lied when he made his presentation to the community. The architect said that the project will consist of one-family homes." Their attorney continued, "We now see that the proposal is for garden apartments." When it was my turn to testify, I stated, "I never said we were building one-family homes". The Judge asked if the Community Board could present the tape recordings of those meetings and my presentation. The Executive Director of the Community Board said he could produce the tapes and would only need about an hour so to get them from his office. The judge adjourned the trial for lunch and to commence at 2pm.

During the afternoon session, the tape was played and the Judge clearly heard my presentation. I stated, "The design of these buildings will be like a one-family home because the entrance of all the buildings will be directly from the street. That includes both the first-floor and second floor of these garden apartments." When the Judge finished hearing the tapes, he stated, "It seems very clear to me that the architect was not lying in his presentation, case dismissed". The project continued and was completed on time and within budget. It turned out to be a very successful new shining community in an area that was previously a disaster.

There was one short incident, during the beginning of construction that I found very interesting and amusing. On the end of the very first day of construction, all the contractors put their equipment in a storage container that was locked up for the evening. When they arrived the next morning, they found that the storage locker was broken into and all the tools and equipment was missing. The construction Super for this project was a savvy guy who has been around construction sites for a long time. He quickly put the word out that he is hiring local security guards for the project. It didn't take long for a number of young men to approach the site in an effort to be hired as a security guard. The Super told the assembled young man they will all be hired and well-paid under one condition; that all the stolen tools and equipment was returned. The next morning everything was returned, in piles, in front of the storage locker. The young men were there, to be hired as security guards, and so they were. After this incident, there were no more thefts or any other problem from the neighborhood. My partners and I owned a piece of that project for approximately 20 years until a large real estate consortium purchased the entire project from us.

Armenian Earthquake

One of the highlights of my career as an architect was the following adventure that opened my eyes to the rest of the world. In 1988, a massive earthquake hit Armenia. It devastated the city of Leninakan, which was part of the Soviet Union. The earthquake lasted 26 seconds and was rated 7 on the Richter scale. Roughly 85% of the city was destroyed or severely damaged, 55,000 people were dead, 20,000 injured, 500,000 homeless, 4000 children lost one parent, and 500 children lost both parents. Huge areas were completely wiped out. Entire buildings ended up as piles of rubble. The devastation was pretty complete. One school collapsed in 20 seconds, killing 997 students and teachers.

The Joint Distribution Committee (JDC), a non-sectarian organization, provides humanitarian relief around the world for victims of earthquakes, floods or other catastrophes. The JDC is an arm of the United Jewish Appeal and funded by the Jewish Federation. When the JDC received word of the Armenia earthquake, they geared up and traveled to Armenia to provide needed humanitarian aid.

If you remember your history, in 1988, Ronald Reagan was President of the United States. The climate between United States and the Soviet Union was in a very dangerous position. It was the cold war. The Soviets were boasting about their Inter-Continental Ballistic Missiles that could reach every community in the United States. The hostility between these two countries was at a point where nuclear war could possibly happen. Ronald Reagan was talking about building a complete shield over the United States, from the Pacific to the Atlantic, to protect us from incoming missiles. The Star War feeling that prevailed at that time was very scary.

The Executive Director of the JDC got the bright idea that the earthquake in Armenia might be able to bring the countries together in an effort to avoid a nuclear war. He felt that if a coalition of western governments, got together as a group, and provided humanitarian aid to the Soviet Union to help the Armenia earthquake victims, the political effect from this good-will mission could help nullify the threat of nuclear war. He managed to call a meeting for all interested governments to join together in this effort. As a result, a meeting was held with the Russians,

Israelis, British and United States in attendance. This assembly of countries all agreed to provide the humanitarian help that the Armenian people desperately needed. The British pledged to build a school that would replace the one that collapsed. The Israelis pledged to send teams of doctors to stay in two-year shifts to provide for their medical needs. Israelis were experts in providing artificial arms, legs, and rebuilding all kinds of body parts, due to their experience in all the recent wars. The United States pledged to build a hospital for the Israeli doctors to work and teach the Armenian doctors their methods.

The JDC, in conjunction with United States State Department, searched to recruit an architect to assemble a professional team to design and build this hospital in Armenia. My office was contacted in an effort to enlist us to volunteer our services in this endeavor. After a short meeting with my partners, we agreed to volunteer our services in this effort. It was agreed that I will be the architect in charge of putting the team together to build the hospital.

I recruited all the engineers that I would need to produce this project as well as a construction company that worked on an international level. I met with the Executive Director of JDC, to work out the details of my visit to Israel to help me understand the needs of the entire medical program, and then to Armenia, to get all the information I needed in reference to the site, availability of utilities etc. My team was put together. All the information required by the various governments was submitted to the Russian embassy. They would prepare all the visas and other documentation that we would need. JDC made all the addition travel arrangements for the entire project. I was told that it would take about one month to get everything put together for this international adventure.

In the meantime, I started to research Armenia, to familiarize myself with that part of the world. About three weeks passed and I contacted the Executive Director of JDC to find out how the travel visas were coming along, since we were scheduled to leave in about one week. I was told everything will be delivered to me shortly. Due to the bureaucracy of the Soviet Union, the visas for my entire team were delivered to my home, the night before we were scheduled to be at the airport. My wife, being an avid reader, checked all the visas. She realized that her visas had a lot of writing in Russian and mine had very little writing. This concerned her. I don't know how she was able to work it out, but her visas allowed her to travel to Israel, then to Armenia, then to Moscow, then to Leningrad, and back home. My visas however, allowed me to travel to Israel, then to Armenia, and that was it. Since there was no time to do anything about this, we just went to sleep, got up early in the morning and went off to the airport. At the airport, we were greeted by a representative of Israel. He took us into a private room outfitted with great snacks and coffee while we waited for our flight. I mentioned the visa problem to him and was told that the minute we get to Israel, they would look into it.

      We arrived in Israel at about 2am, tired and weary from a long flight. At the airport, a car, driver, and representative waited for us and took us to our hotel. At the Sheraton Tower Hotel in Tel Aviv, we checked in, and were taken to our suite to get comfortable, for what was left of the evening. We gently fell asleep. About 5am, we were awakened by a knocking sound that was coming in from one of the open windows. Putting all my energy together, I got out of the bed looked out the window. To my amazement, the sun started to peek its brightness over the beach area below the hotel. There, even so early in the morning, were a great many people on the beach having the time of their lives. They were playing some sort of game. They each had a paddle and were hitting the ball to one another and back and forth, even though there were no nets to get the balls over. What kind of game was this that I don't know? However, where I come from, in the middle of the week, at 5 o'clock the morning, no one is out on the beach playing ball. This seems like a country that likes to have fun.

Morning activity at the beach.

Now that we were up, we showered and got dressed and went down for a hearty breakfast. We were treated as VIPs. We did not receive a bill for the food. By this time, it was about 9 o'clock. Our contact from JDC met us to start the day and get the program moving. I mentioned the problem with my visas. I was told that the minute we get to Armenia, we will have it all straightened out, at our first meeting with the Minister of Health. We set the agenda of all the meetings that we would need to have. I needed to have my hands into the entire program, so that I could design a good hospital. It has to fit well with its intended purpose.

It will take almost two weeks in Israel to meet all the people involved and for me to see the type of medical and surgical procedures that will be performed in the proposed hospital. The first meeting was scheduled take place in Rambam Medical Center in Haifa. This hospital was a 900-bed facility that served 1,100,000 people plus the U.S. Navy's Sixth Fleet. There we met Dr. Chaim Stein, Chief of Orthopedic Surgery. He was also involved with the Military Rehab Hospital and was the head of the team of doctors that went to Armenia to assess the medical situation.

Dr. Stein filled me in on the conditions that he experienced on his visit to Armenia. The following is a direct quote by Dr. Stein, written down by my wife Harriet, who was taking notes, of what he encountered when he visited the earthquake site. It should be noted, that his visit toke place six months after the earthquake struck. What he saw were the results of the lack of medical attention that the Soviet Union provided to all of these victims. "I found human beings in a physically broken state with multiple injuries and this at six months after the earthquake. I found many of the people with legs missing from the hip down, remaining bones projecting through the skin from various angles, similar cases were found with missing arms, backs, hips and severe spine injuries, still others having infections. Any hope of living useful productive lives for these people, if kept in this condition, where non-existent." Dr. Stein and his team took 61 patients, with the worst damage to their bodies, to the airport to be brought back to Israel, accompanied by a relative or aid. Once back in Israel, all these patients received the necessary surgery and were outfitted with prosthesis, so they will be able to live out their lives as independent human beings.

Dr. Stein told Harriet and me to follow him. He wanted us to meet the 61 patients that were under his care. I expected to be taken to some form of hospital room or area where recuperating patients were residing. He took us to a large outside garden area. To my amazement, I saw 61 people walking around, socializing, smiling and having a wonderful afternoon in this park-like setting. Please note that this was about six weeks after Dr. Stein brought those 61 people to Israel. I looked at Dr. Stein and said, "You created this situation in six weeks?" "No", he said, "I did all this in a little under three weeks. We are all here waiting for you to get with the program, so that we could all go back to Armenia together."

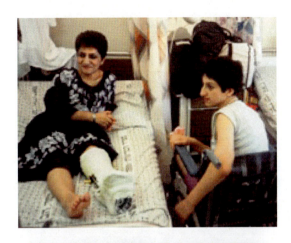

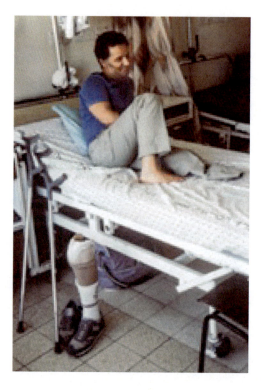

      This blew my mind. I served on the board of a teaching hospital for about 10 years. In addition, I underwent two hip replacement surgeries. I never witnessed results in the United States that were achieved here in Israel. I started to visit with some of the patients, when I realized there was a large press corps on the property. A number of television and newspaper reporters from Armenia, Israel and the United States were gathering stories. I met a woman who was walking with a cane and her legs still had some bandages on them. She gently walked to a bench, sat down, unhooked her leg to show me the prosthesis, then hooked the leg back on, stood up, and walked away. We met another fellow who was a commercial artist. His hand had been crushed in the earthquake. He thought he would never be able to make a living with his art anymore. There he stood, with the new arm and hand painting away with a smile on his face and ready to get on with his life. We met a young man about 13 years old with a crushed pelvis and a missing right leg from the hip down. The doctors designed a complete pelvis out of leather and other materials that could be adjusted as he grew, as well as outfitting him with a new leg. Seeing these people, my wife and I had tears rolled down our cheeks.

We started the series of meetings that would take us to three other hospitals within the next couple of weeks. One of the other hospitals that we visited was the Alyn Hospital in Jerusalem. There we met Dr. Shirley Meyer, the Medical Director and Orthopedic Surgeon. This was a 120-bed hospital that handled about 24 outpatients that arrived by ambulance every day. Quite a few of the very handicapped patients lived on the premises, in a special rehab section. My visit to all these hospitals was a fantastic learning experience for me. It was so different than my experiences with the medical profession in the United States. I was amazed at how far advanced the Israelis were in running hospitals and treating people. I felt that United States hospital administrators should spend some time in Israel and see how they treated patients.

Through all of the interviews and meetings with the various doctors, administrators and directors of various departments, two thoughts kept popping up all the time. Number one; everything that I design in the hospital must be patient friendly. That means, little items like in an exam room, there must be a mirror on the wall, so when the patient is finished with the examination, they can check to see that they're well put together. They can check their hair and makeup. There should be a shoehorn with a long handle in the room, that help people put their shoes back on. There must be a shelf in the bathrooms, so the patients will have a place to put their clothes, while washing or bathing. Who wants to use a bathroom without a clean place to set down your clothes? I noticed in the United States, in a number of hospitals, the patient has to put their clean undergarments on the toilet seat. We discussed many items of this nature that must be in the new facility. Every patient must be kept in a happy condition.

The second requirement was that a patient must never, under any circumstances, be left for more than one hour without knowing the status of their medical condition, what procedures are going to be done, and everything about their stay in the hospital. When the patient is not completely informed at all times, they start imagining all sorts of conditions. They can work themselves up into an unhappy situation. I noticed this in many hospitals in the United States. When a patient is admitted to the hospital on Tuesday, and a doctor does not do rounds until Friday, the patient is laying in their bed for days with nothing to do but worry and imagine the worst. Well-informed, happy patients have much better outcomes than ones that are left to worry.

The Israelis ran their hospital like a military attack operation. When a military attack plan goes into operation, everyone synchronizes their watches, the Air Force is put on high alert and prepares for the signal, the infantry is on high ground waiting for the action to begin and the tanks are in the valley awaiting orders. Then, at the right moment, the orders are given, and each group swings into action, as called for in the design of this operation.

The same approach is taken when a new patient is getting ready to arrive at an Israeli hospital. The patient is given a date and time to arrive. The admitting section has all the information ready to receive the patient. When the patient arrives, they are quickly escorted to their room, which is ready and waiting for them. The minute they enter the room, they are made comfortable in bed and allowed to rest for no more than one hour. Within the hour, the doctor and his team will visit the patient, and explain the entire procedure that is going to happen during their stay at this hospital. The doctor describes all of the tests that will be performed and everything else the patient would want to know. The doctor introduces the two or three of his assistants that are with him (or her). They explain that during the patient's entire stay, the doctor or one of these assistants will visit, to keep the patient up-to-date. The patient will never be forced to lie in bed, for hours, or days without knowing what's happening.

Everything in an Israeli hospital moves like clockwork, because it had been arranged prior to the patient's arrival. In the situation of a surgical patient that is to be fitted with a prosthetic, all measurements will be done before the surgery. The technician will manufacture the prosthetic, in a lab, inside the hospital. After surgery, the prosthetic will be ready for fitting, without any delay. This is far different to similar situations I have seen in the United States. Here, the prosthetic is built in a facility far from the hospital. Here, there will be delays at every step of a patient's care. Here, the patient has to wait days or weeks for the process to be completed.

After that never-ending week of meetings and demonstrations, my head and attaché case were filled to the rim with information and details. I had a good understanding of the type of hospital and facilities that they required. I worked out a schedule of approximate square footages and floors, etc. This information is used to calculate the size of this site that would be needed for this project. This is vital information for the upcoming meetings with the authorities in Armenia.

On August 13, 1989, Dr. Stein informed me that in two days, the 61 patients and their aides would be ready to return to Armenia. The medical team, my team & I, plus the press corps, were given details about the flight to Armenia. When the time came, the patients and their aides were the first to board the plane. When they were comfortably settled, the rest of us boarded. I should note that throughout our visit, the press corps was busy with video cameras and interviews. This press corps covered us wherever we went and whatever we did.

While on the plane, I walked through the cabin and had some informal chats with some of the patients. One woman took her arm off and put it on her seat's tray table. She told me the horror stories of that horrible day and the earthquake. She told me about the members of her family that had died. The saddest part of all their stories was that during the earthquake, and the days that followed, there was practically no help from any government agencies. Even 6 months after the earthquake, these people hadn't received any medical attention. They confirmed what Dr. Stein had described to me when we first met. They told me about watching their friends and relatives slowly die from their wounds, one by one. The one thought they all had was, "Will I be next?" It was hard to believe that the Soviet Union was not able to provide any medical attention to all these people that were in such desperate need.

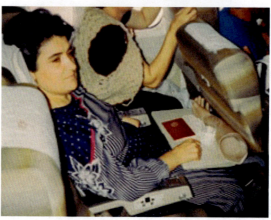

When our plane was getting close to arriving in Armenia, a patient delegation of two people asked to speak with me. They explained that when the Israelis first took the 61 patient's to Israel, they were strapped onto stretchers and hoisted onto the El Al airplane for the journey. Their relatives watched them be loaded into the plane like slabs of cargo. After six weeks of treatment in Israel, they were returning to Armenia as vital human beings. They were able to disembark the plane under their own abilities. They asked to be the last ones off of the plane. They wanted to wait a few minutes to add a little drama and theater to the situation. They would all walk down the large staircase from the plane to the ground, carrying themselves and their belongings, without any help from their aides. They wanted to make sure that the families watching this miracle from the windows of the terminal saw them as vital independent people. They were just about to give up and die, but were now fully capable of living great lives.

I agreed to their request, notified the flight attendant of the procedure that we would be following to disembark the plane. The plane landed and came to a stop on the tarmac. It was quite some distance from the terminal. The staircase was rolled up to the exit door of the plane. My wife and I, and everyone else that was not a patient exited the plane. When we reached the tarmac, we met the Commissioner of Health and a number of other dignitaries that greeted us. The women in our group were handed flowers as we were all welcomed to Armenia.

After a few moments of drama, we all looked up at the door of the plane for the first patient to start down the staircase. The press was stationed all around the staircase and video cameras recorded the event. Reporters were ready with their pencils for taking notes. Then it started. Each patient walked out the door and down the stairs, all on their own, with huge smiles. Some of them carried packages with them. The crowd was so quiet that you could hear a pin drop. No one in the audience, including myself, or any of the relatives watching through the terminal window, wanted to look at one another. This would reveal the flood of tears that were running down everyone's cheeks. It seems that during this entire precession, the world stood still. This was truly a miraculous event. After all the patients disembarked the plane, the reunion in the terminal was a loud, tearful, and joy filled event.

As soon as everyone was assembled in the terminal, government security personnel quickly separated all the VIPs, as we were called, from the patients and relatives. We were herded into a large room and waited for our luggage to appear. The Commissioner of Health notified us that we would be taken for a State reception in our honor, at a nearby catering hall. We were told to leave our luggage in this room and board the bus for our formal reception. We would be brought back to retrieve our luggage after the festivities. Since we were in a foreign country, we did as we were told. We boarded the bus. We proceeded through the crowded traffic for about a mile.

All of a sudden, a small yellow Volkswagen, drove up to the front of our bus, and forced the bus to the sidewalk. We watched, as three men jumped out of the Volkswagen, and quickly entered our bus. Everything happened so fast that there was no time to react. My first thought was that we were under attack by some dissidents. We could only guess that these people were unhappy with us interfering in their country's business. I thought they were going to pull out guns and shoot us all dead. Our interpreter spoke to the young men. These men saw us on television. They wanted to personally thank us for coming to their country to help them in their hour of need. They walked down the aisle of the bus, shook hands and thanked everyone, in their native tongue. This incident was extremely touching to our delegation. We sat down quietly with moist eyes and reflecting on this entire adventure. The three-man welcoming committee backed up their vehicle and our bus continued on its way to the catering hall.

At the catering hall, we were surrounded by local press. They got interviews for the local television station with their microphones and cameras. After a few minutes in the limelight, our security guards ushered us to our tables. Let the festivities begin.

As soon as we were comfortably seated, I noticed a line of waiters with a bottle in each hand. I soon found out that one bottle had vodka and the other Cognac. The waiters asked us all what we favored. I took the vodka. The Commissioner of Health stood up holding a glass and made a toast. In one gulp, she downed the liquid in her glass. I noticed that all the local dignitaries did the same thing. I am not much of a drinker so I slowly took a sip. Within a split second after that sip, the waiters that were standing behind us quickly filled the glass again. Then, a gentleman presumably from the American Embassy stood up and made his toast. And again, the fast gulp and my slow sip. Once more the glasses were quickly filled by the waiters. It seemed like an army of people made toasts, as each course of food was served. Finally this ritual came to an end. Everyone had calmed down and got ready for the formal speeches. I finished my small glass of vodka and pushed it away from me. After a while, all those little sips turned into a pretty big headache. I looked at my wife, who was staring into space with bulging eyes. I knew exactly how she felt. She was like me, and not much of a drinker. After the long plane ride and the emotional arrival, this was way beyond my physical capabilities. I am thankful that the speeches went on for a long time. It allowed us the chance to feel almost normal again. Finally, this welcoming adventure came to an end. We boarded the buses and went back to the airline terminal.

Harriet finished her toast.

At the terminal, my wife went to use the ladies room. Upon her return, she was shaking her head in a gesture of disbelief. "What was the problem?" I said. "You're not going to believe this, but in the ladies room, on the floor was a bucket. The bucket was loaded with strips of a newspaper, you know, cut up Sunday comics from the local newspaper. That was the toilet paper. One of the locals said we are lucky to have that." My goodness!! God bless America!!

We eventually found our luggage. I asked one of the security guards who spoke English, about getting someone to help us bring out luggage upstairs and out to our buses. He looked at me as if I was a stupid American. He explained in this country, they do not have luggage handlers. Everyone there carries their own luggage. He pointed to the large stair case. He pointed out a 2 x 8 wooden plank that was lying on the stairs. That is there, so you could drag your luggage up the wooden plank, to the main floor. He said that when you get to the exit, you will see another plank going down the stairs on the first floor to the street level. This arrangement makes it very easy for travelers to move luggage from one area to another. This was another 'I don't believe it' scenes. Please note that we were in Yerevan, the capital of Armenia, at the time. Could you imagine this happening in any American airport?

Once we made it up the staircases and into the bus, the bus driver loaded the luggage in the compartments under the bus. We all entered the bus and found our seats. We were off to our hotel. The bus driver told us that our hotel is the finest hotel in the Capitol of Armenia.

As we drove up to the hotel, the first thing I noticed was a large, splendid, architecturally designed building, in keeping with the time period of its construction. That indicated that this could be the finest hotel in Yerevan the Capitol of Armenia and a pleasant place to stay. Then I noticed, on the front steps leading up to the lobby, a 2 x 8 wooden plank for us to slide our luggage up into the hotel. Well, I thought, this hotel looks good on the outside.

Once we entered the lobby, the realities of the Soviet existence came to light. Everything I saw was dirty and broken. It seemed that the furniture was bought before the Art Deco era and was still in use. The windows were so dirty, that it was hard to see daylight. Just standing there and looking around the lobby, I could not help feeling the truth of a dark, dingy, un-cared for bureaucratic system of maintenance.

After dragging our luggage to our rooms, it was quite clear that the dingy feeling at the entrance, permeated throughout this entire facility. Upon entering the room, we found, much to our horror, the bed that we were to sleep in. It was really not a bed, but a glorified cot. There was no attempt at decoration or trying to make the resident feel comfortable.

Harriet went to the bathroom and started to close the door when I heard a loud scream. I rushed into the bathroom. In the bath tub, to my amazement, were about a dozen huge cockroaches, trying to up climb the sides of the slippery tub to escape. I guess I do not have to say this was not a very good welcome. I removed the strainer from tub drain and washed all the bugs away. There was no television set in the room. I did notice a small radio.

By this point, I was pretty cautious of everything in the room. I picked up the radio and examined it. I checked to see if it was plugged into the wall outlet. I looked for the end of the electric cord, and much to my surprise, there was no plug. Bare electric wires were jammed into the wall outlet. This is a number one fire hazard. This hotel was a horror. But that was daily life in the Soviet Union.

It seems that nothing was ever fixed or cleaned or attended to in any shape, means or manner. Out in the hall, on every floor, was a small card table with a matron in attendance. I learned later, that the duties of this matron, was that of a government spy. I was warned by a non-Soviet person that I should be very careful not only on the phone because the phones were all bugged, but remember normal conversation can be overheard. As they say, "When in Rome...", well you know the rest.

Harriet and I unpacked and got ready for the evening meal. To my surprise, when my suitcase was empty, I kept staring at it in hopes that all my shirts would appear. Just my luck, there were no shirts. When I packed my luggage in Israel, I evidently forgot to open a drawer in the dresser where my shirts were snuggled in. They are probably still there, waiting for me to pack them for the trip to Armenia. Harriet looked at me with a smile and said, "A shopping we will go."

So off we went to the bank to change dollars into the local currency. I gave the cashier $100 USD and he gave me the equivalent in local currency. I figured $100 I should be able to get three or four shirts. I made some inquiries as to where I could find stores that sell shirts. I was notified, with a smile, that they don't shop in stores in Armenia, because all the stores are completely empty of everything. They shop on the black-market.

This lovely young lady then took us by the hand for a walk just about two blocks from the hotel. We made a left turn for about 50 feet, then another left turn into an alley where the black market was. All the shirts you want were there for purchasing. I picked out three shirts that looked halfway decent and were in my size. Not knowing what the cost was between the local currency and the US dollar I just handed them the $100 worth of local currency. The woman selling the shirts got very angry. She grabbed two shirts back, said something that sounded very nasty to me, and kept the hundred dollars of local currency.

Our guide notified me that the amount of local currency I handed for the shirts was not worth hundred dollars. "But I made this exchange in a bank", I said. She laughed so hard. I just didn't understand what was going on. When she got control of herself, she said, "Nobody exchanges dollars in the bank. The bank pays the exchange rate that's listed by the government. This rate is calculated in favor of the local bank. Everyone goes to the black-market." We started back toward the hotel. About a block before we got to the hotel, she introduced us to a young man. He was about 25 years old. He exchanged more than five times the amount of local currency for each dollar then we got at the official bank. I was so amazed at how the black-market operates, in the open, all over the place, and not bothered by any government officials.

Just to spike your attention, later on in this book, I will inform you of the horrors of life under communism, when we started construction of the hospital. I learned the shocking realities of why everyday living conditions are so bad in the Soviet Union. Now that I have your interest, you will have to read the rest of this book, to find out exactly why these conditions exist.

We had the misfortune of having to stay at this hotel, but it was the best that they had. Our stay was for about a week. We made the best of the situation that we could. I needed the time to attend all the meetings in this bureaucratic country, and to get permission to travel all around the earthquake site, as well as other areas. At the earthquake site, I would need access to all their engineering and building department personnel, to obtain all the information I needed to design and build this hospital.

The next day, we were ready to start work. Harriet was with me, as a secretary, took all the notes, and created a great volume of this entire trip from beginning to end. It was because of her work, including all the detail, dates, names of people we met, plus times and places etc., which I was able to put together into a complete lecture series. I gave these lectures to a number of hospitals in the United States.

At our very first meeting, we met the Commissioner in charge of providing all the transportation, drivers, and interpreters that I would need. He also made arrangements at the earthquake site, so the people I needed to see, were available when I arrived. Since this Commissioner was responsible for this type of work, he was the guy that I needed to take care of the visa problem I discussed early. I showed him the discrepancy, with my wife having documents to travel to Armenia, Moscow, Leningrad and then back to New York, while I only had documents for Armenia. He said, "No problem. Give me your passports and visas and I will take care of it." He got on the phone, and called an aide who came rushing in very promptly. He explained what had to be done to take care of my problem quickly. The aide took all the documents, and off he went.

My team and I were being set up with meetings with his staff. I should note now that the Executive Director of JDC was with me and my team at all the meetings. At our first meeting, I informed these bureaucrats of all equipment and personnel that I needed to do my work. My first need was enough cars or a bus with drivers and interpreters to be made available during my stay in the area. I also requested that he contact the Mayor of Leninakan, where the earthquake was, and have him ready to meet at 10am the next day, with all of his department heads from the building department, engineering department, and representatives of all the utilities in the town. I also requested an in-depth tour of the entire area affected by the earthquake, in an effort to select the proper location to build this hospital.

     These bureaucrats, who were charged with getting me whenever I needed, looked puzzled. The one who looked like a leader said, "We can't do that." I explained that we are here volunteering our services to build a hospital, free of charge, to treat all of your people that were so terribly injured by the earthquake. With the shrub of the shoulder he said, "That's very nice of you, but I can't give you what you want." I sat there looking at them, in the state of amazement. This bureaucratic explained to me, that the original team assigned to this project was reassigned. He and his new team is what we have to work with. He told us that he knows nothing about the earlier arrangements and could not carry out my wishes.

     I failed to mention the name of Executive Director of JEC was Aryeh Cooperstick. He said that he was at the original meeting, with the Prime Minister of Armenia, in New York, when this project was agreed upon. Mr. Cooperstick asked the bureaucrat to call the Prime Minister's office, let him know that we are here and to request a meeting. With a look of horror on the bureaucrats' faces, they said, "No, We could never do that." Mr. Cooperstick picked up the phone, dialed the operator, and in a very determined voice of authority stated that he must contact the Prime Minister. The problem was that the request was made in English, but the operator did not speak English. The head bureaucrat started to laugh and felt that the Prime Minister would never agree to see us. In a very cocky manner, he picked up the phone and made the same request, in his own language. The operator told him to hang on and they will make the connection. This bureaucrat sat there with the smug face, waiting for the results. He was sure that no meeting would be arranged. All of a sudden, this bureaucrat's face turned white, as I heard him say, "Yes Sir. We will be right up." He instructed us to follow him.

     We went out the door, down the hall, and walked up about three floors. It was decorated in a fashion that indicated that this is where the big man did his business. We were directed into a waiting room. A young lady was waiting for us. She smiled as we walked in. She said, "The Prime Minister is waiting for you." Harriet, I and Aryeh were the first ones to enter the room. All the bureaucrats entered the room behind us. The

Prime Minister, with a big smile on his face, went up to Aryer Cooperstick and gave him a big hug. He said that he was very glad to see him in his country and that the hospital we were going to build was desperately needed. He turned to Harriet & I and gave us an extremely warm welcome. At that point, the Prime Minister pivoted around and faced the bureaucrats. In a commanding voice told them to sit on the chairs in the back of the room.

We were escorted to the soft chairs surrounding a table where an aide brought in all sorts of local snacks for our enjoyment. Needless to say, the bureaucrats got nothing. After some small talk, Aryer told the Prime Minister that, "Mr. Efron is head of the team to build the hospital." He said that I have requests that would be needed in order to carry out the mission. The Prime Minister said, "Don't tell me what you need. I will take care of that." He turned to the bureaucrats sitting along the back wall and told them to "provide Mr. Efron with anything he requests, in a very expeditious manner". He said, "If any report comes back to me that Mr. Efron is not pleased, you will feel my wrath." We said our goodbyes, thanked the Prime Minister for his help, and left.

I again gave the bureaucrats a list of all my requirements, including the cars, drivers and interpreters. The next morning, at 9 o'clock, everything we asked for was sitting in front of hotel, bright and shiny, waiting for us to take charge. I gathered my team and boarded the 4 large vehicles. Each one had a driver and interpreter. They notified me that we will need to stop for gas for the long trip.

At the gas station, I was surprised to see the way it was designed. It had a round center stanchion with four gas hoses equally spaced around it. There was a car located at each gas hose around the stanchion filling their gas tanks. Our vehicles lined up behind the vehicles filling their tanks. I noticed cars lining up behind us waiting for their turn to fill their tanks. The problem with this design was very evident. When the first car was finished filling the tank, they could not back out, because we and the cars behind us would block their way. This was happening at all four gas hoses. A number of young employees came out to direct traffic. They struggled to maneuver the cars by requesting some cars to move little to the right and some to the left, in an effort to obtain space so the first car could back out of this tangled mess. It took quite some time until we were able to fill our tanks and be on our way. This ridiculous situation, due to a horrible design of this filling station, went on all day, every day. I learned from one of our guides, that there were quite a number of gas stations designed this way. It is hard to believe that the designers of these stations did not realize the problems they are causing, and replicated this awful situation in many locations anyway.

All along the route as we were driving, you could see that the entire economy was run by the black market. All the official stores we passed were completely empty. There was nothing to buy in any store. However, all along the route, there were cars parked with their trunks open, selling everything imaginable from meat and vegetables, to toys and computers. Whatever you wanted to buy, you just drove up to the car with the item you needed. There were rows and rows of tables set up, selling all kind of vegetables and fruits. Nothing had a price, we noticed. Everything was a matter of bargaining. The problem with products like meat, sitting in the back trunk of a car, in the sun, waiting to be purchased, is that it did not look very sanitary. But life went on.

As we drove, we went past many housing developments and communities that were not affected by the earthquake. After about 2 hours of driving, I looked out the window, and saw nothing but a large open field of debris. There were no sidewalks, no roadways, just huge open fields with extremely large piles of destroyed building materials. My guide said, "This is it. You're in the earthquake area." As we drove, we started to see large apartment house structures with their entire exterior walls gone. You could look directly into all of the apartments. You could see whatever furniture had remained that was not thrown out by the earthquake. We saw cows grazing where the lobbies of some of the buildings use to be. We rode quite a long distance, and all we saw was the ruins of their buildings.

I was told that the destroyed buildings were built after the communists took over. We saw other large structures that looked more like government buildings that had very little damage. We were informed that the relatively undamaged buildings were built prior to the takeover of the communists. Later on, I did some research on the construction in each era. The buildings constructed before communism were built using standard approved proper engineering and construction methods. The buildings constructed under communism were built by people who had no knowledge of construction. Maybe someday I'll write another book about all the construction methods that I saw. I wondered why many of these buildings didn't fall down long before the earthquake.

We arrived at a portion of the town, or what was left of it, that contained the city government. As we drove up, we were mobbed by the people who were suffering this calamity. They asked if we were the Israeli doctors. They needed the doctors. They needed the Israelis. We notified them that we were the design and construction team to build the hospital for the Israelis. We were overcome by all the hugs, kisses, and crying by the people we met. Harriet sat down in one area with a group of women. Each one told her their stories of their husbands and/or children that were killed in the earthquake. Some of these people were relatives of the 61 people that the Israelis brought back to life. When word got around that the 61 people returned from Israel and were living and walking human beings again, the entire community felt that there might be life after this earthquake.

Constructed before Communism

We were wined and dined in whatever facilities they had where food could be served. We were taken to the back of what used to be a restaurant. It seems that the back end of this structure did not collapse. The Mayor and his senior staff did their best to provide a festive welcoming lunch. The meal was finished, and all the customary toasts were complete. We were preparing to leave when the Mayor stood up and said one more toast. I thought, "Oh my God. This is going to last forever." The Mayor lifted his glass, which was filled again with vodka, and toasted this wonderful flower amongst us. Everyone looked at him and wondering what is he talking about. And then he turned to the only woman in the room, which happened to be my wife, Harriet, and toasted this wonderful flower amongst us. You should have seen the smile on her face. That incident was something that she never forgot.

    Now it is time to get to work. We drove around the earthquake site as the Mayor went into detail of what happened in each area. He took out a map of the area. He and I examined the map, and looked out the window at the area, in an effort to ascertain a possible site for the proposed hospital. My structural engineer and the Deputy Mayor were with us in the back seat of the car. My structural engineer noticed two Russian soldiers that passed by, dressed in fatigue uniforms. They wore working fatigue hats with the Russian insignia of the hammer and sickle. My engineer casually said, "Boy I would love to get one of those hats as a souvenir." With that, the Deputy Mayor opened the car door, jumped out of the car, and took the hats from both soldier's heads. He came back and gave my engineer one of the hats and handed me the other. I had no idea what was happening, because I was concentrating on the map and talking with the Mayor. When he gave me the hat, I didn't realize what it was. I grabbed it and felt this material thing, and felt some sort of grease on the inside. After examining this prize, I realized it was a soldier's hat and this soldier used a lot of hair cream. After our day's activity examining all the sites, we went back to our hotel. I washed the hat, dried it off, and packed it in my luggage. That hat now proudly hangs on the wall in my computer and photography den.

Harriet, the flower amongst us.

When we were in Israel, I calculated the square-foot and cube needed for the building. I kept this in mind while selected the site, so it would be adequate to construct the building. The site I selected was as close to the area with the largest population of people. I felt the hospital should be located where would be easiest for the patients and families to commute.

The next day, we had a meeting with the Zoning and Building Code Commissioner. He gave me a lecture on the building location size and construction, in such a beautifully bureaucratic way that it made me smile. His first thought was that he wanted the hospital located as far out of town as possible. He felt that a hospital is a negative place and should not be located in town. I explained to him that hospitals are a place where people go to take care of their medical problems. The hospital should be convenient to the majority of the people that need the facility. Most of the people traveling to the hospital have all kinds of handicaps, so that the location should not require long distances of travel for the patients. We must've spent at least an hour or more debating this philosophy, until I finally convinced him to move the hospital much closer to where the majority of the people were. I guess this was a compromise.

The next thing he told me was that 'a hospital is not a happy place'. They have negative feelings and therefore we cannot call this building a 'hospital'. He dictated that this building will be called a "children's rehabilitation building'. Okay, I gave him that one. The next demand was that the building could not be more than one story high. This blew my mind. If you speak to any hospital architect or administrator, they will tell you to never build hospital one story high. Communication between different departments would be far, inefficient and very difficult. In Tucson, Arizona the community forced the Tucson Medical Center to be one story tall, so that it would not block the view of the people living in the area. That hospital is a horror. I know this from firsthand experience. When my wife had her first stroke, she was taken into Tucson Medical Center. Every time I went to visit her, I got lost. Walking within TMC feels like miles. The staff has to use golf carts to get around. I looked for the golf carts to bum a ride, whenever I was there. Every time I left, I could never find the same way out. It was quite a chore to find where I parked my car. TMC's floorplan is humongous. Simple things like getting equipment from one room to another or serving food from the kitchen are a disaster. I tried to explain this to the Commissioner without success. "The building must and will be one story high." he said.

Another problem with hospitals is that they are living and breathing entities. Hospitals are always in a state of construction. It's just the nature of the business. Every time you hire a new doctor, they come with a new program and different equipment. This requires an alteration to the building. Space for additional construction should always be considered and made part of the original building. A one-story building makes it difficult to expand without having to add area to the site. Expansion on a single story building will require the acquisition of additional land. It is always more efficient to build up than out.

I pulled a fast one. I was able to sneak a 2nd story rough-in past the building department bureaucrats, and it was built in. At the entrance of the building, which enclosed the middle third of the entire first floor, I designed a very high ceiling that was called an atrium. The height of this atrium just happened to be high enough to accommodate a second floor. I told the authorities that this additional height was needed to get light into the center of the building from the windows. I laid out the structure in such a manner that in the future, to create a second floor, you just have to install factory built reinforced concrete planks of standard size that will fit perfectly with the interior concrete beams. I made provisions for the installation of 2 staircases, one on each end and also for a one-story lift. I also arranged the plumbing, electric, utilities etc., to be bundled so that they could easily be extended up to the second floor. The building plan sheets showing how to add the 2nd floor were given to the Israeli doctors only. They weren't included in the set submitted for building plan approval.

Back to the Commissioner's requirements: Since he felt that a hospital had a negative impact on the community, I was directed to make sure that the design of the building did not look like a hospital, but like a large one-family home. At this point, I was a little tired of the debate, so we granted him this wish.

The last requirement, he said, the building must be built with reinforced concrete and clad with tufa stone. The tufa stone request was no problem. About 95% of all construction in Armenia uses tufa stone. This particular stone has a brown finish that is quite pleasing. In addition, the stone is found everywhere in Armenia.

However, the reinforced concrete request for a one-story building is idiotic. Reinforced concrete columns and beams are much larger than steel and therefore not very efficient in a one-story building. Reinforced concrete is most efficient in high-rise buildings. The Commissioner told me that the Armenians are experts with concrete. They never use steel in this country because there are no steel facilities in Armenia. All steel would have to be imported at great cost, while concrete is easily available and very inexpensive. This point I lost. The building was designed as a one-story reinforced concrete building.

He mentioned that wood was nowhere to be found in Armenia, so he instructed me to not use wood construction in any place in the building. He said, all I have to do is to conform to these requirements, and all the rest I want to do could be done. The building department will not interfere.

Now that I know the building is going to be one-story, all my calculations of square footage & cube went out the window. Switching quickly, I had redo my calculations, and coordinate with the site that we selected, to make sure that there is enough room to fit the building, walking areas and outdoor rehab gardens, etc. After another four days of meetings, I had all the information needed to design this building.

When we got back to our hotel at the capital, I was notified by the Commissioner who was taking care of my visa problem, that everything was squared away. I was told to stop off at his office and get the documentation. I thanked him and off I went, back to the hotel, to meet Harriet, and pack for our next stop, which was Moscow. We slid our luggage down the 2 x 8 ramp from the hotel. The driver put it in the luggage compartment. We drove to the airport and boarded our plane.

Within the first 5 minutes on the plane, I felt maybe we should get off this rust bucket and try to make other arrangements. However, being in a communist country, you can't do things like that. The seats were broken, seatbelts were nonexistent, it was filthy, and had the worst interior of any plane that I have ever seen. We were notified, due to the shortage of fuel, we would have to make at least one stop. Depending upon how much fuel we were given for each leg of the journey, we might need additional stops. I didn't feel reassured. The hope was that on the first leg of the journey, we would have enough fuel to land someplace to refuel before taking off again.

On the plane were some civilians. The seat next to me was occupied by a lovely young man who was trying to learn English. He showed me some of the English words and phrases that he was studying. The first one was "Mary had a little lamb ". As I turned the pages of this little study book, all the rest of the teaching examples were very similar to good old Mary. He tried to communicate with me but it was hopeless. No way could we have any type of conversation.

We finally landed in Moscow, safe and sound. There to greet us, was a driver and guide/interpreter in a large black limo. The driver spoke very little English but our guide/interpreter spoke fluent English. We drove to our hotel which was located near Red Square. We were taken into the lobby and seated in a lounge area near the check-in desk. Our guide took our passports and other paperwork to the front desk to check us in. We sat there for quite a while and I noticed there was a lot of conversation going on. It seemed like there was an argument between our guide and the person behind the check-in counter.

Our guide came up to us and said we have a problem. "What's the problem", I said. It seems when we left the hotel in Armenia, I was supposed to go to the front desk to officially have my documents stamped to check out. I did not know that. The Commissioner who gave me the paperwork told me that we were all set, and should go right to the plane. I never formally checked out from the hotel. She said, "You cannot check in here, because you are not in Moscow according to the paperwork. You are still in Armenia." Oh, this is a wonderful bureaucracy. I said, "What am I supposed to do, go back to Armenia?" Our guide said, "No, You cannot do that, because you do not have a visa to go to Armenia." What a beautiful dilemma! I said to our guide, "We are guests of your government. Your country invited us here for the humanitarian work we are doing in Armenia. Your country is paying for all the hotel costs, food, travel and any other incidental costs. It is up to you, and/or someone else, to wake up a big shot politician to straighten this out." After another half hour or so, our guide came back with a number of papers for me to sign. They basically said in Russian, I was told, that I am here legally and will abide by all rules and laws of the country. I signed, we smiled, and were taken up to a room.

As we entered the room, a maintenance person quickly pushed by us, unplugged the black phone that was sitting on the dresser, and installed a red phone. My guide notified us to be very careful with everything we say on the phone because it is all being recorded. I told Harriet, "Let's not use this phone."

We looked out the window and there was a fabulous view of Red Square with those magnificent onion domes glowing in the moonlit evening.

The next day after some introductions, we met with some government officials. They were trying to find ways of doing business with the United States to improve their economy. We spoke about a proposed hotel to be built at the outskirts of Moscow. It seems that because of the growth around Moscow, new facilities had to be provided to satisfy the need around that area. The Russian government was willing for the Americans to take over the entire project with the exception of the supply and installation of all concrete work. It seems that concrete is a specialty in Russian. After much conversation, we learned that all the money and profits that were earned in building this project were not allowed to leave the country. Because of this mandatory condition, it does not make sense to get involved in such a deal. They explained that the way to get your money out of the country is to first buy Russian government surplus trucks and tanks. These can then be sold to other countries in Europe. That way profits could be taken out of Russia. I think you can now realize why we ended the meetings without making any deal.

We were taken to the famous GUM department store. This was really not a department store. It was a huge, and I mean a HUGE, glass enclosed shopping mall right off Red Square. As we went through the area, passing shop after shop, we saw that all of the stores were completely void of any stock. Every store was completely empty, except for a couple of employees that stood there, wasting time. All of a sudden, we noticed a huge line in front of one store. We were told, that for some reason that store has something to sell. So everybody lined up, with hopes of getting in, before whatever it was they were selling, was sold out. I asked, "Why are so many people standing there? They do not know what was for sale". It didn't matter. Whatever it was, they needed it. They had very little-to-nothing. They had money to spend, but there was nothing to spend it on.

To satisfy my curiosity, we went into a jewelry store. The store clerk smiled and asked, "Can I help you?" Our interpreter was always with us doing her job. I said, "Yes, You can start by showing us what you have to sell." Our interpreter past our remarks over and the clerk just looked at us with a puzzled expression and pointed to the empty showcases. She said, after it was interpreted, "I think we do have something in the back." She went into the back room. She came out and gave us a small lapel pin. We thanked her and left. It was of no use to us.

GUM Department Store.

     Our guide told us that buying in retail stores is not the thing to do in the Soviet Union. Whatever you need, you make an application to the government and in time, if approved, they will give you a voucher to purchase that item. She said, "My son needed shoes, so we submitted for a voucher. About three months later, we got the approval to buy the shoes. The problem was to find a store that has shoes to sell. I had to wait until it was announced that shoes were available at a particular store. Then I could purchase the shoes with the voucher.

     When received the notice of the location of the store, I was working as a guide for a tour group. Here's the dilemma, do I leave the tour group and maybe get fired, or stay with the group and not get the shoes?" When the people in the tour group found out about the problem, they told her to go get the shoes. They waited where they were until she got back. She thanked them and rushed down to the store.

It had an extremely long line. Everybody had the money and the voucher and wanted to get shoes. She was able to meet someone in authority that she was friendly with, who managed to get her up front of the line and in within a reasonable amount of time. She got the shoes for her son. She went back to the tour group to continue the day's travel. Now the question comes up, what about her husband's shoes? What about her shoes? What about sweaters, jackets and all of the rest of the clothing? This is a very hard life.

She told us that before our group goes to any restaurant, she has to notify the restaurant that we are coming. This is because we are VIP guests of the government. The restaurants have been directed to get whatever food we order. She opened her large pocketbook to show us all the plastic bags that she kept. She told us to order as much food as we want, plus an extra amount. She wanted to take home the food that was left over. She was going to stuff the plastic bags she was hiding. We ordered a good amount of food and made sure she filled those plastic bags.

Then I did a stupid thing, I asked for a second couple of coffee. Our guide said something in Russian to the waiter who walked away with an angry face. She told us that they do not have coffee in their country. The only coffee available is for VIPs like us. And only one cup is allowed. So when I asked the second cup, the waiter was very upset.

The thing that I don't understand, is why all of these people, living under these conditions, did not revolt years before. Instead they accepted these horrible conditions. This was a real eye-opener for me. Based on what I saw, I decided that doing business with the Soviet Union is not for me. At that time, they were still fully Communist but were starting to look to the West in an effort to make whatever deals they could.

We were taken to a store that was run by the United States government and only allowed United States citizens to shop in the store.

When we entered, we were amazed at all the items for sale that were non-existent to Soviet citizens. Harriet and I did some shopping and bought two cartons of cigarettes, as a gift for our driver and interpreter. When we got to the car and gave them the cigarettes, they both grabbed the package and wanted to keep both cartons of cigarettes. I managed to make sure that the driver got one carton and our interpreter got the other carton.

The next day I was told, as a treat for us, arrangements were made for us to go to Leningrad or Stalingrad, whichever it was called at that time. Our guide and driver took us to the railroad station and told us that a driver and interpreter will pick us up at the other end. We boarded the train for the overnight trip to Leningrad. We were given a private compartment. This sounds great, but it was extremely small and uncomfortable. It was impossible to sleep, because I swear the train's wheels were square. All the banging and noise that I heard as this train roared down the track, could only be achieved with square wheels. It was a blessing to get to Leningrad and out of that train.

We were given a private tour through some fabulous buildings that were restored in keeping with the era that they were build. All the buildings were kept in fantastic condition. The whole history of Russia was experienced by us going through these buildings with a very knowledgeable guide. All visitors had to remove their shoes and put on these woolly socks, as not to scrape the floors. We met a number of local people and were taken for a great lunch to finish off a day of sightseeing. We had good sleeping quarters that evening. The next day we were flown back to Moscow to catch a flight back to the US.

We were standing in line at the airport, slowly working our way to check-in, where our credentials and luggage were inspected. We got to the point where there was just one man in his 30s in front of us. When they checked his luggage, the inspector pulled out a book. I did not see the name of the book as it was quite small. The inspectors had a quick conference and then they both seized the young man, turned him around and a guard put handcuffs on him. The guard grabbed his luggage and off they went and disappeared into a back room. Where they went, what he did, what happened to them, we don't know. We took a great sigh of relief, once we were sitting in our plane and were in the air leaving the Soviet Union.

When I got back to my office, I started the process of designing this building. The first problem I faced was that we use feet and inches for our measurements in the United States, but the Armenians use the metric system. It makes it easier for me, and will save me a lot of time, I thought, if I use feet and inches, then have someone from my staff convert it to metric before sending it out to the client. The major problem is that you cannot build a building if you just convert the numbers. As an example, if the plans call for a 3/4" pipe and you convert that to metric, you'll need a 1.905cm pipe. They don't make that size of pipe. It would need to be rounded up to 2cm. But is that correct when you consider the inside diameter of the pipes? It can get complicated. We had to re-design so things were in sizes for the building materials that they could buy.

The big problem that really scared me was that the standard method of designing a building was not available to me. Usually I design a building in a very rough form and create what's known as a schematic plan. I sit down with my client to review the plan to make sure my interpretation meets all of the client needs. At that point, any changes, errors or omissions can be corrected. It's a good point to get feedback and direction from the client and any other people that are involved. I take these adjusted drawings and create what's called a preliminary drawing, which is the same drawing, but in much more detail. Again we have a chance to review it with the client and make sure everything is correct so we can all stay on page. Once that is done, I'd proceed with documents that are used for construction. In this case however, I do not have a client with me at this early stage of the design process. The people needed for decisions are in Armenia and Israel. All the information that I have is either in my head, or on the tons of notes that I took.

Here I am, all alone to design this building basically from memory. I better get it right. Anything wrong could be a negative reflection on the United States Government. When the building plans were completed, we took all the drawings and specifications, packed them up, and turned them over to the New York headquarters of our construction company. They sent the plans out to the construction crew in Armenia to start work.

After a few days, I started to get daily progress reports. Each report I received said the same thing, "No work done today". I contacted the President of the construction company to find out what was going on. He said, "Al, sit down." He described the Soviet system of construction. It was used not only for construction, but for maintenance, cleaning, or any other work that has to be done. The system is as follows:
The Commissioner of Employment is given a list of the type of employees; electricians, carpenters, etc., and how many are needed. The Commissioner assembles these people from a government list. He notifies them where and when to report for work. When the people arrive at the work site, they are given a form to sign. It basically says they reported for work. This form is sent to the Commissioner of payroll. When the Commissioner of payroll receives all the forms for the day, he issues checks to the workers for that day. In the meantime, no work was done. So now that the worker received his or her check, they politely go home. As far as the employees are concerned, the work is complete for that day. The next day, the same thing happens and on and on and on.

It seems there is no Commissioner to check to see if any work is actually done. No one knows. No one cares. It just works that way. That's why in every hotel or public space, everything is broken or in terrible condition. The people at the hotel, or any building, put in a work order. The personnel are assigned. They sign-in at the site, get their check and go home. The work is never done.

This is very hard to understand and to believe but this is exactly what was happening. I said to the President of the construction company, "What are we going to do? We made a commitment, not only to the JDC, but also to the United States State Department." He said, "Al, don't worry. I will handle this. I have an idea how to do it. I will make sure that this building is built in accordance with your drawings. That is my commitment to you."

About four or five days went by until I received another daily report. To my great delight, it said "Construction is moving ahead at a rapid pace". Every day the daily reports went into detail of all the work that was being done. I had to find out what miracle he performed to create this change. I found out the simple truth. The contractor quickly delivered to the site, enough money to cover the cost of paying all employees a second check, equal to the check that the government was paying them. The employee was given this second check, if the worker put in a full day's work and moved the construction job forward very rapidly. They felt it was worth it and the crew started actually working. The good old saying holds true, "Money Talks". The building was finished ahead of schedule and on budget. It was a one story building, built of reinforced concrete and clad in tufa stone. It was not call a hospital. It was called the Children Rehabilitation Center.

When the building was completed, I was invited back to witness the opening ceremony of taking over the building. I did not have the time to be able to attend the building opening. As I heard later, the building worked well and was very successful. A great many people will be human again with prosthetic arms, legs, pelvises and whatever the Israeli doctors were capable of doing in that building.

Shortly after, I was back in my office, and into the usual business and practice of architecture. I received a phone call at 9am from two diplomats that I met while in Armenia. They informed me that the Prime Minister sent them to the United States in an effort to recruit me to work with them. They wanted to start a business arrangement for our two countries to work together. They informed me that they were authorized to offer me the position of an official representative of Armenia.

Notice the raised roof clear story, to accommodate a future second floor

I asked where they were. "We are about three blocks from your office and would like to come up and talk to you." I invited them to come right up. They arrived a few minutes later with big smiles on their faces, saying they were glad to see me. During our preliminary conversation, I learned the most bizarre facts of their visit. Their government sent these two diplomats to the United States without making any arrangements for a hotel for them to stay. In addition, they were not supplied with any money that they would need to book a hotel, pay for meals, or any other normal travel & living expenses.

My first thought was, "What to do with these two gentlemen?" I remembered a very nice young man I met who worked for the embassy when we were first planning this trip. I contacted him to see if he could provide lodging and some funds for these two diplomats. He informed me that he would be able to make arrangements for quarters for them for that evening. In addition he will try to get the necessary funds that they would need for their stay in New York. He asked me if I could entertain them for the rest of that day, to give him time to put this package together. He gave me an address where I could bring the man that night after 10pm.

I took the two diplomats on a short tour of New York City and showed them some of the buildings that I designed. One building was a high-rise apartment house, which also contain the four-story Mormon Church, plus the Museum of American Folk Art located on the ground floor. This building was located in the Lincoln Center area. After touring the facilities, I took them to the gift shop. I wanted to buy them each a gift that represents the United States. They both selected a wood carving of Uncle Sam, painted in red, white and blue. I purchased these two items. The clerk put them in a plastic bag for each of them. When they gave them each this gift, they had a quick conference, and then approached me with a request. They asked for some of the plastic bags the gifts were put in. They saw the look on my face and realized that I was not aware that plastic bags were a premium in their country. I spoke to the clerk. She graciously gave me a large stack of plastic bags for these foreign guests.

It was still quite early. I decided to bring them to Staten Island, where I can give them an in-depth tour of the Staten Island University Hospital, of which I was a board member. I spoke to our CEO who made all the necessary arrangements. The staff of the hospital prepared a VIP tour of the facilities. They were blown away by what they called a high-tech operation. To us this was just standard hospital facilities and procedures. I took them to my house to say hello to my wife and freshen up for dinner. I call the manager of our country club and told him about these foreign visitors. He told me he would provide a very special dinner for the four of us for the evening.

At dinner, these two diplomats were utterly amazed and shocked at the amount of food and the quality that was served. They told me that everything I was able to show them on this visit was so far above the standards that they had back home. That evening around 10pm, I dropped them off at the address given to me. We found everything in order for their visit. During the next week, I set up meetings with various business people to see if there was any interest in doing work in Armenia. The big problem that developers from the United States encounter in trying to do business with the Soviet Union, is the fact that you could not take any profits out of the Soviet Union. At the end of the week they thanked me for the wonderful time and experience that they had in the US. They returned to Armenia, and I went back to the practice of architecture.

US/Europe Consortium

The architectural practice of Shuman, Lichtenstein, Claman & Efron was growing into a very large office. We designed many successful luxury high-rise apartment buildings in Manhattan, major shopping centers and a great number of hospital and nursing home projects. We also started to work overseas. We were preparing to do huge projects in China and the Soviet Union. Both these communist countries were in the early stages of trying out democracy and were looking for arrangements to work with the United States.

One day, I had a phone call from an architect in London trying to form a consortium of architects throughout Europe and the United States. The basic idea was that if any architect within our consortium gets a job in another country, then the consortium architect from that country will become the eyes and ears of the original architect. Harriet and I flew to London to meet the architects in an effort to put this consortium together. We did manage to set up this arrangement. Our hosts managed to create a fabulous time for Harriet and I in London.

The one thing in London that blew my mind was when I got into one of their cabs. I couldn't help but look around at all the space that was in the interior of the cab. We felt like we were sitting in a limousine. I realized that London cabs do not have trunks. The space that is usually the trunk in American cars are converted into space in the passages section.

While riding in the cab, the cabdriver turned around and asked me, "How is your black mayor doing?" I looked at the driver and asked him, "First of all, how you known I am from New York? And second of all, how do you know the mayor is black?" He turned around, looked me squarely in the eye, and said, "Young man, you have a very thick New York accent, and our newspapers cover everything that's going on in your part of the world." I couldn't help but to wonder, "Do New York City cabdrivers know what's going on in London?"

Un-Ethical Lawyers

The vast majority of the projects that we designed were very successful. We created a reputation that allowed us to work for a great many of the major hi-rise residential developers, federally funded projects through the Department of Housing and Urban Development (HUD), hospitals, nursing homes, shopping centers, etc. Along with all the great things that we were doing, it is inevitable to hit some bad projects.

I remember we designed and built a high-rise luxury apartment house next to a lot that had a one-story building on it. Manhattan real estate is too expensive for an old one-story building to sit on a piece of property. Eventually another luxury apartment house will replace the one-story building with a high rise right next to ours. It just so happens that in one of our apartments, we ended up with a large storage closet whose exterior wall was facing the open space above that one-story building. It is against the building code to have a legal window required for ventilation on a lot line wall. A living room, bedroom, or kitchen is required to have a legal window. A closet is not considered a living room and therefore does not need a window. We reasoned it would be nice to have a small window in the closet to bring in some light. When a new building is put up on the adjacent lot, then this window will have to be blocked. In order to make it legal, we worked out an arrangement with the Department of Buildings. The window would contain wire glass to prevent any breakage and therefore if there was a fire, the adjacent building would not be affected. In addition we put a sprinkler head above the window as added protection to keep fire from spreading to another building. That's what our drawings had shown and that's what was approved for this closet by the New York City Department of Buildings.

This building was built in conformance with the approved drawings. This apartment was sold to a family who used that large room as a closet as it was designed. Years later, the building was sold and that apartment became empty. When the renting agent examined the apartment and noticed that large closet with the window, he came up with a brilliant idea to call this closet a 'Junior Bedroom'. A 'Junior Bedroom' is designated as a living room and therefore requires a legal window. Making this change creates an illegal condition. This renting agent had no idea what he was doing and sold the apartment under those incorrect conditions. Lo and behold, the owners of the adjacent one-story building, demolished the building, and put up an apartment house. The people that were living in that apartment and using that closet illegally as a 'Junior Bedroom', found a brick wall about 1 inch away from the window. To make a long story short, they hired an attorney to sue us for designing an illegal situation.

At the deposition, it became very clear that we did not make any error. It was a renting agent's mistake. The young opposing attorney said to us that he could never win this case because we did nothing wrong. He went on to say this is his first case. The experience of going through a complete legal case, handling all the paperwork and everything else that goes into it would be great for him. It's in his best interest to continue with the lawsuit, even though he knows he will lose, just for the experience. We told this young attorney that we are not his father and we do not have to support his education. What he was doing was completely unethical. All this was to no avail. The suit went on until it was finally thrown out of court.

However, we had $100,000 deductible as part of our errors and omissions insurance. This law suit cost us quite a bit of money. I don't remember the exact amount, but usually we spent somewhere around $30-$40,000 for legal fees with a nonsense cases like this.

I Am On The Hook

I remember another great story in reference to a project I was working on that kept me up many nights. I am the type of architect that does everything for my clients. When I meet with any government department, I work out all deals and sign all statements necessary to make sure the project moves ahead.

My client owned property in Westchester, New York. We were given the commission to design and build an apartment house on his property. When I filed with the Building Department, I discovered that there was a large, terra-cotta sewer pipe that was installed in the 1800s and ran right through the middle of the property. The Building Department Commissioner was concerned that if this pipe was ever broken, it could be very expensive and difficult to repair. The Commissioner was also concerned with the vibrations from the piles that we will have to drive into the ground because of the poor soil conditions. I showed the Commissioner how we could lay out the piles, so they would not affect the existing pipe. The Commissioner looked at me and said that he would approve this drawing, if I personally sign, that if anything goes wrong, I am personally responsible for all costs and conditions to repair the pipe. I quickly signed. I called a meeting at the job site with the contractor. I explained the situation. I showed him the drawings that the Building Department approved, and if they follow the plans, they would not damage the pipe when they drive in the piles. I also told the contractor that I am personally responsible. If they screw up, I'll be on them so hard they will feel like it's the end of the world.

I am not sure if the pile driver held my drawing upside down or what he did, but the first pile went right through the middle of the pipe. Needless to say, my phone rang and it was the Commissioner telling me, in all this beautiful language, that he needs us to fix that pipe. After a hard meeting with the pile driver, everything was agreed to and a specialist was called to fix the pipe. Once that was done everybody was happy. Whoever paid the bill, I don't know but it wasn't me. The Commissioner allowed us to continue with construction. Construction can be a tough business.

Again The Mafia?

Every day in the practice of architecture, there is a new adventure. This new adventure took place on a sunny afternoon, at a meeting that I had called on the construction site. The building was a luxury apartment house in Manhattan that was ready for occupancy. The plastering contractor did a horrible job. I could not in good conscience, approve of the work. At this point, the plastering contractor had submitted his requisition to receive final payment. I turned down the payment until he corrected all the disapproved conditions. I called the meeting with my client and the contractor to review together the corrective work that I demanded the plastering contractor do, in an acceptable manner, before I would approve this payment.

It so happens that my partner Peter Claman was with me that day because we had another meeting when this one was finished. Peter stood on the sideline while I was working with the client and the contractor. When I started the meeting, the contractor interrupted me, and said he would like to wait a few more minutes because he invited someone to be at the meeting with us. A few minutes later, a large black limo pulled up to the job site. A large man, who looked like he enjoyed his food and was dressed in a very sharp suit, joined the meeting. I described and pointed out all the defects that I wanted corrected. When I was finished speaking, the large gentleman in the sharp suit said to me, "Mr. Architect, what you see, is what you get." I looked at him and was about to express my opinion, when my partner grabbed my arm and pulled me aside. He told me that I was speaking to Fat Tony, the boss of the Plasterer's Union and one of the senior Mafia bosses. Peter said, "Al, you did your thing. Now let's get out of here." The rest was up to the owner. And off we went. The next day, I called the owner to find out what happened. He told me, in order to keep everyone happy, and to stay in one piece, he paid the contractor in full and released him from the project. He hired another plastering contractor to make the necessary corrections.

About six months later, I read in the New York Times, that Fat Tony was found in a large vacant lot in New Jersey with the bird in his mouth and the bullet in his head. That's a typical result of a Mafia member saying the wrong thing to the wrong person.

BAGEL?

It is time for a story that creates a laugh. My firm was commissioned to build a major project at Lincoln Center in New York City. This building contained a high-rise upscale New York City apartment house. It also contained a four-story Mormon church and the ground floor was occupied by the Museum of American Folk Art, as well as an open gallery for retail stores and pedestrians. I started a number of meetings with all interested parties of this multi-use building.

At my first meeting with the representatives of the Mormon Church from Salt Lake City, I was informed of their theory of church design. The same interior was to be used in all church facilities around the world. Their main concern was that whenever a church member travels anywhere in the world and a visits a Mormon church, upon entering, everything should look familiar and they should feel like they're at home. Therefore, my design for this church needs to incorporate all the items for the interior decorating.

They wanted to ensure that every architect that designs a Mormon Church building throughout the United States incorporates and coordinates their philosophy. A conference was scheduled for architects to meet to discuss and coordinate the interior design of the buildings. It so happens that the conference that was scheduled was to be held at a Mormon Church located on Staten Island, New York. I had been living on Staten Island about 35 to 40 years by that time. I never knew there was a Mormon Church located in our community. It was a beautiful, well-designed church, setback in a large wooded area, on the South Shore of Staten Island, hidden from view of the general public.

On a bright sunny morning on the day of this conference, architects from around the country assembled in the auditorium. There were a number of young executives from the Mormon Church that flew to Staten Island from Salt Lake City to run this conference. A handsome young man from Salt Lake City, who was appropriately dressed, including a handsome crewcut, addressed the gathering of the architects. He walked up to the microphone and greeted us with assuring smile to make us all feel welcome.

He notified the audience that they had provided breakfast for all those interested. He pointed to the left side of the room and announced, "We'll be taking a break in a few minutes and can all help ourselves to the cereal, milk, all sorts of breads and cakes, etc." He continued by saying, "We also have on the breakfast table, special delicious type bread. You will see this bread. It is round and has a hole in the center. I think they call them beegels or bagels or something like that." He said, "However you pronounce that bread, you got to try it. It's very good." The audience then started to chuckle as politely as they could. We all wondered what hole that young man lived in to not know such an item as the world renowned bagel. This put us all in a good mood. It was a long and interesting day learning the ways of the Mormon Church.

The construction of the Mormon Church at Lincoln Center had a very rough start by angry protests from the community. The community's main concern was a policy of the Mormon Church to not accept Hispanic people as members of the Church. After a great many meetings and demonstrations by the community, a solution was worked out that satisfied both groups. As the architect for the building, I was not part of those deliberations. As far as I remember, special services and use of the building for Hispanic people were agreed to and by accepted by the Mormon Church.

The design of the building was full speed ahead to meet all schedules for the construction. The biggest problem I had during the design process was entertaining the various delegations from Salt Lake City that came to visit my office and visit the construction site. The problem was taking these delegations for lunch. Due to their strict dietary rules, it was hard to find the proper restaurant to satisfy their culinary needs. It took a while, as I tiptoed through this minefield, and was able to find the proper places to entertain those delegations.

When the building was completed, a delegation from Salt Lake City was taken on a tour through the entire facilities. Their main concern was that they felt the same in this new building as they would feel in any other Mormon Church around the world. With a sigh of relief they thanked me for doing a great job and all was well.

Back To Photography

One day, for an unknown reason, I said to myself it is time to get back into photography. But this time, as a hobby. Someday you too will be retired and photography could help make those days enjoyable. I did some research on the latest technology. You must remember, a huge amount of time had passed since I was a professional photographer, straight out of high school. Today's photography is a high-tech endeavor. The days of using basic and simple cameras are over.

A client of mine, Danny Regan, was deep into photography. I looked to him to get up to speed with all the great things that were now on the market. I purchased my first Nikon camera, did some experimenting, and I was then on my way to this new exciting technology. My first Nikon camera was still using film. Digital photography was about two to three years in the future. At that time, I was on the board of five non-profit organizations. These organizations needed photography. I was the man they looked to for all the photography they needed, free of charge. This work gave me the experience in handling the camera and all the new gadgets that were built into them. None of these organizations realized that they were my guinea pig, because everybody was happy with the work I was doing.

Wild Eyes

One day I read an article about this place called Wild Eyes. It seems that when professional wildlife photographers go out to the jungle, or wherever on assignment, they cannot always get the shots they want. Sometimes you could be out in the field for days and not see any signs of wildlife. Sometimes they need some fill-in photographs. They can go to a place called Wild Eyes in Montana.

At Wild Eyes, the owners get newly born animals. The animals are given to a handler. The handler bonds with the baby animal and becomes somewhat of the animal's parent. They keep the animal away from other human beings as much as possible. When the baby animal grows up, they let them run loose through the woods and fields. The animals are trained, so when the handler calls them, they would dutifully come running back to the handler. Any photographer can go to Wild Eyes, tell them the type of animal they need to photograph, and without the need to go back to the jungle, can fulfill their assignment.

I contacted the owners of this facility and said I would like to spend some time to photograph wildlife. "No problem", they said and we set a date. I was ready for my first big adventure. I landed in Montana, rented a car, and started my journey to find the ranch. It was summertime, so the roads were free of winter snow. Being from New York, I never before in my life saw so much open space. I found the place, checked into a lovely apartment, and got ready for the next day's adventure. At breakfast, I met a commercial cinema photographer, who was there to gather a lot of footage of a various number of wild animals. I hooked up with him and his aides and off we went.

One evening, we were sitting by the fireplace and talking. The owner asked the cinema photographer if he would come back in the winter and do a commercial of this operation. The photographer agreed and then turned to me and said that I am going to be the star of this commercial. He said he'll contact me around December of the next year and will be in business. It sounded like a great adventure. I figured that when he got back to his studio, he would forget about me and that will be the end of it. The following December, I got a call saying he is sending me airline tickets. I should appear at the ranch and be ready to be his star. I would not be paid for my services, however all travel & lodging costs will be taking care of. When the time came, off I went.

Remember now, this was December in Montana. The weather gets cold and the snow gets deep. You better bundle up or you will freeze to death. You're all bundled up, but still have to use the camera and other equipment. We were still using film. The digital age has not yet appeared. On the first day of shooting, I was all decked out from head to toe. I was lugging my equipment and trying to keep my gloves on, as we slid down an embankment to get on this frozen lake. We walked across the solid frozen lake, covered with snow to the line of the woods. We were ready for the owner to let the animals loose.

The first animal was a wolf. The sound man, who was part of the cinema photographer's team, installed a microphone, right under my chin, attached to my jacket. When shooting wildlife, you must get down low to shoot directly into the animal at their level. You cannot stand up and shoot downward, because everything flattens out and you do not get a professional shot. I was told to photograph the animals as they are running through the woods. They'll be photographing me with the cinema equipment. I got down with my knees in the deep snow resting on the frozen ice. We waited for the wolves to come flying by. The wolves came by very quickly. I started to shoot. The wolves zoomed by me and I photographed them until they were out of my range. I was supposed to get up and run about 20 feet to follow the wolves. However, I just couldn't stand up. The weight of the camera and other equipment kept pulling me down. If I put my hand in the snow, it just sunk down to the ice below and I could not get any leverage.

At this point, I was talking to myself in what I thought was a low voice. However, the microphone was right under my chin and picked up every word I said. The sound man heard my talking, saw my problem and I heard him yell out, "We need a Sherpa for Al." They appointed a Sherpa to go with me to help me get up out of the snow so I could get to the next location.

The next problem was that my jacket was getting cold and frozen and was making a crackling noise when I moved. The sound man made some adjustments and so we continued our photographic mission. There was a lot of laughter as I started to get my act together. By the end of the week, all the photography was captured and sent back to his studio to be edited. We had a going away party. I was given a beautiful heavy jacket with "Wild Eyes" embroidered in big letters and the face of a tiger. I was also given a beautiful hat to match. About three months later I received a copy of the edited commercial, on cassettes, as was used in those days. It was very exciting to watch myself on the television. He did a good job of editing, because I looked pretty good.

National Parks Photo Shoots

I learned a lot about the new photography technology. I came home after the week in Wild Eyes with a great number of photographs of wildlife that I never thought I would ever be able to do. After that great adventure, I did a number of other photo shoots on my own. I went to Glacier National Park in the summer and Yellowstone National Park in the winter. I went to Alaska with my son, and flew into the back country on small propeller planes. We landed on a lake to photograph wild grizzly bears in Katmai National Park. They were all great adventures, which I will always remember. I got many great photographs. I went on a number of smaller photo shoots which were also very enjoyable.

At this time I must tell you of an incident that I had when in Yellowstone National Park in the winter. At that time of the year, the snow in some areas was about 8 to 9 foot high. The temperature was approximately 5 below zero. That time of year, the park is closed. The only way you can get into Yellowstone in the winter, is to hook up with an outfitter who has an SUV without wheels but tracks like you find on a military tank. I hooked up with the proper organization and out we went in the wild blue cold yonder.

The photography was great and I enjoyed every minute of it. However, nature called and I had to urinate. About 10 feet from where I stood, there was what they called a 'latrine'. This outhouse facility has three concrete walls and a metal roof that started about 2 feet above the top of the concrete wall. On the open side of this outdoor toilet, was a concrete block wall that served as a vanity wall about 4 feet away from this building entrance. The end result, was that if the temperature outside was five below zero, then the temperature in this latrine was also five below zero. I entered, flipped my two cameras to each side to get them out of the way, opened my jacket, opened my sweaters, open my long shirt, opened my silk heat stabilizing underwear, opened my regular underwear, and then said to myself as I looked down, "I know I had one. I came in with one." Looking down I continue to say, "I can't find it. I know it must be there someplace." I hope you, the reader, understand what I'm talking about and went through. It took some time but finally I found that I did have one, and with success in locating that very cold shrunken object, and I did what I came for. I almost froze to death until I closed everything up. Now you know that it's not all fun and games doing wildlife photography. Life can be hard at times.

Staten Island Zoo & The South American Amazon Adventure

A friend of mine named Tony Gattulo, was the Executive Director of the Staten Island Zoological Society. He knew about my passion for photographing wildlife. He asked me if I would like to serve on the Board of Directors of Staten Island Zoological Society. Since I believe in joining every organization possible, my answer was definitely yes. About an hour before my first board meeting, Tony took me on a tour of the zoo. It was a great little zoo that had a world renowned snake collection. I found it disturbing when I observed a large lion in a cage that I felt was too small for this creature. I said nothing at the time and continued with the tour. I was really impressed with all the animals and facilities that they had for the care and maintenance of the entire collection.

We went to the board room and I was introduced as a new board member. As is my policy when I am new with any gathering, I sit quietly and listen to everyone's opinions, thoughts, objections and everything else about the people that I am serving with. At about my third or fourth board meeting, I brought up the subject of having that large lion in that small cage. There were some other large animals that I also felt should not be displayed in such tight quarters. After much discussion, I realized that most of the board members felt as I did. We asked the staff if they can do some research in relocating some of the larger animals, so they can be housed in a proper environment.

As I remember, in about four or five months of research, the staff found that a new zoo had just completed construction in Mexico. This new facility was a very large, state-of-the-art zoo, and had the opportunity of housing large animals in a great outdoor setting. The problem that this new zoo had is that they ran out of money. They could not purchase animals for their new shining facility. At the next board meeting we all agreed that we would donate all our large animals to Mexico and redesign our zoo with displays for smaller animals. The Mexican zoo's Board of Directors accepted our donation. We had the large animals that were going to be transferred to Mexico examined medically. They were given all the necessary medical treatment in conformance with all laws and regulations of the United States and Mexico. We assembled the necessary cages to house the animals for the trip. It was also agreed that our staff, who had been working with all these animals over the years, attend the trip to Mexico. They would stay there until the animals were comfortable in their new home. This entire operation was put into action and very successfully carried out.

We hired a zoo architect who specialized in this type of facility. The architect created a fantastic design. It felt like the animals were out in the open and we, the viewers, were in the cage. Part of the design contained trees and rocks to replicate the natural outdoor environment of the animals. The funds for this redesign were obtained from a special grant from the City of New York. A company specializing in building trees and rocks for displays was located, as I remember, in the Midwest. When all the displays were completed and ready to be sent to the zoo, the City of New York insisted that a member of the Board of Directors of the zoo examine all displays at the factory for approval before the City will pay the bill. I was selected as the board member to go with the Executive Director to visit the factory, and sign off on the finished product.

When we arrived at the factory, we were greeted by the owner and a number of his artists that created the displays. We went onto a large open area and were shown the trees that they created. I had a puzzled look on my face. I was sure that I was staring at trees that were real and growing in that yard. The owner assured me that these trees were man-made.

They took me into the factory to observe the creation of a tree. The artists created the trunk of a tree using wire mesh foundation. They sprayed the entire wire mesh foundation with a foam material that will dry and harden. It can be sculptured to create a beautiful tree trunk. They created the branches and leaves using another type of material that was assembled to the trunk. When all was completed there was a real tree standing in front of me. These artists created magnificent work.

We were taken to another area to check out the large rock formations that were to be installed at our zoo. I looked at the rocks and inquired how they are going to ship these heavy rock formations to Staten Island. The owner went up to one of the rocks and lifted it with one hand. He handed it to me. As I grabbed the rock, I realized it weighed much less than a half a pound. They showed me the process they used to create these rocks. Their artists went out into the field and found the perfect rock formation that they wanted to re-create. They painted a liquid material and covered the entire existing rock formation. After the liquid dried and hardened, it formed a rubber mold. They sprayed the inside of the mold with a special spray gun. They coated the inside of the mold with the combination of glass fiber and liquid matrix that would harden to became a lightweight rock.

At the end of the day everything was approved for shipment to the Staten Island Zoo. Once everything was installed, the transformation of the zoo was like a miracle. All the animals were the proper size for the environment that was created. The number of visitors to the zoo increased dramatically with adults and children from all over the City. The entire board felt that it was a job well done and we were proud.

About two years later, it was agreed that the Board of Directors would be taken on a trip through the South American Amazon jungle. It would be of some value for board members to see wildlife in its natural habitat. Arrangements were made for the board members as well as representatives of the Staten Island Advance, our local newspaper, to take the trip.

The professional tour guide that was going to accompany us on this trip, held a prep meeting, to explain what we were going to see, do and what we should bring. He made it clear that we would be living in the jungle, in conjunction with the local natives. There will be no towns or hospitals or any conveniences that we now enjoy in our daily lives. This is going to be the raw jungle. We will be eating mostly jungle food prepared by local chefs. Freshwater will be flown in to us and dropped by airplanes.

He suggested that we bring some gifts to trade with the local tribes, as they don't use money. He handed us a list of suggested gifts that are needed by the local people in the jungle. The list contained items like fishhooks, T-shirts, caps, utensils, etc. I thought to myself, that everyone on this trip is going to be bringing the same items from this list. I should bring items that are not on the list. I'll find items that I think would be more appealing to the natives.

On 14th Street in New York City, there were many stores that sold cheap items such as hammers, pliers and other tools for one dollar each.

They also sold very inexpensive items like cigarette lighters & flashlights, etc. One afternoon I visited these stores and stocked up for an interesting day of dealing with the natives in the jungle of the Amazon. It turned out to be quite a heavy container with the metal tools. I lugged this heavy container in my luggage half way around the world.

It so happened, that the day we were to leave for this new adventure, it was also Harriet's birthday. Since I was leaving for this two week trip, I felt that I should do something to keep Harriet in good stead. So I went to the famous pearl jewelry store in Manhattan named Mikimoto. I purchased a high-quality pearl ring and had it gift wrapped. I hid the ring in our basement in a location that Harriet would go to. I made up a large sign, "from your Amazon lover" with the gift. Harriet drove me to zoo to meet the rest of our tour group. At this point Harriet was not aware of the gift I left. With hugs and kisses, I got on the bus, and we were off to the airport.

At the airport, we went through the usual security, boarding the plane, and were off to South America. After a long, tiring flight, we arrived in Iquitos, Peru. Iquitos was a 'Rubber Baron' town in the 1800s, when rubber sap was being harvested from the trees in the jungle. It provided rubber for sale worldwide. Iquitos is surrounded by jungle and does not have any roads into the city. The only way to reach this town is by air.

We checked into our hotel for our first night stay. All the members of our group paired up to shares hotel rooms. However, as my kids call me, I'm a snob. I want my own room. I always get what's called, single supplement. I spent a pleasant night in an air-conditioned room.

In the morning I took a nice hot shower and was read to do the town. We spent that first day touring the sites of the area. It was amazing being surrounded by all those street vendors selling snakes and other useless items to the tourists. In the shopping area of town, there were many street vendors set up all along the sidewalks. It was a disturbing view because all sorts of body parts from a variety of jungle animals were presented for sale. The other view that we were not accustomed to, were uniformed soldiers with heavy automatic weapons on every street. The most amazing part is that the soldiers looked like they were 15 or 16 years old. We had a pleasant day buying trinkets and eating local dishes in their restaurants.

The next day we packed up our gear and were taken down to the waterfront at the beginning of the Amazon River. At the dock, there was a very large canoe with a straw canopy to protect us from the sun. On the back of this large canoe was an outboard motor. On top of the outboard motor was a toilet seat. When that outboard motor was turned on full speed, it propelled us up the river, and the need to use that toilet seat tugged on our stomachs. If you sat down and relieved yourself, the Amazon River would splash up to greet your rear end. I do not remember seeing any females in our group using that facility.

After about a two hour run up the river, we turned onto a small extension of the river, which took us to our first village. Our lovely canoe was tied up to a small pier. We collected our personal gear and hiked through the jungle for about a half-hour. We reached our first home away from home. We all stood there looking at the so-called 'building' where we will be living for the next few days. It was just a platform about 20 feet off the jungle floor, with the ladder to climb up to the platform. The platform was constructed of some sort of reed that grows in the area. As you walk, you felt as if you could rip right through the floor. There were poles that supported a grass roof to protect us from the sun and rain. There were no walls. It was wide open to the jungle.

In one corner, there was a bucket of water underneath a small shelf with a dish. I did not see any toilet facilities or any other facilities located on this platform. On one end of the platform, was a row of very thin mattresses, with a small mosquito net covering each. The netting was tucked under each mattress. These bunks were set about 3 feet apart. Our guide informed us that we each get one of the bunks. We all looked at one another. Male / female? Privacy? Out of the question. I told the guide that I paid extra for single supplement, so I can have my own room. He told me to look at the beginning of the row of tents. He said, "Notice, these are 3 feet apart. At the end of the row, they are 5 feet apart. That is your single supplement."

At this point, I had two choices; either cry, or get into that tent at the end of the row. After some consideration, I took the tent. The next question was toilet facilities. He pointed to the jungle floor about 15 feet from the platform. There we saw what looked like an enclosure that was ready to collapse. "In there you will see a wooden box with a hole in the top, covered by a toilet seat." This straddled a hole in the ground. I noticed on the floor, or I should say, on the dirt, were a variety of little crawling insects. They were searching for food right next to the roll of toilet paper.

About 10 feet to the left, was a large metal container supported by four posts. It was open on top. There was a showerhead attached to the metal container. This is a rainforest. It always rains and fills the container. When the sun shines on it, you get hot water. In the evening or on cloudy days, you get cold water. All you have to do is stand under the container and pull the string.

We were ready to change our clothing and get ready for sleep. We looked at each another and basically said, 'What the hell'. We got undressed. Modesty flew out the window. We each got into a tent and went to sleep. One person in our group was a loud snorer. That sound just added to our adventure.

In the morning, we got dressed and lined up by the bucket and dish on the shelf. We took turns to brush our teeth and do whatever other cleaning we had to do. When each of us was done, we dumped the bucket into the jungle below. The rest of our bodily functions I leave to your imagination.

For the next couple of days, a local native guide took us around the jungle to observe the wild life. We went by foot or by dugout canoe. At one point, I said to our guide, "I don't see any monkeys." He told everybody to sit still, not move a muscle, or make any sound. We sat that way for about four or 5 minutes. All of a sudden, the trees were swarming with small monkeys. They were chattering as loud as they could, as they swung from tree to tree. The guide clapped his hands. Instantly, the monkeys disappeared. It was impossible to see any of the monkeys that were there just moments ago.

We saw lots of parrots, capybaras, pink dolphins, sloths, piranha and a host of other wildlife. The sky was full of all sorts of small and large birds. We were given some string with a fish hook at the end and some meat to put on the fish hook as bait. We were ready to fish for piranha.

Within seconds of dropping the hook into the water, these little fish with huge sharp teeth were grabbing at the hooks. We just kept pulling them out of the water and into the dugout. That evening our cook served the little fish. Since I am not a fish eater, I did not take part in that feast. It's just as well, because those fish were 95% bones, skin, and teeth, with very little edible flesh.

    We lived in this facility for two days. On the third day, we were told to pack our gear and stack it on the side of a tree, where a number of young natives were standing. These young men took heavy cloth, fit it around their forehead, while their buddies loaded our gear into the cloth on his back. When each guy was loaded, they took off in a run through the jungle to our next camp. The natives worked as a team and moved all our gear.

    We started walking through the jungle and followed our guide. We began hearing some strange sounds, and since we were in the rainforest, it must be rain. However, we did not feel any rain drops at all. The sound of the rain got much louder. Our guide told us to have patience. It takes a while for the rain to work its way through the thick growth above us. We kept on walking through the jungle for about another 10 minutes. All of a sudden, the rain finally worked its way through the thick vegetation. It was coming down in buckets. We ran for shelter.

    When we reached the village, we were able to get into one structure that had a grass roof. Amazingly, that grass roof did not allow any rain water through. We dried ourselves as best we could then enjoyed hot coffee and cookies, while waited for the rain to stop. Believe it or not, but it eventually stopped raining. We found our gear and settled in for the night.

    This place was much better than our first experience. We each had a small enclosure with a door, a cot and a window. We felt that we were now in a high-class New York hotel. The next day we went out to explore the jungle. We were taken to the canopy, where researchers use to examine life at the top trees. In order to get to the top of the trees, we climbed a ladder attached to a tree trunk that took us up about 10 feet to a platform. From this platform there was a rope bridge, slowly swinging in the wind. It went up at an angle to another platform anchored to a tree about 50 feet away. We continued to another rope bridge to another tree and so on until we reached the very top of the jungle.

Walking on that rope type bridge was very difficult. As I got higher and higher, I was holding on for dear life, as it was swaying with the wind. I proceeded up to the top, hanging on as tight as I could to this frail rail. I successfully came to the very top platform.

I was amazed at the sight before me. I could see for miles in all directions at all the treetops. It was a spectacular view. We noticed a large variety of vegetation all around us. We were told that most of this vegetation was not part of the tree, but was using the tree for its foundation and nourishment. It was also benefiting the life of the tree. How the tree benefited from all those varieties of growth that were living off the tree was beyond me. I just listened to the explanation and enjoyed the moment immensely.

We had to a walk down the same rickety way we came up. When we hit the bottom, we all took a deep breath of relief.

The next day we were taken to a village where actual natives lived. The children were all running around completely nude. The adults wore a variety of dress, from nude to blue jeans & t-shirts. I guess us visitors were here to supply the blue jeans & t-shirts. We started to do our bargaining. We lined up and took out all the goodies they were going to trade. I took out my tools and all the other good stuff. It did not take more than a few seconds for the natives to realize that everyone except me had the same stuff, from the suggestion list. I had the best stuff. In a few seconds, I was mobbed by the entire town. I noticed when we first got there, that the natives had nothing much to trade with us. So I just dumped all my stuff on the dirt and got out of the way. I let them fight amongst themselves and take the stuff I brought, as a free gift from me. When things calmed down, the natives noticed the other people in our party. They slowly went over to see what else they could acquire.

The only things that I got as mementos of my visit were a small 3-inch long hand carved dugout, and a small functioning blowgun. We were given a demonstration on how to use a blowgun. I was amazed at the length of these blowguns. They seemed to be about 5 or 6 foot long. This one young man took a small box about the size of a cigarette pack and attached it to a tree. He went back about 100 yards and faced his target. He put a dart in the blowgun and with one puff, shot his dart and penetrated the box on the tree. He gave us instructions on how to use a blowgun. We had a chance to try our skill. When it was my turn, I put the dart in the blowgun and puffed, and puffed, until I had a blue face, but that stupid dart would not travel the full length of that blowgun and exit. After a few more tries I was able to get the dart to travel about 6 inches past the end of the blowgun. All the natives were laughing. I bowed and gave them back their blowgun.

We spent another two days with this tribe. We had a good understanding of how they lived and their family life and values. They might be naked people living in the jungle, but they were just as intelligent, and had an understanding of life, that I felt made us all equal as human beings.

After this enlightening experience, we continued on to the next village. To my surprise this village had a large soccer field. It seemed that soccer was the center of some of their lives, just as football is to us. We watched the kids as they had a tournament. Their skills moving the ball with their feet were unbelievable, considering that they were all barefoot. This village was a little more contemporary. Everyone was dressed with some sort of slacks and t-shirt. We spent time eating with them in their environment, by sitting on the floor and using our fingers instead of forks.

We were told that we could borrow any of the dugouts to explore the surrounding communities by water. For a short moment, I thought of getting in a dugout and exploring. However, if you look closely at these dugouts, they were designed for the native population. These natives are much smaller and lighter than any of us. Some of our group tried to get into the dugout. It started to lower in the water because of the excess weight of the white American and it seemed like it would be under water in no time. At that point, I change my mind about exploring the area in a dugout.

Two guys in our group got in to a dugout very gently. They sat quietly in that dugout and did not move. The water level was right up to the top of the dugout. When they gently put their paddles in the water, the dugout simply got too low and filled with water. These two heroes found themselves swimming, laughing, and having a great time splashing in that muddy water. I yelled to them, "That water is filthy. You don't know what kind of germs are swimming in there with you. I wouldn't stay in there if I were you." They just laughed and kept on swimming. They must've enjoyed themselves for about 15 to 20 minutes.

The next day as we were exploring the jungle, we noticed the two guys who went swimming were not very happy. They were off hiding the jungle vomiting and moving their bowels. They were both in very bad shape. Remember now, we are in the jungle. There were no doctors or emergency care or anything to help these poor guys. For the next three days, I thought these guys would never live. They finally recovered, but did not feel well for the rest of the trip. Needless to say, I am glad I did not get in that dugout or swim in the water.

The rest of our group continued on to visit a school that served a number of tribes living in the area. It was a simple, fairly large one room building, with a grass roof and no walls. We did not have the opportunity of witnessing a class in action, but were told they had basic books to teach the children to read Spanish as well as learn math and geography.

That evening we had a great meal in the living area of one of the families. The food was mostly vegetables and fruit with a small amount of some kind of meat. The next day we were on our way for a long hike through the jungle. One of the women in our group was on the heavy side and was not able to walk very fast. It did not take her long to figure out how to keep up with the group. She was always the first one in front of the group whenever we started to walk. Little by little she would fall behind. By the time we would reach our destination, she was still with the group but at the very end. She proved that with a little thought, you can always find a way to solve your problems.

Going through the jungle was very primitive. There were no streets or sidewalks or direction signs or bridges over streams, etc. When we came upon a stream that we needed to cross, we would look for a tree that had been cut down many years ago that straddled the stream. Since the tree was in that position for a long time, moss had grown around the full length of the tree. There was no such thing as a guide rail or handrails to be found. Our native guide quickly walked across the tree trunk over the stream with the ease of a gymnast.

Our group started to follow. It was a hilarious sight to the locals. They watched us trying to keep our balance walking over that wet slimy tree trunk. It was the only thing preventing us from taking a swim in the muddy stream rushing below us. One of the men in our party lost his balance and reached out and grabbed a bush to steady himself. As his hand close tightly on the bush, he gave out a yell of pain. Our guide grabbed him and pulled him to safety. When they examined his hand they found a large number of thorns embedded in his hand. His hand was very painful and started to swell. The first thought we had was to pull out the thorns. As he pulled on one thorn, the pain increased and the thorn would not come out. He asked if there was any kind of medical help somewhere in the jungle. The answer we all knew was no.

The natives had their own ingenious way of healing. It so happened that our guide was also a "medicine man". He quickly found a special kind of leaf that was growing in the area. He took a handful of these leaves and tied them together. He then started a small fire so that he could heat the leaves. The medicine man passed the smoking leaves around the patient's painful hand, so that the smoke was in full contact with the hand. After a couple of minutes the pain started to slowly disappear. Our medicine man took the smoking leaves aside, and gently removed the thorns. To our amazement, there was no pain or blood. The thorns just slipped out. Once all the thorns were out, the swollen hand gently calmed down to its normal size. Our patient was all healed and ready to continue our adventure. It is hard to believe that this type of medicine works. However, seeing is believing.

That evening, our local guide took us down to a special section of the Amazon, where large canoes awaited us. We all got into the canoes. These were much steadier than the little dugouts we encountered previously. We traveled up the Amazon River in the dark as our guide was lighting the way with large lanterns. After a while, we noticed a great many glowing eyes all around us in the water. Our guide explained those were a type of crocodile called caiman. It seemed like all those eyes glowing under the light of the lantern were waiting for one of us to fall in the water so they will be provided with dinner.

The next day we climbed into those large canoes and slowly worked our way up the Amazon River. Our guide pointed out all the wildlife that we passed. There were many multicolored birds, sloths, monkeys and a variety four-legged pig like rodents called Capybara. After about an hour trip we reached our destination. We were going to visit a jungle factory.

This jungle factory in no way resembled a factory that we are used to seeing in our form of life. The factory itself was just a large open area. The floor was just the raw jungle. There were posts that held up a grass roof for protection from the sun and rain. In the center of this open area was a grindstone with a rod projecting out of the center, going up towards the roof, and attached to a gear contraption. A large leather strap was attached to the gear, extended out, and attached to a saddle fitting on a horse. The horse was encouraged to walk in a complete circle around the grindstone. As the horse walked, the one and only worker in this factory fed corn into the hopper above the grindstone to create cornmeal. I felt sorry for that poor horse that had to walk in a circle all day long to keep the grindstone crushing the corn. The worker took the cornmeal to another section of the so-called factory to a large pot mounted over a fire that was filled with some sort of liquid. The cornmeal was put in the pot and mixed with a dark liquid to be cooked to create molasses. When the molasses was completed, half of the batch was bottled for sale and distribution to the various villages. The other half of the molasses was turned into an alcoholic drink that was also for sale and distribution to the villages. We were given the privilege of tasting both final products. Much to my amazement, the molasses and the alcoholic drink were both very good. These people were able to produce a great product without the use of a modern day computerized factory.

At the end of the day, we were taken to our last destination of this fantastic trip. The young men that carried our gear, delivered all our gear to our last station. All the occupants of this village were there to greet us with songs of the jungle. They were very melodic and put on a great show. We were served a great last meal and told stories of their daily lives. They seemed be very happy people. After all the festivities, we packed the gear to be ready to leave early the next morning. About 9 or 10 the next morning, after a hearty breakfast of jungle fruit, we reported to the large, motor driven canoe, we first experienced at the beginning of this adventure. When we reached Iquitos, buses were waiting to take us to the airport. We checked in, went through security and had about a half-hour to kill until it was time to board the plane.

Almost as in our country, there were a great many vendors selling all sorts of local junk. I could not help myself when I saw this young boy selling these large dried jungle bugs, with huge horns and other menacing growths. The young man told me if I bought these bugs, when I got home, I should keep them in the freezer for about a week, to make sure that there is nothing still alive within the shells. I could not resist.

When I got home and displayed this magnificent purchase, I was greeted with the choice that Harriet said I had to make. I could put the bug in the freezer and live in the cellar for the rest of our marriage, or I could get rid of the bug and come up to bed. After much deliberation, I'm sure you know what the final decision was.

Third-Party Lawsuits

Third-party lawsuits are when the person doing the suing is not part of the original project's ownership, design or construction. An example of a third-party law suit is when a stranger walking on the sidewalk in front of the building under construction slips and falls. Or let's say they trip over some construction debris. When that person gets up, even if they do not have an injury, they take out their iPhone and photograph the building sign. As required by law, the building sign lists all the parties involved with the construction; the names and contact info for the owner, architect and contractors. The person simply contacts a lawyer and starts a lawsuit against everyone on the building sign. Some of the people on the building sign have nothing to do with incident. How could the architect be considered to be liable for a slip and fall? How about the interior decorator? These frivolous lawsuits are almost always thrown out of court. However the person being sued still has to spend legal fees and court costs. This can be in the area of $40,000 to $60,000, just to defend yourself.

The following are some examples of third party lawsuits that I had to live through in my professional life:

About 20 years after we had built a bank building in Brooklyn, New York, we received a subpoena in reference to a lawsuit that was being filed against us. My partners and I were puzzled about being sued for a building that had been successfully operating for 20 years. My partners were very happy when I agreed to handle this problem. Our professional liability insurance company was notified about the lawsuit. The sad part is that our policy stated that we were responsible for paying the first deductible up to $100,000 for legal fees.

An attorney was assigned to the case by our insurance company and the deposition procedures of the lawsuit began. It seems that the front entrance plate glass window fell into the bank and injured a woman customer standing there. I was completely puzzled by the fact that the building had been in use for 20 years without any incidents. This situation could not be a design or construction error. Any faulty design or improper construction would have occurred years before. I checked our architectural drawings to make sure that we designed and specified the proper system for the construction of that bank storefront. I requested the manufacturers of that storefront system to examine my drawings to ensure we created the proper system. After the manufacturer of the storefront equipment examined my drawings, I was told that everything that we designed was in keeping with the proper design and construction of the system and should have never failed. They agreed to file that statement to the court.

After I received the depositions from all the people involved, I slowly read every word of testimony to fully understand just what happened. Our attorneys also read all the testimony and were puzzled by this entire incident and were hard-pressed to find a defense for our portion of this suit. When I carefully read the testimony, I noticed one statement made by the security guard when he said, "He saw the sign flying and the window crashing in." It seemed that no one questioned the statement. I wondered, "What sign he talking about that was flying?" I wanted to find out if that was a very windy day that could be responsible for this mishap. I made arrangements to hire the television weatherman on Channel 9 to research the weather conditions that particular date and time of day. The weatherman's final report stated that there were very heavy winds then. Upon further research with the maintenance people from the bank that cleaned up the broken glass, we discovered that they also cleaned up and discarded a large wooden sign.

It was plain to see the problem was that the weather had caused the sign to be ripped from its anchor and smashed through the window. This was proof that there was no faulty design or construction of that storefront. After I provided my attorney all the information that clearly proved my office was not liable, Harriet and I left for our 10 day per month visit to Tucson Arizona for a joyful time of golf and great weather. My attorney called to notify me that the judge decided that no one was liable for the situation. However, the customer of the bank was hurt through no fault of her own. The judge decided that all parties should chip in a portion of the judgment to help pay for the injured parties medical expenses. I was told that my contribution was to be $2000. I told my attorney that since my firm did nothing wrong, and was not liable for any judgment; I refused the request of the judge. I felt that if I paid that $2000, this payment would be on my record. It could be legally interpreted that I was guilty of "errors and omissions".

My attorney informed me that he could provide the proper wording in the judgment that would clearly exempt us from any responsibility. I still felt uneasy about the situation and instructed my attorney to tell the judge that I will not be party to his proposal. My attorney then said he would pass the word on to the judge but felt I was making a mistake. About three days later my attorney called and notified me that he spoke to the judge and told them my decision. The judge told my attorney that if I did not agree to pay the $2000, he would hold me in contempt of court, issue a warrant for my arrest and haul me into court in New York in handcuffs. My attorney also mentioned that when the judge made his statement, his face was red and he was banging on the desk. "Al", my attorney said, "Pay the money." I reluctantly agreed and I paid the money.

Thinking this case was over and behind us I got back into the practice of architecture. About three months later, I get a call from an investigator from the New York State Education Department. He inquired about my possible malpractice in relation to that lawsuit. I was in a state of shock as I held that phone to my ear. After a few seconds to gather my wits, I requested a meeting with the investigator and my attorney. The investigator agreed and we set a date for the meeting in my office.

At that meeting, my attorney made it clear, noting that the evidence showed there was no malpractice. The investigator said that he will be dropping the case because it is quite evident everything was in order. I asked the investigator, since this was a third-party suit that seems to happen quite often, and I as the architects are always found to be not guilty of any malpractice, how does that affect my license to practice architecture? He said that if this happened a number of times, it tells them there must be some malpractice involved, and they can take your license away. After this incident, on many other third-party lawsuits, I never agreed to any payment that could be misinterpreted. If the judge feels I should be arrested, I am ready to go. Thank goodness this situation never occurred.

Unethical Lawsuits

My office was commissioned to design a major area shopping center in northern Philadelphia. One of the buildings of this complex was to be two stories with a basement catering hall. During construction, one of the contractors set up his scaffold on the steps of this large monumental stair case. It went from the basement level, up through the first floor, and continued up through the second floor. The contractor was working on the perimeter walls of the staircase. It seems that when the contractor set up his own scaffold, it was not seated solidly on the steps. After working a few minutes, his scaffold tilted and he fell off the scaffold and rolled down the steps to the next landing. The contractor was badly hurt and taken to the hospital.

This contractor set up his own scaffold, for him to work on, and evidently did not do a proper job of setting up his own scaffold which caused his accident. It is clear that there is no liability from any of the design team of this project. However unethical lawsuits always raise their nasty heads. This contractor sued me as the architect, the interior decorator who selects paint colors, the owners of the shopping center and the general contractor. Here we go again.

There was absolutely no malpractice or any other wrongdoing by anybody involved in this construction project. My design or my building plans had nothing to do with his fall. I remember the interior decorator calling me and being very disturbed as to his involvement in his lawsuit. He said, "All I did was select furniture, wall treatments and paint colors. Why am I being sued?" The simple answer is because of our legal system, anybody can be sued. A situation like this is quite evident that no one could be held responsible for the error by the contractor in setting up his own scaffold. However everyone being sued had to defend themselves and therefore were penalized the cost of legal fees and court costs. We had to prove our innocence and were vindicated at the end of the trial. But the lawyers made money with this legal battle. They generated billable hours by including us as defendants. Life is fun and games.

Arrogant Lawyer

I could continue with about 10 or 15 more of these lawsuits, but that might become boring. I might lose my reading audience. There is one more lawsuit that I must document. It proves the failing of a great many lawyers. They feel so impressed with themselves that they never seek professional advice when it comes to cases involving other professions.

My office was commissioned to build a large addition to an existing hospital. This hospital addition was to be built on a new structural steel frame, attached to the existing building. It should be noted that the design of all components of the structural steel frame are custom manufactured for this particular project. The design of the entire project was completed and submitted for competitive bids. Contracts were awarded and construction began.

While the general contractor was working on the site, the structural steel fabricator was manufacturing the components of the structural steel frame. The site was ready for the installation of the steel frame. The steel was shipped to the site. The construction crew organized the installation. The surveyor marked the locations on the site, and the work began. The steel frame installation began at the far end of the addition and worked its way back to the existing hospital. However, much to everyone's horror, when it came to tying the addition into the existing hospital, the steel was short of reaching the existing building by 6 inches. This is a catastrophe condition. This meant that new steel had to be designed and manufactured which will take some time. At a meeting with all responsible parties, the blame for this error was strongly suggested to be that of the architectural drawings. I got together with my structural engineer and we carefully went through all the calculations and checked everything on the architectural and structural drawings to see if we could find the error. We could find no error. The construction drawings were perfect. If the construction was done in conformance with these drawings, there should be no problem. However there was a problem.

In order to determine responsibility and obtain the necessary funding for the redesign and construction of the new steel pieces, a lawsuit started. The lawyer for the owner was one of these attorneys who felt they were infallible and were an expert in all fields. In preparing for this trial, the attorney examined my drawings. He did not consult with an architect, as an intelligent attorney would do.

      I was called to testify at the trial. I was quite nervous because I had no idea where the error was. I was called and sworn in. The attorney approached the table in front of me with the huge roll of my drawings for the entire project. It should be noted that there were over 100 sheets in this 30" x 42" drawing set. You must remember, this all took place in the days before we had computers. The attorney dropped the drawings on the table, with showman's flair, and flipped them so they would roll open. He proudly asked me, "Mr. Architect, are these your drawings?" I looked at the drawings and said, "Yes those are my drawings." He asked, "How do you know that?" I pointed to the title block at the lower right-hand corner of the drawings that had both my name printed out as well as my signature. He pointed to a dimension on the first drawing. As he pointed to that dimension, bells, whistles, and horns of joy rang out in my head. I just figured out exactly what the problem was. The lawyer said, "Mr. Efron, what does that dimension say?" I proudly stated, "The dimension says 30 foot minimum." He said, "If the surveyor put his starting point at 30 feet from the property line, would the steel frame lineup as required?" I enjoyed the moment while this arrogant attorney was setting a trap for himself. I said, "No it would never lineup." He looked at me puzzled. I continued, "Why are you looking at this drawing?" I waited a few seconds and then continued, "If you look at the lower right-hand corner at the title block you, will see in addition to my name and my signature, that the title of this drawing is 'Zoning Calculations'. This drawing, as all architects know, was prepared solely for the use of the Building Department to show the building design conforms to all zoning requirements. That is why the dimension you proudly pointed out to me says '30 feet minimum'. That means this building cannot be built closer to the lot line than 30 feet. If you turn the page (I flipped over the page with showman flair), you will see that this drawing is titled 'site plan'. If you look closely at that dimension you proudly asked me to verify, you will see it reads 30'8". It is quite evident that the surveyor was probably not experienced enough and made the mistake, just as you did, and was looking at the wrong drawing. If the surveyor used this starting point at 30'8" the building would close out perfectly."

I sat there and looked at the attorney. He was looking at the drawing with the horrible expression of disbelief of his error. If this high-end and mighty attorney would have bothered to ask an architect to check if he was interpreting the drawings correctly, this would never have happened. The lawyer looked up at me, and after a few private moments, said to the judge, "Your honor I request an adjournment to give me time to investigate this new evidence." I have yet to be contacted in reference to this issue. Some behind the scenes maneuvering must've taken place because the money for the repairs was found, the new steel was designed and installed. I think its best if I don't say any more about my feelings of the legal profession.

Non Thinking Construction Workers

While I am on a roll, let's talk about the stupidity that often occurs in the construction process, the ones that create heartburn for all of us architects. I mentioned earlier in this book about the lawsuit in reference to the poorly set up scaffold. Another building in that complex was a freestanding bank building. Part of the requirements for the design of this building, was that an underground vault had to be completely waterproof for customer lock boxes, as well as a money counting room. I specified that the entire underground foundation was to be completely encased in a waterproof envelope and covered by foam boards, to protect the waterproof envelope from damage during the backfill process.

I was on the construction site for a periodic observation which was part of my contract. The workman had installed the waterproof envelope around the entire cellar of the building. They were trying to adhere the foam boards to the waterproofing and were having trouble making them stick in place. The problem was that it was a very hot day and the adhesive was not sticking in the heat. They decided not to use the foam boards. I happen to be standing near this building when they started to backfill and I noticed that there were no foam boards. I stopped the backfill process and told them to get another adhesive that was adequate for the high temperature. I had to leave for a meeting and told them I will be back later.

About an hour later, I returned to the site and found that the workman, to my horror, were taking large concrete cut nails and nailing the foam board through the waterproofing into the concrete foundations. In doing this they destroy the entire integrity of the waterproofing system. They told me they could not find the proper adhesive so they decided to nail the boards in place. I just cannot understand the stupid thinking in a situation like this. To make a long story short, a complete new waterproofing system had to be installed. This stupid situation only cost money. Stupid situations in construction that cause human injury or life are another story. And so, I'm going to tell just one more.

School Conversion To Apartment House

One of my clients obtained an abandoned school building in Westchester County, New York. This project involved changing the use of this building from a school, to senior citizens housing under a federal program. In addition, to make it economically viable, I was to add one additional story to the existing building. I went to work and redesigned the entire building from the school to an apartment house and additional story. After all contracts were awarded, the construction process started.

During one of my periodic observation visits, I noticed that the new exterior masonry wall of the added story was not constructed in an acceptable manner. There was missing mortar between the bricks and daylight shone through those openings. This condition was on all the walls of the entire new floor. During this visit a representative of the bank that was providing the mortgage money was on the site. He was waiting for my approval, so he could make the monthly requisition payment. I refused to approve this condition and outlined a massive correction procedure that had to be done to my satisfaction before I provide the approval.

The gentleman from the bank was very upset because he could not make the payment. The bank's sole purpose is to get their money out to the builder so the interest payments can start flowing to the bank. We broke for lunch so they could think of what to do.

My client and I were the first to return to the job site after lunch. I was standing in the street, waiting for the contractor and the bank representative to return. All of a sudden, I heard a loud voice yelling and screaming and I turned to see what was happening. To my horror, it was the contractor, who happened to be a very large strong individual. He was yelling and cursing at me as he was approaching. His body language told me that he was on the verge of becoming violent. We stood nose to nose. He kept yelling and I just stared him down. I stood my ground on the outside but my insides were a volcano eruption. I did not back down, because I felt that if I did, he might get violent. Finally a couple of construction workers came running out. They calmed the contractor down and saved the day.

The gentleman from the bank said we have to settle this right now so he could make the payment and construction can continue. The contractor said that he guarantees all of this construction work. I said that if the contractor wants to sign a letter that he will be responsible, then I'll sign off. We wrote up a document allowing them to continue. It had the condition that since I don't feel it will be watertight if left as is, the contractor would be fully liable for any leaks. If there are any problems, then the contractor, at his own expense, will do all the reconstruction that is needed to ensure the building is watertight, to my satisfaction. The contractor agreed, the document was signed by all parties. Payment was made. Construction continued.

The first time it started to rain, the building leak like a sieve. The bank and I pulled out the signed document. I outline a method of construction that he was to perform, as per the agreement. It was a very expensive situation that the contractor had to correct.

Another problem the contractor had was that his backers from the Mafia were putting pressure on him for payment of money. They made him hire two young men just off the boat from Italy. They had no construction experience in any form or manner, and did not speak a word of English. He set them up on a scaffold that was hung by ropes to an anchor on the parapet wall above. They were instructed to apply the waterproofing that I specified. Since these two young men were not experienced in working on the scaffold or applying this material, they made the mistake of pushing too hard on the wall. When they pushed on the wall, the hanging scaffold was forced away from the wall, leaving a large gap that both men fell through to the ground below. One of the men died and the other was severely injured. Now this contractor had many problems.

As far as my client and I were concerned, we had enough money held out from the contractor to cover the situation. We called in a reliable contractor to finish the work. Some months later we learned that the contractor had passed away. Why and how he passed away, I do not know. I leave that up to your imagination.

Non-Thinking Bureaucrat

One sad day, Harriet's stepbrother passed away at a young age. After the funeral, his wife, Alice received the official Death Certificate. She also got an additional 9 copies for a total of 10 documents. To collect on the life insurance policy, she notified and sent the insurance company a copy of the Death Certificate. An agent of the insurance company called her and said that they could not pay on this policy because the Social Security number on the Death Certificate was not that of the deceased. She then examined the other nine copies and discovered that that bureaucrat making out the death certificate used the credit card number in place of the Social Security number on all of the documents. The widow called the city department responsible for issuing Death Certificates in an effort to have this corrected. After many calls and speaking to many bureaucrats, she couldn't get this fixed. She called me to help her. I called the Commissioner, who was a friend of mine, and explain the situation.

I asked him if he can help correct this error. He said, "Al, for you. No problem." He told me to have Alice bring all the copies down to his office and ask for him. The next day I got a phone call from Alice explaining the bizarre happening. She went down to the office and asked for the Commissioner as she was told. The Commissioner came out of his office with a big smile and greeted Alice. He then took one of the death certificates, took out a pen from his pocket, crossed out the credit card number and replaced it in ink with the correct Social Security number. He then instructed one of his subordinates to do the same thing on the rest of the copies.

I'm wondering if this was legal or not. Alice sent the corrected death certificate to the insurance company and, lo and behold, she got paid. If that's all it took, why didn't one of those bureaucrats simply do it? Maybe Alice should have just tried this herself.

The Desert Gold Diggers

One year, Harriet and I happen to be on Staten Island in November, my birth month, getting ready to leave for Tucson. Our mail lady rang our doorbell and delivered a package. I greeted our mail lady with a hug because she was also considered a friend. I went into the kitchen and opened the package. Harriet joined me in this package opening activity. It was a gift for my birthday, from our son Paul. We carefully opened it up, and looked into the box with a puzzled expression. I remove a plastic green platter and examined it wondering what the hell this was. After further digging into the box, we found a certificate making me an official member of the Gold Diggers Association of America. We removed a video cassette that we assumed will inform us what this is all about.

The video was a course in how to pan for gold, just like the prospectors did in the 1800s. We saw an elderly gentleman sitting on a rock with his feet in the water as he filled the pan with dirt just below the waterline. He swirled the dirt around in a dynamic artistic motion. Lo and behold, he showed us bright shiny gold that he just acquired from the stream. I was trying to figure out why Paul sent me this stupid gift. After thinking about this a while, I felt it might be a great new adventure to start gold prospecting when we got back to Tucson.

We got back to Tucson and met Paul in our house. We all got excited and were ready to get rich from all the gold we were going to take out of the streams. We sat down and planned our attack. Paul said he met a geologist in a bar who told him that a good place to find gold was in Canada Del Oro, which is a river wash in Oro Valley located northwest of Tucson. Paul was told that there is a heavily mineralized area near Biosphere 2. Just a side note, I never heard of Oro Valley before, and I now live there. 'Oro' means 'Gold' in Spanish.

Paul did some research and got a geologic map of Canada Del Oro wash, and sure enough, it did appear that there was a heavily mineralized area. We wanted to rent a metal detector for our attack and found a local store dedicated to the gold mining hobbyist. He suggested we join the Desert Gold Diggers. It's a club located in Tucson.

We packed our equipment into Paul's 4WD truck including our pans, sluice system, stack of large black plastic garbage bags, food & water, etc. Off we went to Oro Valley to the heavily mineralized location. By this time we got to our destination, it was 12 noon and to me that means lunch. I opened the lunch package that we brought and started to munch away. Paul took the metal detector and started to work.

As I was eating my lunch, I looked down on the ground. I could not believe what I was seeing. The ground seemed to be covered with very small gold flakes shining in the sun. I called Paul over and showed him what I discovered. He got all excited and said, "We hit the mother lode."

Setting up the sluice system and cleaning the dirt takes a while. We figured it would be better use of our time, to take as much dirt as we could with us and clean through it at home. We took out the big plastic bags and filled them with as much dirt at the bags would hold. We loaded up Paul's truck with as many of these bags that the truck could carry. His half ton truck was rated for 1,100 pounds. We headed back to Tucson to return the rented metal detector.

At the store, the proprietor said, "How come you're back so soon?" We proudly announced that we hit the mother lode. This store had a huge trough filled with water to demonstrate and practice gold panning. He suggested we bring in a sample and we'll clean it out in the trough. Paul grabbed a sample from the truck. The proprietor quietly took a handful of our gold laced dirt, dumped it into a gold pan and started cleaning it in the trough. He asked us, "Where is the gold?" Paul and I stared in the gold pan and saw all the gold flakes floating merrily around on the top of the water. Gold is very heavy and will always sink to the bottom. The proprietor said one word, "Mica". Then he said, "Biotite Mica actually." Paul and I then looked at one another, realized how stupid a mistake we made and started laughing hysterically. We were laughing so hard and could not control ourselves. We both ended up on the floor of that store in a hysterical laugh. We gained a small amount of control able to go out to the car. We continued to laughing and couldn't stop. It took us another half hour to calm down enough to be able to drive.

Now we heard of 'Fool's Gold'. That's Iron Pyrite and is something different. Neither of us had heard of Biotite Mica. We drove to Paul's house and dumped the dirt in the plastic bags with all the fortune of Mica in his backyard.

We waited for the next meeting of the Desert Gold Diggers club. We joined and learned more about ways of gold prospecting. This club owned several gold claims and arraigned for groups to go prospecting together. We perfected our battery-operated pump/ sluice box system and looked like real professionals. We went on several excursions, but found nothing but tiny specs of gold. I keep those flakes in a small jar of water for display.

At every meeting they raffled off a gold nugget. I guess someone upstairs felt sorry for us because at one meeting we had the winning ticket. We can say that at least we came away with a real piece of gold. It was a great adventure and a lot of fun spending that time together with Paul, even though we did not get rich.

Another Stupid Construction Worker

Yes, I know I said no more construction stories, but this incident popped into my head and I just couldn't ignore it. This is a quick story of personal stupidity by a construction worker. The building designed by my office was a high-rise office building in Manhattan. In keeping with the upscale design of the structure, we decided to create a reflecting pool as part of the large lobby.

In order to keep this reflecting pool watertight, our specifications required the installation of a standard system containing a plastic sheet called a Nervastral embedded in a coat of thick liquid called Nervaplast to be installed as per manufacturer's directions. This is a standard and approved system for this type of installation. The workman diligently covered the entire pool with the Nervaplast, then installed the Nervastral sheet and finished with another layer of Nervaplast. At that point they took a portable blowtorch, as required by the manufacturer of this waterproofing system, to heat the seams so they will fuse together. The instant the blowtorch flame was lit, the entire area was ignited creating a quick puff of flame which lasted about a second or two. The workman received burns to his skin from the quick flash of fire.

As a result, a lawsuit was filed against us for not warning the contractor of the danger in using this material. At the trial, I testified that our specifications required that the person installing this system shall do so in strict conformance with the manufacturer's directions as noted on the material's packaging. These directions are easily found, if the workman bothered to read the instructions on the can. It is also common practice for people working with materials that they are not familiar with, to read the manufacturer's directions. I read the manufacturer's directions that were boldly printed on the can, out loud to the court. They stated that the workman shall wait about 5 minutes after installing the liquid to allow the vapor to evaporate. My testimony was simple and clear-cut allowing the judge to rule in my favor. This is a good example of people not taking personal responsibility for their actions.

Pre-Jupiter Developers

One day in the winter season, the builder of our house in Tucson, was on our block overseeing another house that he was building. He approached me and said that he has a proposal that could be beneficial to both of us. He said, "Since your son Paul is an engineer and a hard-working young man, I propose that we form a partnership. We will both invest equal amounts of money to buy land in an upscale area and build high end homes together. Since Paul is an engineer and knows the design portion of construction, and I know the construction in the field part of the process, we will make a good team. I will teach Paul my end of the business and you, Mr. Efron, as an architect, can provide the design knowledge to round out the team. We will then split profits 50% for me and 50% for Paul." He said, "You Mr. Efron, will be the banker for Paul's portion of the investment." He did tell us upfront, that all of his past partners wind up hating him, I we probably will too. After further conversation and negotiations, we made the deal. Paul started Jupiter Development Corporation.

We bought a number of lots in the upscale area of Tucson known as the foothills. Design and construction of the first house started. Paul was rapidly soaking up all the knowledge of the construction end of the business. When the house was finished and sold, Paul received his 50% and things were great. We started construction on a second house. Paul notified me that we have a problem. It seems our partner was not a very nice person, and was treating Paul not as a partner, but as a low grade employee. At this point I will spare the reader all the gory details. We decided to dissolve the partnership. I was in New York and our partner was in Tucson. The breakup negotiations were being conducted via telephone. It was very hard, nasty yelling, and everything else that you can imagine. We finally came to an agreement where we were to divide the lots that we co-owned equally and settled the financial portion of the deal.

Paul would be on his own as the builder. He felt very confident that he had the knowledge and ability to be successful in the business. It turned out that Paul became an excellent builder and a great negotiator with everyone in the construction trades. He did well with sales of our new homes.

The next winter season arrived and Harriet and I were back in Tucson. One day I was out in front of our house and the builder was across the street on his way to a building down the block. I waved to the builder and said hello with a smile on my face. He looked at me with a puzzled expression and said, "Mr. Efron, I thought you would never speak to me again." I informed him that I would never enter into any business agreement with him because I don't trust him. "We could still be civil to one another. When I see you walking down the street, I do not want to hide or feel uncomfortable. Isn't it better that we smile and greet one another and avoid any aggravation or negative feelings? Let's enjoy life." Later, when I was with Harriet and Paul back in the house, they said they would never talk to that son of a bitch again or even greet him in any manner. I think my way is better.

Jupiter Developers

Paul was now building on his own. We sold some of the land that he obtained as part of the partnership breakup. We purchased other land that Paul felt was in a better location. The money we received from the sale of the land was deposited in a local bank that had to be cleared through a bank in New York. That money was going to be used for the purchase of the new land. We were to go to the closing on the new land in about three days. Just to make sure everything was in order, I checked with the bank in Tucson to verify that the deposit went through and we would be able to issue a check against that money. I was informed that they had no record of the deposit. It seems that when Paul deposited the money, he used the ATM machine. I quickly called the New York bank to see if they cleared the money. Yes, I was told the Tucson bank did forward the money and they did clear it so everything is in order. I checked back with the Tucson bank and again they said they did not receive any approval from the New York bank.

At this point I asked to speak with the bank manager. I was politely told that I cannot speak to the bank manager because she was very busy working on the float for the rodeo parade that is held just before the beginning of the rodeo. This parade is always held on opening day of the rodeo. It is a very important event in the lives of people living in Tucson. After a moment of silent shock I demanded that she get her A ***!!! back to the bank so we can straighten out this mess. I am going to a closing tomorrow morning and that money must be available to close the deal. Finally after much time, the manager appeared. I demanded that the manager call the bank in New York that cleared the money for the Tucson bank to honor. After many heated words, they called the New York bank. They realized their error. I was told there would be no problem. We can issue the check and the bank would approve the payment.

Now all is well, Paul and I went to the closing. We issued the check and everybody smiled and went home. About three hours later I got a call from the escrow agent stating that the check bounced. I explained the situation and told escrow agent I will call the bank and that check will go through. I got the bank manager on the phone and with a firm voice asked what happened. I stayed on the line as the bank manager went to check the situation. She said that the escrow agent deposited the check in another branch of their bank. It seems that these computer systems do not talk to one another and did not transfer the information to all the branches. I instructed the branch manager to personally call the escrow agent and tell them that the error was all on the bank's side and to get that money paid. Everything was finally worked out and I poured myself a little Canadian Club.

Paul then went on to build a number of other houses, made a lot of money, and retired at the age of 43. All's well that ends well.

This is what allowed myself and Paul to retire. Him at 43!
Floor plan and listing for Jupiter developers.

My Genius Brother Who Was Not Very Smart

Since my brother, Ed, was nine years younger than me, his teen years were during the post-depression times. Therefore, he had the opportunity of going to college. One day he met with a career advisor at Brooklyn College to help them plot out the course of his professional life. The career advisor informed my brother of this new technology that is in its infancy which he felt will grow and change the world. This new technology was known as electronics. The word computer or calculator did not exist at that time. My brother took his career advisor's advice and signed up for classes in the new wonder known as electronics.

At the time my brother graduated college, there was an urgent need for engineers in the new electronics corporations. There was an urgent effort to hire qualified electronic engineers. The day after graduation, he received invitations from a number of corporations to visit their facilities for an interview. These corporations paid for his airfare, hotel accommodations, and other incidental costs for him to visit their facilities. It seemed that the world was upside down. But since there were so few qualified electronic engineers available, the law of supply and demand was in full bloom. His first job was with IBM. He managed to work himself up to a high management position. Then, these employment agencies that specialized in top management positions, known as headhunters, signed my brother up. He started his rise in the industry by working for Sony, and a number of other organizations. He became the CEO of a computer manufacturer located in California.

An opportunity came his way when IBM and Panasonic joined forces to form a new corporation to convert existing black-and-white movies to color. Ed was recruited to become the CEO of that corporation. During that time, he invented his own technology to revolutionize the movie industry. His new invention, which he had patented, would use computers in all aspects of creating movies. My brother had a friend who was the father of Steven Spielberg. My brother told his friend about his invention. His friend then told his son, Steven Spielberg, about my brother's invention. Steven Spielberg was very much interested in this new technology and asked his father to arrange a meeting so he could meet my brother.

At the meeting, Steven Spielberg felt that Ed's technology was truly revolutionary. He proposed that he and my brother become partners in this new adventure. My brother will provide the technology and Spielberg will provide the money and they will be off and running. It should be noted that in all of my brother's business experience, he was always an employee, regardless of this title, and received a weekly check.

My brother, with all his non-intelligence, asked Steven Spielberg, "How much are you going to pay me in salary every week?" At that point, Mr. Spielberg read the personality of my brother, told him very politely that the deal is off, and good day sir. When I heard the story, I said to my brother, "What in the hell is the matter with you?" You just talked yourself out of a fabulous opportunity. My brother said, "I have to get my weekly pay or am not happy."

I tell this story so you can understand the following saga. He went working in the corporate world. A headhunter approached my brother saying they have a great opportunity for him to work for Bayer Corporation as head of their medical instrument division. Ed followed through and took the job as CEO of Bayer. He noticed that they had many instruments. Each drew a different liquid such as blood, urine, or other bodily fluids and used a different controller. He designed one controller that could do all the work that is required for each different instrument. This change allowed Bayer to save a huge amount of money.

Ed was then summoned to corporate headquarters in Germany, so the senior partners could meet this genius computer engineer. They wanted him to lecture all their facilities around the world of his management style. My brother was not just a dummy at some things, he was also very shy. He turned down their request. Turning down the request of top senior management in the corporate world is a no-no.

He contacted a headhunter who got him a job with Disney. Disney was building their Florida amusement park and getting ready to build an amusement park in France. When Eisner, the CEO of Disney, interviewed my brother, they discussed my brother's invention of a computerized movie studio. Eisner was very interested in investing in Ed's technology. However, he first wanted my brother to take over the computer operations during the design and construction of their Florida facilities, and then do the same thing for their facilities being planned for

France. When both are complete, they will put all their efforts into my brother's invention.

When Florida was finished and France was beginning, my brother was commuting back and forth from the US to France. Eisner informed my brother that he, and his family consisting of his wife and 5 children, should move to France, at Disney's expense, so he could more effectively get that facility built. My brother and his wife did not want to move to France for the year. He told Eisner that they would like to keep everything as it is. This was another no-no, so my brother was let go. That's another great opportunity down the tubes.

Ed was looking for another employment opportunity. Bally, the manufacturers of gambling machines found out about my brother's controller that he designed when he was at Bayer. Bally offered my brother the opportunity of creating a new corporation that would design controllers for their various computerized gambling equipment. The deal was set, and signed, stating that my brother would be the CEO of this corporation in full control. The agreement also noted that any patents would be exclusively assigned to the Bally Corporation. My brother would be given a substantial salary plus a Cadillac. My brother, not being so smart, signed that agreement. My brother went to work, designed the controllers, set up the manufacturing facility, and started turning them out. Bally installed these controllers into their various machines. The result was a resounding success. Microsoft heard about my brother and his controllers and contacted him to try to work out some sort of business arrangement. Much to my brother's shock, he was notified that since Bally owned the rights to the controllers and the patents, Microsoft will do business with Bally. Once the controller designs and manufacturing facility for Bally's were completed, Bally realized that they did not need Ed or the Corporation that he set up anymore. They gave him notice and he was out.

My brother was in a panic and called me for advice. I could not figure out why on earth he gave them control of his patents. As far as I was concerned, this looked like a great opportunity. I told Eddie that I will get a number of investors together. We will buyback the patents and the corporation before it is dismantled. You'll be back in business. My brother was very happy with my proposal and I put this operation into full blast. I set up a number of luncheons and dinners with various investors that I knew in the construction industry. I contacted Bally and told them the proposal. They agreed to give me time to put this deal together to buy them out. I was spending all kind of money on the lunches and dinners as well as with attorneys to put this whole package together.

The bottom line was that my brother would be Chairman of the Board, President and CEO of the corporation. He would receive 55% of the stock. The investors would receive 45% of the stock. This arrangement means that my brother will own this company and have the final say on anything. The investors with only 45% of the stock, therefore not have a voice in the corporation. Everything was put together. The investors wanted to meet my brother. A conference was arranged and we all sat down at the table together. After the usual small talk, we got down to business. My genius stupid brother said that he has some requirements that have to be in the contract. He went on to say that he must receive a Cadillac. As he finished that sentence, I looked at my brother in disbelief. I said, "Eddie, this is your company. You can always buy yourself a Cadillac. It's just the car." "No", he said, "Every position that I had always came with a company Cadillac.

All of my investors were looking at me with nervous looks on their faces. Ed said, "The other requirement that I must have, is that if this corporation should fail, I want two years severance pay." I could not believe my brother's brain, or lack of a working one. I said, "Ed, owners of corporations do not get severance pay. Only employees get severance pay.

After a couple of seconds, we all started coming out of a state of shock. One of my investors said, "Al, if we do this deal, I insist that we have a co-CEO of my choosing, so we know what's going on. At that point, I stood up and said, "Gentleman, my humble apologies, but this deal is off." I looked at my stupid brother, who just gave up the chance of a lifetime, because he wanted a Cadillac. Over the next couple of weeks, I finalized the end of this adventure by paying off the attorneys and other bills associated with this disaster. Bally closed down the corporation and still has the patents. When it was all over, I said to myself, all I lost was money and not my health, so things are good.

Lesson One: How To Blow You Self Apart

One bright sunny morning, I was having my first cup of coffee in my office when my phone rang. It was a friend of mine who was a New York State Commissioner working for the State Senate. He started right to the point without and small talk by saying, "Al, I desperately need your help. Yesterday afternoon there was a huge explosion in a housing development located in Westchester, New York. There were a number of deaths and much damage. This incident is very sensitive with great political concerns. I need somebody, basically you, to go there, assess the damage and fix it, so it's back to normal as fast as possible. The political pressure is shaking up every elected official associated in that area." I told him that type of work was really not my field. There are companies out there that handle such catastrophes. He said, "This is too politically sensitive to bring in anyone else. This needs someone like you." He used the four magic words, "do me a favor". How could I refuse?

I drove right away to the apartment house. I met the superintendent who was waiting for me. He explained to me what happened. "This event is the most bizarre happening by a human being with a thinking brain. It seems that the gentleman in the apartment came home from the hospital to recuperate after major surgery. He was in bed and connected to an oxygen machine to keep him breathing. He quietly took out a cigarette and lit it. It didn't take more than a second for the oxygen to explode, killing him and blowing his wife out a window off the balcony to her death below. Their daughter was just coming home. She started to open the door when the blast occurred. It destroyed the corridor. The daughter ran away and was missing. She was found three days later roaming the streets, completely disoriented."

The oxygen tank blew right through the concrete block wall separating the apartment from the public corridor and went right through the concrete wall on the opposite end of the corridor going into the next apartment. The damage was massive and there were concerns of possible structural damage to the building. At a meeting with some of the local officials, they all pleaded, as well as demanded, that this entire area gets back to normal as fast as possible. By the way, I forgot to mention that my friend, the Commissioner, said there were no fees for the work that I was to do. I swung into action. I used those four letter magic words to recruit my structural and mechanical engineers to help me assess all the damage, and what I had to do to create the documents to get the contractors to put this place back together. I won't bore you with the details, but we worked fast and put it back together and everyone was happy. I tell the story only because of the unbelievable stupidity of that man; to light a cigarette when on oxygen.

Conditions Non-Locals Are Not Aware Of

I had a client who got control of a piece of property in glorious West Virginia. He decided to build an apartment house on that property. We had a meeting to discuss the type of building he wants to fit in with the economic conditions of the area. We came to an agreement and I got to work designing the preliminary drawings for this proposed project. I made an application with the National Council of Architectural Registration Board (NCARB) to get my Architectural license for the State of West Virginia. Once you are approved by this organization as a Licensed Architect, they file to receive your license in other states for you, omitting a lot of red tape for me. After my preliminary design was approved by my client, I scheduled a trip to West Virginia to obtain all the information I needed in reference to their zoning and building code requirements.

I met with a very nice young man who was a Building Department Examiner, to obtain all the information I needed. He gave me the necessary zoning and building code publications and examined my preliminary plans. This lovely Building Department Examiner said, "Let me take you to lunch. We have a fabulous soup restaurant a block away. I never heard of a restaurant that just sells soup, or a bureaucrat taking a customer to lunch. We walked down the block to the restaurant. It was clear to see this was a fast food soup operation. We got on line and examined the menu on the wall behind the service counter. They served hundreds of different kind of soups. I looked up at that massive menu and said at random, "Number Five". I just didn't have the patience to read through that whole menu to make a decision on a fast food lunch. We got a bowl of soup, went to the counter for the free bread or crackers, and sat down to a great meal. The restaurant did not impress me as much as the great attitude of this government employee.

Back in the Building Department office, we finished with my requests, and he asked me if I had the underground survey. I looked at him puzzled, because I never heard of an underground survey. He said, "It's okay. Don't be embarrassed. I know you're not from this neck of the woods. Everyone living in West Virginia knows that the entire underground in this state is honeycombed with coal mines that have been dug over many years. It is quite common for the fumes and vapor within those mines to catch on fire. Once the fire starts, it spreads through the mines and burns for years on end. If your property happens to be above one of these mines that are on fire, you cannot build anything on that site." He put me in touch with a company that conducts underground surveys.

Once I acquired all the information as to the fees and time it takes to conduct the survey, I packed up and was on my way home. I enlightened my client of this problem. It could cause him to own a piece of property that could not be built on. Needless to say, my client was not a happy camper. To make a long story short, I later saw a survey that showed a blazing fire under his proposed site. This fire had been burning for 10 years. The survey said that there was no end in sight for the fire. The only positive thing on this adventure was I became a licensed architect in the State of West Virginia, to add to my other state licenses.

AIA National Design Award

One bright and sunny day, as most literary stories begin, my office received notification that we had been awarded an American Institute of Architects National Design Award. This award would be given to us at the next annual national convention. The building we were receiving the award for was an office building located on Fifth Avenue in New York City. The design of this building was a joint venture between my office and the architectural office of the Dean of Architecture of Columbia University. Since I always have been derelict in record keeping, I sadly cannot remember the name of the architect with whom we were sharing this design award.

A few weeks before the national AIA convention, I received information in reference to the presentation of this design award. This was the first convention that Harriet was not able to attend with me. I was on my own. Since I am not a slow, in-depth reader, but tend to skim very quickly, the event of tragedy is always staring down on me. I read the instructions that stated, "A rehearsal session shall be conducted at 1pm at the Convention Center." This convention was being held in San Antonio, Texas. For those of you, who are unfamiliar with the weather in San Antonio, Texas, in the summer months, there is a hot, thick, unbearable humidity that all the residents have to endure. I put on light weight pants and a lightweight golf shirt to attend the rehearsal session. Remember, I didn't read instructions carefully and Harriet wasn't with me. She would have read the instructions.

I walked about five blocks from the hotel to the Convention Center in the punishing humid heat. Upon entering the Convention Center, I quickly noticed that the men were dressed in business suits and ties. I asked one of my friends, "Why are you dressed in a suit and tie in this heat and high humidity? Suits and ties are for the activities tonight." I heard the words that shook me. "Al, didn't you read the instructions?" I said, "Yes", in a hesitant voice. "Then you read that they do not allow photographs during the actual presentation. This afternoon is a rehearsal and photo session."

Complete disaster. I asked if I had time to go back to the hotel to change. The answer was yes, if I go extremely fast. I ran those five blocks through the steam bath of humidity and dashed up to my room. Gallons of water from perspiration were dripping off me. I got dressed in a suit and tie. I ran as fast as I could the five blocks back, fighting my way through the humidity. I arrived at the Convention Center just in time to hear them calling my name. My co-architect and I went on stage. There I stood, soaked from sweat, head to toe, and tried very hard to not collapse. My handkerchief was so soaked with sweat, that it was useless to try to dry myself any further. I stood like a drowning rodent, smiling for the cameras, as my co-architect and I were being presented the award.

After, I sat down and tried to compose myself. My client, who was also attending these festivities, said to me, "Al, how about a round of golf?" I was in no condition to be able to go out on a golf course and try to hit the ball. However, in the business world, you never say no to a client. I agreed and wondered if I will be able to live through this day. My client said he would make all the arrangements and let me know what time and where to meet. I said, "Great, I will be in my hotel room to clean up and change for golf." A half hour later, I got a call from a client who said he had bad news. He told me the bad news that he couldn't get a starting time because they're booked solid. My eyes looked to heaven and under my breath I was saying thank you, but on the phone I said, "Oh, that's too bad." I showered and fell on the bed for a long rejuvenating sleep.

Back on Staten Island, when I told this incident to Harriet, she said, "You need to slow down and read all the words."

A Change In Life Style To Enjoy Life

My partners and I built up a pretty active architectural practice. We had about 90 to 100 professional staff of architects, draftsmen & clerical people, etc. We operated on two floors of office space on Broadway off 14th Street in Manhattan. At one point, we were so well organized, that when my partners and I brought in a new client and completed the preliminary design of the building, our great and capable professional staff took over. Every morning, I would check the progress of my projects with my project architects. That way I always knew what was going on. When there were no problems, the staff just kept moving along at a very fast pace. However, whenever there was a problem, I got involved. At one point, I was not doing architecture anymore. I was only putting out fires. I remember discussing this problem with my partner Peter Claman. After a short discussion, we agreed to take some time off and start enjoying life. The solution was simple. We would both take off 10 days every month throughout the winter. I had the beginning of the month; Peter had the end of the month.

We both eventually bought homes in Arizona. I located in Tucson and Peter located in Carefree. When we first started with these winter vacations, Harriet and I stayed at the historic Arizona Inn. We did this for 3 years. This hotel was built in 1929, when Tucson was a very small cowboy town and the rest of the area was desert.

We moved to an apartment that was owned by our son Paul for a few years. Then we build a house on the grounds of Skyline Country Club, which is a gated community. We joined Skyline Country Club to begin a great lifestyle. We made quite a few new friends very quickly because the slogan of Skyline Country Club is that 'there are no strangers here'. Those 10 days every month in the winter was a great relief from the everyday pressures of the construction industry. After a number of years of this very long commute, we decided to retire and become snowbirds. For six months of the winter, we avoided the snow and cold of New York City by living in Tucson. We spent the glorious summer in New York and avoided the hundred plus degrees in Arizona. It was the best of both worlds.

I had to find new mental stimulation in Tucson. We made Skyline Country Club the center of our lives. We got deeply involved with golf. Harriet was a very active golfer and played almost every day of the week. We think she could have held a record for number of golf games played per year, if anyone would have bothered to keep track. Harriet played with many women friends. I played with the men. We were also involved in various tournaments that involved couples which were a lot of fun. There was a lot of discovery of interesting places in and around Tucson. In order to add variety, we got involved with the entertainment committee of Skyline Country Club. We planned various themed parties and events. It gave us the opportunity to intermingle with the many members of the Club who were not golfers. Being part of this committee was all fun.

One day a member of the Board of Directors asked me if I would set up a photography club for the members of Skyline. I agreed and formed a small committee. The big incentive for having members join the Club were the classes that I taught. I covered the technical and art of photography, for beginning and advanced members. In a very short time, we had a good size group of about 20 members. I taught the basics of photography to bring all members up to speed in the use of cameras. I got into the art of photography and finally the use of the computers for editing. From time to time, we invited guest lecturers that covered various fields of photography.

When I felt everyone had enough knowledge to start doing serious photography, I started a series of photo shoots in and around Tucson. We arranged with the Club to have a photo exhibition every year for the month of April. Skyline provided the room and our members hung their photographs for public viewing. On opening evening, the Club provided a great display of hot and cold hors d'oeuvres for the event. This exhibit became a very popular event which still happens every April.

Retirement

If I had the opportunity to go through life once more from the beginning, I wouldn't change a thing. Not one thing, action or any other situation would I want to change. As the wise man said, "If it ain't broke, don't fix it." One Friday morning, upon completing a meeting with my client and a number of contractors, I sat in my office and took a 5 minute break. The night before, Harriet asked me what I wanted to do for my 70th birthday that was coming. Then it hit me, 'I'm going to be 70 years old and I'm still working'! I realized that according to tradition, I am supposed retire at age 65. What am I still doing here? I called my accountant for some economic information. I told him I am thinking of retiring. My next big question, with retirement in the balance was, "Can I afford to retire?"

Peter Claman and I with our second generation of partners. Picture taken in our conference room, upon my retirement.

To my astonishment my accountant started to laugh when I asked that question. He said it was a dumb question. He told me to talk to Harriet. Through all of my working life, I gave Harriet my earnings for her to be bookkeeper of our personal finances. I had no idea of our personal financial condition. My working thoughts were always on my business and my client's needs. My accountant advised me to keep my house and Country Club membership on Staten Island then go to Tucson and buy another house and join another local Country Club. At that point he said, you will be an official snowbird. Enjoy your new life spending six months during the summer on Staten Island, and six months during the winter in

Tucson, Arizona. That information was music to my ears. At the end of the day I anxiously got into my car and drove home for a serious conversation with Harriet to plan our future.

The minute I came home I asked Harriet, "could I afford to retire?" She opened a large journal book to the first page and told me to start reading. To my amazement, I had no idea the amount of money that Harriet showed we had. All the money that I had earned and turned over to her, she brilliantly and successfully invested to allow it to grow. We looked at each other and said, "We are going to be snowbirds." The next day at the office I informed my partners that I am going to be starting my next career as a retired person. I suggested that we take one of our senior project architects that had been working closely with me and my clients, and make him a partner to take over my position.

Everything was agreed to by all parties. A smooth transition took place without any disturbance to our architectural practice. At the beginning of the next winter season, Harriet and I were off to Arizona to either buy a house or have one built. We joined Skyline Country Club in Tucson on the top of a mountain where you can see the world as we played golf. We first started to look for houses within the gated community where Skyline Country Club was located. All the houses that the real estate agent showed us were very large houses with fantastic views. As we visited all these homes, one thought that always popped up in my mind was Harriet's voice telling me that my job would be to vacuum the carpet. As I studied each home and observed the acres of carpet, I felt it would take so much time that I would not have the ample time left to play golf. I said to myself, "We have that large house on Staten Island that requires a lot of maintenance. Why in my retirement would I take up other domestic chores? There must be some smaller, but upscale homes that the two of us can enjoy."

So we informed a real estate agent of our new requirement. One day Harriet and I were having lunch on the exterior deck of Skyline Country Club. As we were enjoying our lunch we heard a lot of construction noise that seemed to be coming in the area not too far from the first tee. After a little investigation we found that a developer was building new homes in the area that was a short block's walk to the first tee of the golf course. After lunch we went to visit that developer and look at his model homes. That house was perfect for us. It was a three bedroom two bathroom house about 2,500 ft². The backyard patio faced the eighth green on the other side of a small stream that provided us privacy. It did not take us long to make a deal with the developer for him to build one of those homes for us. Once construction was completed, we moved in and started our new adventure in life. From that time, every winter was a joy for us in Arizona, and every summer was another joy for us on Staten Island.

Harriet's Stroke, Angel Alice & Tommy

After about 10 years of being a snowbird, Harriet experienced her first stroke. It was devastating. But we still made the long commute every six months back and forth between Staten Island and Tucson. We did this for about two years, and then Harriet had her second stroke. She recovered well from the second stroke, but it became too difficult to travel, so we became permanent residents of Arizona. I tried to hire help with the everyday chores of taking care of Harriet, but could not find the right dedicated trustworthy health care workers to help me out. So I did the chores 24 hours a day, seven days a week, for about eight years.

One day, a friend came to visit Harriet for the afternoon. That gave me the chance to visit a friend of mine who had just move into a recently built Continual Care Retirement Community. My friend, Irving Olson, who was in his 90s, introduced me to the Marketing Director of this new facility. She gave me a whole stack of literature to read. I had absolutely no thought of buying an apartment in this type of facility. Harriet and I went through the literature, just to see what they had to offer. After looking at all those pretty pictures, we started to soften. We struggled over the thought of selling our house in Tucson and the house on Staten Island and buying a large apartment in this new facility. I felt that I might be able to get more help in this type of community then living by ourselves in a private house. And so we made the change. We moved in to an independent living unit. It is a great apartment about 3000 ft.² with all the amenities that you need. However, since this was an independent living unit, getting the help I needed was not available. There was an assisted living area and a nursing home section as part of this facility for those who could not live in the independent units any longer. This place could have done a better job at servicing our needs.

You must remember that our architectural firm designed and built a great many nursing homes and hospitals. I am very familiar with the entire operation of these institutions. I served on the board of a very fine nursing home for 15 years and of a teaching hospital for about 20 years. I had a lot of experience in all facets of the nursing homes, health care and hospital businesses. I call them health business because in this country, we do not have a health profession any longer.

I never wanted my wife to have to spend any time in a bad environment. One day I met an angel named Alice Gilligan. Alice is a healthcare worker that was employed by a healthcare agency that provides assistance to those in need, in their own home. She was recommended by a friend who strongly urged me to interview her.

Alice, the angel

The minute she walked in the door, and I read her body language, I was blown over. Her bright open eyes and warm expression on her face, the way she walked over to Harriet, the whole package was telling me that this was a wonderful person. I was convinced this woman knows how to practice her profession. She could provide all the services that I dreamt of. I thought I would never be available to find a great person to help me care for Harriet. She walked over to Harriet, got down on one knee and looked straight up at Harriet with love and understanding. Harriet fell in love with her without hesitation. About two minutes passed and I said, "You're hired." This is the type of woman that I was looking for to help Harriet, for about 10 years. The person who brought Alice to us said you did not interviewed her yet. I said, "I saw enough in a few minutes to know we have a winner here."

After a couple of weeks went by, I realized that the agency Alice worked for could take her from us and send her to another client. It didn't take me long to realize that I must hire this woman to work directly for me full-time. I offered her a job for life, if she quits her agency and comes to work for me. I would create a legal home care agency so that she could get her Social Security, workers compensation, a retirement plan and all the other benefits of working for legitimate organization. She would be off on the weekends & holidays and get vacation time, and anything else we both agreed to. When I said 'a job for life', I meant, that if I survived Harriet, and even if I do not need help, she's to report every Thursday to pick up her check. If the time comes when I need help, then she will have regular hours. I agreed to pay her almost 3 times the salary that she was making at the agency. How anyone can survive working for those agencies at minimum wage is beyond me.

The problem I had is that Alice signed an agreement with her agency preventing her from working directly for one of their clients. If she left the agency, she could not work for any of their clients until after a two-year period. I met the owner of the agency and said I wanted to buy Alice out of her contract. He knew we had me and said he wanted $10,500 to free her to work for me. I gladly made out the check and I now had a full-time fantastic person to take care of Harriet. With the help of my son, Paul, we legally set up Arista Home Care LLC. This new agency is legal under federal and Arizona law. My long-term insurance company investigated my new agency, found it legal and acceptable and agreed pay our health care benefits to Arista. We were in business.

As Harriet got worst, we had to hire more help. At one point Arista Home Care LLC had a staff of 6 caregivers for around the clock care. Alice was my Chief of Staff. Alice and Paul worked together to find, hired and schedule our staff. Alice set the schedules and made sure the girls came on time to relieve the girl going off duty. There were times when the midnight-to-5am girl couldn't show up at the last minute. When Alice couldn't get one of the other girls to cover the shift, she stayed. I woke up one morning and found Alice sitting on the couch. Alice made life for both Harriet and I a joy. Harriet started to go downhill and Alice made her feel very comfortable during this tough time. It became time to call in hospice. One evening Harriet fell asleep and never woke up.

After the funeral, everything calmed down and all fell into place. I told Alice that since I am still in good shape and don't need her help, she is to stop by every Thursday to pick up her check as I promised. I told her I never make a promise that I do not intend to keep. She didn't say anything. The next morning at 9:30 she was there. She stayed with me until about 3 PM and went home to take care of her husband and household chores. At the writing of this book, Harriet has been gone for over two years. Every Monday to Friday, Alice shows up about 9: 30 and spends a day with me. We go to the movies, have lunch, go to some organizations that I am involved with, and some evenings when I'm entertaining someone for dinner, she goes with us. It is now to the point where I couldn't survive without her. My doctors don't talk to me anymore; they talk to Alice because they know Alice will get the information and know exactly what has to be done. That's why at the beginning of this little saga, I called her an Angel and so she is.

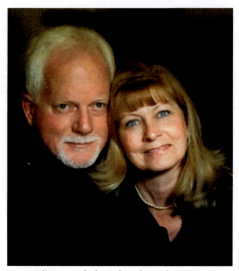

Alice with her husband, Brian

One time Alice and I were having lunch with a couple of our friends from Skyline. I said to my friends, "Did you know that God is a woman?" They looked at me puzzled and I just pointed to Alice. I must say that her husband, Brian, is also an angel for allowing his wife to spend so much time with me. I do not consider Alice as an employee, I think of her more as a loving daughter.

Every day I say to myself that this aging process is not affecting me mentally or physically in any manner. I reasoned that if I keep saying that, it will be true. However, to ensure that I maintain my mental capabilities, I go on photo shoots and volunteer with non-profit organizations. I provide photographs and use Photoshop to process all my work. I felt that I should have a computer guru on call for those moments when computer problems arise. I needed someone I could call.

I made some inquiries with the people manning the front desk of our facility. One young man handed me a business card. It did not take long for my computer to tell me it's time to get that card out and call for help. I made the call and we set a date for him to come to my apartment and take care of my computer problem. He told me his name was Tommy. When the time arrived, he rang my doorbell. I opened the door, and in walked Tommy. With a smile, he said, "Take me to your computer." I stood there for a moment not believing what's happening. Just like with my Angel Alice, when she walked in and I read her body language, I knew she is a real Angel. The same thing happened with Tommy. "Oh my", I said to myself, "Can I be that lucky?"

Tommy, and his love Stephanie

After working with Tommy, I think by the third visit, I said, "You have to be working directly for me on a part-time call basis." I offered to pay him a fixed salary, once a year. It would cover his expenses, time and profit, so that he could be on-call whenever I needed. I agreed to make sure that my needs do not interfere with his current job as the IT expert with the Indian gambling casinos. He accepted my offer. Not only is he a great computer guru, he turned out to be a great friend. He is in my apartment taking care of my computer at least once a week. But he and his lifetime mate of 15+ years, Stephanie, have joined Alice, I and others on a number of great vacation trips together. Again I say, "Life is good."

Living in a Continual Care Retirement Community, such as Splendido, was a new experience for us. We tried to fit in to this style of living. We had lunch in the café and dinner in the dining room. We attended some of the lectures that were given. They covered subjects in keeping with the age of the audience. Art lessons were part of my schedule as was displaying some of my photographs in the art shows that were held from time to time. We really tried to fit in. However, we found all the activities not in keeping with our lifestyle and to be honest, we found them to be boring. The food in the café was passable and convenient. However, the food and the service in the dining room, to be polite, were not up to our standards.

I found that the operation established by the corporate, was run by a group of bureaucrats and lawyers, whose only concerns were that no one should be able to sue them for any reason, and the all-important bottom line. The residents that live here, the ones that pay the bills, the people that allow them to make a profit, are the last concern that they have. The people are on the bottom of the list of all their decision-making. A quick example of management's thinking was when a resident went to the front desk and requested a Band-Aid. They were told that they cannot give out Band-Aids. The concern was that if they gave you a Band-Aid, and you develop an infection, you could sue them. They also have a policy that the nursing home may not issue Band-Aids. This is the height of stupid irresponsible bureaucracy. We ran into many other issues like this that should be a normal situation for this type of institution.

It did not take long after we moved in, to realize that the entire construction of this building was substandard. The first problem arose when I started to prepare for the evening and getting ready for a good night sleep. After spending a few minutes in the master bedroom, I noticed an odor of sewer gas. I called the front desk. They sent a maintenance employee to check out the situation. He told me that this apartment had been vacant for a long period of time probably causing the water in the plumbing trap under the bathtub to evaporate. He poured some chemicals down the drain and flushed it out with water. He told me everything should be fine. Less than an hour later, the sewer gas was back. After a number of other attempts, the director of maintenance decided to break open the wall in an effort to see if there was any damage to the piping.

Once the wall was open, the cause was plain to see. Our apartment is on the ground floor and has concrete slab on grade. It appears that the plumbing contractor missed blocking out some space in the concrete slab for the plumbing trap during construction. They did not have enough room to install the plumbing trap after the slab was poured. They didn't bother to cut the concrete to get the trap in place. Some unscrupulous contractor just connected the tub drain to the sewer without the trap. There was nothing from stopping the sewer gases from coming into the bathroom. This was never noticed, because we were the first people to live in this apartment. It sat vacant from the initial construction and was used as a conference room before we moved in.

The director of maintenance said he would have to break open the walls and remove the bathtub and reinstall everything to have the tub working in a legal and proper manor. Harriet or I never took baths. We preferred showers. Our apartment has 3 showers. I told them to seal up the bathtub drain to stop sewer gas from entering the room. I took this approach to enjoy the apartment in lieu of going through the major construction process.

A week or so went by. My son, Paul, and I were in the third bedroom that I use as a studio and office. We were working on the computer. We were talking to each other having a normal conversation when the phone rang. It was my neighbor whose bedroom was on the opposite side of the wall. He politely asked me if I would turn down the television set because the volume was up to loud preventing him from falling asleep. I told him that I do not have a television set in this room. We are just speaking with our normal voice. I told him to put the phone down. I said, "Lee is the phone down? Can you hear me?" To my surprise, I heard, "Yes Al, I can hear you clearly." We could talk right through the wall. Again this place was built with substandard construction. There was no sound insulation built into the walls separating the apartments. I later learned that this problem is throughout the building.

The management was well aware of the situation and did correct the situation in a number of locations, but did not correct it here. A solution was sought and found not to be acceptable to my neighbor. Since the majority of the time I am alone in the studio, I decided to forget about the problem. However if someone else is in this room with me, we try to speak with a low voice.

Another deficiency in construction was the installation of an adequate hot water system to all the apartments. When you want to get hot water for a shower or other needs etc., you have to let the water run for about 5 to 10 minutes. If you're lucky, you'll get hot water, but you could easily get semi-warm water. In the mornings when a lot of people shower, hot water can be sketchy.

I was seriously thinking that now with Alice as part of my life, I should buy a house in the area. I started to look around at new houses. I eventually decided the physical act of packing, moving, unpacking, redecorating and going through the entire moving horror was not worth the effort. After Harriet passed away I made some major changes to my living at Splendido. I gave up my meal plan and receive a $200 credit on my monthly expenses. I started to get more deeply involved with community and political activities outside of Splendido.

I Am In My Father's Footsteps

I find it hard for me to believe that I am actually a senior citizen. Not only by age, but also my actions, needs and wants. In addition, I am following in my father, Milton's footsteps. I remember so clearly when my mother passed away. My father, being a senior citizen, felt alone. He felt uncomfortable living alone and concerned that if there was any type of emergency, he might not be able to help himself. Harriet and I flew out to California where Milton was living, to help him find a Continual Care Retirement Community to live in. After some research and visits, we found the perfect one for my father. Milton moved in to a lovely apartment with a balcony.

Al with Angels Mary Kay and Alice

It was a typical operation that provided three meals a day, all the activities and entertainment, plus nursing care to make sure he takes his medications, etc. Milton was living there for about three months when Harriet and I made the trip to California to visit him. When we arrived at the building, the manager saw and came over to speak with us. She said, "We never see your father. He does not eat here, nor does he take part in any of the activities. We don't know what he does all day and we're getting concerned. Please let me find out what he's doing." We went up to my father's apartment and were met with greetings and hugs. I asked him how he was feeling. He said he feels well. Everything is good and he is very happy. I asked him what he does all day. He said, much to my surprise, "In the morning, I go out to get breakfast at a nice little restaurant couple blocks away. In the afternoon and in the evening I go to the hospital cafeteria right down the block to eat my meals. I spend some time in the lounge reading and talking to the people that are there visiting their family members in the hospital. Sometimes I go to the loading dock of the hospital and talk to the nice guys that unload the trucks.

Then he said, "I have a story to tell you. It's hard to believe but one day when I was at the retirement home, one of the ladies that lives above me asked me to go to the movies with her. I looked at her and said 'you should be ashamed of yourself, at your age asking me for a date'. Can you believe that?" "Pop", I said, "There's nothing wrong with socializing at your age."

I continued, "Why aren't you eating at the home where the meals are paid for?" My father looked at me and said, "You want me to sit in that dining room with all those old people? All they do is cough and hock and are very boring. At the hospital I find people that are interesting to talk to." I was amazed at my father's attitude and did not understand his feelings. Now, much to my horror, I am doing the exact same thing as him. I do not eat at this facility because it is loaded with old people, the food is horrible, and I find it a stagnant existence. Since I do not eat in this facility and food is included in my monthly charges, I receive a monthly credit.

Just like my father I find all the lectures and activities in this facility to be boring and mindless. I watch them playing cards or bingo and you can hear a pin drop. It seems that they are playing these games, but are not really enjoyed life. It fills in the time, I guess. I get mental stimulation through the various organizations that we attend and by associating with young people. I also enjoy eating in good upscale restaurants and love their culinary delights.

As far as socializing with women, I had a similar experience in Splendido as my father. One of the female residents told me to sit down on the couch next to her. Not realizing what was happening, I sat down. She took my arm and put it around her shoulder and snuggled into my chest. I was in a state of shock and jumped up to get out of her clutches. I said, "It's time to go." Believe it or not, I'm behaving just like my father.

The Horrors Of Medicine

One morning, when I woke up, I became aware that the big toe on my left foot just did not feel right. I called my podiatrist, who told me to come into his office that morning. After he examined me, he said that I had an ingrown toenail that became infected. He put some medication on it and gave me a prescription for antibiotics that I should take the next few days. In time, the infection was gone and everything turned back to normal.

About two months later, that same toe became infected again. This happened because my podiatrist did not cut my nails properly to prevent the second infection. This time the podiatrist said the infection was so bad that I had to see a vascular surgeon. I quickly made an appointment with a vascular surgeon. Upon first meeting this vascular surgeon, I felt very uneasy with him. I was concerned because of his body language. Looking at this doctor, I could see an arrogant, self-impressed jerk that could care less about his patients and more about collecting fees. When I read a person's body language, I find that I am right on the button about 90 to 95% of the time. I questioned myself with this doctor. Are my first thoughts in the 90 to 95% correct area, or am I making a mistake in my reading of this man's personality. It turned out that I was right on the button again.

He told me that I have very poor circulation in my feet. He's going to operate to try to open the veins and arteries to allow a better flow of blood. On the way to the operating room, the doctor told me that if I am fortunate enough to have my legs outlive me, then there is no problem. However if my legs do not outlive me, then he would have to amputate both legs from the knee down. He concluded that it might be desirable to do the amputation in a few weeks. At that point, I knew my impression of this doctor's body language was 100% correct.

He operated to try to increase the circulation. After the operation he had his physician's assistant look after me as he went on vacation. The incisions from the operation were not healing well. Puss was running down my leg that would not stop. The doctor's partner was made aware of my problem to see if he could stop the infection. This doctor did nothing and did not ever meet me in the hospital. Finally, my doctor came back from vacation and looked at the situation. He said we have to call an infection specialist.

The doctor that specializes in infections examined me and prescribed some pills for me to take. Nothing was helping. Then, another angel came into my life. This angel's name is MaryKay, a close friend of my son, Paul. She came to visit me at the hospital to see how I was doing. I told her my tale of woe. She told me that her brother had terrible trouble with his feet and amputation was once considered. She told me that her brother was saved from amputation and was cured of his foot problem by the SALSA institute (Southern Arizona Limb Salvage Alliance).

I immediately checked myself out of this horrible hospital with that horrible doctor. The nurse told me that I could not leave the hospital. I quickly informed her that I have a lot of experience with hospitals. "I have designed and built many hospitals. I'm on the board of a hospital. You cannot tell me that I have to stay in this hellhole. Get me your standard form that states I am leaving this hospital on my own and against medical advice."

I quickly made arrangements to get to the emergency room at University Medical Center. When I arrived at the hospital emergency room, I asked to see Dr. Armstrong, the director of SALSA. I said that if he isn't available, please get one of the other SALSA doctors. The nurse started to check on this.

While I was waiting, I noticed the emergency room only had a few people waiting. I mentioned that I was on the board of a teaching hospital and our waiting room was always packed to the gills. The clerk told me that she contacted the SALSA Institute and a doctor will be right down. I was taken to an exam room.

The next nurse looked at my records and asked me who I knew in this hospital. "I don't know anyone in his hospital. Why do you ask?" "Well", she said, "On your records, it's marked 'VIP'." She said, "I guess I have to treat you like a VIP." What I think happened was at check-in, when I said, "I was on the board of a hospital", the admitting nurse misunderstood me and thought I said, "I am on a board of this hospital". I said nothing to correct the situation and enjoyed the preferential treatment.

Dr. Nicholas Giovinco from the SALSA Institute came down to examine me. He ordered intravenous antibiotics. The Doctor informed me that tomorrow morning I could leave the hospital and go home. I will become an outpatient of the SALSA Institute. He said the infection should be all cleaned up by tomorrow morning.

Believe it or not, but by the morning the infection was completely gone. I had a car pick me up and went home. Monday morning I received a call from the SALSA Institute with a date and time to come down to meet Dr. David Armstrong for a complete in-depth examination of my condition. Once he took control, my troubles were over. Dr. Armstrong had another specialist on his staff, Dr. John Hughes also examine me. It should be noted that I was wheelchair bound during all of these examinations. When Dr. Hughes finished his examination, while two of his aides stood by, he got down on his knees and put my socks on. Dr. Hughes pushed my wheelchair out to the front desk and instructed the appointment clerk to make an appointment for my revisit as soon as possible. He also informed the clerk to call my ride home to pick me up in the front of the hospital and call for an aide to push my wheelchair down to the hospital entrance. In all my years associated with the medical profession, I never saw a doctor treat a patient in such a wonderful way. From that moment on, I knew I was in the right place/ There they know how to care for the patient.

All was cured within a few visits to the hospital without any talk of amputation. Dr. David Armstrong and his team saved my feet. I will never forget them. By the way it should be noted that I consider MaryKay to be another one of my unofficial daughters. We have been good friends for many years and continue to be. The moral of this story, don't blindly accept one doctor's treatment plan. If I had the doctor amputate it would have needlessly taken several of my toes, if not my entire foot or leg.

Mental Stimulation Over The Years

At the beginning of this book, I noted that the personality, genes, and other properties that create how a person thinks and acts, is a gift of nature. This gift dictates how we are going to live our lives. In my case, I am on the hyperactive side. Sitting quietly and reading a novel is torture to me. I need a lot of physical action and mental activity. I call it, my need for mental stimulation. I was always able to fill my waking hours by being involved not only in my practice of architecture, but also enjoying every organization that I was a member of. When two people got together and I became the third, we were off and running as a new organization.

If you have the opportunity to look at my resume, you will see a great variety of organizations that I was active in or on their Board of Directors. They satisfied much of my mental stimulation craving. Part of my mental stimulation was satisfied by some of the lectures that I gave at various organizations and conventions, such as the New York State component of the American Institute of Architects, the National Homebuilders Association Convention, Western Parks Association, Oro Valley Library, Staten Island Chamber of Commerce, and various political organizations.

I also spoke at Richmond County Country Club, Skyline Country Club and at Splendido. I have four favorite lecture subjects. My first favorite lecture subject is Photography. This works out to be more than a lecture, but a two session class, lasting 3 hours each. My other three favorite subjects are; The Art of Public Speaking, Networking, and Understanding Body Language.

In the past, I was fortunate enough to enjoy photography and wild life photo shoots that took me all over the world. I have a few dozen photo albums of our family vacation cruises and bus excursions.

The crowning glory of my photographic experiences were not only mentally stimulating but self-gratifying. I volunteered on many non-profit boards and incorporated my photography into my service to these organizations. A number of these organizations included work for the blind, deaf, handicapped, and others who were not fortunate enough to have the mental or physical capabilities to enjoy life as we do. I also had the opportunity to serve on the Board of Directors of the American Institute of Architects, New York Society of Architects, Staten Island Zoological Society, Staten Island University Hospital, Wagner College, Eger Nursing Home, Tibetan Museum, Snug Harbor Cultural Center, New York City Building Congress, and New York City Council of Senior Centers and Services. Living in Tucson, Arizona, I had to leave all of the organizations I was involved with back in New York.

There came a time in my life when I took care of my wife after she became a stroke victim. I did everything I could for her with a loving heart. During all the wonderful years of our marriage, Harriet did everything for me with her loving heart. Not having the mental stimulation during this period was not a problem for me. My time was filled helping the wife I love.

Then came the day when Alice came into our lives. She brought buckets of sunshine and love into the Efron household. Alice gave me the opportunity to have my own time. Being caregiver to another is an exhausting full time job. Knowing Harriet was being well taken care of in the loving hands of Alice gave me some freedom.

I was able to get involved with organizations again. One morning I sat down at the computer and Googled 'Organizations in Oro Valley' and 'Southern Arizona'. My search found the Oro Valley Historical Society (OVHS). I looked at their website and said to myself, "Al, this looks as good as any other organization". I made contact, paid my dues, and was invited down to a board meeting to meet the members of this organization. When I arrived at the meeting, I was asked to give an introduction of myself and to note my qualifications.

I learned about Steam Pump Ranch at the meeting. This ranch sounded like a great undertaking and opportunity for me because of the real estate. It is so similar to my past organizations although Steam Pump Ranch is on a much smaller scale. It's on less than 20 acres, with half a dozen small single-story adobe buildings. As a comparison, Sailor's Snug Harbor was a historic preservation site on Staten Island that I was involved with. It was on 85 acres, contained 50 large four-story reinforced concrete buildings.

Steam Pump Ranch

Towards the end of the meeting they started to discuss the 10-year anniversary celebration of the granting of the Pusch family title of the property as a historic preservation site. Being new to Oro Valley, I had never seen or heard of Steam Pump Ranch. One of the problems with the proposed anniversary party was that they lacked the funds to even buy a sheet cake to serve all the dignitaries that were expected to attend. It was hard for me to believe that any organization such as this one does not have the funds for a simple cake. I gladly volunteered to pay for the cake. Needless to say I became the hero of the day.

The day of this great celebration was the first time that I was on this historic preservation site. I stood there, looking around trying to understand how and why this ranch became a historic site. I learned some of the basic history and agree that the ranch definitely qualifies as historic site.

The adjoining property is a shopping center. In order to enter the ranch, you have to drive through the shopping center. A second item that struck me as odd was that the celebration is noting their 10-year of existence as a historic site. On close examination of what was there, the deteriorating ranch looked like it was a bombed out broken down facility.

It looked like it had been vacant for many years without any maintenance or repair of any manner. When I think back about Sailor's Snug Harbor, the comparison is amazing. The Staten Island project was tremendously larger with 50 large four-story concrete and masonry buildings that were in complete disrepair when we took over. At our 10th anniversary, we had raised all the necessary money from foundations and had completed all construction. All the buildings were occupied and the entire site became a historic education and art center. Here in Oro Valley, after 10 years, as far as I could see, absolutely nothing had been done. I quietly mentioned my experience with Sailor's Snug Harbor to some of the people in attendance. I said we can do the same thing here for Steam Pump Ranch. After all of the speeches and the eating of the precious cake, the announcement was made of the next board meeting and we all went home.

At the next board meeting, the Vice President had stepped down for personal reasons. The President called for an election and asked for nominations for VP. As I sat there quietly, I was taken back by hearing someone in the audience say "I nominate Al Efron". My reaction to his surprise nomination was to say, "Are you sure you want to nominate me? I know very little about this organization. I don't have the history that's needed to be an officer." To make a long story short, I became Vice President.

At my first executive meeting, I roughly outlined the program that we followed on Staten Island. It enabled us to raise the millions of dollars from foundations and bring all the buildings up to date in a safe and approved New York City Building Department code condition. After the renovation, we moved in all the various artists, museum, botanical garden, and other art groups. I emphasized the fact that we accomplished all this in the first 10 years.

During the time between my first and second board meeting I did some homework. Getting into all the details and the creation of this historic district I learned that the Oro Valley Historical Society does not own or have any legal rights to Steam Pump Ranch. It is owned by the Town of Oro Valley. It is the Mayor and Council of Oro Valley that did nothing in 10 years to help preserve and to restore the ranch.

It's easy to know why Oro Valley did nothing. They didn't want to upset the voters by spending money on a historic preservation project. They want their taxpayer money to be spent on police, fire, health, education, parks & recreation, highways, bridges and streets, etc. Historic preservation is not a need for the community to spend taxpayer dollars on. It doesn't provide necessary services on the people. The money for historic preservation should come from foundations and donations to a non-profit organization, such as the Oro Valley Historical Society.

I proposed to the OVHS that I would host a cocktail party for the Mayor, Council, Town Manager, senior staff people and members of the OVHS. At this meeting I would make a presentation; explain what we did on Staten Island, and how we should recreate that here. Everyone was in agreement. A date was set. Notices went out to all the people that we were inviting. I made arrangements to rent a room large enough to hold all attendees and to provide food & drinks for the evening.

When the evening arrived, we had a very good showing of Council people, staff people, the Town Manager and various other interested people. After everyone had their drinks & food, we all calmed down and got ready for my presentation. I started by explaining what we did on Staten Island and how to replicated that here. I explained that in order to be able to accept foundation money, we have to have the legal rights expressed from the Town of Oro Valley as the owners of the property. We can't start or carry out a construction project on property that they do not own. We need a simple legal document giving us permission to work on the site. The rough plan is for us to get the funding, then repair and/or stabilize the existing buildings. We'll build new facilities. We'll eventually move the stock pile of historic artifacts into a functioning museum. We could make this a place for tourists from around the world to see what life was like in the early days of the West.

A second and very important step is that the foundation must get a well detailed preliminary drawing of the entire project. This is needed to generate a reasonably accurate construction cost estimate. Plus the drawing and estimate are important documents to be able to sell the project to foundations for funding.

This is what happened on the Staten Island project. A partnership was formed between the City of New York and Sailor's Snug Harbor. The City of New York took ownership of the land. They were responsible for cutting the grass and for all roadways sidewalks and parking lots. All the buildings were owned by the Sailor's Snug Harbor Board. I, as an architect, was appointed Chairman of the Architectural and Construction Committee. We hired, initially on a part-time basis, an architect and historian manager. Preliminary drawings and a construction cost estimate were created. The manager had the help from some volunteers qualified in that field. We requested a grant from the State of New York to get this program started and were awarded, to the best of my memory, $40,000 of seed money. We went to work.

I brought photographs of Snug Harbor as well as photographs of a working ranch here in Tucson for use in my presentation. I explained my vision of what we could do to totally complete the historic preservation of Steam Pump branch within the next 10 years. After the meeting, a number of City Council people approached me and requested to have lunch meetings, so that we could get this project moving. I set up a number of lunch meetings, as well as meetings with the Town Manager and his professional staff to try to get everybody on the same page. We also had meetings with our attorneys and the Town, so that we could get a document giving the OVHS the legal right to raise money from foundations and spend it for construction on the Town-owned property.

I also suggested a number of changes to the OVHS bylaws. The bylaws initially stated that the maximum of nine people can serve on the Board of Directors. In order for this organization to move ahead we must have more talent on the board than only nine members. The board members are also a good source for fundraising, so more is better. So the bylaws had to be changed to allow 21 members on the board. With this change, we could recruit other talented people to serve on the board, such as the president of a bank, the owner of insurance company, an architect, various engineers, and any other business types. I call them community makers and shakers.

The next thing we need is a professional fundraiser who works with foundations. This type of professional person knows which funds give for historic preservation, the amount of money they give, and a host of other requirements. This person also prepares the documentation and makes the submissions to obtain the funds. I felt very confident that we could make this project move ahead quickly.

Little did I know, but these people were not like the makers and shakers that I worked with in New York. I soon discovered that the Town of Oro Valley was run by incompetent bureaucrats. I should note my definitions of 'bureaucrat' verses 'maker & shaker' are as follows: A 'bureaucrat' is a good person who has a job and does not want to make a mistake. This person will never think for themselves or make a change that may create a problem. If a minor change occurs that is not in keeping with the original instructions, the bureaucrat stops working. They then go their superior ask for directions to proceed. A 'maker & shaker' is a good person who when given a project, does not need in-depth instructions, just a good understanding of what needs to be done. Once the maker & shaker has what they need to do the job, get the hell out of their way and let them do it. That's the way things get done.

In working with the Town of Oro Valley, all I heard was "you can't do that". When I hear those four words, I get very angry. There was no such thing, as far as I'm concerned, that you cannot do. You can do whatever you want to do, if you look for a solution. If you don't look for a way, then you can't do it. At every meeting, I heard the senior leadership of the town say "you can't do that" phrase over and over. I showed them how we could do 'that' to their amazement.

One incident that blew my mind was the stupidity of a bureaucrat in a senior management position. The conversation went like this: I asked the manager when the building that they promised to fix up for us would be ready. I wanted to set up the OVHS office first, and get all the artifacts displayed later. This person said, "You can't do that". I looked puzzled and asked, "What can't I do?" The answer, "You can't have an office in a historic preservation project." It was just amazing this person could think that way. I said, "We are going to get a project manager that will be running this museum. Can that person be in this museum?" "Oh yes", the bureaucrat said. "Don't you think we should put a desk and a chair someplace for the manager to sit?" "Oh. No problem. You can do that." "What about a phone. Can we put in a phone for the manager to use?" "Yes. You can put in a phone." "When our manager is on the phone or having a meeting, they'll need some privacy. Can I put a simple wall around him with the door for privacy?" "Yes. You can do that." I very angrily said, "So why the hell are you telling me we can't have an office in a historic preservation site? We are a museum. Every museum in the world has a number of offices; for the manager, for director of maintenance, for the fund raising director. The program director will also need an office. There will be a number of classrooms and conference rooms and theaters and everything else that makes up the use of the museum. We'll also include toilets believe it or not." I looked at this person's face and just saw a blank stare. I wondered why this person was holding a job that they were not fit to have.

After so many meetings and agreements, I was so disturbed to find out after two years nothing was done. Meeting after meeting, we discussed the same problems, came to the same conclusions, everyone agreed and then left for home. Nothing was done again until it was re-discussed again at the next meeting. We had a group of nothing but bureaucrats who were afraid to make a decision.

At the writing of this book, the ranch had been declared a historic site 15 years ago. The deterioration is rapidly destroying the place. The OVHS has no preliminary plan. The OVHS never received a legal document giving them the right to spend foundation money for construction on the Town's land. I and a couple of other board members were on the verge of surrender.

We gave it one more shot. I had a meeting with the Town Manager and he agreed with requirements for the legal document for ownership. He stated that he will meet with his attorneys and work out a document, as I requested. He notified me that within a month he would be leaving his position for a job in Colorado. But he promised we'd have our document before he leaves.

We did receive a document from the Town. It said we had the right to use of one building to display some artifacts. There was nothing about ownership or foundation money or repair/stabilizing/construction of the site. It was completely inadequate for our needs. It actually made it unlawful for us to do any of the things needed.

About a week later, Alice and I were having lunch at a restaurant called The Overlook. It was owned and operated by the Town. At that lunch, the Town Manager, who was sitting at another table, approached Alice and I to invite us to his farewell party. He asked if we got the document he sent. I stood there for a minute, looking at him, and I was considering if I should kick him in the groin, or just say nothing. I chose to say nothing because it's safer. There was no other way to sum up this incident other than the man was lying to me. At that point, I said I give up. I resigned my position as Vice President but stayed on as a member of the board. As a member of the board I was to get some mental stimulation but didn't spend much time.

I had one incident in relation to Steam Pump Ranch that I found very challenging. What if the OVHS could get the Oro Valley Chamber of Commerce to relocate their facilities onto Steam Pump Ranch in conjunction with the restoration project? It would benefit both parties. I arranged a meeting with the CEO of Oro Valley Chamber of Commerce to discuss our proposal. The CEO of the Chamber liked the idea of relocating to Steam Pump Ranch. At that time they were renting space in a small office complex. It really wasn't adequate for their operation. But the Chamber didn't have the finances to construct a new building. I made them a proposal that would solve the problem. Thinking out-of-the-box, I proposed that I would seek two or three investors, including me, to provide our own money or obtain a construction loan to build the Chamber a new adequate headquarters. The chamber would rent the building from us at a pre-arranged monthly rate. The monthly rent would pay the investors. After the investors were repaid their total investment plus reasonable profit, the building ownership would then be turned over to the Chamber of Commerce. Under this scenario the Chamber will own the building that was designed for them and would not cost them any money. The CEO was very much interested in this proposal. He told me he would bring this up to the Board of Directors for their approval.

In the meantime, Steam Pump Ranch historic preservation was slowly becoming a dead issue, in my opinion, due to the dysfunctional Oro Valley government. It became quite clear to me, as well as to the CEO of the Chamber of Commerce, that Steam Pump Ranch will never happen. The Chamber decided to form their own non-profit organization and obtain construction money from foundations. They hired a real estate company to find them the proper site.

More Mental Stimulation Activity - Special Olympics

Now that I decided to let Steam Pump Ranch fade away, I got back on the computer and found the Special Olympics. It's a very good cause that's badly needed to help these handicapped children. I made a donation and volunteered to be their photographer. I went to my first photo assignment at their big bowling tournament. It was a fabulous experience for me and was very mentally stimulating. Seeing the great smiles on the children's faces as they released the bowling ball and watched it travel down the alley, is all the compensation I need for my efforts.

For those youngsters that are wheelchair bound, there was a solution for them to have full access to join the bowling fun. A portable unit was created by assembling two metal pipes to form a track. The end of the track sat at the starting line of the bowling alley. The bowler puts a ball in the beginning of the track. The youngster adjusts the track from right to left in an effort to line up the ball. They lift up on the track and watch the ball travel down the track, down the alley and strike the pins. I saw such joy and excitement when I watched the youngsters adjust the track and release the ball.

During this entire afternoon, the excitement was overwhelming. I captured photographs of some great smiles that tell the story of the Special Olympics. I must admit that volunteering to photograph Special Olympic events not only gives me the mental stimulation that I crave, it also gives me a great feeling of helping those beautiful human beings.

Democratic Politics

One day, I got a phone call from a member of the State Democratic Party, here in Tucson. I did not know this individual or how he got my number to call me. But he called and invited me to a working session of the State Democratic Party in preparation for the elections that were coming up. He told me this meeting will be held at the exclusive Mountain Oyster Club.

On the date of the meeting, Alice and I drove down to find out what this was all about, and how I came to be invited. When we entered the room, we were greeted warmly and introduced to all the participants. We engaged in some small talk while we ordered lunch. We were offered some pre-lunch drinks and continued with small talk until lunch was served. Finally the meeting started. A lovely young lady, I would say about 22 years old, started her presentation on organizing the workers she was hiring in a Get-Out-The-Vote effort. She was honest and sincere in what she was doing. However my experience as a political leader on Staten Island was in direct conflict with this lovely young lady and what she was trying to sell. I politely expressed my views in a positive manner as well as congratulating her on the honest and sincere efforts that she is making. At the end of the meeting, a Senior Vice President of the State Democratic Party rushed over to me, handed me his business card, and said, "Al, we have to sit down and have lunch together."

About a week later, we arranged lunch at the historic Arizona Inn. Alice and I enjoyed a working lunch with a gentleman named Bill Roe. He suggested that I meet with a woman named Jo Holt, Chairlady of the Pima County Democratic Party. He told me he is going to pass my name onto her and she will contact me. She did and we had a number of meetings where I expressed my experience and how I set up the Democratic Party that was under my control. At that point I became an unofficial advisor to the Democratic Party. I was introduced to a number of candidates. We spoke about the process of getting elected.

On election night 2016, we were invited to a private party at a hotel in town. With Jo Holt's permission, Alice, my son Paul, Tommy, Stephanie and I went to this event. It was a very exciting evening. A number of local candidates were elected, however the real, as they say, kick in the gut came with the election of Donald Trump. My heart dropped with deep concern for the future of this country and the world. Time will tell whether my feelings are right or wrong.

About a month later Jo Holt invited me to attend a working session in her office. We met four members of her senior staff. They made a presentation about the organization they were setting up. When they finished, I was wondering if this was a working session of the democratic party, or of a huge international bureaucratic corporation. It seems that in Arizona, everybody works by creating huge bureaucratic documents, going in detail about a bunch of nonsense, that's meaningless for the operation of a local political organization. You only need that huge bureaucratic approach in order to keep control of huge corporations with facilities around the world. I expressed my opinion that paper does not get out the vote, people get out the vote.

During the discussion, the point came up that Jo Holt was being challenged for her position as Chairperson of the Pima County Democratic Organization. I told them to throw away all the paper. All you have to do is count the votes. The voters in this case are the elected district precinct leaders. This type of election calls for one simple action. Get a list of all the voters, check the ones you feel will be on your side, the ones that you feel are not on your side, find out if they have a political job with the Congressman or State Senator, etc. If they do, and that Congressman or State Senator would be on your side, contact them to get the word out to their people to vote for you. You have to contact all the other voters too and start working on them to win them over to your side. This is pure hardball political procedures. Nothing else counts, just the vote.

We left the meeting with the hope that she does the right thing by getting in the gutter, playing hardball politics, and get those votes. About a week later I learned that a whole series of classes were being set up to teach the precinct committee people the strategy of running the organization as I did on Staten Island. I am sure if all participants follow through with the teachings in these classes, the Democratic Party will prosper in Arizona.

Phony Salespeople

For those of you who have known me for a number of years, know that I am not a violent type of person. I always try to listen to the other person's point of view, and always look for common ground. However, there are times when my opponent is either lying or presenting a phony argument that hits the wrong button. Earlier in this book I mentioned my understanding of body language. If someone's body language that tells me the person I am dealing with is not honest, it can set me off. Brace yourself for two episodes where I just had it.

Living in Splendido I decided that I needed a second car. Alice had a truck that rode high off the ground and Harriet couldn't get in and out of it. The second car would be for Alice to take Harriet places. It could also be used by Paul when he is in town. He could take Harriet places too. It so happened, that Paul's business partner's brother was a manager of a Jim Click car sales lot. So off we went to visit Paul's partner's brother.

At the lot, the brother, being a manager, turned us over to a salesman. I explained to the salesman that to me, cars are just wheels. I don't care what it looks like. I'm not interested in the color, or the seats, or the hubcaps etc. My only concern is that it is a quality car and has all of the latest safety features. In the conversation, the salesman told me that a car we were looking at was "loaded" with all the latest safety features. At that point I controlled myself when I heard the wrong word that he used, "loaded". That is baloney talk that salesmen use to get you think that you getting more than you really are. As he used the word "loaded" I noticed his hands held one another in front of the stomach just for very short time. He used the wrong word, "loaded", and his body language told me that he is lying. I asked him, "If I'm in a parking spot, and I back out as a car is coming behind me, will both side view mirrors start blinking to warn me that a car's approaching?" "No," he said, "That feature is not on this model." I said, "In entering my garage and I'm getting close to the front wall and boxes on the sides, does a diagram light up and show on the monitor to warning me that I am approaching something blocking my way?" "No," he said, "That feature is not on this model." This proved enough for me to know the word 'loaded' is nonsense and assured me that I did not misinterpret his body language.

We head back to the office, and my son, Paul, is ready to buy the car. I'm walking and thinking and getting angrier. I feel that this salesman is a bum. Should I pin him to the wall or just let it pass? When we got into the office and sat down, I looked straight at the salesman and I said to myself, "I can't let this go." I pulled my chair very close to his. He watched me and wondered what I was doing. I bent over so my face got close to his face. I took my hand with two fingers pointing to my eyes and I said "Look closely at me. Do I look like an 18-year-old kid buying my first car and not knowing anything about how cars are sold?" I let that sink in a couple of seconds. "Look closely", I said, "You see the face of the senior citizen. You should know how many cars I bought and sold over all those years. In my heyday I had a minimum of four cars going all the time. Just about every year I was trading in a car. I heard all the loaded nonsense and other tricks that you guys use to sell cars. You should learn to read body language before you tangle with a guy like me." At this point everybody was quiet and in a state of shock. Paul's partner's brother came running over to calm the situation down. I turned to him and said, "I am not buying a car today. If I come back next week and see you, will you sell me a car?" Paul's partner's brother said, "Yes". I got up and walked out.

The next week I came in to buy a car. This time it was entirely different story. Paul's partner's brother was excellent. I was given all the details that I wanted and shown all the prices that were involved and the price that I was to pay. Everything was now plain simple and out in the open and I bought the car.

Another of these rare occasions, when I got excited, was when Harriet and I were selling our first house. We bought it in 1953 and lived in it for 25 years. We originally paid $18,000 including all of extras. The economy changed drastically over those 25 years and this house was worth a $109,000. The real estate broker found a buyer who was interested and willing to pay the asking price. A meeting was set up with the buyer, their attorney, Harriet, our attorney, and I. Everyone was in attendance at the designated time except for the buyer's attorney.

We waited about 10 minutes and the buyer's attorney arrived. He took off his coat walked to the table, did not sit down, took a stack of papers, and with the flair of violence, slammed them on the table. He said, "There's a lot we have to talk about in reference to this price." Here we go again. I listened to his words and body language, and knew that there was no negotiating with this type of tactic. Without saying a word, I gently stood up and slowly walked to the door. Harriet followed my lead and was right next to me. "Where are you going?" he shouted. "We're leaving. The house is not for sale with you in the room. When the whole attitude changes, give us a call and we'll come back." We walked to the door and slammed it shut.

My lawyer ran after us. He tried to calm me down. "Tell them", I said, "The deal's off. I am not interested in selling with that guy around. If the buyer wants the house, then they will have to work with me with an ethical attitude."

About a week went by and I got the news. I hope it was not any of my doing, but the buyer's attorney died of a heart attack. A new meeting was set up with a new attorney for the buyer. We all sat down and spoke in a legitimate manner and the house was sold. The moral of these stories are, 'Don't let the tricks of high-pressure salesman suck you into something that you don't want to do.'

After Operation Bureaucracy

During the years 2000 & 2001, I underwent two surgeries to replace my right and left hips. A few weeks after my second operation, my doctor discovered an infection between the ball and socket of my right hip. My doctor gave me three options;

Option Number One: Have another operation to remove the entire hip that was infected and replace it. Hip replacement is a major surgery. It means having to go through to the entire rehabilitation program, to get me to walk, again.

Option Number Two: Have a simple operation to remove and replace the inner plastic lining in the socket where the ball rotates. The rehabilitation on this operation was much easier. However I would have to have daily antibiotic injections, to prevent any further infection, for about six months. A PIC line, in simple layman's terms, is a very small long plastic tube that is inserted in my arm and continues somewhere around my heart area. The beginning of this line is exposed on my arm with an opening so that the antibiotic drug can be injected by anyone. In my case, 'anyone' would be my darling wife, Harriet.

Option Number Three: No surgery, just antibiotics through the PIC line for six months. The problem with the third option is that in a number of cases, it does not successfully remove the infection. It didn't take me long to reach the conclusion that I will take Option Number Two. The operation was done, the PIC line was inserted, and Harriet was proficient in her job of injecting the medicine.

It became time to take our journey to Tucson, Arizona. Being a member of the Board of Directors of the hospital, the staff gave me a huge shopping bag full with hypodermic needles and two separate medicines which were to be injected. They wanted to make sure that I had enough supplies to last me for the six months that we would be in Tucson. When I looked at this package, I wondered how I could get past the inspection at the airport with all those hypodermic needles. No problem, I was told. The hospital gave me an official card stating this was a medical necessity and must be allowed on the plane.

We arrived at the airport. It was my turn in the x-ray machine. My two metal hips had showed up which was fine. My luggage was examined, and I was stopped for questioning. "What is in this jar?" he asked. I looked at this guard in amazement. I had a huge bag of hypodermic needles and he was worried about a jar of hand cream, which was sealed closed, and clearly labeled by the manufacturer. His concern was that the jar was a few ounces larger than allowed. I was still wondering about the hypodermic needles. I can't do much with that jar of hand cream but I can jab a lot of people with those needles. This guard confiscated the jar of my hand cream and sent us on our way. Bureaucracy is the scourge of society.

In Conclusion

To wrap up my experiences and feelings in my journey through life, it can be expressed in one word "TERRIFIC". I was fortunate to be able to share that trip with a great family named Harriet, Meryl Joy and Paul David. On the way we had our ups and downs. The ups were fabulous and the downs were very mild and did not take away from the ups in any manner or form. Harriet and I never, in the 63 wonderful years of marriage, until her passing, ever had an argument. We did have disagreements. We were always able to discuss these disagreements with intelligent conversation and come to a mutual solution of the problem. Quite honestly it always ended with my stating this simple phrase "Yes Dear" and all was well. Both Meryl and Paul had good times and bad times, good things and bad things, but all things were great things. There was never any heavy anger or violence or any other such negative feelings or actions. There were never any problems involving the law or society in any negative way. All the bad things were just not so bad things and always laughable when those things were past things.

Meryl, a practicing dentist by profession, was deeply involved in all facets of the community. She was the Director of the Dental Residents Program at Staten Island University Hospital and President of the New York City Dental Association. She also served on a great many non-profit boards and community organizations. She was also a fantastic fundraiser for those groups. She was well known and respected by all professional and community organizations. Upon her untimely passing at the young age of 55 she was remembered and honored by the community with a street dedicated in her name, "Dr. Meryl Efron Way". If you visit Staten Island and are in the vicinity of Richmondtown you will be able to see and drive down the dedicated Street.

Paul on the other hand took a different direction on his journey through life. He is a licensed Professional Engineer and more of a thinker, doer, creator and inventor that made life interesting and exciting. He was a very successful builder in the foothill section of Tucson Arizona as well as a mechanical engineer. Much to my pride and astonishment he was able to retire at the age of 43. He had the correct attitude that was to enjoy every moment. And so he did.

I remember when he graduated college. The economy was in a steep downturn. Recruiters from large corporations that usually hire these young graduating engineers were nowhere to be found. Paul decided to seek his fortune by driving around the country to find opportunities in other states. One day he called me and said he was in Tucson, Arizona. He went on to say how much he liked Tucson. He found an apartment to rent with another guy. He told me that he intends to stay in Tucson. I asked him, "Where did you get a job so fast?" He said he doesn't have a job yet. That blew my mind. In my generation, the thinking was you first got a job, and that is where you would settle down. Paul went on to say quality of life is very important. He said he'll always be able to find a job. After some deep thought of what Paul was saying, I concluded that he was completely correct. I also stopped to reflect on his early retirement at 43 which enable him to get deeply involved in a number of his creative activities.

My Photo Gallery

These are a collection of my photographs,
as they hanging on my studio wall

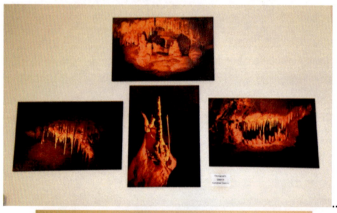

Wonderful Memories
Hawaiian Cruise, Harriet, Alice, and I

Al's 80th birthday party!
Skyline Country Club

Our Adventure in China with the McLeod's

The Efron's and their Bermuda cruise!

Mary Kay,
hosting Harriet and my anniversary dinner

A day in the caboose
on the Verde Canyon Railroad.
Clarkdale, AZ.

Our visit to Bearizona Wildlife Rescue, Williams Arizona

Our trip down Route 66

Out of Africa

Our adventure at the Gallipolis Islands

About The Author

My First Profession - Photography.
In my early years, during the Great Depression, about 1939, I became a professional photographer. I started as a great number of photographers do, by shooting weddings and high school graduations. I partnered up with a friend and grew our business. In March of 1951, I found myself drafted into the Army to fight in the Korean War. After fulfilling my two year obligation, and was still alive in one piece, I was honorably discharged from the Army in March of 1953. I went back into photography on a more professional scale by acquiring work from advertising agencies doing fashion and product photography. One day, two tough looking guys entered the studio and proclaimed that they are starting a union. It was quite evident that this was the Mafia. I wanted nothing to do with The Mafia, so I changed professions.

My Second Profession - Architecture
It took me 12 years of working for an architect before I became qualified to take my State board exams. Becoming a Registered Licensed Architect changed my entire life. Three architects and I reorganized a small existing architectural practice and became Shuman, Lichtenstein, Claman & Efron Architects. Through the years we were able to build up a large international practice. I found architecture a very rewarding and exciting profession.

My Third Profession - Back to the first.
After retiring at the age of 70, I returned to wildlife photography. I hooked up with a number of specialists that organized wildlife photo shoots around the world. I was shooting side-by-side with the professionals whose work appeared in National Geographic, etc. The walls of my computer studio are covered with photographs from those wildlife adventures. My last photo shoot was when I was 83. My son and I flew into northern Alaska on a small single engine aircraft that landed on a lake. We were able to photograph wild brown bear in their natural habitat fishing for salmon.

Made in the USA
San Bernardino, CA
29 August 2017